MBS

THE RISE TO POWER OF

MOHAMMED
BIN SALMAN

BEN HUBBARD

WILLIAM
COLLINS

William Collins
An imprint of HarperCollins*Publishers*
1 London Bridge Street
London SE1 9GF

WilliamCollinsBooks.com

HarperCollins*Publishers*
1st Floor, Watermarque Building, Ringsend Road
Dublin 4, Ireland

First published in Great Britain in 2020 by William Collins
First published in the United States by Tim Duggan Books in 2020
This William Collins paperback edition published in 2021

1

A catalogue record for this book is
available from the British Library

ISBN 978-0-00-834058-2

Book design by Simon M. Sullivan

Typeset in Janson Text LT Pro
Printed and bound in Great Britain by
CPI Group (UK) Ltd, Croydon

MIX
Paper from
responsible sources

FSC
www.fsc.org   FSC™ C007454

BEN HUBBARD has spent more than a dozen years reporting in the Middle East, where he is the Beirut bureau chief for the *New York Times*.

Praise for

MBS

"Detailed and disturbing ... Clear and convincing ... the book's strength is the thoroughness of its reporting ... Hubbard does a brilliant job helping us understand Khashoggi the man as well as the operation that killed him"   *New York Times*

"A fine account of the crown prince's rise ... Hubbard delivers a highly informed portrait, leavening his narrative with well-deserved scepticism, and leaves the reader wondering what lies ahead for the prince and his kingdom ... sheds light on MBS's role in molding and shifting Saudi foreign policy ... Definitely worth the read"

LLOYD GREEN, *Guardian*

"Full of chilling detail ... Ben Hubbard's account of the life, machiavellian style and ambitions of the de facto ruler of the largest and wealthiest country in the Gulf is a fine example of talented and dogged reporting. He also speaks and reads Arabic, not something you can take for granted among western Middle East journalists or even 'experts' ... An impressively well-sourced work. There is a fascinating account of Barack Obama confronting [bin Salman] ... Another riveting chapter is devoted to the three-week tour of the US by the crown prince in the spring of 2018 ... It would be surprising if the crown prince came out much better in later drafts of history than this impressive first one"   IAN BLACK, *Guardian*

"A revealing portrait ... With his years of on-the-ground reporting, Hubbard pinpoints the simultaneous realities of the kingdom that so few of its critics and admirers seem to be able to grasp"

LOUISE CALLAGHAN, *Sunday Times*

"He has spent more time in the kingdom than most other working western journalists ... Moves at a brisk pace through the key events: the lifting of the women's driving ban, coupled with the arrests and torture of the women who campaigned for it" *The Times*

"In this engaging account, Ben Hubbard shows both sides of the story, bringing his narrative alive with a host of insights, conversations, anecdotes and details ... Lucidly recounted" *Financial Times*

"Excellent ... gripping ... compelling ... an accessible biography that does not stray into sensationalism but helps make sense of all the recent headlines around the impulsive—and, one could argue, dangerous—young prince" KIM GHATTAS, *New Statesman*

"An elegant writer, the multilingual veteran Middle East correspondent Ben Hubbard is exactly the right person to draw this portrait of the most important leader in that part of the world today. His fast-paced narrative never flags or avoids dark corners. I found it riveting" ADAM HOCHSCHILD, author of *King Leopold's Ghost*

"Can we trust this mysterious prince with our oil supplies, with our friendship—with the prospects of peace in the Middle East? If anyone can give us the answers to these life-and-death questions, it is the brilliant and compulsively readable Ben Hubbard" ROBERT LACEY, author of *The Kingdom* and *Inside the Kingdom*

"A rare and penetrating look behind the curtain of the world's most important family and its dangerous new leader. Ben Hubbard brings all the strands together in this absorbing biography" LAWRENCE WRIGHT, author of *The Looming Tower*

To my parents,
for always keeping so many books around

And let it be noted that there is no more delicate matter to take in hand, nor more dangerous to conduct, nor more doubtful in its success, than to set up as a leader in the introduction of changes.

—NICCOLÒ MACHIAVELLI, *The Prince*

Ask the young. They know everything.

—JOSEPH JOUBERT

CONTENTS

AUTHOR'S NOTE

THIS WORK IS based on hundreds of interviews in a half-dozen countries over six years; a range of English, Arabic, French, and Turkish publications, news accounts, and social media posts; and my experiences during multiple trips to Saudi Arabia between 2013 and 2018. It is a work of nonfiction, and in no place have I altered names, details, or facts to hide the identities of sources or enhance the narrative. The reader can find citations in the endnotes, as well as supplementary information.

The realities of working as a foreign journalist in Saudi Arabia changed substantially over the course of the events depicted in this book—first for the better, then for the worse. In addition to Saudi Arabia's treatment of Jamal Khashoggi, the kingdom has imposed travel bans on thousands of Saudis and jailed and prosecuted citizens for expressing themselves online or communicating with foreign journalists. This has led me to err on the side of caution with the identification of Saudi sources, granting many anonymity. I am aware that this affects the transparency of the work, but I prefer that over endangering those who chose to share their stories, thoughts, and information with me.

For the rendering of Arabic names and phrases in English, I have followed no standard rules, but tried to ensure clarity for the nonspecialist reader.

Mohammed bin Salman declined to be interviewed for this book.

INTRODUCTION

B Y THE TIME the young prince who was running the Arab world's richest country was due to speak, a standing-room-only crowd of international investors, businessmen, millionaires, and billionaires had packed a luxurious hall under massive crystal chandeliers to await his appearance. It was fall 2017, and all had come to Riyadh, the capital of Saudi Arabia, for a lavish investment conference that had unofficially been dubbed "Davos in the Desert" to give it the same ring of exclusivity and consequence as the annual meet-up of global powerbrokers in the Swiss Alps. This conference, however, had a different goal: to convince the assembled moneymen that the time was now to bet big on Saudi Arabia.

Over the previous days, the kingdom had worked hard to convince its thousands of guests that any preconceptions they had about Saudi Arabia were not true, or were at least on their way to not being true. The country was changing, they were told, opening up and shedding its past as a hyper-conservative, insular Islamic kingdom.

Saudi Arabia had long been known for two things: oil and Islam. The first was pooled in such great quantities under the kingdom's sands that it had turned its royal family, the Al Saud, into one of the world's richest dynasties, giving the country that bore their name a geo-strategic importance it otherwise would have lacked. The massive oil wealth had shaped the Saudi economy, giving an elite class of princes and businessmen tremendous wealth while most citizens either stayed home or earned salaries from government jobs that paid well and often required little work.

The official Islam of the kingdom was not any Islam, but Wahhabism, the ultraconservative and intolerant interpretation that was woven into the kingdom's history. It taught the faithful to be wary of non-Muslim "infidels," saw murderers and drug dealers beheaded in public squares, and deprived women of basic rights. The kingdom was far stricter than most other Islamic societies, but its status as the guardian of Islam's holiest sites, in Mecca and Medina, gave it unique clout among the world's 1.8 billion Muslims.

Saudi leaders knew their kingdom's troubled reputation, so the conference had been carefully planned to challenge how attendees saw the country. Guests had dined on grilled lamb and chocolate truffles at private dinners hosted by princes and officials in opulent homes with swimming pools, art galleries, and hidden liquor cabinets. Women featured prominently in the program and mingled freely with men in the coffee shop of the Ritz-Carlton, with no obligation to cover their hair, as they had to elsewhere.

Slick presentations courted investors for grand initiatives. Saudi Arabia would become a global shipping and transport hub. Entertainment options for its 22 million citizens would proliferate, with amusement parks, cinemas, and concert venues, all of which had long been forbidden for religious reasons. Tourism would boom, with the development of long-neglected historic sites and the creation of a world-class eco-resort in the Red Sea. And in case anyone doubted that the changes were real, the kingdom was finally going to reverse the regulation that had long stood as the primary example of its oppression of women: In June 2018, it would let them drive.

The message was clear: Titanic changes were afoot in Saudi Arabia, and the man driving them was a mysterious, workaholic son of the king, named Mohammed bin Salman. He was 32 years old and out to remake the kingdom—and the wider Middle East—as fast as he could.

Seated in plush chairs or on the tan carpet, the conference attendees had come to take the measure of the young prince. Was he for real? Was he a visionary leader who would drag Saudi Arabia from its conservative past or a rash upstart who would drive it into the ground?

Murmurs raced through the hall as a side door opened, and the prince appeared. He wore the standard outfit for Saudi men: a long white gown with snaps down the front, known as a *thobe;* a red-and-white-checkered headdress held in place with a black cord; and black sandals. He was chubby, due to his fondness for fast food, and he wore a scruffy beard that climbed high up his cheeks, telegraphing that he was too busy working to waste time on superfluous grooming. Flanked by aides and trailed by photographers and television cameras, he ascended the stage and sank into a white armchair.

He had emerged from obscurity less than three years before, a prince among thousands of princes, who had charmed and plotted his way to the top of the kingdom's power structure. When his elderly father, King Salman, ascended to the throne in 2015, he gave his son oversight of the kingdom's most important portfolios: defense, economy, religion, and oil. Then, shoving aside older relatives, he became the crown prince, putting him next in line to the throne. His father remained the head of state, but it was clear that Prince Mohammed was the hands-on ruler, the kingdom's overseer and CEO.

To distinguish him from the mass of his royal relatives, Saudis and Saudi watchers referred to him by his initials, MBS. He was a large man with a presence that filled up rooms. In public and private, he dispensed with the formal Arabic customary among Arab leaders and spoke rapidly in dialect, gesticulating with his large hands, his voice deep like a growl. He often overflowed with energy, his thoughts coming so fast he interrupted himself mid-sentence. During audiences with foreign officials, he would sometimes hold forth on his vision for the future for an hour or more without pausing for questions. One foreign official recalled that the prince's leg never stopped bouncing during their meeting, making him wonder if the prince was nervous or on some kind of stimulant.

On stage that day, MBS addressed the moderator in English to show his foreign guests that he could, then switched to Arabic to unveil yet another hyper-ambitious project: NEOM, a city that would rise from an isolated plot of desert near the Red Sea, where businessmen would write the laws and entice the world's top minds to innovate on Saudi soil. Planning for a post-carbon future and taking advantage of the Saudi sun, the city would be powered by solar energy and staffed by so many robots that they might outnumber the human inhabitants. NEOM, MBS said, would cost $500 billion and be a place for "dreamers." It was not an economic development project, but a "civilizational leap for humanity."

The lights dimmed and the audience watched a flashy video about the proposed city. Then the moderator, a foreign woman journalist, asked whether the kingdom's religious conservatism would hinder a project so focused on the future. MBS dismissed the idea that intolerance was part of Saudi history, insisting that the kingdom sought to engage with the rest of the world for the benefit of everyone.

We were not like this in the past. We are only returning to what we were, a moderate, balanced Islam that is open to the world, and to all the religions, and to all traditions and peoples.

Seventy percent of the Saudi people are younger than 30 years old. With all truthfulness, we will not waste thirty years of our lives dealing with any extremist ideas. We will destroy them today, immediately. We want to live a natural life, a life that translates our religion into tolerance and our good customs and traditions, and we'll live with the world and contribute to the development of the whole world.

Such a vow had never been made in public by a Saudi leader. The audience erupted in applause.

TWO WEEKS LATER, a harsher reality set in. Over a few days, officials from the Royal Court and the secret police rounded up hundreds of Saudi Arabia's wealthiest and most powerful men, including a number of MBS's royal relatives—and even some who had attended his wedding. They were stripped of their cellphones, guards, and drivers and locked in the Riyadh Ritz-Carlton, turning the investment conference's luxury setting into a five-star prison. There was a new future on the way for Saudi Arabia, and it would involve more than robots and women driving.

The government said the detentions were a crackdown on corruption, and many Saudis welcomed the idea. They had long watched princes and businessmen muscle their way into lucrative contracts or run other schemes to siphon fortunes from the government's coffers. Some of those locked in the Ritz were among the worst offenders.

But other well-known offenders remained free, raising doubts about the crackdown's true goals. Other aspects were strange, too. While the arrests were taking place, the committee leading the investigations was announced. It was led by MBS, the source of whose own wealth had never been scrutinized. Hadn't the prince himself spent nearly a half-billion dollars on a yacht? What about his French château, hailed in magazines as "the world's most expensive home"? Later, a proxy buyer said to be acting for MBS plunked down $450.3 million for a Leonardo da Vinci painting.

The detainees in the Ritz were told they were guests of the king, but their treatment was far from benign. As their ordeal dragged on, their loved ones cautiously reached out to me to curse MBS. One was from a storied Saudi business family who said she had heard nothing from her detained relative for weeks until he suddenly called.

"I am fine," he told her, convincing her that he was anything but.

The call ended in three minutes.

She saw the crackdown as a ploy by MBS to commandeer the kingdom's capital for his own ends while tarring the reputations of all who might challenge him.

"He is a psycho. He has spite. He wants to break people. He doesn't want anyone to have an honorable name but him," she told me. "He is a devil, and the devil is learning from him."

IN ONLY A few years, Mohammed bin Salman had become the dominant force in Saudi Arabia and one of the most dynamic and scrutinized leaders in the world. His prominence was not preordained.

For much of his life, he was lost in the crowd of richer, more experienced princes and low down the totem pole in a family where seniority reigned. So how did he do it? This book tells the story.

MBS could prove to be Saudi Arabia's most momentous ruler since his grandfather founded the kingdom eight decades ago and made it a key partner of the United States. MBS's rise came six decades after his grandfather's death, during a time of serious threats to the Arab world's richest country. The oil price was crashing, sapping its economy. Two-thirds of its citizens were under age 30, scrambling for jobs and chafing under strict social restrictions. In the wider Middle East, the jihadists of the Islamic State were rampaging through Iraq and Syria and bombing the kingdom. Iran, Saudi Arabia's nemesis, was taking advantage of the region's turmoil to expand its influence.

Exacerbating these challenges were doubts about the commitment of the kingdom's most important ally: the United States. President Barack Obama had little fondness for the place. Before becoming president, he had dismissed Saudi Arabia as a "so-called" ally and criticized its exportation of Wahhabism for fueling intolerance in the Muslim world. His administration would forge a nuclear deal with Iran while Congress passed legislation allowing Americans to sue Saudi Arabia over the terrorist attacks of September 11, 2001; fifteen of the nineteen hijackers, as well as their leader, Osama bin Laden, were Saudis. Both moves were stinging slaps to a kingdom that depended on the United States for protection, spent billions of dollars on American weapons, and expected a certain loyalty in return.

MBS would attack all these problems and more, plunging the kingdom into a war in Yemen; launching a plan to overhaul the economy; charming executives from Wall Street, Hollywood, and Silicon Valley; detaining another country's prime minister to force his resignation; and forging a strong and unlikely bond with President Donald Trump and his son-in-law, Jared Kushner. Inside the kingdom, he would defang the clerics, open cinemas and concert venues, and shatter traditions, locking up other royals—including his own mother—and putting in place a technological authoritarianism that would put his spies in people's phones, manipulate social media, and lead to the state becoming involved in the gruesome murder of a journalist that would shock the world.

MBS's rise rode the waves of global trends. As more of the world's wealth was concentrated in fewer hands, populist authoritarians used nationalistic rhetoric to rally their people while shutting down outlets for opposition. Like the Communist Party in China and rising dictators from Egypt to Hungary, MBS saw no need for checks on his power and crushed all threats to it, perceived or otherwise. His was an era of Saudi Arabia first, and he would stop at nothing to make Saudi Arabia great again, on his terms.

The nationalistic tide rose in Western nations, too. Britain's vote to leave the European Union and the election of President Trump in the United States turned their citizens and governments inward, cutting their authoritarian allies considerable slack. Those two events also showed that in politics, truth often mattered less than the passions one could stir on social media. That was a lesson that MBS learned well, and put to use in his own kingdom.

MBS is a hugely divisive character, praised by supporters as a long-awaited game-changer in a region aching for it and dismissed by foes as a brutal dictator in the making. Inside Saudi Arabia, he is a giant whose face is everywhere—printed on cellphone covers and hung over entrances to shopping malls—and whose every initiative is sold as a masterstroke by loyal boosters and journalists. But much about him remains mysterious. Waves of arrests have shut down public discussion of his background, the wisdom of his plans, or his ability to carry them out. In some sectors, enthusiasm abounds, as social life loosens up and women get jobs their mothers never dreamed of. But fear is so widespread that a stray social media post or a private comment could lead to arrest or jail that many Saudis avoid talking on the phone or put their devices in the fridge when they meet.

MBS is at the root of both phenomena, driven by two tendencies that came into focus in late 2017 when he nearly simultaneously charmed the investment conference and locked people in the Ritz. He is determined to give Saudis a shining, prosperous future, and exercises an unflinching willingness to crush his foes. Combined in different doses, those attributes will likely guide his actions far into the future.

Some may consider it unwise—if not foolhardy—to write a book about such a young leader who could rule his country for decades. This book does not seek to tell MBS's full story, but to narrate his remarkable rise and its effects on the kingdom, its relationships with the United States and the wider Middle East. MBS will determine where his story goes next. Here is how it began.

MBS

THE KINGDOM

_____

I N 1996, A British-Algerian man teaching at an elite school in Jeddah on Saudi Arabia's west coast got a unique job offer. A prince named Salman bin Abdulaziz was coming to town for a few months with one of his wives and her children, and the family was looking for an English tutor.

The teacher, Rachid Sekkai, knew a bit about Prince Salman. He was the governor of Riyadh Province, which put him in charge of the Saudi capital, and he was a son of the king who had founded Saudi Arabia, granting him high status among the thousands of princes and princesses who made up the royal family. The job sounded interesting, and would probably pay well, so Sekkai accepted, and for the next few months a chauffeur picked him up from school at the end of the workday and drove him to the royal compound where Salman and his family were staying.

Entering for the first time, Sekkai saw "a series of jaw-dropping villas with immaculate gardens maintained by workers in white uniforms." He passed a parking lot full of luxury cars, including what appeared to be the first pink Cadillac he had ever seen in real life. At the palace, he met his charges: Salman's four sons from his second wife, the eldest of whom was a mischievous 11-year-old named Mohammed bin Salman.

The young princes clearly had more interest in playing than in studying, but Sekkai did his best to keep the younger boys focused, an effort that collapsed when MBS showed up.

"As the oldest of his siblings, he seemed to be allowed to do as he pleased," Sekkai recalled. During the lessons, MBS would take a walkie-talkie from one of the guards to make "cheeky remarks" about his instructor and joke with the guards on the other end of the line to regale his siblings.

After a few lessons, MBS informed Sekkai that his mother considered the tutor "a true gentleman." Sekkai was surprised, as Saudi Arabia's gender segregation had prevented him from meeting the mother, much less giving her a chance to assess his character. Then he realized that she had been watching him through the surveillance cameras on the walls.

That left him feeling self-conscious, but he pressed on. The boys did not make much progress in English, and into his late twenties, MBS avoided speaking the language in public. They made even less progress in French, which the princes' mother requested that Sekkai add to the curriculum. But by the end of his tenure, Sekkai had grown fond of the spirited young MBS, years later recalling his "imposing personality." Sekkai assumed it came from his status as the eldest of his mother's sons and the attention his immediate family lavished on him.

"He was the admired figure, which gave him that sense of 'I am in charge here,'" Sekkai said. "In that palace, he was the one that everybody looked after. He got the attention of everybody."

MBS's FATHER, SALMAN bin Abdulaziz, was a handsome, hardworking prince with jet black hair, a goatee, and a reputation for rectitude and toughness. When he traveled abroad, he sported suits with wide lapels and striped ties that invited comparisons to Wall Street bankers or characters from James Bond films. At home, he wore traditional, princely regalia and presided over the Saudi capital and surrounding areas as the governor of Riyadh. Residents joked that they could set their watches to the sight of his convoy heading to work in the morning, hours before other princes got out of bed. To run the capital, he kept tabs on the area's tribes, clerics, and big clans—including his own. For years, he was the disciplinarian of the royal family. If a fight between royal cousins over a piece of real estate got out of hand, if a princess bailed on an astronomical hotel bill in Paris, if a prince got drunk and caused a scandal, it was Salman who would bring down the hammer, locking up egregious offenders in his own private jail.

"I have several princes in my prison at this moment," he bragged to the British writer Robert Lacey. An American diplomat wrote that Salman had stopped one of his brothers from complaining about a new regulation by telling him to "shut up and get back to work."

No one would play a greater role than Salman in propelling MBS's rise.

Salman traversed the titanic changes that revolutionized life in Saudi Arabia during the 20th century. He was a scion of a dynasty that had twice failed to create a kingdom in central Arabia before succeeding so phenomenally that the desert-dwellers who had pioneered the idea would have had a hard time believing how it ended up.

In the mid-1700s, in a sunbaked oasis of mud houses and date palms, Salman's ancestors had made the first attempt, when a chieftain named Mohammed Ibn Saud created the first Saudi proto-state around his home village of Diriyah. Mohammed was not from one of the major tribes that formed the primary social structure of Arabia at the time. Instead, the Al Saud were settled farmers who grew dates and invested in trade caravans.

Battles between tribes and clans were common, but Mohammed got an edge by forming an alliance with a fundamentalist cleric that underpinned how Arabia was ruled for generations to come. Sheikh Mohammed Ibn Abdul-Wahhab preached that Islam had been corrupted by traditional Arabian practices such as the veneration of idols and trees. He called for a purification of the religion by rooting out "innovations" and returning to the practices of the Prophet Muhammad and his companions centuries before. The sheikh's views got him chased from his hometown, and he sought refuge in Diriyah, where the Al Saud bound his religious message to their political project.

The alliance benefited both parties. Backed by Ibn Abdul-Wahhab, the Al Saud were no longer just another Arabian clan out for power, but crusaders for the one true faith. In exchange, they gave the sheikh and his descendants control over religious and social affairs. The alliance proved to be potent, and as the first Saudi state grew, those communities that refused the sheikh's message were branded infidels who deserved the sword.

When the state's territory expanded to include the Islamic holy sites in Mecca and Medina, the Ottomans struck back by sending troops that toppled the state, reduced Diriyah to rubble, and scattered the surviving members of the Al Saud. Their descendants tried to reestablish the state in the 19th century in the nearby town of Riyadh, but the effort collapsed in infighting over who should be in charge.

In the early 20th century, a descendent of the Al Saud named Abdulaziz—MBS's grandfather—revived the campaign to conquer the land of his forefathers. He led troops on camelback and reestablished the alliance with the descendants of Ibn Abdul-Wahhab, who provided religious justification for his rule. Over three decades, Abdulaziz brought much of Arabia under his control, ruling it from the new capital, Riyadh.

But the rise of this new, fundamentalist polity disconcerted the Western powers who were establishing themselves around the Persian Gulf, and King Abdulaziz faced a choice: to continue expansionary jihad, which would have invited conflict with the British, or to create a modern state. He chose the latter, and declared the Kingdom of Saudi Arabia in 1932.

Saudi Arabia would most likely have remained a desert backwater of minor interest to the rest of the world had it not been for the discovery of oil in 1938. That attracted speculators, technicians, oil companies, and representatives of Western governments seeking access to the kingdom's black gold, including the United States. In a secret meeting in 1945 between President Franklin D. Roosevelt and King Abdulaziz aboard an American warship in the Suez Canal, the two leaders hit it off, laying the groundwork for a lasting agreement that guaranteed American access to Saudi oil in exchange for American protection from foreign attacks. That arrangement became a pillar of American policy in the Middle East into the next century.

The influx of oil wealth turbocharged the inheritances from the kingdom's history. The Saudis financed the international propagation of Ibn Abdul-Wahhab's teachings, making Wahhabism a global religious force. Saudi Aramco, the kingdom's oil monopoly, became the world's most valuable company—by far. The Al Saud became one of the world's wealthiest dynasties. By the time of his death in 1953, King Abdulaziz had married at least eighteen women and fathered thirty-six sons and twenty-seven daughters. His offspring did not skimp on procreation either, expanding into a sprawling clan whose country bore their name and who enjoyed tremendous wealth and privilege.

There were thousands of them, all subsidized by the Saudi state. In 1996, an American diplomat visited the office that distributed their monthly stipends and found a stream of servants picking up their masters' allowances, which varied based on their status. The sons and daughters of King Abdulaziz received up to $270,000, his grandchildren up to $27,000, and his great-grandchildren $13,000. The most distant relatives got $800. Princes also got million-dollar bonuses to build palaces when they got married, as well as perks for having children. The diplomat estimated that the stipends cost the state more than $2 billion per year, but that was merely a guess.

Much of that money trickled into society to earn the royals the loyalty of the population. One of Salman's sons said he spent more than a million dollars of his own money during the holy month of Ramadan, hosting feasts for his subjects. But the royals still lived large, commanding fleets of yachts, building palaces from Los Angeles to Monaco, and taking foreign vacations so lavish that they caused economic booms in the communities where they landed.

The royals were so numerous that they formed a micro-society that functioned according to its own rules, including deep discretion and a respect for seniority so ingrained that they memorized one another's birthdays. That is what allowed them to shuffle into line from oldest to youngest at functions with the ease of geese forming a V to fly south for the winter.

The mud walls and ramparts of Diriyah, the oasis where it all began, still stand a short drive from Riyadh—now a modern capital of 8 million people, studded with malls, skyscrapers, and broad motorways.

It was there that Salman spent his life—and prepared his son for the future.

• • •

SALMAN WAS BORN three years after the foundation of Saudi Arabia and would recall later in life that when he was a child, his family had still lived in tents for part of the year. But by the time he was a young man, oil wealth had transformed the royals into palace-dwellers and players on the world stage.

The family respect for seniority shaped how the kingdom was ruled. After King Abdulaziz died in 1953, rule passed to a succession of his sons, from oldest to youngest, with some brothers skipped over because they did not want to rule or because the rest of the family deemed them unfit. (Women had no political prospects.) Under the king, the country was run by senior princes who shared the main portfolios: internal security, the military, the National Guard, and foreign affairs. They made major decisions by consensus.

Salman was the twenty-fifth of his father's thirty-six sons, which put him so low in the royal pecking order that, for most of his life, the prospect of his becoming king was remote. There were simply too many others ahead of him in line. Nor was he put in charge of a powerful ministry that he could use to promote his sons. Instead, in his twenties, he was named the governor of Riyadh Province, a job he would hold for nearly fifty years as the city grew from a desert outpost to a metropolis.

Running Riyadh made him a key interface between the royals and society. He maintained relations with the tribes and knew their genealogies, rivalries, and histories. Riyadh was the largest city in the Wahhabi heartland, the region of *Najd*, and Salman often hosted the clerics in his court. But Salman's main job was receiving subjects who appealed for help. Those with ailing relatives sought money for operations. Businessmen solicited contracts. Farmers came for mediation in land conflicts. Families with sons on death row appealed for intercession to prevent beheadings.

Over the years, Salman fathered an impressive brood. His first wife, Sultana bint Turki Al Sudairi, hailed from a prominent family and bore him five sons and a daughter. The eldest, Fahd, attended universities in California and Arizona and got involved in British horseracing, which familiarized him with the West. After Saddam

Hussein invaded Kuwait in 1990, Fahd spoke often with the Western reporters who flooded into the kingdom to cover the war.

The next son, Sultan, was a colonel in the Saudi Air Force who became the first Arab and the first Muslim to go to space, on the shuttle *Discovery* in 1985. He loved skiing, ran the kingdom's tourism commission, and was so fond of the United States that he once told an American diplomat, "Some of the best days of my life were in the U.S."

Next was Ahmed, who studied at the Colorado School of Mines and graduated from Wentworth Military Academy before also joining the Air Force. He later attended the University of California, Irvine, and served as the chairman of the family's media company. In 2002, he caused a horseracing upset by buying the thoroughbred War Emblem for $900,000 three weeks before it won the Kentucky Derby. Acquaintances recalled him as "an elegant man with clipped mustache and pocket handkerchief, unexpectedly casual for a member of Saudi royalty."

The next son, Abdulaziz, was a rare royal to work in the kingdom's oil sector, where he championed efforts to modernize the industry and was later named energy minister.

The youngest of Sultana's sons, Faisal, earned a PhD from Oxford, was a research fellow at Georgetown, founded a Saudi investment company, Jadwa, and also had a taste for thoroughbreds.

Salman's first wife had one daughter, Hassa, who worked with the kingdom's human rights commission and later ran into legal trouble in France after a plumber accused her of ordering her bodyguard to kill him.

At some point, Sultana developed a kidney ailment that worsened over time, leaving her surrounded by doctors and sending her frequently abroad for treatment. So Salman married Fahda bint Falah Al Hathleen, a short woman from a prominent tribe who would bear him six more sons. (Salman also had a short marriage to a third woman that produced one son, Saud.)

Fahda's eldest son was Mohammed bin Salman, born August 31, 1985.

As a prince, MBS grew up steeped in inherited and unearned privilege, socializing in palaces, shuttled about in convoys, and fussed over by nannies, tutors, and retainers. Only close friends and relatives called him by his name. To everyone else, he was *tal omrak*, short for "May God prolong your life," or "Your Royal Highness." But if his father was far down the royal pecking order, MBS was even farther. As the sixth son of the twenty-fifth son of the founding king, there was little reason to expect that he would rise to prominence. And for most of his life, few people did.

MBS later said that his father oversaw the education of him and his siblings, assigning each child a book each week and then quizzing them on it. His mother brought in intellectuals to lead discussions and sent her children on educational field trips. Both parents were strict. Showing up late for lunch with his father was "a disaster." His mother was harsh, too.

"My brothers and I used to think, 'Why is our mother treating us this way?' She would never overlook any of the mistakes we made," he said.

He later concluded that such scrutiny made him stronger.

MBS has rarely spoken publicly about his youth, nor have others who knew him at the time. That makes it hard to paint a detailed picture of his early life. Exacerbating the challenge is the power he would wield later, guaranteeing that public utterances about him would be complimentary and that anything scandalous would be buried. But to get a sense of where he came from, I have spent the last few years tracking down Saudis and others who knew or crossed paths with him in his youth. Most still live or have relatives or business in the kingdom and so spoke on condition of anonymity to protect themselves.

Salman lived with his first wife near the Royal Court in a palace with a white-columned façade; people jokingly called it "the White House." MBS's mother and her children lived elsewhere, but she had ambitions for them that could be achieved only through their father, so she packed them off frequently for lunch at "the White House" so they could be close to him. But MBS and his brothers were not warmly welcomed by Sultana, who looked down on the children of the second wife for their tribal background (and probably out of jealousy toward their younger, healthier mother). She did not hide her contempt, which her children sometimes echoed, mak-

ing fun of MBS while leading jet-setting lives and filling their résumés with businesses and foreign degrees.

MBS's trajectory was profoundly different—largely domestic and
deeply Saudi. But through his teens, he was mostly lost in the crowd
of royals, with few obvious ways to elevate his standing. That would
change because of two series of deaths in the family.

IN 2001, SALMAN's oldest son, Fahd, who had helped out reporters
during the Gulf War, died suddenly at age 46. A year later, his
brother Ahmed, the Kentucky Derby winner, died, too, at age 44.
The declared cause in both cases was heart attack, but the underly-
ing reasons were never made clear.

The sudden, untimely deaths of two sons threw Salman into deep
mourning. While his older children were off pursuing careers and
taking care of their own families, MBS, then 16, stuck close to his
father in his time of pain, deepening the bond between them. MBS's
mother pressed Salman to spend more time with MBS, and the
young prince often shadowed his father as he ran the Saudi capital
as governor. It was an immersive education in the state of the kingdom, as MBS saw who came and went, learning who mattered in
which tribe, which clerics held which positions, which businessmen
had tapped which parts of the economy, and which royals had found
innovative ways to rip off the state.

One member of the family's entourage during that time recalled
that MBS's social life centered around using his royal privilege to
build bonds with the people. In the summer, his family would de-
camp for the Red Sea coast, where MBS would rent a fleet of Jet
Skis for the young men. In the winter, they would set up camp in the
desert, where MBS would have the biggest camp, serve roast lambs
on huge platters of rice, and keep fleets of buggies for the Bedouin
who dropped by to greet the royals. MBS's world was Saudi Arabia,
and he seemed to love it as much as his cousins loved London, Geneva, or Monaco. His father appreciated his fondness for the kingdom, and their bond grew stronger, as MBS accompanied him at
weddings and funerals and prayed near him at the mosque.

MBS's mother and her children eventually moved into their own mansion, and some summers, Salman would vacation at a palace built by his brother, the late King Fahd, in Marbella with his first wife and her children, then pop in to see his second wife's family in Barcelona. Later, MBS's mother would take over a portion of the Hôtel Plaza Athénée in Paris, shunning its French cuisine for Saudi food prepared by cooks she brought from home.

In his teens, MBS developed a reputation for misbehaving. Fellow royals and others who knew him say he seemed frustrated and angry, erupting at times in fits of rage. At least once, he dressed up as a police officer and went to an outdoor mall area in Riyadh to show off. The actual police officers could do little because they knew he was the governor's son.

Accompanying his father immersed MBS in contemporary Arabia, but he was also a son of the twenty-first century. As with many Saudis of his generation, his sense of the rest of the world was shaped by Hollywood movies, American and Japanese cartoons, and social media. Old friends said he would sometimes lose himself in videogames and was the first in his circle to become addicted to Facebook.

MBS was 16 when the hijackers dispatched by Osama bin Laden attacked the United States on September 11, 2001. He told a delegation of Americans years later that his mother had called him to see the news and he had reached the television just in time to watch the second plane crash into the south tower of the World Trade Center. While MBS did not want his comments during that meeting to be directly quoted, the delegation's head, Joel. C. Rosenberg, told me his impression was that MBS recalled feeling a sense of horror that the world was going to hate Islam because of the attacks and that it would be harder for Saudis to feel comfortable abroad.

That feeling may have affected how he ruled later on.

"I think he grew up deciding," Rosenberg told me, "'I don't want to live in a country that the world thinks of this way, and that I think of this way, and I'm going to hunt down anyone who could think up something like this or who could lead us to be perceived as a backward, crazy country.'"

Instead of going abroad for university, MBS stayed in Riyadh and studied law at King Saud University. One of his classmates said it appeared even then that he wanted to be a leader, directing discussions among friends and once telling a group that he wanted to be the next Alexander the Great. Another prince of the same generation would see MBS at weekly dinners their uncle, Prince Sultan, hosted for his nephews.

"He always talked about the government and how he wanted to get involved and what he wanted to change, but I thought he was just saying that because he was the son of the governor of Riyadh," the prince recalled. "He always wanted to be the one speaking. He always wanted to be in the lead."

He was also into Margaret Thatcher.

"He always enjoyed talking about the Iron Lady and how she enhanced the economic system of Great Britain," the prince said.

But MBS remained far off the radars of the foreign diplomats and experts who studied royal dynamics to anticipate who might come to power in the future. In 2007, the American ambassador to Saudi Arabia visited Salman, who asked for help with U.S. visas for his family. His first wife had trouble traveling to see her doctor, and although Salman's other children put up with the stringent application process, MBS "refused to go to the U.S. Embassy to be fingerprinted 'like some criminal.'"

MBS graduated from university fourth in his class in 2007 and spent two years working for the Bureau of Experts, a research body for the Saudi Cabinet. After two years, he was due for a promotion but King Abdullah blocked it, so he returned to work for his father. He married a cousin, a petite princess named Sarah bint Mashour, and celebrated at a luxurious hall in Riyadh.

To outsiders, all Saudi royals appeared wealthy, but inside the family, there were vast gradations, and MBS was, yet again, far from the top. His father was well known, but MBS realized during his teens that compared to other senior royals his father had no fortune. As he moved into adulthood, the differences in wealth began to burn, as his cousins descended on European capitals with fleets of luxury cars and entourages that took over entire hotels. The cash wielded by some royals was mind-blowing, enabling them to vacuum up fancy homes and field house calls from Harrods salesmen with chests of jewelry for their wives and daughters.

They gave thousand-dollar tips to bellboys, passed out $100,000 stacks of cash to their entourages if they happened to land near a casino, and could drop $400,000 on watches during a single shop visit.

Part of what the royals paid for was protection from public scrutiny of their lifestyles and spending habits, but details often leaked out. Marbella, on Spain's Costa del Sol, was a favorite summertime destination, and royal cash drove a high-end economy. Some threw banquets with lamb, shellfish, and caviar that cost as much as $1,000 a head. Bloated hotel bills were further inflated with rented yachts, helicopters, and private jets. Most royals behaved well in public, but hospitality workers noted that many indulged pleasures in Spain that they had to forgo at home, such as alcohol, pork, and all-night parties.

"In the early hours of the morning, it appears the corridors of some hotels look more like catwalks for fashion models," a local journalist wrote.

Sometimes, scandals drew attention to royal excesses. One princess, Maha al-Sudairi, left behind nearly $20 million in unpaid bills in Paris, including nearly $400,000 to a luxury car service and $100,000 to a lingerie store. Three years later, she was back and tried to slip away without paying a $7 million bill at the Shangri-La Hotel, where she and her entourage had occupied forty-one rooms for five months. The next year, her son celebrated his graduation by booking entire sections of Disneyland Paris, where his dozens of guests were entertained by rare Disney characters. The bill for the three-day blowout came to $19.5 million.

MBS didn't have that kind of money, but he began playing the Saudi stock market as a teenager. Once he entered his twenties, he dabbled in business to build his wealth.

Real estate had long been an easy way to generate princely wealth, and MBS tried that, too. MBS clearly managed to make some money. A retired diplomat recalled asking a luxury car dealer around 2011 about the market for high-end rides.

The dealer broke it down.

The lower princes bought Porsches or BMWs.

The next level up got Maseratis or Ferraris.

The big spenders purchased Bugattis, which cost a few million dollars each.

"Who buys those?" the diplomat asked.

"I just sold one to this guy called Mohammed bin Salman," the dealer said.

The diplomat had never heard of him.

"He's the governor's kid."

But during MBS's mid-twenties, there was still little reason to expect that he would become more than a middling prince who dabbled in business and pitched up abroad now and then for a fancy vacation. Then a second series of deaths in the family vaulted his father up the ladder—and MBS with him.

IN JULY 2011, Salman's first wife lost her long battle with kidney disease and passed away. His full brother, Prince Sultan, who was next in line to the throne, suffered from cancer, and Salman stayed with him in New York until he died later that year. Another brother, Prince Nayef, became the crown prince, but he had coronary heart disease and died in 2012. King Abdullah then named Salman the new crown prince, and suddenly MBS's father was next in line to the throne and well positioned to empower his favorite son.

MBS has never publicly discussed when he began plotting his political career, but he has talked about his desire to be a new kind of ruler, one who disrupted the old order like the giants of Silicon Valley, instead of one who followed the traditional ways.

"There's a big difference," he said. "The first, he can create Apple. The second can become a successful employee. I had elements that were much more than what Steve Jobs or Mark Zuckerberg or Bill Gates had. If I work according to their methods, what will I create? All of this was in my head when I was young."

King Abdullah, however, saw MBS as an upstart whose experience fell far short of his ambitions. He named Salman minister of defense, but barred MBS from joining his father in the ministry. The king later relented to Salman's request and named MBS the head of the crown prince's court and the director of his father's office at the ministry, a cabinet-level position.

Much still remains unclear about how MBS spent his twenties, largely because he did so little that drew attention at the time and because so much effort would later go into retroactively polishing his reputation. But what is clear is everything MBS did *not* do before he burst onto the scene in 2015. He never ran a company that made a mark. He never acquired military experience. He never studied at a foreign university. He never mastered, or even became functional in, a foreign language. He never spent significant time in the United States, Europe, or elsewhere in the West.

That background would shape how he wielded power later on. His deep understanding of the kingdom and its society would enable him to successfully execute moves that few thought possible before he pulled them off. But his lack of experience with the West gave him weak instincts for how allies, particularly the United States, functioned and thought—a blind spot that would frequently lead him to miscalculate how they would view his riskier gambits.

The drastically different backgrounds of MBS and his older, more experienced half brothers poses the question of why his father chose MBS to follow in his footsteps. Salman has never publicly explained his choice, and as an absolute monarch, will never have to. So we are left with little more than informed speculation.

Salman may have shared the views of his own father, the kingdom's founder, who had rejected the suggestion by an American businessman that he educate his sons abroad.

"In order to be a leader of men, a man has to receive an education in his own country, among his own people, and to grow up in surroundings steeped with the traditions and psychology of his countrymen," King Abdulaziz said.

That jibed with the theories of two close associates of the Salman family who spoke to me on the condition that I not identify them.

One felt that the older brothers, with their foreign educations, British accents, and horse ranches, had lost touch with their father, who, in the end, was a Saudi traditionalist who liked the desert and

eating meat with his hands. So did MBS, and his father appreciated it.

The other said that although MBS's rough style grated on many
of his relatives, it never bothered his father, who may have seen in
the young prince a toughness he felt the kingdom needed going
forward.

The associate summed up the thinking this way: "To deal with a
Bedouin, I need a Bedouin."

IN THE SPRING of 2014, Joseph Westphal arrived in Riyadh as President Obama's ambassador to Saudi Arabia. Then 66, Westphal had
led a career that moved back and forth between academia and government, working at a number of universities and serving for a spell
as the acting secretary of the army. He was a tall, large, avuncular
man whose back-slapping style annoyed more hard-driving members of the administration. But it worked well with the Saudis, who
appreciated that he liked to chat before getting down to business.

As Westphal settled into his post, someone showed him an old
video of Salman getting a tour of some public facility—a factory, or
a water treatment plant—elsewhere in the Middle East. Salman was
dressed like "a Wall Street banker," Westphal recalled, and made
sure that those giving the tour explained everything to his son, who
jotted down copious notes on a small pad.

That was MBS, and Westphal was intrigued.

"There is something very special about this young guy," he
thought. "There was no question that he was the apple of his father's
eye."

King Abdullah was busy and often ill, so Westphal frequently visited Salman and noticed MBS, usually standing to the side but never
speaking. So Westphal requested a meeting with the young prince
and got the impression that MBS was excited, because no one as
prominent as a U.S. ambassador had ever asked to meet him before.

The two men hit it off, chatting about their families and backgrounds, and the ambassador became convinced that the young man
was off to do big things.

"I did believe from the very beginning that this was a young, ambitious guy who was destined to be a leader," Westphal recalled later. "And he had the platform."

ARRIVALS

I KNEW NOTHING ABOUT these royal machinations when I made my first visit to Saudi Arabia in 2013. I had recently been hired as a Middle East correspondent for *The New York Times* after living and working in the region for seven years. I spoke and read Arabic, lived in Lebanon, and had reported in Egypt, Syria, Iraq, Libya, and elsewhere, giving me a broad understanding of the region's dynamics. But Saudi Arabia was a black hole, its murky politics dominated by men in identical white robes with seemingly interchangeable names, its society opaque, reduced in most writing to generalities about the birthplace of Islam and outrage over the treatment of women.

I had grown used to hearing Arabs blame Saudi Arabia for all manner of ills, from the rise of particular political parties or trends, to funding or inspiring terrorist groups like the Islamic State and Al Qaeda, to the spread of social conservatism. But the mechanics of Saudi influence seemed invisible, as if the kingdom's power emanated across the Middle East at some subsonic frequency that affected everything but remained inaudible to the naked ear.

For the next five years, my assignment was to figure the place out. During dozens of visits to the kingdom and trips to many of its provinces, I met and got to know hundreds of Saudis from different parts of society: clerics who thought the kingdom was the best place on earth; young people who longed to escape; princes and princesses who were oblivious to their privilege; women who wanted to drive; women who could not care less about driving; and others who were proud to be Saudi even if they wished the place would lighten up a bit.

Over that time, I wrote hundreds of articles exploring Saudi politics, foreign policy, culture, and religion. I saw remote historic sites.
I watched horse races at the king's track. I met the Grand Mufti, the
top religious authority, who told me to become a Muslim. And I
made friends with a range of Saudis who helped me understand how
they saw their homeland and where they wanted it to go. But it was
my early visits to the kingdom that showed me the old Saudi Arabia,
giving me benchmarks I could use after MBS showed up and tried
to change everything.

In 2013, I checked in to an old-fashioned hotel downtown that
had large, framed pictures of the king, the crown prince, and the
founding king, Abdulaziz, in the lobby. All the employees were men,
from India, Pakistan, and other Arab countries. The only Saudis in
sight were men in white robes who were always reading newspapers
in the lobby. Why were they there? Were they secret police, keeping
an eye on who was meeting whom? Or did they just like the ambi-
ence? I never knew.

My room looked as if the wallpaper had been hung in the 1970s
and the carpet laid before that. There was a speaker next to my bed
that I could turn on to get the call to prayer piped in five times a day.
Not that I needed it. There were so many mosques around that I
could hear the call clearly, even with the window closed. On Friday
afternoon, the city shut down for communal prayers and the sermons were so loud that I could follow them word for word inside
my room.

I didn't know anyone, so I reported to a functionary at the Ministry of Culture and Information who dealt with foreign press. I began
to tell him about the articles I hoped to report, but he cut me off,
saying that I should have sent him a fax with my "program" a month
in advance. Since I had not, he could not help.

"I am very sorry," he said, not sounding very sorry at all.

He served me tea in a plastic cup.

"Enjoy your time in Saudi Arabia."

I had a list of phone numbers I had inherited from colleagues who
had covered the kingdom before, so I got to work, cold-calling Saudis to ask for meetings. Most were surprisingly welcoming, offering
to meet me at my hotel or sending their drivers to bring me to their

homes or offices. There was nothing secretive about it, and the newspaper guys in the lobby never seemed to care. At that time, Saudis had no reason to worry about speaking to a foreign journalist.

The kingdom was clearly wealthy, and many of the Saudis I met seemed to have a lot of money without doing a lot of work. But it was also shabbier than I expected, with perpetual roadwork snarling highways and poor lighting as soon as one left the main drag. At the time, the kingdom was at the end of a ten-year bender, during which oil prices had remained high, piping cash into the government, which trickled down to everyone else. Had there been no oil, there would have been almost no economic activity whatsoever.

Non-Saudis did most visible jobs. Foreigners made up about one-third of the kingdom's population, and they did the economy's heavy lifting. Checking in to a hotel, one was likely to meet an Egyptian or an Indian. Take a taxi and the driver was often Afghan. Construction sites were packed with Bangladeshis and Pakistanis. The professional class was full of Arabs, with engineers, managers, accountants, and doctors from Iraq, Egypt, Syria, and Lebanon. A smaller number of Westerners worked in banks, large firms, the oil industry, or as advisers to wealthy royals.

I was struck by the kingdom's conservatism and how Wahhabism shaped every aspect of life. In public, nearly all women wore baggy black gowns called "abayas" that hid their forms, turning them into billowing black figures, indistinguishable but for the high heels or tennis shoes poking out below. Nearly all covered their hair, and most covered their faces, leaving only thin slits for their eyes. Mixing between unrelated men and women was forbidden, and to prevent it, restaurants were divided into sections for "families," where related men and women could sit together, and for "singles," who were all men. I would learn that many Saudis mixed in private, and men and women could usually meet in hotel lobbies with little problem. Others did not want to mix and saw gender segregation as part of their culture. In some conservative circles, men went their whole lives without seeing the faces of women other than their immediate relatives—even their brothers' wives.

Shops and restaurants shut their doors when the call to prayer sounded, even if their proprietors hung out in the back and killed time on their phones instead of going to the mosque. They had little choice but to shut their doors, to avoid the wrath of the Commission for the Promotion of Virtue and the Prevention of Vice, the so-called "religious police." Its stern, bearded fellows patrolled public areas to harass women whose clothes were deemed not concealing enough and to seek out those drinking, doing drugs, or engaging in unsanctioned *ikhtilat*, or "mixing," with the opposite sex. Local news sites reported when they stormed a basement where Indian Christians were holding a covert church service (the kingdom banned the practice of any religion other than Islam), or when they broke up a birthday party where young Saudi men engaged in "inappropriate dancing" (birthday celebrations were considered un-Islamic).

That meant there was not much to do. In fact, it was excruciatingly boring. No movies. No music. Few parks. I felt cooped up in my room, and so walked to the mall for a change of scenery, but was not allowed in because it was "family time" and I was a single male. So I sat outside and watched young Saudi guys try to glom on to visiting families to sneak inside, where they might see some girls. I tried to work in coffee shops, but got kicked out when prayer time came. Once, I took a seat outside and a policeman tried to hustle me off to the mosque.

Since there were so few public places for young men to hang out, they pooled their money to rent simple salons where they could gather to talk, drink tea, and watch television. Before I got there, the more daring would steal cars and engage in a unique kind of Saudi drifting called *"tafheet"* that birthed its own subversive subculture. Like rave organizers, the drifters organized pop-up events where drivers entertained crowds with risky car tricks. Filling out the scene, poets praised their favorite drivers, who competed to expand their entourages. It was dangerous and illegal, but exhilarating, like drag racing during the James Dean era, and it gave the city's underclass, who had benefited little from the kingdom's wealth, a way to push back. But by the time I got to Riyadh, the government had plastered the city with surveillance cameras so the police could shut down the drifters before they got going.

Young women had even fewer options, so they mostly met up in homes or went out to eat. There was lots of fast food, and lots of eating. But if the ladies' drivers were occupied and no male relatives could drop them off, they stayed home.

A few days after I arrived, there was a driving protest, although the organizers insisted that it was *not* a protest, because the government *hated* protests. Small groups of women had been challenging the driving ban now and then for decades, and a group of activists had chosen October 26, 2013, for their next campaign. The idea was simple: Women who had legal foreign licenses would drive and post videos of themselves online to show that it was not a big deal.

But news of the non-protest got out and conservative forces mobilized to remind the kingdom of the perils of women behind the wheel. One religious scholar on TV blasted the activists as "a great danger" whose goals were "suspicious and threaten the homeland." The clerics had banned women from driving, he said, "because of the political, religious, social, and economic problems it entails" which could "open the door to evil." Another cleric led a delegation of more than a hundred men from around the kingdom to warn King Abdullah about "the conspiracy of women driving."

As the big day approached, hackers defaced the women's website, filling it with insults and posting a video by an Israeli-American activist calling on women to drive and sarcastically accusing "Zionists" of using the issue to weaken the kingdom. The government warned that it forbade all that "disturbs the social peace, opens the door to discord, and responds to the fantasies of those with sick dreams among the biased ones, the intruders, and the predators." The security forces would respond "with all force and determination," it said, to punish anyone who sought "to split and divide society." Security officials called the activists to tell them to stay home.

But on the day of, some still drove. The organizers said they received videos from dozens of women, but it was hard to know how many there were, and in any case, it was minuscule in a country with 22 million citizens. I got the feeling that day that there were more foreign journalists looking for women drivers than there were drivers to be found.

But the videos were charming. One showed a young woman grinning as she sped through Riyadh, giggling as her father filmed her from the passenger seat.

"This is Loujain Al-Hathloul who just arrived in Riyadh and is on her way home. She is driving and happy," he said. "God willing, after ten years we will laugh at this image."

I spoke to a number of the participants. One was a 60-year-old photographer and psychoanalyst named Madeha Alajroush, who told me the women's request for an audience with King Abdullah had been turned down. That annoyed her, since it seemed like clerics got to see the king whenever they wanted. All she wanted was to drive herself to a café.

"We are looking for a normal way of life, for me to get into my car and do something as small as get myself a cappuccino or something as grand as taking my child to the emergency room," she told me.

On the morning of, her driver took her to a Costa Coffee, where she was to meet a friend to drive with. But two men were following them, so they aborted the mission, sought refuge in a mall, and bought a yellow toy car, which they presented to the men as a gift. The men stormed off.

The hubbub surrounding the issue bugged her.

"This is not a revolution," she told me.

I also spoke with a linguistics professor at a Riyadh university, Eman Al Nafjan, who wrote a blog about Saudi women. She didn't have a license, so she filmed other women as they drove. But she did own a car, a beige Ford, and she explained her transportation setup.

"There is a little room outside my house, and in that little room is a little Bangladeshi guy," she said. "He drives me around."

I laughed, and she laughed, too.

"That's Saudi for you," she said.

In the coming years those three women and their quest to drive would collide with MBS's rise in unexpected ways.

By the end of the day, no women had been jailed, society had not collapsed, and the biggest news ended up being a music video posted on YouTube by a group of Saudi artists. To the tune of Bob Marley's "No Woman, No Cry," they sang an a cappella version that urged "no woman, no drive."

"I remember when you used to sit, in the family car, but backseat . . ."

They mocked a cleric who argued that driving damaged women's reproductive organs.

"Ova-ovaries are safe and well, so you can make lots and lots of babies."

It was funny and went viral, its criticism so clever that it didn't enflame tempers or get anyone arrested.

"Heeeeeeey, little sister, don't touch that wheel! No woman, no drive!"

That was one of many incidents during my early visits that made it clear that the kingdom was bursting with young people who were branched in to the outside world through entertainment and social media and who saw the kingdom in drastically different ways than their elders.

I kept meeting young Saudis who challenged my assumptions of what it meant to be "liberal" or "conservative." One religious man I got to know sported a long beard and no mustache, the signs of a *salafi*, a hyper-conservative who imitated the practices of the Prophet Muhammad and his companions from centuries before. I once caught him reading Hillary Clinton's autobiography.

"You don't even believe women should be in politics, right?" I asked.

True, he said, but irrelevant.

"She's an important figure and I want to know how she thinks," he said.

The next time I saw him, he was reading *The Da Vinci Code*.

I asked what he thought.

Its history was bogus, he said, but he didn't care. "Great story!"

I made friends with a judge whose day job was applying Sharia law. We met to discuss an article I was reporting, but when we paused for tea, he leaned in and asked, "Do you watch *Breaking Bad*?"

As I got to know him, he confided that for vacation, he liked to take his wife and daughter to California, where they would rent a car and drive around Hollywood. He had effectively been drafted into the judiciary after university and was trying to get out, which was not easy. I wondered what life he would have chosen had he been able to.

The mantra in King Abdullah's Saudi Arabia, repeated ad nauseam by government officials and Saudi academics, was "evolution, not revolution." The kingdom was politically stable, as far as anyone knew, and the old king was a reformer, in his way. He had lifted regulations to allow women to enter the workforce; appointed a group of women to the Shura Council, a royal advisory body; and vowed to let women vote and run in municipal elections. Most Saudis welcomed those changes but were keenly aware of the chaos that the Arab Spring uprisings had unleashed in neighboring countries. That made them happy to take it slow and leave governance to the royals, as long as they kept paying the bills.

But building quietly was a looming challenge to the monarchy. As the younger sons of the founding king grew old and died, it was not clear who would take over once they were gone. The throne would eventually have to pass to the next generation, but how? The third generation contained thousands of princes, so who would choose from among them?

In 2009, a well-known Saudi journalist who had spent decades with kings and princes and had a good feel for royal dynamics laid out the issue to an American diplomat.

The kingdom was "a country in transition," the journalist said, facing tough questions about its future. Within ten years, he predicted, Saudi Arabia would have a young ruler from the "new generation." The problem was, "No one knows who this will be."

The journalist's name was Jamal Khashoggi.

He was right.

CORONATION

<hr>

O N JANUARY 23, 2015, King Abdullah succumbed to a long bout with lung cancer and died in the National Guard Hospital in Riyadh. One of his sons emerged from the emergency room to inform relatives and courtiers that the king had passed, and many broke into tears. As word spread through the kingdom, princes from other branches of the family passed by to pay their condolences. Among them was Salman, who arrived with Mohammed bin Salman. At some point, the young prince took the seal used on Royal Court documents from the powerful man who had run it under King Abdullah, an early sign of who would be in charge going forward. The royal guards who had brought Abdullah to the hospital left with Salman. Abdullah was laid to rest in a simple grave and Salman became Saudi Arabia's new king. He was 79, one of the last surviving sons of King Abdulaziz, and the last of his generation to rule the kingdom.

Despite the jubilation in Saudi Arabia at the ascension of a new monarch, with celebratory programs flooding the television stations and green fireworks bursting over Riyadh, it was a troubling time for the kingdom. The popular uprisings known as the Arab Spring had shaken the regional order the Saudis were used to by toppling autocrats in Tunisia, Yemen, Libya, and Egypt. Their departure had left behind a murky picture of who would wield power where and how they would relate to the kingdom.

A new, Saudi-backed dictator had taken charge in Egypt, but the Arab world's most populous country faced an economic crisis. Libya was in chaos, with two competing forces seeking to impose their rule on a shell-shocked country. Scrappy rebels known as the Houthis had seized control of northwestern Yemen, including the capital, Sanaa, and territory along the Saudi border. Farther afield, a brutal civil war raged in Syria, where Saudi support had failed to help rebels oust a Saudi foe, President Bashar al-Assad.

In the meantime, the jihadists of the Islamic State had rampaged through eastern Syria and western Iraq, seizing territory the size of Britain, using phenomenal violence to terrify enemies, and declaring the creation of a caliphate, or an Islamic government they hoped would unite the world's Muslims. In reality, most of the world's Muslims, including the Saudi leadership, abhorred the jihadists, but their rise posed challenges for the kingdom. It drew unflattering attention to Saudi Arabia's own intolerant interpretation of Islam, which also shunned "infidels" and practiced public beheading. There were significant differences: Wahhabism did not call for the establishment of the caliphate, encouraged obedience to rulers, and did not oppose interactions with the West. But the similarities on most religious matters were so great that the jihadists used Saudi textbooks in their schools. Nevertheless, the jihadists blasted the royal family as hypocrites and sellouts while recruiting thousands of Saudis to their ranks, some of whom launched deadly attacks inside the kingdom.

At the same time, Iran was taking advantage of the chaos across the region to increase its influence through covert support for militias in Lebanon, Syria, Iraq, and Yemen. Saudi Arabia and Iran were competing lodestars for Islam's two largest sects. The Sunni kingdom considered itself a Vatican of sorts for the world's Muslims and saw Iran's Shiite faith as an aberration. For its part, Iran, ruled by a revolutionary Shiite government, saw Saudi Arabia as a prime adversary in its quest to export its revolution and undermine American and Israeli interests.

Hampering Saudi Arabia's ability to confront these threats, the global oil price had begun a precipitous decline that would keep it well below $100 per barrel for years to come. That sapped the kingdom's budget, giving it not only less money to throw at its problems, but also damaging its economy. The country was overflowing with young people who had grown up during the oil boom and had high expectations, but the government could no longer employ them the way it had their elders.

Further exacerbating the kingdom's fears was a sense that the United States, on whom it had relied for its security since President Roosevelt met King Abdulaziz during World War II, was not as loyal as the Saudis hoped. The Saudi leadership did not like or trust President Barack Obama, and had little reason to believe that he liked them much either. They had grown angry with him in 2011 for saying that President Hosni Mubarak of Egypt should leave power amid mass protests against his rule. Their frustrations grew when Obama did not provide more support to the rebels in Syria and declined to bomb President al-Assad after he used chemical weapons on his people in 2013, a tactic that Obama had previously declared a "red line." They then learned that the Obama administration had engaged in intensive negotiations with Iran about its nuclear program. The talks had been kept secret from the Saudis, solidifying the feeling that they had been betrayed by their most important ally.

As these challenges mounted, Salman ascended to the throne, with MBS in tow. Few Saudi watchers knew much about the young prince at the time.

Salman put in place a new royal lineup, elevating to crown prince Muqrin bin Abdulaziz, a younger half brother whom King Abdullah had placed in the line of succession. Muqrin had an impressive background, having trained at a British air force academy and held a number of governorships before serving as the head of Saudi intelligence. Foreign officials who worked with him suspected that he owed his later prominence to King Abdullah's fondness for him. Muqrin was a raconteur and joke-teller, and King Abdullah had liked having him around. He was the youngest surviving son of King Abdulaziz, but his mother was a Yemeni concubine, which normally would have disqualified him from becoming king.

Salman also appointed as second in line to the throne Mohammed bin Nayef, a nephew and head of the Interior Ministry, who was best known for spearheading the kingdom's campaign against Al Qaeda. The elevation made MBN, as he was known, the first of the grandsons of King Abdulaziz to be directly in the line of succession.

While most of the attention was focused on the well-known royals filling the top jobs, 29-year-old MBS stepped out of the shadows. Salman named him minister of defense, giving him oversight of the military, and put him in charge of the Royal Court, which gave him control over access to his father and the royal purse strings. MBS would leverage both jobs to increase his power.

MBS and his aides would later describe how they got to work immediately to confront what they recognized as a looming crisis born of low oil prices and exacerbated by poor management under the previous monarch. From 2010 to 2014, when oil prices were high and as King Abdullah's health declined, constraints on government spending had fallen away, with increasingly large contracts slipping through with little or no scrutiny.

After King Abdullah died, MBS pulled together four advisers, who worked through the night to come up with a plan to restructure the government—and begin centralizing power under MBS. The next day, MBS ordered up a royal decree that abolished a range of government bodies and replaced them with two supreme councils, one for economic development, the other for security. MBS took charge of the first, giving him vast powers over the kingdom's economy. He would later take over the second.

"From the first twelve hours, decisions were issued," MBS said later. "In the first ten days, the entire government was restructured."

One of MBS's economic advisers later estimated that between $80 billion and $100 billion, or one-quarter of the Saudi budget, had been lost every year to inefficient spending. In the first few months of Salman's rule, when the low oil price forced the kingdom to dig into its reserves to pay the bills, MBS's team discovered that that trajectory would leave them "completely broke" in two years. The gravity of the looming crisis put the adviser "on the verge of having a nervous breakdown."

Over the course of that first year, MBS would slim the government budget, reimpose spending controls, and take other measures to slow the kingdom's race toward insolvency. But old habits died hard. Less than a month into his reign, King Salman decreed the payout of a two-month salary bonus to every government employee, soldier, and university student at home and abroad as part of a vast spending package estimated at $32 billion—more than the annual budget of Nigeria, Africa's largest economy. For a leadership that would make fiscal responsibility a central talking point, it was a bald bid for popularity through royal largesse.

The naming of MBS as the minister of defense did not immediately draw much attention, because the Saudi military had little history of fighting wars. Instead, it had served to employ large numbers of Saudi men and enabled princes to sign massive weapons contracts with the United States and other Western countries to underpin alliances and enrich networks of middlemen.

MBS saw little reason not to put the military to work. On March 26, he ordered the Saudi Air Force to start bombing Yemen, the kingdom's poor, dysfunctional southern neighbor, in an effort to drive out the Houthi rebels who had taken over the capital and restore the government they had toppled. Senior U.S. officials received little notice that the intervention was coming before Saudi officials asked if they could count on American support. Saudi diplomats, including Ambassador Adel al-Jubeir, flew to foreign capitals to convince the kingdom's allies that the war would be over in a matter of weeks. That prediction turned out to be woefully off-base, and the war in Yemen was an early sign that MBS would take a new, hands-on approach to the region.

More royal decrees followed. One changed the name of the Yemen operation from "Decisive Storm" to "Restoring Hope," a linguistic switch to suggest that the heavy lifting was over and it was now time to mop up. The king also removed Muqrin, the noted raconteur, as crown prince, saying it had been at his request, and replaced him with Mohammed bin Nayef, the esteemed security chief. The move was well-received in Washington because MBN had coordinated with the United States on security and was close to the Central Intelligence Agency.

MBS also moved up. His father named him deputy crown prince, putting him second in line to the throne, and made him the head of the board that oversaw Saudi Aramco, the kingdom's economic crown jewel.

Had a figure as unknown as MBS come to power so swiftly in the United States and immediately restructured the government and launched a new war, there would have been a scramble for information about him. Newspapers would have dug into his background, tracking down old friends, acquaintances, and bosses while seeking out the details of his personal life and financial dealings. In Saudi Arabia, none of this happened. The king had chosen his son, and it was the citizens' job to praise him, not to question his qualifications.

The Saudi news media published profiles with scant details about MBS's past: his stint as a government researcher, his jobs under his father, his positions with youth and heritage organizations. No one publicly questioned his qualifications to oversee the oil industry or the military. Foreign officials knew even less. For months, even his age was unclear. Publications, including *The New York Times*, repeatedly said he was "believed to be about 30." *Politico* noted that he was "something of a mystery to U.S. leaders, but he serves as the Saudi defense minister and has a hawkish reputation. He is believed to be King Salman's favorite son and often is referred to as 'MbS.'"

IT WAS NOT long after his elevation to deputy crown prince that Washington got its first glimpse of MBS. In May 2015, the leaders of the Gulf Arab monarchies came to Washington for a summit at Camp David with President Obama. It was an awkward visit, not least because of the rustic conditions. American presidents since Franklin D. Roosevelt had slipped away to the rural Maryland retreat to host high-profile dignitaries far from the hubbub of the capital. That history meant little to the Gulf royals, who were accustomed to palaces and luxury hotels. Sleeping in rustic cabins, walking dirt trails, and riding through forests on golf carts was not their idea of a good time. And relations were already sour, due to Obama's push for the nuclear agreement with Iran. The Americans were well aware of the Gulf leaders' bruised egos, so the meet-up was designed to reassure them that the United States remained committed to their security.

Although he had been expected to attend, King Salman stayed home, but he sent both MBN and MBS, and Obama welcomed them in the Oval Office before the summit. It was the first time top members of the Obama administration met MBS, and a number of them recalled that he appeared uncomfortable and out of place. He spoke little, deferring to his older cousin, who was comfortable in English and was used to such situations. When Obama addressed MBS in English to bring him into the conversation, the young prince responded nervously through an Arabic translator.

But right after the meeting, Adel al-Jubeir, who had been promoted to foreign minister, asked Susan Rice, the national security adviser, for a private meeting with MBS. She agreed, and they met in Rice's office, where MBS warmed up, speaking at length about his wife and family and declaring that he planned to advance women's rights in Saudi Arabia.

It was clearly an effort to charm her, a targeted pitch to a powerful woman who could have continued into a future Clinton administration. White House officials were struck by MBS's strategic move, but also confused. As soon as he had appeared on the scene, American spies had gathered information about him for a personality profile, as they did of all foreign leaders. That had turned up a perplexing situation: MBS had locked his own mother in a palace with two of her sisters. Even more perplexing was that he was hiding his mother's whereabouts from his own father, the king.

At the time, MBS's mother was the king's only remaining wife and he was fond of her. But when he would ask where she was, MBS and his aides would proffer excuses, usually saying she was abroad for medical treatment.

Other members of the royal family had also noticed the apparent disappearance of MBS's mother. Around the time that Salman became king, she had stopped showing up at family weddings, funerals, and holiday celebrations, leading them to conclude that her son had locked her up somewhere. But, like the Americans, they didn't know why.

There were a number of theories. American officials and some plugged-in Saudis thought MBS feared his mother would interfere with his rise because she worried that his ambition would split the royal family. Others proposed wilder scenarios, such as MBS suspecting his mother of using black magic on the king to promote other members of her family.

Saudi officials deemed any inquiry into the whereabouts of the king's wife highly offensive and never provided any information. Other royals considered it inappropriate to inquire, as did American officials, since it did not affect affairs of state. But many wondered what MBS's ability to confine his own mother and hide her from his father said about his character.

YOUNG PRINCE RISING

W HILE MBS REMAINED a relative mystery, the new crown prince was a known quantity at home and abroad. Mohammed bin Nayef was a reserved man in his mid-fifties with glasses and a brush mustache who avoided the media other than allowing journalists to photograph him when he visited wounded security officers in the hospital. For more than a decade, he had been the giant of the kingdom's fight against terrorism, first as deputy to his father and later as the head of the Interior Ministry, which oversaw Saudi intelligence and the conventional and secret police.

In 2003, Al Qaeda had declared war on Saudi Arabia, launching a wave of attacks on civilian targets, including compounds where foreigners lived. The threat was so great that the United States withdrew diplomats' families from the kingdom. MBN oversaw the response, launching a campaign of raids on militant hideouts that dismantled Al Qaeda's network in the kingdom and stopped the attacks. By the end of the decade, the diplomats' families had returned.

That fight, which was closely coordinated with the United States, gave MBN deep relationships in Washington, especially in the Central Intelligence Agency. American officials who worked with MBN praised him as serious and hardworking, a spy chief dedicated to the kingdom's security and to its partnership with the United States.

Inside Saudi Arabia, he was hailed as a hero and known as a deft manager of the kingdom's religious figures, including many whose views bordered on, or veered into, extremism. The security services he oversaw were unflinching when it came to those who engaged in violence at home. But for everyone else, he championed a carrot-

and-stick approach aimed at neutralizing their threat to the state. Homegrown ideologues were to be managed, not stamped out. Even young Saudis who fought with extremist groups abroad were treated as citizens who had been misled and who could, with the proper education and incentives, reintegrate into society.

That approach was put into practice at reform centers in the kingdom's prisons that bore the prince's name and used religious teaching, psychology, and cash to put wayward Saudi men on a new path. The centers found wives for the bachelors and granted married prisoners conjugal visits in a facility built like a hotel, with magnetic door cards, playgrounds for kids, and room service. There was never an independent audit to verify the approach's effectiveness, but American officials came to appreciate it, and Saudis argued that it was more humane than locking people up indefinitely or killing them on the battlefield with drones.

MBN once told a visiting American dignitary that it had pained him to learn that Saudis had played an outsized role in the September 11 attacks.

"Terrorists stole the most valuable things we have," he said. "They took our faith and our children and used them to attack us."

His approach to dealing with militancy extended to the families of dead militants, who were told their sons had been "victims," not "criminals." That helped families deal with the social fallout caused by having militant offspring and sought to break the cycle of radicalization.

"If you stop five but create fifty" terrorists, MBN said, "that's dumb."

That focus on engagement almost killed him. In 2009, the brother of a storied Saudi bomb maker who was hiding out with Al Qaeda in Yemen announced that he wanted to return to the kingdom and surrender to MBN in person. The prince received the man in his palace, ordering that he not be searched to avoid humiliating him, and sat next to him. Then the man detonated a bomb hidden in his rectum, killing himself and giving MBN what were described at the time as light wounds.

The next year, MBN provided further proof of his importance as a partner to the United States when he warned the White House and the CIA that powerful bombs hidden in cargo containers were headed for the United States. The bombs were intercepted in Dubai and the United Kingdom and defused.

That history made American officials grateful that the kingdom's planned future ruler was someone they knew. MBN's appointment as crown prince was also hailed as a smart way to pass power from the sons of King Abdulaziz to his grandsons. MBN was popular at home and had only one wife and two daughters, which many assumed would allow him to focus on governance, not on promoting his sons.

But indications soon emerged that MBN's position was not as secure as it appeared. King Salman collapsed the crown prince's court into his own, depriving MBN of a major perk of his position and a platform to build ties with subjects. From then on, there was only one Royal Court, overseen by MBS.

That summer, Adel al-Jubeir, the longtime Saudi ambassador to Washington who had been named foreign minister, flew to Nantucket to see Secretary of State John Kerry and spoke to him of MBS as the future of the kingdom due to his focus on reform. Kerry made it clear that the United States would not take sides in a princely struggle over who would inherit the kingdom.

MBS was also little known in the wider Arab world, including among Saudi Arabia's closest neighbors. Like its fellow smaller monarchies in the Persian Gulf, the United Arab Emirates had long viewed Saudi Arabia warily as the region's giant, whose wealth, power, and population dwarfed its own. For years, the Emiratis had wanted to step out of the Saudi shadow and develop their own national standing, and their leaders privately looked down on their Saudi counterparts as elderly conservatives wedded to ossified ways. An American diplomat wrote that Emirati leaders described the kingdom as "run by cantankerous old men surrounded by advisors who believe the earth is flat."

The de facto ruler of the Emirates was Sheikh Mohammed bin Zayed Al Nahyan, the crown prince of Abu Dhabi, a helicopter pilot and sharp tactician known by his own three-letter moniker, MBZ. He was tall, kept in shape, and maintained a modest demeanor that was uncommon among Gulf royals, sometimes rising during meetings to serve guests coffee or tea. MBZ had worked to give his country international clout that outweighed its size. The Emirates had fewer citizens than Dallas, Texas, and a relatively small army. But he equipped it with billions of dollars' worth of American weapons and built special forces units that fought alongside American troops in Afghanistan, Somalia, and elsewhere. While few Americans had heard of his country or its leader, he had poured huge sums into lobbying efforts in Washington to make sure that his views on the Middle East reached the centers of power.

King Salman's appointment of MBN as crown prince did not bode well for the Emirates, since MBN did not get along with MBZ, who had once insulted MBN's father, saying that the older prince's clumsiness proved that "Darwin was right."

But MBZ was curious about MBS and summoned regional experts to see what they knew. He was impressed and deputized his younger brother to get to know the young Saudi. A desert camping trip was arranged so that the two could meet, and they hit it off. It was a deft move on MBZ's part that laid the foundations of a strengthened regional alliance. Both men benefited. MBS got a powerful mentor who supported his quest to become Saudi Arabia's future ruler. In return, MBZ impressed his vision of the region on the inexperienced young Saudi, particularly his animosity toward Iran and the political Islam of the Muslim Brotherhood.

MBZ began selling MBS to any American official who would listen. MBN was the past and MBS was the future, he argued, suggesting that the administration invest in that future by choosing an official to build a relationship with MBS. President Obama's policy was that the United States would not take sides in an issue as weighty as who would become the next Saudi king. But there was talk inside the administration of finding an "MBS whisperer" who could mentor the young prince. John Kerry was suggested, but was too busy. Ash Carter, the secretary of defense, was MBS's natural counterpart, but wasn't interested. Vice President Joe Biden was discussed, but deemed too old.

In the end, the idea never took off—at least not until a young Jewish real estate investor from New Jersey named Jared Kushner entered the White House with the next administration.

• • •

As MBS's POWER grew, so did his interest in tremendous wealth and its trappings. If he had spent his youth watching his wealthier cousins amass fortunes, take lavish vacations, and drop mind-blowing sums on prime real estate, his turn had now come.

His father was king and so could spend as he wished, and MBS's position enabled him to create new income streams. One involved the Saudi national airline, Saudia, which had planned to buy fifty jets from Airbus, earning a bulk discount while upgrading its fleet. Instead, MBS arranged for a company overseen by his younger brother to buy the jets and lease them to the airline, rerouting the discount and other profits to his family.

In June 2015, the same month that deal was inked, MBS took a group of friends on vacation to the Maldives, a collection of palm-studded islands scattered like strings of pearls in the Indian Ocean. They set up camp at a hyper-luxury resort called Velaa Private Island, where accommodations normally ran from $1,500 to $30,000 per night. To ensure their privacy, the entourage rented out the whole place, giving them exclusive access to its amenities. These included the sandy beaches that ringed the island; the villas with thatched roofs on stilts in the sky-blue ocean; a spa with a cloud-shaped pod that rocked guests into deep relaxation; and the only "snow room" in the Maldives, where vacationers could take a break from the sun and surf with some manufactured arctic chill.

The developer had built the place from scratch, tearing out the native bushes and papaya trees and bringing in paneling from Borneo, deck chairs from Italy, and paving stones from the Jordanian desert that would not burn the feet no matter how long they sat in the sun.

"I always had this idea that our guests would find themselves stranded on a deserted island, and by coincidence, there is this unique resort," the resort's Czech architect said.

But relaxation, snorkeling, and watching baby sharks and dolphins visit the coral reef were not the only diversions. MBS also hosted a string of blowout parties, with headline talent ferried in to entertain the guests.

Psy, the South Korean singer, performed "Gangnam Style." The American rapper Pitbull was photographed in sunglasses and a tan suit being escorted to a seaplane. A few days later, someone photographed the Colombian singer Shakira in a black T-shirt and tights being taken to a VIP terminal at the airport.

"The party has been going on for some days now and we don't know exactly how long it would last," a local news site said.

"The Maldives is heaven like, thank you Mr. Smejc," Pitbull wrote to the resort's financier, Jirí Smejc, after his trip. "The island was unforgettable. Look forward to the next trip."

MBS's vacation came three months after Saudi Arabia had launched its military intervention in Yemen, which fell under his purview as the minister of defense. A number of American officials who reached out to him during that time found him unreachable. Then American intelligence reports came in, explaining that the prince was on vacation in the Maldives.

The parties eventually died down, and the flap they caused may have encouraged MBS to look for a place of his own, where local reporters would not pry into his affairs and post photographs of his guests on the Internet. He found it a month later, floating in the Mediterranean off the coast of France. Near the Port De La Ciotat on the French Riviera was *Serene*. She was not just any boat, but a superyacht, a tad under 440 feet long, with navy blue sides, white upper decks, and a helipad on her nose. When she hit the water in 2011, an industry publication hailed her as "one of the ten largest yachts ever built in the world and one of the finest in terms of sophistication and technology." She had a helicopter hangar, water-level hatches for speedboats, and a submarine dock. And she was massive, with 48,000 square feet of internal space, more than the base of the Parthenon or the concourse of New York's Grand Central Terminal.

Much of that space, distributed over seven decks, was jammed with luxury amenities for two dozen guests. A glass elevator carried them from level to level. A spiral staircase landed in a dining room with a grand piano. There was a gym, a cinema, a climbing wall, and an outdoor hot tub with commanding views. One sundeck had a glass floor over a seawater pool so that those chilling up top could watch their friends below.

The summer before MBS bought the boat, tabloid journalists had reported that Bill Gates chartered *Serene* for a family vacation near Sardinia, where a helicopter had spirited him out to sea after a tennis match. But the boat's owner was Yuri Shefler, a Russian tycoon best known as the proprietor of Stolichnaya brand vodka. So it was to Shefler's people that MBS dispatched a confidant to buy the boat. The deal was done within hours, for a total of €420 million, or more than $456 million.

MBS's father, the newly crowned king, was also living large. That summer, King Salman landed in the south of France for a three-week vacation with what journalists called his "inner circle." That turned out to be an entourage of a thousand people, who booked up local properties and rented hundreds of luxury cars. The king slept in a sprawling beachfront villa in Vallauris, where Rita Hayworth had married Prince Aly Khan of Pakistan in 1949. Local businesses feted the influx of so many wealthy Saudis, but other residents were less pleased. About 150,000 signed a petition against the closing of the public beach in front of the villa, and the town's mayor complained to the French president after workers poured a slab of concrete on the sand to install an elevator for the king. So after eight days, the king packed up and moved his vacation, and much of his entourage, to Morocco. A Saudi official said the move had nothing to do with the negative media coverage.

Later, on a beach in Tangier, workers built a new vacation palace for King Salman, with blue helipads, a string of guest villas, and a giant tent.

Other properties also caught MBS's eye. A company linked to the prince's money managers bought a 30,000-acre game ranch in South Africa that workers ringed with a double-layered electric fence. Land inside was allocated for twenty villas and a runway long enough to land 747s bringing in guests to hunt big game.

In late 2015, MBS laid out more than $300 million for a French château that *Money* magazine called "the world's most expensive home." In 2014, Kim Kardashian had stopped there for a photo while reportedly considering the château for her wedding to Kanye West. Built on 56 acres and surrounded by forests in the Paris suburb of Louveciennes, the Château Louis XIV had been built from scratch in place of an older palace and combined seventeenth-century craftsmanship with twenty-first-century technology.

"The result is an opus of architectural art with an exclusive royal touch," its developer said.

The château's grounds boasted intricate flower beds, a gold-leafed fountain, and a hedged labyrinth. Crowning the reception hall was a domed ceiling painted with winged creatures. It had a string of luxury suites, a sauna and spa, a movie theater, a nightclub, a wine cellar, and a moat with glass walls, through which guests could gander at giant fish. The only thing missing appeared to be the proprietor, whom neighbors said they never saw at the property.

After MBS was revealed as the château's buyer, a neighbor who had once foraged for mushrooms on the grounds complained that they were now off-limits.

"Before, it was a ruin only for ghosts," she said. "Now it is brand new for ghosts."

COURTING OBAMA

PRESIDENT BARACK OBAMA came into the White House in 2009 hoping to turn a new page in the United States' relationship with the Muslim world. He understood, and talked about, how the United States' focus on terrorism had led it to neglect other problems in the Middle East and spoke about the Israeli-Palestinian conflict in a way that suggested sympathy for the Arab point of view. His first television interview was with a Saudi-owned network; he delivered a high-profile address to the Islamic world from a university in Cairo; and he spoke directly to Muslims in his inaugural address.

"To the Muslim world, we seek a new way forward, based on mutual interest and mutual respect," he said. "To those leaders around the globe who seek to sow conflict, or blame their society's ills on the West, know that your people will judge you on what you can build, not what you destroy. To those who cling to power through corruption and deceit and the silencing of dissent, know that you are on the wrong side of history, but that we will extend a hand if you are willing to unclench your fist."

Despite the rhetoric, the Saudis were ambivalent about Obama, and their view got worse over time. During my early visits to the kingdom, I heard growing frustration with how Obama had handled the Arab Spring, how he had failed to support the uprising in Syria, and how Saudi Arabia and its Gulf allies needed to pursue greater independence from the United States. That attitude became more entrenched after the announcement of the Iran deal, which left

Saudi Arabia feeling that its protector was engaged in a dangerous dalliance with a wily foe.

In September 2015, King Salman and MBS came to the United States for a visit deeply colored by those differences. During a meeting in the Oval Office, Obama pressed the king on human rights, suggesting that increasing the margins for expression and granting more freedoms to women were necessary for the kingdom to develop. The king grew animated, pushing back and arguing that Obama did not understand Saudi society.

A smaller meeting was also held, with just the king, MBS, Obama, and Susan Rice, the national security adviser. As soon as they were alone, the king turned the floor over to MBS, who laid out grand plans for the future of the kingdom, which included opening up society and diversifying the economy away from oil. Obama and Rice listened, but refrained from giving the full-throated American endorsement their Saudi guests seemed to be hoping for. That plan would later be released publicly as Saudi Vision 2030, the centerpiece of MBS's ambitions. But at the time, Obama and Rice felt that the goals were laudable even if the plan itself seemed shallow.

"He knew how to say the right talking points about reforming the kingdom, but he didn't seem to know what was underneath them," Ben Rhodes, Obama's deputy national security adviser, recalled later. "He had all the right buzz words, but if you tried to probe them like they did, he didn't seem to know what they meant."

During the same visit, Secretary of State John Kerry hosted MBS for dinner at his mansion in Georgetown. The evening began with a chat in the ground floor sitting room. At one point, MBS eyed the piano. Kerry asked if he played, and MBS sat down and performed a well-practiced classical piece, surprising everyone in the room. Given Wahhabism's animosity toward music, MBS's hosts had not expected that he played. The group then moved downstairs to a dining room overlooking the back lawn. During a discussion of Middle East politics, MBS surprised his host again by suggesting that he could determine who ruled where in the Arab world.

"If I want Sisi out, he'll be out," he said, referring to President Abdel Fattah el-Sisi of Egypt.

None of the Americans present knew how serious he was, but

when the official report on the dinner made its way around the White House, many were taken aback by the prince's cockiness.

At the time, a range of officials and opinion-makers in and outside the United States had noticed MBS's growing power, and their early assessments of him varied widely. In late 2015, *New York Times* columnist Thomas Friedman spent an evening with MBS and wrote the first in what would be a procession of breathless columns by foreign commentators lauding him as a much-needed change agent.

MBS, Friedman wrote, "wore me out" with talk of proposed innovations few expected in Saudi Arabia. The prince planned to improve government performance through an online dashboard that would track Key Performance Indicators, or KPIs, for each ministry. The kingdom was too dependent on oil, so MBS would reduce subsidies for wealthy Saudis and institute a value added tax and "sin taxes" on cigarettes and sugary drinks. The government would privatize key sectors and charge fees for undeveloped lands, meaning, MBS argued, that even if oil fell to $30 a barrel, the state would still have enough cash.

Political reform played no role in the prince's plans, Friedman noted, but MBS said that the connection between the royal family and the people was enough.

"A government that is not a part of the society and not representing them, it is impossible that it will remain," MBS said. "People misunderstand our monarchy. It is not like Europe. It is a tribal form of monarchy, with many tribes and subtribes and regions connecting to the top."

Those relationships guided governance, he said. "The king cannot just wake up and decide to do something."

Soon after, a starkly different assessment emerged from Germany's foreign intelligence service. In a one-and-a-half-page memo sent to German news organizations, the BND warned that a new, assertive Saudi Arabia could destabilize the Middle East.

"The cautious diplomatic stance of the older leading members of the royal family is being replaced by an impulsive policy of intervention," the report said. This had led Saudi Arabia to pursue an increasingly confrontational stance toward Iran through proxy wars in Syria and Yemen.

"Saudi Arabia wants to prove that it is ready to take unprecedented military, financial, and political risks in order not to fall into a disadvantageous position in the region," it said, adding that MBS risked doing too much too fast.

"The concentration of economic and foreign policy power on Mohammed bin Salman contains the latent danger that, in an attempt to establish himself in the royal succession while his father is still alive, he could overreach with expensive measures or reforms that would unsettle other members of the royal family and the population."

ON THE SECOND day of 2016, the world woke to the news that forty-seven men had been executed in Saudi Arabia, the kingdom's largest mass execution in thirty-six years. Most of the men who were killed that day were Sunni Muslims who had been convicted of links to Al Qaeda attacks in the kingdom. But a number were members of the kingdom's Shiite minority, and one was famous. Sheikh Nimr al-Nimr was a thin preacher with a salt-and-pepper beard who wore a large white turban and had a reputation for diatribes against the royal family.

An estimated 10 percent of Saudi citizens were Shiites. They lived mostly in the kingdom's Eastern Province, where they faced consistent discrimination. While most kept their criticisms of the government to themselves, some participated in protests against the state, which during the Arab Spring grew more ardent and sometimes violent.

Al-Nimr hailed from the village of Awamiya, which had a history of opposition to the monarchy. After more than a decade abroad for religious studies in Iran and Syria, he had returned to his village and taken up at a local mosque, where he delivered fiery calls for Shiite rights. His reach was small at first, and many in his community avoided him, fearing trouble. In a diplomatic cable, an American diplomat said locals dismissed the sheikh as "a secondary player in local politics."

But his star rose with the Arab Spring in 2011. Inspired by protesters elsewhere, Shiites in Saudi Arabia and the nearby island nation of Bahrain joined the movement, clashing with security forces. Young Shiites who felt their elders' quiet efforts to win concessions had failed coalesced around al-Nimr, who overflowed with anger. He argued that Shiites deserved a fair share of the country's oil wealth and suggested that they secede from the kingdom. In one sermon, he called on the downtrodden to rise up against "oppressors."

"In any place he rules—Bahrain, here, in Yemen, in Egypt, or in any place—the unjust ruler is hated," he said. "Whoever defends the oppressor is his partner with him in oppression, and whoever is with the oppressed shares with him his reward from God."

He enraged the Saudi leadership by attacking the royal family, comparing its members to villains in Shiite history and branding them "tyrants" who should be toppled.

"A crown prince dies, put a new crown prince! What are we, a farm? Poultry for them?" he shouted in one sermon. "We don't accept the Al Saud as rulers. We don't accept them and we want to remove them."

The Saudi authorities arrested al-Nimr in 2012, shooting him in the leg during a raid. Pictures of the cleric wrapped in a bloody cloth fueled further protests. A Saudi court sentenced him to death for charges that included breaking allegiance to the ruler, inciting sectarian strife, supporting riots, and the destruction of property. The United States, the European Union, and the United Nations all expressed concern about the trial's fairness.

His arrest and trial elevated al-Nimr from a small-town firebrand to a lightning rod in the growing rivalry between Saudi Arabia and Iran. To Saudi Arabia, al-Nimr was a dangerous rabble-rouser who personified the kingdom's fears of Shiite insurrection and Iranian meddling Iran and its allies saw the cleric as an invaluable domestic foe to the Saudi ruling family, and they amplified his message, making him a regional figure.

As news of the cleric's execution spread, protesters chanting "Death to Al Saud" threw firebombs at the Saudi Embassy in Tehran, smashed windows and furniture, tossed papers from the roof, and set the building alight. Saudi Arabia cut diplomatic ties with Iran and gave the Iranian ambassador and the country's other diplomats forty-eight hours to get out. Iran followed suit. Saudi Arabia and Iran had long been at odds, but the episode marked a sharp escalation in the regional Cold War that would fuel regional tensions for years to come.

A few days after the executions, MBS sat down with journalists from *The Economist* magazine for his first full-length interview, giving the world the most detailed description yet of his ambitions for the future of the kingdom. He defended the executions, including that of al-Nimr, saying they were the result of a legal process the rulers could not intervene in. But the interview focused on his economic vision, which had developed since he pitched it to Obama the year before. The kingdom was overhauling its economy, he said, privatizing health care and education to take pressure off the government budget; developing a domestic military industry; turning undeveloped state land into a valuable asset; and increasing religious tourism to Mecca and Medina. The plans were hugely ambitious, and the prince threw around sums in the tens of billions of dollars as if they were casual investments.

What generated the most buzz, however, was his surprise announcement that Saudi Arabia would sell shares of Saudi Aramco, the state-run oil monopoly and the world's most valuable company.

"I believe it is in the interest of the Saudi market, and it is in the interest of Aramco, and it is for the interest of more transparency, and to counter corruption, if any, that may be circling around Aramco," he said.

It was an eye-popping statement. For anyone familiar with the oil industry, it was clear that the proposed transaction would be massive. No outsider knew exactly how much Aramco was worth, as it had never had a formal valuation and the kingdom's oil reserves had never been audited. But the Saudis estimated its value at between $2 and $3 trillion and said they would sell shares of up to 5 percent of the company, earning more than $100 billion. If those numbers worked out, it would be the largest initial public offering in history.

Others zoomed in on two words MBS used to describe the plan: *transparency* and *corruption*. The first was significant because Aramco's finances had always been opaque, especially when it came to the share of its profits that went to the royal family. Exposing those details would reveal one of the kingdom's most closely guarded secrets. The second drew notice because in a kingdom rife with mismanagement and corruption, Aramco had always been seen as the cleanest, best-run institution. Did the prince have reason to suspect foul play?

The proposed IPO lit up energy and financial markets whose analysts and dealers would spend the next few years scrambling to get information on the kingdom's plans and angling for a piece of the action.

MBS summed up his interview with a description of the Saudi Arabia he dreamed of, for himself and for the kingdom's other young people. It was a place that would not be dependent on oil and would have a growing economy, transparent laws, a strong position in the world, popular participation in decision-making, and would participate in "facing the obstacles and the challenges that face the world."

"My dream as a young man in Saudi Arabia, and the dreams of men in Saudi Arabia, are so many, and I try to compete with them and their dreams, and they compete with mine, to create a better Saudi Arabia," he said.

It was heady, grandiose talk, the likes of which the kingdom had never heard before. But what to make of it? He was still only number three in the kingdom's power structure, and the barriers to everything he wanted to accomplish were numerous—and deeply embedded in his own society.

NO SUCH THING AS WAHHABISM

D URING MY EARLY visits to Saudi Arabia, I became friends with a Saudi businessman who had returned to the kingdom to live after studying in the United States. He was a charming blend of cultures, a fan of dirty jokes and hamburgers who hailed from a prominent family and fasted during Ramadan. We would go out to dinner and discuss current events. I got the feeling that being with an American reminded him of his old life, and I appreciated his insights into Saudi society.

One day, he was angry when he picked me up. I asked what was the matter, and he delivered a tapestry of insults at the religious police, the force officially known as the Commission for the Promotion of Virtue and the Prevention of Vice.

"The Commission," as Saudis called it, was deeply woven into the kingdom's history as part of the alliance between the royal family and the clerics. It owed its existence to the Quranic injunction to build a religious society by encouraging good behavior and stopping bad. The Commission had come to exert great influence in Saudi society, a force of stern, bearded men (it did not employ women) with offices and patrol cars who reported to the king and roamed public places imposing what they saw as proper Islamic conduct. It bothered them little that their rules were much more strict than those practiced in nearly all other Islamic societies.

They included preventing unauthorized *ikhtilat*, or "mixing," between unrelated women and men; enforcing a ban on music; making sure that merchants closed shops during prayer times; herding people to the mosque when the call to prayer sounded; castigating men who wore their hair long; and ensuring that women dressed modestly in public, which meant shrouding their forms and covering their hair. If they covered their faces, too, that was a plus. If not, the men of the Commission would trail them, sometimes wielding batons, commanding, "Cover up! Cover up!" and insulting the women's honor.

The Commission were the on-the-ground enforcers of Wahhabism, and Saudis had no choice but to heed their injunctions or pay the price, as my friend had learned.

The day before, he told me, his wife had been returning to her car from the grocery store with her hair covered but her face showing, and carrying their baby. A man from the Commission spotted her and told her to cover her face, insulting her. She locked herself in her car, snapped a photo of the man, and sent it to her husband to let him know she was being harassed.

He rushed to the supermarket in a rage but couldn't find his wife's car. He spotted the Commission's vehicle and worried she had been arrested, so he ran to open the back. The officers shoved him away, he shoved back, and he remembered seeing one of the men "flying toward the Starbucks." He realized his wife was not in the car and went home.

Shortly after, the police called. Cases had been filed against him and his wife for assaulting an officer from the Commission and for distributing his photo. My friend had to report to the police station, which he feared would mean jail time. So he spent the next few weeks working his connections to get the cases dropped, a process he finalized by paying a hefty fine (he called it a bribe) to the Commission. The experience left him so bitter that he considered giving up on Saudi Arabia and returning to the United States.

"They are germs," he told me. "Filthy criminals."

By 2016, THE rise of the Islamic State in Iraq and Syria had led to new international scrutiny of Wahhabism, and my editor sent me to Saudi Arabia to explore how it was lived in the modern day.

I had always been struck by the kingdom's unique mix of urbanism and desert tradition, with a determined adherence to a strict interpretation of thousand-year-old scriptures. Tremendous wealth, gleaming skyscrapers, and motorways packed with SUVs existed within an all-encompassing religious regime, in which questions about how to interact with other faiths, handle money, and treat animals were answered with stories about the Prophet Muhammad or quotes from the Quran.

Religion permeated daily life. Images of men and women were blurred on billboards and department store mannequins lacked heads because Wahhabism rejected depictions of the human form. Insurance companies employed boards of clerics to ensure their compliance with Sharia law. Textbooks spelled out how girls should cover their bodies (completely), how boys should cut their hair (short), and how often a person should trim his or her pubic hair (often).

There was no public trace of any other religion, because the men of the Commission actively suppressed other faiths. Jews working in the kingdom kept it to themselves. Christians didn't wear crosses. There were no churches, and not even a Church's Chicken (they called it "Texas Chicken"). Saudi officials denied that this showed intolerance, arguing that the kingdom was a unique place for Muslims, with its own rules, as the Vatican was for Christians. (It did not seem relevant to them that women in headscarves or men in turbans could visit St. Peter's Basilica without issue.)

As in any country, personal religious practices varied, but even those who followed the state's official creed were alarmed by the tendency among Westerners to equate it with extremism and insisted that they supported "moderate Islam." That was a slippery term. In Saudi Arabia, it meant beheading criminals, jailing "apostates," and barring women from traveling abroad without the permission of a male "guardian."

Gay rights? Not so much.

The kingdom had championed foreign jihad in Afghanistan in the 1980s (in cooperation with the CIA), but that idea had gone out of style by the time I arrived, and government clerics focused their teaching on another tenet of Wahhabism: obedience to the ruler. I heard little disparaging talk about Christians and Jews, but the clerics persistently attacked Shiites, for ideological reasons and as part of the rivalry with Iran.

The only Saudis who ever called me an infidel were children.

A Saudi journalist once introduced me to his 9-year-old daughter, whom he had enrolled in a private school so she could learn English.

"What is your name?" I asked.

"My name is Dana."

"How old are you?"

"I am nine."

"When is your birthday?"

She switched to Arabic.

"We don't have that in Saudi Arabia," she said. "That's an infidel holiday."

Alarmed, her father asked her where she had learned that, and she retrieved a government textbook and flipped to a lesson listing "forbidden holidays": Christmas and Thanksgiving. Her teacher had added birthdays to the lesson.

Another time, I was having coffee with a conservative friend and his two young sons when the call to prayer sounded. My friend excused himself to pray, and his sons looked at me wide-eyed, wondering why I did not follow.

"Are you an infidel?" one asked.

DESPITE THESE OVERWHELMINGLY visible signs, Mohammed bin Salman consistently argued that Wahhabism didn't exist.

"No one can define Wahhabism," he said. "There is no Wahhabism. We don't believe we have Wahhabism."

He was not the only one. The hardest part of discussing Wahhabism with Saudis was their tendency to deny its existence, for a range of reasons. Even the most devout Saudis did not identify themselves as Wahhabis and argued that Muhammed ibn Abdul-Wahhab had not established a new creed, but merely restored Islam to its roots. Others noted that Wahhabism was often used as a blanket slur against a range of practices or beliefs that the person wielding the term didn't like.

But Saudi and foreign academics and Muslims from other societies found the word useful to describe the ultraconservative interpretation of Islam born in Saudi Arabia and propagated by its
government at home and abroad. Under that definition, it would
have been hard to find a truer Wahhabi than Hisham al-Sheikh, a
direct descendant of Ibn Abdul-Wahhab, the cleric who had started
it all hundreds of years before.

"There is no such thing as Wahhabism," al-Sheikh told me the
first time we met. "There is only true Islam."

Since Ibn Abdul-Wahhab's death, his movement had mush-
roomed into a massive religious establishment inside the Saudi state.
It included a legal system that applied Sharia law; a network of universities that cranked out graduates in religious studies; a council of
clerics that advised the king; tens of thousands of mosque imams
who delivered the government's message from the pulpit; and, of
course, the Commission, to police public behavior. In addition, a
complex web of organizations worked to spread the faith abroad,
from Texas to Tajikistan.

Al-Sheikh's life had been defined by the religious establishment.
His uncle was the Grand Mufti, the kingdom's top religious official.
He had memorized the Quran at a young age and studied with
prominent scholars before completing a PhD in Sharia law, writing
a thesis on how technology changed its application. Now he wore a
number of hats, all of them religious. He advised the minister of
Islamic affairs; wrote studies for the clerics who advised the king;
served on the Sharia board of the MedGulf insurance company; and
trained judges to serve in the kingdom's courts. On Fridays, he
preached at a mosque near his mother's house and welcomed visitors who came to see his uncle.

When I met al-Sheikh, he was a portly man of 42, with a long
beard and no mustache, in imitation of the Prophet Muhammad,
and in the middle of a shining career. We met in the music-free
lobby of a Riyadh hotel, where we sat on purple couches, ate dates,
drank coffee, and chatted, with al-Sheikh glancing from time to
time at his iPhone.

"I am an open-minded person," he told me.

It was clear he hoped I would become a Muslim.

He had traveled extensively abroad and loved the United States. He had been to Oregon, New York, Massachusetts, and California and visited a synagogue, a black church, and an Amish community, whose adherence to strict religious rules he admired. The hardest part had been during Ramadan, when he struggled to find a restaurant open late that did not have a bar.

"All I had was IHOP," he said.

He told me that Islam did not forbid doing business or being friends with Christians and Jews. He frowned when I asked about Shiites, but said it was wrong to declare *takfir*, or infidelity, on entire groups. Each person would be judged individually.

The issue of birthdays was complicated. He didn't oppose their celebration, but his wife did, so their four children did not attend birthday parties thrown by less strict Saudis. Instead, he showed me a video on his phone of the family's own celebration. They gathered around a cake bearing the face of his 15-year-old son, who had memorized the Quran, a major milestone. They lit sparklers and cheered, but did not sing.

Many strict Wahhabis forbid music, but al-Sheikh kept an open mind, relatively. He allowed for background music in restaurants, but opposed music that put listeners in a state similar to drunkenness, making them jump around and bang their heads.

"We have something better," he told me. "You can listen to the Quran."

Since much of what shocks outsiders about Saudi Arabia is its treatment of women, I wanted to talk to a conservative Saudi woman, which was a challenge because most would refuse to meet an unrelated man—let alone an infidel foreign correspondent. So I had a female Saudi journalist I worked with contact al-Sheikh's wife, Meshael.

She agreed to meet me, so I asked her husband for permission.

"She is very busy," he said, changing the subject.

So Meshael and my colleague met at a women's coffee shop, where they could uncover their faces and hair and talk freely.

Meshael and al-Sheikh were cousins and their marriage had been arranged when he was 21 and she was 16. They met once for less than an hour before they were married, and he had been allowed a glimpse at her face before making his final decision to wed.

"It was hard for me to look at him or to check him out, as I was so shy," she said.

He had accepted her condition that she be allowed to continue her studies, and she was now completing a doctorate in education while raising their four children. She disputed the idea that Saudi women lacked rights.

"They believe we are oppressed because we don't drive, but that is incorrect," she said. Driving would be a hassle in Riyadh's traffic anyway. "Here women are respected and honored in many ways you don't find in the West."

She, too, was a descendant of Ibn Abdul-Wahhab and said proudly that one of her ancestors had founded the religious police.

"Praise God that we have the Commission to protect our country!"

THE PRIMACY OF Islam in Saudi life had fed the growth of a huge religious sector that extended beyond the state's official clerics. Public life was filled with celebrity sheikhs: old sheikhs, young sheikhs, sheikhs who used to be extremists and now preached tolerance, sheikhs whom women found sexy, and a black sheikh who had compared himself to Barack Obama. They competed for followers on social media in the kingdom's hyper-wired society, and a number of them, including the blind, elderly Grand Mufti, had their own television shows.

This embrace of technology ran counter to the history of Wahhabi clerics rejecting nearly every innovation as a threat to Islam. Throughout Saudi history, the clerics had sought to ban the telegraph, the radio, the camera, cinema, soccer, girls' education, and television, whose introduction in the 1960s caused outrage.

In areas where it was not entirely clear what was *halal* or *haram*—permitted or forbidden—Saudis turned to clerics for fatwas, or religious opinions. Some fatwas had made international news, such as when Ayatollah Ruhollah Khomeini of Iran called for the killing of the author Salman Rushdie, but most had to do with personal religious practice. Others revealed the lengths clerics went to when applying ancient scriptures to modern life.

Take the cleric who appeared to call for the death of Mickey Mouse and then backtracked. Or the cleric who had to clarify that he had not, in fact, forbidden all-you-can-eat buffets. That same sheikh was asked whether it was OK to take a photo with a cat. The cat was not the problem, the cleric said. The photo was.

"Photography is not permitted unless necessary," he said. "Not with cats, not with dogs, not with wolves, not with anything."

The private fatwa sector sometimes got unruly, so the government tried to impose consistency with official fatwa institutions. But their fatwas provoked laughter, too, like the one that deemed spending money on Pokémon products "cooperation in sin and transgression." Others contradicted government policy. The state, since King Abdullah, had been trying to push more women into the workforce, an effort further advanced by MBS. But the state fatwa organization warned against the "danger of women joining men in their workplace," calling it "the reason behind the destruction of societies."

While digging around on the organization's website, I was shocked to find a fatwa in English from the previous Grand Mufti that called for infidels to be killed or taken as slaves until they became Muslims.

"Whoever refuses to follow the straight path deserves to be killed or enslaved in order to establish justice, maintain security and peace and safeguard lives, honor and property," it read. "Slavery in Islam is like a purifying machine or sauna in which those who are captured enter to wash off their dirt and then they come out clean, pure, and safe, from another door."

I was having coffee with al-Sheikh once and he answered his cellphone, listened intently, and issued a fatwa on the spot. He got such calls all the time, he complained. This query was a simple one: At what point did a pilgrim headed to Mecca have to don the white cloths of ritual purity? Jeddah, he said. But others baffled him, and he declined to rule if he was not sure. Once, a woman had asked whether she could wear fake eyelashes. He told her he didn't know, but later decided it was fine, on one condition: "That there is no cheating."

A woman could put them on before a man proposed and got his first peek at her face—marital false advertising.

"And then after they get married, they're gone!" he said. "That is not permitted."

One Friday, he invited me to visit his uncle, Grand Mufti Abdulaziz al-Sheikh.

We entered a vast reception hall near the mufti's house in Riyadh, where a dozen bearded students sat on padded benches along the walls. The mufti presided in the center in a raised armchair, his feet clad in brown socks and perched on a cushion. The students read religious texts, and the mufti provided commentary. The younger al-Sheikh told me his uncle was 75 and had not been able to see since age 14, when a German doctor had tried to save his eyesight and instead left him blind.

My turn came to ask a question, and I asked one that was on the minds of many Westerners: How did he respond to critics who compared Wahhabism to the ideology of the Islamic State?

"That is all lies and slander. Daesh is an aggressive, tyrannous group that has no relation," he said, using an Arabic acronym for the group.

After a pause, he told me, "You must become a Muslim."

My family were Christians, I said.

"The religion you follow has no source," he said. I needed to accept the Prophet Muhammad's revelation.

"Your religion is not a religion," he said. "In the end, you must face God."

MY REPORTING ALSO led me to the home of a man whose relationship with the religious establishment was more conflicted. Ahmed Qassim al-Ghamdi had spent most of his life working for the Commission, helping to protect the kingdom from secularism, Westernization, and general religious laxity. Some of his tasks had resembled police work: catching drug dealers and bootleggers in a country that banned alcohol. But most of it focused on upholding the kingdom's strict social rules on dress and *ikhtilat*, the hated gender mixing that opened the door to fornication, adultery, broken homes, orphans, and all-around societal collapse.

I met al-Ghamdi in a sitting room in his Jeddah apartment that had been decorated to look like a Bedouin tent, with burgundy fabric on the walls, gold tassels hanging from the roof, and carpets on the floor, on which al-Ghamdi prayed periodically. He was 51 and sported the same signs of a devout Saudi man as al-Sheikh—the long beard and bare upper lip. For much of his life, the beliefs of both men would have lined up, too, but al-Ghamdi had gone through a religious reckoning that had caused him to question his old life and the religious establishment that had defined it.

Little in his background foretold his future as a religious reformer. He had worked at the customs office in the port of Jeddah during university but quit after a cleric told him that Islam forbade collecting duties. After graduation, he studied religion in his spare time and handled international accounts for a government office, a job that required travel to non-Muslim countries. At the time, the clerics recommended avoiding infidel lands, so he quit.

He next got a job teaching economics at a technical school, but became so annoyed that the curriculum did not include Islamic finance that he quit that, too. When he landed a job with the Commission in Jeddah, he thought, finally, a vocation that matched his religious convictions.

In different positions there and in Mecca, he helped catch prostitutes and sorcerers, who could be beheaded. But over time he grew uneasy with the force's methods, feeling that his colleagues' zeal made them overreact, breaking into homes to hunt for contraband or humiliating suspects.

"Let's say someone drank alcohol," he said. "That does not represent an attack on the religion, but they exaggerated in how they treated people."

He got a position reviewing cases and tried to report abuses. One case involved a middle-aged bachelor who received two young women in his home on weekends. The man did not pray at the mosque, so his neighbors suspected the worst. They called the

Commission, which raided his house and caught the man red-handed—visiting with his own adult daughters.

"People were humiliated in inhuman ways, and that humiliation could cause hatred of religion," al-Ghamdi said.

In 2005, al-Ghamdi was promoted to be the head of the Commission for the Mecca region, a big job overseeing scores of stations in a large, diverse area. He worked hard, but worried privately that the force's emphasis was off. He returned to the scriptures and the sayings of the Prophet Muhammad and found a gap between what they contained and what the Commission was imposing. There had been plenty of mixing among the first generation of Muslims, for example, and no one had sought to stamp it out, not least the prophet himself.

Al-Ghamdi came to believe that much of what Saudis practiced as religion was actually Arabian cultural practices that had become mixed up with their faith. It was a startling conclusion, and dangerous for a man of his station. So he kept quiet, at least for a time.

In 2007, SAUDI Arabia broke ground on a new pet project for the monarch, the King Abdullah University of Science and Technology, which was supposed to grow into a world-class university on the Red Sea with the help of a royal endowment of more than $10 billion. To ensure international standards, King Abdullah insulated KAUST, as it was known, from clerical interference. Female students would dress as they wished, and classes would be co-ed.

KAUST followed the precedent of Saudi Aramco, the oil company, where the clerics had also been forbidden to tread, highlighting a great Saudi contradiction: As much as the royals preached Islamic values, when they wanted to earn money or innovate, they did not solicit the clerics' advice. They locked them out.

Most clerics stayed mum on the plan, out of deference to the king, but one member of the top clerical body warned on a call-in show about the dangers of co-education. There would be sexual harassment. Men and women would cavort, distracting them from their studies. Husbands would grow jealous of their wives. There could be rapes.

"Mixing has many corrupting factors, and its evil is great," declared Sheikh Saad al-Shathri, suggesting that the king would stop it if he knew.

But the mixing at KAUST had been the king's idea, and he promptly fired the cleric.

The ordeal frustrated al-Ghamdi. He felt that the clerics were not supporting an initiative that was good for Saudi Arabia. So after praying about it, he put his thoughts in two articles about religious practices that were published in *Okaz* newspaper in 2009.

They were the first volleys in a prolonged battle between al-Ghamdi and the religious establishment. He followed with other articles, and faced off on TV with noted clerics who countered him with their own evidence from the Islamic scriptures. His colleagues at the Commission shunned him, so he requested—and swiftly received—early retirement.

Once off the force, he cast doubt on other practices, arguing that it was not necessary to close shops during prayer times, force people to go to the mosque, oblige women to cover their faces, or bar them from driving. Women during the time of the prophet had ridden camels, which he argued was more provocative than driving SUVs. At one point, a woman asked him if she could not only show her face, but wear makeup. He replied, Why not? To prove that he meant it, he went on a popular talk show with his wife, Jawahir, her face bare and adorned with a dusting of makeup.

His arguments went off like a bomb inside the religious establishment, shaking the foundations of the social order that gave the clerics their power. Condemnation rained down from the senior ranks. Some attacked al-Ghamdi's credentials, saying he was not really a sheikh. That was a dubious accusation because there was no standard qualification for sheikh-hood. Others questioned his résumé, arguing, correctly, that he had no degree in religion and pointing out, also correctly, that his doctorate was from Ambassador University Corporation, a diploma mill.

"There is no doubt that this man is bad," a member of the kingdom's top clerical council said. "It is necessary for the state to assign someone to summon and torture him."

The Grand Mufti, who years later would beseech me to become

a Muslim, addressed the issue on his call-in show, saying that the kingdom's television channels should ban content that "corrupts the religion and the morals and values of society."

The clerical attacks were loud, but the social blowback hurt more. Angry callers yelled at al-Ghamdi through his cellphone. He got death threats on Twitter. His tribe disowned him as "troubled and confused." A mosque where he preached asked him to stop coming. Vandals scrawled insulting graffiti on the wall of his house. A group of men showed up at his door, demanding to "mix" with his women-folk. His sons—he has nine children—called the police.

Al-Ghamdi had not broken any laws and faced no legal charges, but the attacks shook his family. The relatives of his eldest son's fiancée called off the couple's wedding, not wanting to associate their family with his. His sister's husband left her after she stood by her brother. A boy at school taunted his 15-year-old son, Ammar, saying, "How did your mom go on TV? That's not right. You have no manners."

So Ammar punched him.

BY THE TIME I met al-Ghamdi in 2016, the hubbub had mostly died down, although he kept a low profile because strangers still insulted him when he appeared in public. He was publishing columns in foreign newspapers, but was otherwise jobless—a cleric whose positions had rendered him unemployable in the Islamic kingdom.

It was a bad year for the Commission. A video of its officers confronting a girl in a mall parking lot had gone viral. It showed her being thrown to the ground and yelping as her abaya flew up, exposing her torso. For many Saudis, "the Nakheel Mall girl" personified the Commission's overreach. Then the Commission arrested a popular talk show host who had criticized religious figures, and photos of him appeared online in handcuffs with bottles of liquor. It appeared that the photos had been staged and leaked by the Commission in an attempted character assassination. The outrage grew.

Those incidents highlighted the irony of al-Ghamdi's ordeal: Many Saudis, including important royals and even some clerics, agreed with him that the kingdom's strictures had gone too far. One of them was MBS, who recognized that clerical control was a major barrier to his development plans. So in April 2016, a surprise royal decree stripped the religious police of their powers. Henceforth, they could not arrest, question, or pursue subjects except in cooperation with the actual police. And they were advised to be "gentle and kind" in their interactions with citizens.

When the news broke, I contacted a number of Saudi friends for their thoughts, but no one knew what to make of it. Was it for real? It seemed too good to be true, and the Commission too powerful to merely fade away. But over time we realized that, yes, it was real. With a single royal decree, MBS had defanged the clerics, clearing the way for vast changes they most certainly would have opposed.

GRAND VISIONS

THE CONSULTANTS CAME in droves, wearing well-cut suits with power ties, flying in first-class from Dubai, Beirut, or London, and checking in to the Riyadh Ritz-Carlton or the Four Seasons. They put in long days extracting information about the Saudi government and economy and refining it into detailed reports and flashy PowerPoint presentations. When the time came to present their findings, they showed up at the Royal Court and waited in its ornate, high-ceilinged sitting rooms, where they inevitably found crowds of consultants from competing firms ahead of them in line. As they waited, servers brought endless cups of tea or saffron-flavored Saudi coffee. Often, they were given nighttime appointments, told to come at 10 P.M. and made to wait until 2 A.M. before being dismissed and told to return the next day. For many, it was a frustrating, grueling routine, but the money was great and there was no alternative if you wanted to pitch your services to the highest-spending customer in the Middle East: Mohammed bin Salman.

As MBS formulated his plans to remake the kingdom, he realized not only that he had to defang the clerics who would oppose change, but that he needed experts to figure out what had to be done and how. So he turned to management consultants, opening the taps of Saudi cash so crowds of highly educated foreigners could advise him on everything from diversifying the economy to streamlining military procurement to reformatting school curricula.

In many ways, it was a match made in heaven. Saudi Arabia lacked human capital in many domains that MBS wanted to reform, and he himself had little relevant experience for much of what he wanted to do. So why not bring in graduates of Oxford and Harvard who had worked on similar issues in other countries to help him out? They could synthesize past experiences, the thinking went, and give more unvarnished advice than the prince could expect from fellow Saudis.

MBS came along at a time of uncertainty for the consulting industry in the Middle East. Many firms had lost business in Egypt, Libya, and Yemen when their governments were toppled and economies roiled during the Arab Spring. So they had shifted toward the wealthy Arab monarchies of the Persian Gulf, which were stable, with small domestic professional classes and lots of money to spend. MBS turbocharged that shift, because of the size of Saudi Arabia's economy and the faith the young prince had in what foreign experts had to offer.

He commissioned the biggest companies, McKinsey & Company, Boston Consulting Group, and Strategy&, as well as smaller boutique firms, to handle public relations and implement projects. Some firms kept permanent offices near the Royal Court, so they could be summoned quickly and sometimes turn around projects in twenty-four hours, much faster than they normally worked. MBS would pit them against one another, giving the same project to competing firms and making them present in front of the others, a live battleground of ideas.

"It's like a beauty pageant," said a consultant who worked with the higher reaches of the Saudi government.

And the budget for it boomed. The kingdom's spending on consultants increased by double digits the year Salman became king, and it would continue to grow, with MBS spending more than $1 billion per year on foreign expertise.

But there was often a culture gap between the consultants, who valued punctuality, transparency, democracy, and open markets, and the Saudis, whose work ethic and schedules were unreliable and who lived in a highly secretive absolute monarchy. After the Arab Spring, there had been discussions inside McKinsey about the ethics of working with dictators, a former consultant there told me. But the company's leaders had ignored the risks, instead viewing their work as an opportunity to play a positive role in the development of countries such as Saudi Arabia.

"There was no question about working with MBS," the former McKinsey consultant told me. "They were all-in."

THE CONSULTANTS NEVER had trouble entering Saudi Arabia to work. I did.

For my first visit to Saudi Arabia, when I had written about the women defying the driving ban, I had received a press visa—one week, single entry, nonrenewable. When it expired, I struggled to get back in. I applied for a new visa and it came through a few months later—two weeks, single entry, nonrenewable. So I went, did a few stories, and waited another few months for my next visa.

During one period, the only way I could get in was to apply for conferences, which were sponsored by powerful organizations working to build their profiles. Most of the events were hugely boring, packed with dull panels about increasing competitiveness and building a knowledge economy, but once I was in, I could work as I pleased.

At one point, I received a visa—one month, single entry, nonrenewable—to attend a two-day conference, but its organization was so poor that I didn't receive the visa until the day the conference began. I flew to Saudi Arabia that evening, attended the conference's second day, and had 29 days left, during which officials I called refused to speak to me because I was not there to do interviews.

Journalistic access improved after Salman became king. Transparency was a talking point of the MBS era, and that affected openness with journalists, at least initially. I did some stories the Saudis liked. I traveled to Buraidah, a staunchly conservative town, and wrote about how clerics intervened in death penalty cases to save criminals from getting their heads chopped off. I wrote about a long-running program at the National Guard Hospital in Riyadh that separated conjoined twins who came from poor families around the world. After those were published, I got a new visa—three months, multi-entry, nonrenewable—which felt luxurious.

As 2016 got under way, momentum built toward the release of MBS's grand plan for the future of Saudi Arabia. Consultants had been heavily involved in it at all levels, and a think tank associated with McKinsey had produced a report diagnosing the challenges facing the kingdom and proposing a range of fixes. It was seen as a trial balloon for various initiatives under consideration.

Then Saudi officials and the local news media began talking about the National Transformation Plan, MBS's road map for the future that was being drawn up by McKinsey. After its release was delayed several times, MBS commissioned a competing firm, Boston Consulting Group, to create an alternative document to launch his proposed reforms. It was called "Vision 2030," and a date was finally set for its release, the week after my visa expired. The guys at the Information Ministry told me I would get an extension, but it never came, so I left. Two days later they called late at night to say they wanted me to cover the launch. They did get me a new visa—five years, multi-entry, nonrenewable—but it was issued the day of the big event, so I put the visa in my passport and watched the release on TV from my office in Beirut.

The vision itself was an extensive document, with subheads and bullet points detailing how MBS planned to restructure Saudi Arabia's economy and change the lifestyles of its citizens. It was grandiose and optimistic, packed with targets.

"We will begin immediately delivering the overarching plans and programs we have set out," its forward declared. "Together, with the help of Allah, we can strengthen the Kingdom of Saudi Arabia's position as a great nation in which we should all feel an immense pride."

The kingdom would take advantage of its place in the Arab and Islamic worlds, transform itself into a global investment giant, and establish itself as a hub for Europe, Asia, and Africa. Sector by sector, the vision laid out what would change. Aramco would grow from an oil company into an energy conglomerate. The kingdom would create a mining industry to employ Saudis, manufacture its own military equipment, and offer improved health, housing, and educational services. There would be recycling, e-government, and renewable energy.

The vision acknowledged, remarkably, that Saudi Arabia wasn't a very fun place to live.

"We are well aware that the cultural and entertainment opportunities currently available do not reflect the rising aspirations of our citizens and residents, nor are they in harmony with our prosperous economy," it said.

So the kingdom would expand entertainment and encourge Saudis to exercise.

The Vision may have been written by foreign consultants, but when it came time for the rollout, it all belonged to MBS. The day of its release, he gave an extensive television interview, throwing around gigantic numbers and speaking about what his plan meant not just for Saudi Arabia, but for "planet Earth." The kingdom had "an oil addiction" that had impeded development, but that would end soon.

"I think that by 2020, if the oil stops, we'll be able to live," he said. "We need it. We needed it. But I think that in 2020 we'll be able to live without oil."

The privatization of Aramco was on the way, he said, through "the biggest IPO in the history of the world." The holdings of the kingdom's Public Investment Fund would be so great that it would be "an essential mover on planet Earth." A proposed bridge across the Red Sea between Saudi Arabia and Egypt would become "the most important land crossing in the world."

It was ambitious, heady stuff, and many of my Saudi friends welcomed the prospect of great change. But in mapping out all the needed reforms, the Vision detailed how poorly the kingdom had been run and how ill-prepared its citizens were to participate in a diversified economy. Would a country that was ready to blast off in the way that MBS described need to "build a culture that rewards determination, provides opportunities for all, and helps everyone acquire the necessary skills to achieve their personal goals"?

The plan also made light of the huge challenges its implementation would face. The kingdom was decades behind its neighbors in building the infrastructure to be a regional hub. And it had a deficit of human capital, both in terms of skills and work ethic. There was little industrial base that was not connected to oil, and no domestic working class to speak of. Foreigners held nearly all the blue-collar jobs. They held many of the white-collar jobs, too.

Critics dismissed the Vision as an exercise in personal branding by MBS or as hugely unrealistic, like an obese man with no college degree announcing his intention to become a vegan triathlete tech pioneer. There was reason to doubt. I remember thinking at the time that at least MBS was planning a positive future for his country. That was more than one could say for most other Arab leaders. But as my experience with the visa operation had shown, the kingdom's bureaucracy had a long way to go to function as MBS planned.

A ROLE FOR JOURNALISM

Soon after Mohammed bin Salman released his vision for the future of Saudi Arabia, he held a private reception for the leading lights of Saudi society. They broke down into two groups. First were the clerics, but not the stuffy, elderly scholars whom young Saudis mocked for their fatwas condemning Pokémon or forbidding photos with cats. These were younger, tech-savvy clerics whose moves young Saudis tracked like Western kids followed Hollywood stars. One hosted a popular television show. Another had been the first black man to lead prayers at the Grand Mosque in Mecca. Yet another was referred to as the Brad Pitt of Saudi clerics because of his luscious lips.

They had not always had easy relationships with the authorities. One was the same cleric King Abdullah had fired for criticizing his co-ed university. Others had been thrown in prison, kicked off of television, or put under house arrest for preaching that strayed outside of the ever-shifting red lines. But the assets they brought to the meeting were clear: millions of followers on Twitter, Snapchat, and other social media platforms. MBS knew well that no other group of Saudis could so easily land Vision 2030 on the screens of so many cellphones across the kingdom.

The other group were intellectuals and journalists who played a role in shaping Saudi public opinion by telegraphing the kingdom's views and letting the people know how their leaders viewed regional and international issues. Among them was a large, mild-mannered journalist named Jamal Khashoggi, the same man who had briefed the American diplomat years before on the looming challenge to the monarchy.

Khashoggi was in his late fifties, and his life had traversed the most significant social trends in Saudi Arabia. He would end up playing a larger role in MBS's trajectory than anyone else in the room that day.

He was born in the holy city of Medina to an elite family in the Hejaz region of western Saudi Arabia. His grandfather was a doctor who had treated MBS's grandfather. Another relative was the famous arms dealer Adnan Khashoggi, whose lavish, billionaire lifestyle had filled magazine spreads.

He did not share his uncle's wealth, but he grew up comfortably in Jeddah, whose historic role as a transit point for pilgrims heading to Mecca made it the kingdom's most cosmopolitan city. He had gone to the United States for college, earning a degree in business administration from Indiana State University in 1983. It was there that he became active in the Muslim Brotherhood, the international Islamist organization that seeks to embed its version of Islam in the lives of its followers—and in the states where they live.

Khashoggi was devout and joined an *usra*, or "family," the basic unit of Brotherhood life that operated like a Bible study, combining religious and social activities. It was not uncommon at the time for young Saudis to fall in with the Brotherhood while abroad. They were prominent in Muslim student associations across the United States, including the Muslim Arab Youth Association that Khashoggi joined. And he would have found their style familiar, since Brotherhood members had played a large role in building the Saudi education system. One year, he ran the book fair at the association's U.S. national conference.

After university, Khashoggi worked as a journalist for *Arab News*, an English-language newspaper in Jeddah, and other publications, which gave him an opportunity to cover the biggest international story of the day for Saudi Arabia: the Afghan jihad.

The Soviet Union had invaded Afghanistan, and the United States and Saudi Arabia had intervened to push it back, each for its own reasons. The United States saw Afghanistan as a new front in the Cold War, while Saudi Arabia and others in the Muslim world considered the Soviet invasion an infidel attack on a Muslim land. So the two countries joined forces, the CIA working with Saudi intelligence to fund and arm the holy warriors, or *mujahideen*.

The Afghan jihad stirred the passions of young men across the Arab world in the same way the Spanish Civil War had inspired Westerners such as Ernest Hemingway and George Orwell. Saudi royals paid for young Saudis to join the fight, and Khashoggi rode the wave as a journalist. During reporting trips to Afghanistan, he donned local clothes and traveled with Abdullah Azzam, a Palestinian Islamic scholar and theorist of jihad. Once, he sat next to him in the crowded backseat of a car to protect the famous cleric from potential attacks. He had his photo taken holding a Kalashnikov (to the consternation of his editor back home). There is no record of Khashoggi fighting, but his sympathy for the cause was clear and won him an invitation from another young Saudi who was making a name for himself in Afghanistan: Osama bin Laden.

Bin Laden had also grown up in Jeddah, a son of a wealthy contractor who had built much of the kingdom's infrastructure, including many royal palaces and the compounds around the holy sites. Instead of seeking a role in the family business, bin Laden had used his wealth to set up a training camp in Afghanistan for the so-called "Afghan Arabs" flocking to join the jihad. Bin Laden wanted to spread the word, and invited Khashoggi to write about the place. In an article for *Arab News* in 1988, Khashoggi trumpeted its transnational Islamic identity:

> Maasadat Al-Ansar, Afghanistan—Muslims are one nation. Despite geographical barriers, political squabbles and differences in color and language, they consider themselves brothers. This unique brotherhood is clearly manifested in the attitude of those Arab youths who have joined the Afghan Mujahedeen in their indefatigable struggle against the Communist forces.

Khashoggi described bin Laden as "a famous Saudi contractor" who had become "one of the foremost leaders of the Arab *muhahedeen* in Afghanistan" and quoted him describing glorious battles.

"We sometimes spent the whole day in the trenches or in the caves until our ears could no longer bear the sound of the explosions all around us," bin Laden told him. "War planes continually shrieked by us and their crazy song of death echoed endlessly. We spent the days praying to God Almighty."

Khashoggi also spoke with Jalaluddin Haqqani, who laid out the idea of transnational jihad that would later drive both Al Qaeda and the Islamic State.

"We are proud of these Arab youths," Haqqani said of the camp's recruits. "These Arabs now know the requirements of *mujahedeen* and will serve as ambassadors of jihad in their own countries when they return."

Bin Laden, of course, would go on to found Al Qaeda and plot catastrophic attacks in the United States and elsewhere, while Haqqani would head the Haqqani Network, a designated terrorist organization associated with Al Qaeda. But in the late 1980s, the two men were seen as Muslim folk heroes, taking up arms against injustice.

But as the war descended into factional fighting and warlordism, Khashoggi's dream that the Afghan jihad would improve life in the country collapsed.

"He was disappointed that after all the struggle that happened, the Afghans never got it together," a Saudi colleague recalled. "The infighting, he always talked about that."

When American commandos killed bin Laden in Pakistan in 2011, Khashoggi mourned, not for bin Laden, but for the dashed hope he had once embodied.

"I collapsed into tears a while ago, heartbroken for you Abu Abdullah," Khashoggi wrote on Twitter, using a nickname for bin Laden. "You were beautiful and brave in those beautiful days in Afghanistan, before you surrendered to hatred and rage."

The failure of the Afghan jihad was the first of several political heartbreaks for Khashoggi.

KHASHOGGI RETURNED TO Saudi Arabia and kept writing, a cordial, devout man who led prayers in the office at *Arab News*. When Saddam Hussein invaded Kuwait, Khashoggi drove through the desert to cover the war, running into fleeing Kuwaiti forces who almost shot him before realizing he was Saudi.

He was promoted to editor, which pushed him into a higher level of society, attending private meetings with officials and royals and traveling with the king. But while serving the monarchy, he kept in touch with Islamists around the Arab world and pushed for another private passion: democracy.

In 1992, the Algerian military barred an Islamist party that had won parliamentary elections from taking power, another political heartbreak for Khashoggi. So he and a friend from the Muslim Brotherhood, Azzam Tamimi, founded a group called "Friends of Democracy in Algeria," which placed ads in British newspapers promoting its cause. The group later broadened its mandate to promoting human rights around the Middle East. Tamimi was its public face, while Khashoggi raised funds behind the scenes.

Khashoggi developed a close relationship with Prince Turki al-Faisal, a son of Saudi Arabia's third king, who headed the kingdom's intelligence agency. That relationship, and Khashoggi's trips to Afghanistan, fueled speculation that Khashoggi was an intelligence agent operating under journalistic cover. Prince Turki and Khashoggi's friends denied it, but several acknowledged that he did favors for the Saudis. In 2005, for instance, a group of Western officials met in Beirut with leaders from Hamas, the Palestinian militant movement, and the Saudis sent Khashoggi to be their eyes in the meeting. There was nothing suspicious about it at the time, because most Arab Islamists did not consider Saudi Arabia a hostile power.

Despite his early admiration for bin Laden, Khashoggi was ahead of many in the kingdom in recognizing the danger of Al Qaeda and how Saudi Arabia's intolerance had contributed to the weaponization of Islam. After the terrorist attacks of September 11, 2001, Saudi officials denied that Saudi citizens had led the plot and conspiracy theories coursed through the kingdom that "the Jews" were behind it. Khashoggi never bought them, placing the blame squarely on those he accused of perverting Islam.

"Osama bin Laden's hijacked planes not only attacked New York and Washington, they also attacked Islam as a faith and the values of tolerance and coexistence that it preaches," he wrote.

Over the next decade, debates on social issues raged between liberals and conservatives inside the kingdom, and Khashoggi was a staunch campaigner for the reformist camp. He was appointed editor of *Al Watan* newspaper and used it to push for women's rights while criticizing the power of the religious establishment. He didn't last long. After Al Qaeda bombings killed twenty-five people in Riyadh in 2003, Khashoggi penned an editorial attacking not only the terrorists, but the clerics who gave them cover.

"Those who committed yesterday's crime, which will have a painful impact on the peaceful nature of our nation, are not only the suicide bombers," he wrote, "but also everyone who instigated or justified the attacks, everyone who called them *mujahideen*."

He was fired after less than two months. He received death threats, so Prince Turki, who had been named ambassador to the United Kingdom, took Khashoggi along as a media adviser. A few years later, Turki was named ambassador to Washington, and Khashoggi followed him there, too. Those two jobs helped Khashoggi build a network of contacts among Western journalists and officials he would keep in touch with over the years. While in the United States, he bought a condo near Tysons Corner in Virginia, where he would seek refuge later in life.

He returned home in 2007, where tempers had cooled since his last attempt at domestic journalism. He got his old job back at *Al Watan* and resumed the reformist fight. To expose what he saw as the backwardness of the kingdom's education system, he published a question from a government textbook—"How can you identify a woman who can breed more children?"—and solicited answers from "experts" to show the question's absurdity.

He was an early advocate for women driving, a topic so hot that he could not address it directly in the newspaper. So he did it obliquely, publishing an article that imagined a girl riding a camel to the university and the chaos that ensued. There was no place for her to park, the police weren't sure how to react, and neither were Saudi drivers, since—as with driving—there was no law that explicitly prohibited girls from riding camels. In subsequent weeks, he published similar articles, imagining a girl riding a bicycle, then a donkey. The articles provoked controversy, and Khashoggi got fired again.

His career broadened out. He became a regular commentator on Saudi and Arab talk shows and published widely, writing a column for *Al Hayat*, an international Arabic newspaper based in London. Along the way, he maintained his ties to the Saudi power structure and communicated the kingdom's views to the world.

For most of his career, he was not a reporter in the Western sense, as in a journalist who dug up facts to hold reluctant powers accountable. More accurately, he was an *i'laami*, Arabic for a "media figure," who wrote, ran newspapers, and appeared on television as much to transmit the government's views as to promote his own. Sometimes, that meant writing for cash, as when a contact wired him $100,000 in 2009 to do a sympathetic interview with Prime Minister Najib Razak of Malaysia.

At times, his own views diverged from those of the Saudi leadership, especially after the Arab Spring uprisings spread across the Middle East in 2011. Khashoggi was moved by the story of Mohamed Bouazizi, the Tunisian fruit vendor who had set himself on fire after a confrontation with the police, becoming a symbol of how repressive regimes dashed the hopes of young Arabs. As the uprisings spread, Khashoggi was optimistic that the protests in Tunisia, Egypt, and Syria would pave the way for democracy.

But he maintained a Saudi view of other uprisings. He opposed protests against Bahrain's Sunni monarchy by the island nation's Shiite majority, and he supported the Saudi military intervention in Yemen as necessary to check Iran's ambitions.

The Arab Spring ran off course—another heartbreak for Khashoggi. Egypt collapsed into chaos followed by a military coup, Yemen fell apart, and the Islamic State rose in Iraq and Syria.

It was during this period that I got to know Khashoggi. He was in his mid-fifties then, a tall, rotund man with droopy eyes and an easy manner who cared deeply about the region, liked to discuss ideas, and seemingly never got angry. His media prominence had made him a household name in the Arab world, and he seemed to live on airplanes, traipsing between foreign capitals for meetings and conferences while juggling multiple cellphones that never stopped ringing. Like other foreign journalists working in the region, I took to phoning him regularly to get his thoughts, knowing that, unlike other prominent Saudis, he usually answered his phone.

I kept track of his views. When the Islamic State was at its peak, he spoke of how its ideology overlapped with the kingdom's.

"Islam itself is in crisis today," he told me in 2014. "We thought we had settled the issues of modernization, relations with the West, the world, women, democracy, and elections. But they are back again and open for debate, and it is ISIS who has brought them back."

Along the way, he served as an adviser to Prince Alwaleed bin Talal, the flamboyant billionaire investor who shared Khashoggi's desire for social reform in the kingdom. The prince funded a new Arabic television station and tapped Khashoggi to run it. But the project didn't work out. In February 2015, Alarab television went live with a talk show on which a prominent member of Bahrain's opposition criticized the island kingdom's royal family. Within hours, it was off the air.

After Salman became king, Khashoggi lauded him as a strong leader and argued that the Arabs should rely less on the United States for security. He penned a widely read column called "The Salman Doctrine" that laid out the new king's foreign policy, criticizing what he saw as American resistance to acknowledge the threat posed by Iran.

His opinions sometimes got him attacked online, but he stuck to them and said he was grateful that Saudi Arabia allowed open discussion.

"In the Arab world, everyone thinks journalists cannot be independent, but I represent myself, which is the right thing to do. What would I be worth if I succumbed to pressure to change my opinions? The atmosphere of freedom must be preserved, and I am happy that my government is doing so," he wrote. "The world cannot bring down someone who is free on the inside. I want to be free, to think freely and write freely. I am free to do so."

Khashoggi's inclusion in MBS's meeting with the clerics and intellectuals in 2016 showed that he mattered, that the kingdom's rising new leader saw him as a voice worth winning over. MBS told the assembled men about his economic plans and spoke about politics, warning of Iran's growing influence in Sudan, Pakistan, and Djibouti.

When Khashoggi's turn came to speak, he asked MBS why he did not speak about such issues publicly.

You are the journalists, the prince said. If you want to write about it, go ahead.

The men had convened after the sunset prayer, and the conversation continued until they performed the last prayer of the day together. It was Khashoggi's first brush with MBS, and he came away believing he had been given a mandate to write about, and even critique, the prince's reforms. He wrote later that year: "This is also what the man of the Vision, Deputy Crown Prince Mohammed bin Salman, promised in a meeting that brought together intellectuals, saying, 'There will be a role for journalism in monitoring its implementation.' And we as journalists want that role."

THE TWO MOHAMMEDS

L IKE MOST RECENT American ambassadors to Saudi Arabia, Joseph Westphal was not a career diplomat, because foreign service professionals were not the kinds of people the Saudis preferred to represent their most important ally. Saudi diplomacy favored personal relationships over institutions, so before the king accepted a new ambassador, what he really wanted to know was not how many years that person had served or where, but whether he was close to the president. So American ambassadors to Riyadh were all men, most with links to the president himself.

By late 2015, Westphal had settled into his job and developed a warm rapport with his main interlocutors. Given the importance of the relationship with the United States, the king received him regularly, and Westphal had continued to meet with MBS as his profile had grown. But much of his official business went through the crown prince, Mohammed bin Nayef, the counterterrorism czar.

That fall, Westphal flew to Jeddah to meet the crown prince. When he landed, he found a helicopter waiting on the tarmac, but not to take him to his planned meeting. Instead, MBS's people said the young prince needed to see him and promised that he would be back for his other meeting. So Westphal climbed into the helicopter. He flew farther away than expected, and his meeting with MBS lasted long enough to make him miss his appointment with the crown prince. Many in the White House concluded that that had been the goal: for MBS to muscle in on his older cousin's schedule.

In public, at royal functions and in meetings with American officials, MBS showed deference to his older, more experienced cousin.

He stood behind him, often with his head bowed and his hands clasped at his waist, while MBN spoke, the expected decorum toward the crown prince. Saudi officials insisted, in public and in private, that "the two Mohammeds" had a strong relationship based on the younger's respect for the older. But as time went on, it became clear that that was not the case. MBS was gunning for his cousin's job.

MBS disarmed him over time. For years, MBN had relied heavily on one deputy, a linguist and computer scientist with a PhD in artificial intelligence from the University of Edinburgh in Scotland. Dr. Saad al-Jabri had risen inside the Interior Ministry, earning the rank of major general, serving as MBN's chief of staff, and developing a reputation among the Americans as the prince's "go to" man on a range of issues. He spoke English better than his boss and was more outgoing, so he met frequently with Americans to discuss the Al Qaeda threat, Iran's activities, and developments in Iraq and Afghanistan.

In September 2015, around the time that MBS made sure that Ambassador Westphal stood up the crown prince, MBN and al-Jabri were at work when a breaking news alert appeared on television announcing that the king had fired al-Jabri. Neither man had known it was coming and they could not contest it, so al-Jabri packed up his office and moved out of the ministry, leaving MBN without his most trusted aide.

A few months later, MBS held his first press conference, fielding questions from sympathetic Saudi journalists about another new initiative, an international alliance of Islamic countries against terrorism. The alliance had thirty-four member states, MBS said, with others expected to join later. An operations room would be established in Riyadh to "coordinate and support the efforts to fight terrorism in all regions and parts of the Islamic world."

The plan was half-baked. The United States and the United Kingdom, longtime counterterrorism partners, publicly lent their support, but privately expected little to come of it. A number of countries the Saudis claimed were members soon said they had never heard of the new coalition or needed more information before deciding whether to join. And the predominately Shiite nations of

Iraq and Iran had not been included, giving the initiative a sectarian cast.

Observers across the region and in the United States saw the announcement as something else: an effort by MBS to gain a foothold in counterterrorism, his cousin's signature file.

"As I recall, the reaction was not that it was going to be a substantive undertaking," said Lisa Monaco, Obama's chief counterterrorism adviser at the time. "It was a sign of him moving into a portfolio that had been quite clearly MBN's for a long time, and to good effect."

The Obama administration knew that a struggle was under way over who would become the future ruler of Saudi Arabia, and the CIA was tasked with drawing up an assessment. Some State Department officials saw promise in MBS's youth and ambition, while MBN was a known quantity who had established his credentials over many years. But President Obama's position was clear: It was not up to the United States to pick the ruler of Saudi Arabia, and his administration would not preference one prince over the other.

"We were watching and very attuned to the dynamics," Monaco said. "It was pretty apparent that this jockeying was going on and it was an issue, insofar as we wanted to make sure that we were not putting a thumb on the scale, even though we were thinking that if MBS is going to be the ruler, we also need to be developing that relationship."

But even some of MBN's biggest fans in the United States were realizing that his best days were behind him. He had been wounded more severely in the attack by the "butt bomber" than had been clear at the time, and he had begun taking strong painkillers. They sapped his energy, and he often appeared wiped out, nodding off at least once during a meeting with Obama. American spies reported that he appeared to be addicted to the medication and could have also been using illicit drugs to pep himself back up. Other intelligence reports suggested another vulnerability: a predilection for cross-dressing and homosexuality.

Those allegations were well known among other Gulf royals, including Sheikh Mohammed bin Zayed of the United Arab Emirates, who did not want MBN to become king. During a lunch at his mansion in McLean, Virginia, in 2015, he had spelled out his position to a number of American officials.

MBZ was personally taking MBS under his wing as the future of Saudi Arabia, he said, while alluding to MBN's problems.

"You know why he cannot be king," he said. "He will not be accepted by the Saudis or by any of us. He can't be king. He won't be king."

Around the start of 2016, MBN left the kingdom for his family's villa in Algeria, a sprawling, isolated compound an hour outside of Algiers. He vacationed there most years, and it was one of the things he most looked forward to, a chance to escape his worries over the kingdom's security and engage his passions for hunting and falconry. But this time, he stayed away for weeks, failing to respond to messages from longtime associates in Washington, including John Brennan, the CIA director.

It was a strange time for the kingdom's security chief to be out of touch, with the war in Yemen escalating and the jihadists of Islamic State bombing targets in the kingdom. But a number of American officials assumed he had fled the frictions with MBS, worried that his path to the throne was in jeopardy.

As MBN STEPPED back, MBS stepped up.

He charmed Republican senator Lindsey Graham of South Carolina during a congressional visit to Riyadh in March 2016. Appearing in his full royal regalia, MBS said he wished he had dressed differently.

"The robe does not make the man," Graham recalled MBS telling him.

"I was blown away," the senator said. "What you have is a guy who sees the finite nature of the revenue stream and, rather than panicking, sees a strategic opportunity. His view of Saudi society is that basically it's now time to have less for the few and more for the many."

An often overlooked staple of the U.S.-Saudi relationship is the think tank trip. Throughout the year, delegations from the Washington cognoscenti make their way to the kingdom, where they are treated to a range of briefings with top Saudi officials, who tell them what they want the Americans to hear. In addition to scholars and researchers, the groups are often packed with individuals who have held government positions and could do so again: former ambassadors, congressional staffers, lawmakers, and presidential advisers. They include Republicans and Democrats, and the benefits for both sides are clear. For the Washingtonians, if they can stand the heat and survive without happy hour, the trips grant rare access to important figures. For the Saudis, the trips provide an opportunity to build relationships, and the American participants often mine them for reports and op-eds, helping the Saudis spread their message in the United States.

In August 2016, Saudi Arabia's hottest and least pleasant month, such a group showed up in Riyadh and got front-row seats to the competition between the kingdom's two most powerful princes. The king said little, but the visitors appreciated the opportunity to meet the monarch. They also met the crown prince, who had little to say when asked about the day's hot issues. What was the strategy in Yemen? How were the economic reforms progressing? Where was the war in Syria going? MBN deflected. About Syria and Yemen, he said, ask the foreign minister. On the reforms, talk to the deputy crown prince. I'm the security guy, he seemed to suggest, but he didn't say much about security either. He looked exhausted. The meeting was over in less than an hour.

Then they met MBS. He opened with a soliloquy on the importance of the U.S.-Saudi relationship, then dove into a barrage of other issues: Syria, Yemen, Iran, the Israeli-Palestinian conflict, oil policy, religious reform.

He was energetic and spoke fast. One participant reflected that he appeared sharp, passionate, and "head-of-state-like." On the reforms, he said he sought to "shock the system" and motivate the population. He acknowledged that the kingdom had an image problem in the West, but said it could move only so fast because its society was conservative and it oversaw the Islamic holy sites.

At one point, he surprised his visitors by saying, "Israel is not our enemy." He turned to a military official seated nearby and asked, "Right?"

The official agreed.

"Israelis are not killing Saudis," MBS said.

He took questions, appearing to enjoy himself, and his guests ate it up.

"With MBS, we covered in two hours every issue, internal and external," said Dennis Ross, who had held senior foreign-policy positions under Republican and Democratic administrations. "He wanted to engage. If you challenged him on something, he came right back. The more challenging the question, the more he seemed to relish it."

The message seemed to be: "Here is a chance for me to show you that we have answers," Ross said.

As the meeting wound down, Philip Gordon, a former top official for the Middle East in Obama's White House, commented that MBS seemed to see no hope for mitigating the Saudi-Iranian rivalry and its effects on the region.

"This was at the end of a two-hour meeting, and he could have let it go, but instead, he said, 'Iran. Let's talk about it,' and he just restarted it," Gordon recalled.

The difference in the two performances was striking.

"We probably spent two hours with him, just engaging back and forth in debate," he said. "It was hard not to come away from those meetings thinking anything other than 'That's the guy.'"

AMBASSADOR WESTPHAL WAS less interested than other American officials in the parlor game of which prince would end up on top, and he continued to meet with both men. MBN remained reserved, but Westphal enjoyed smoking cigars with him at his seaside palace in Jeddah. But before he left his post at the end of the Obama administration, Westphal asked both princes who would be the next king.

MBN deflected.

"He gave me a complete nonanswer," Westphal said. "He didn't even try to create some type of answer. He went off on some other tangent, and I knew he didn't want to answer the question."

MBS responded directly, if not entirely honestly.

The Saudi system dictated that the crown prince became king, he said.

"We always followed the line of succession that had been set, so I fully believe that Mohammed bin Nayef will be the next king and I'll be the crown prince," Westphal recalled MBS telling him.

"He got half of that right," Westphal said.

MBS'S WAR

I N JUNE 2015, as Mohammed bin Salman continued to stake his position as the most significant new power player in Saudi Arabia, WikiLeaks dumped a trove of documents online that blew the lid off the kingdom's foreign policy. Hackers who appeared to have been funded by Iran had stolen tens of thousands of documents from the Saudi Ministry of Foreign Affairs, the nerve center of the kingdom's global efforts to win friends, influence people, undermine its enemies, and spread its version of Islam. The documents themselves were an overwhelming tangle of faxes, memos, cables, and reports, but taken together they provided unprecedented detail about the kingdom's interactions with the rest of the world.

Many of the documents were deeply embarrassing, not just to Saudi Arabia, but to those who hit it up for money as if it were the rich uncle of the Middle East. Mohamed Morsi of the Muslim Brotherhood, who would be elected and ousted as the president of Egypt, asked in 2012 for visas to bring his family on a pilgrimage to Mecca. Ayad Allawi, an Iraqi politician who was competing against an enemy of Saudi Arabia for the post of prime minister, was given some unique help to woo constituents: two thousand pilgrimage visas to hand out as he saw fit (he lost anyway). Samir Geagea, a Christian politician in Lebanon, begged for cash to pay his bodyguards, noting that he had stood up for Saudi Arabia in the media and proven "his preparedness to do whatever the kingdom asks of him." The state news agency of the impoverished West African nation of Guinea asked for $2,000, pocket change for many Saudi royals, "to solve many of the problems the agency is facing."

Other requests had higher stakes—and price tags. After the revolution that ousted President Hosni Mubarak of Egypt in 2011, the
Muslim Brotherhood—the country's ascendant force at the time—
told the Saudis that it could prevent Mubarak's incarceration for
$10 billion. But a handwritten note on the document advised against
paying such a "ransom" because the Muslim Brotherhood could not
stop Mubarak from going to prison. In hindsight, that was a sound
assessment. The Muslim Brotherhood would be ousted in a military
coup, and Mubarak would eventually go free.

The documents also shed rare light on the kingdom's foreign
missionary activities. The Saudis' outsized role in Muslim communities across the world had long been known: its construction of
mosques and employment of imams in places as diverse as Tajikistan, the Philippines, the United Kingdom, and Houston, Texas; its
funding of satellite television stations to beam the teachings of its
bearded ideologues into homes; and its distribution of free Qurans
and other religious publications, many of them shaped by Wahhabism. But the leaks provided new detail. An annual report in 2009
said the kingdom had given $22.4 million in aid to 150 entities in
fifty-five countries and built twenty-two mosques and sixteen Islamic centers. Spreadsheets for the two previous years reported that
2,495 people had become Muslims due to Saudi efforts in Canada,
France, and elsewhere, while 1,153 preachers had been "prepared."

The leaks illuminated the extensive apparatus inside the Saudi
government that ran the global missionary operation. Saudi diplomats abroad received funding requests and suggested projects that
deserved support. In Riyadh, officials in the Foreign, Interior, and
Islamic Affairs ministries and intelligence services vetted potential
recipients. The Saudi-sponsored Muslim World League coordinated strategy. Large requests were approved by the king himself.

The operation was breathtaking in scope, if sloppy in implementation. Aspiring students from, say, Mali or Afghanistan were given
full scholarships to study Sharia law at Saudi universities and kept
on the payroll when they returned home to work in mosques and
Islamic associations. The cables named fourteen new preachers to
be employed in Guinea, for example, and said contracts had been
signed with twelve others in Tajikistan. Some clerics had been paid

by the Saudis for decades, such as the Indian-born scholar who helped found the Islamic Sharia Council in Britain.

The funding was not just to promote Islam, but to promote the *right* kind of Islam, which meant undermining the *wrong* kind of Islam. That mostly meant Shiism, the official creed of Iran. Hundreds of thousands of dollars at a time were doled out for programs to stop Shiite expansion in China, Sri Lanka, and Afghanistan. The kingdom gave more than $1 million to an Islamic association in India, and Saudi ambassadors across Africa were tasked with filing reports on Iranian activities in their countries. The Saudi ambassador to Uganda sent a detailed assessment of "Shiite expansion" in that overwhelmingly Christian country. A Saudi diplomat in Sri Lanka sent a report on a private meeting between the Iranian ambassador and a group of local religious scholars.

The release of the documents troubled a kingdom that went to great lengths to make it appear as if public figures loved Saudi Arabia for its merits and not because they were on the take. A spokesman for the Saudi foreign ministry acknowledged that the documents were from an electronic attack on the ministry, while reminding Saudis that they could be prosecuted for sharing them. He tried to muddy the waters about their authenticity, claiming that many were "clearly fabricated," while defiantly noting that they reflected the "state's transparent policies" and its public statements on "numerous regional and international issues."

In hindsight, the documents served as a time capsule of sorts, capturing the kingdom's old ways of doing foreign policy: slowly, behind the scenes, and in cash. This was the system MBS would shove aside as he gained power, in favor of a more hands-on approach.

IN THE FALL of 2016, the photographer Tyler Hicks and I boarded a small United Nations plane in the East African nation of Djibouti and flew across the Red Sea to Yemen to see the most striking example of this new approach. Shortly after being named defense minister a year and a half earlier, MBS had launched the kingdom into a new war. That turbulent flight, meant for aid workers and

U.N. personnel, was the only way to reach the Yemeni capital, Sanaa, because Saudi Arabia and its allies had shut down commercial air traffic.

The war's destruction was clear as soon as we landed. We bounced down the runway, over craters left by Saudi airstrikes that had been hastily filled in with concrete. As we taxied to the gate, I saw the carcasses of destroyed airplanes strewn about like litter. In the distance stood hangars whose roofs and walls had been blown out by bombs. The terminal's windows had been blown out, too, and the place was empty, save for some scattered hawkers of tissues and cigarettes and the officials who came to process our papers.

"Welcome to Yemen," they said.

We moved around the country's northwest, seeing what the air campaign by the Arab world's richest country was doing to its poorest. In the capital, beggars displaced by bombing and destruction thronged our car, pleading for money and food. Buildings reduced to rubble by airstrikes dotted every neighborhood. And since the Houthi rebels had seized government buildings, the Saudis bombed them, damaging or destroying the Defense and Interior ministries, the army and central security headquarters, the Police Academy and Officers' Club, the Sanaa Chamber of Commerce and Industry, and the houses of officials who had joined the rebels.

By the time I arrived, the conflict had split the country, with Yemeni forces backed by Saudi Arabia and its allies holding the south and east, while the Houthis and allied Yemeni army units held the northwest. Everywhere we went, the rebels were in control, their gunmen checking IDs at checkpoints. In Sanaa's Old City, a UNESCO World Heritage Site, with its stunning mud architecture, posters of rebel "martyrs" covered buildings like wallpaper. Trucks with mounted machine guns sped by, their backs full of fighters. Spray-painted on walls and checkpoints across the city was the Houthis' rallying cry: "God is great. Death to America. Death to Israel. Curse on the Jews. Victory for Islam."

THE WAR IN Yemen had not begun with the Saudi intervention in March 2015, but the year before, when the Houthis, an Islamist group from northern Yemen, had allied with parts of the Yemeni military and seized the country's northwest.

In 2012, an Arab Spring uprising had pushed Yemen's longtime strongman, President Ali Abdullah Saleh, from power, and the United States and Saudi Arabia had helped install his successor, Abed Rabbu Mansour Hadi, hoping his government would hold the country together. But the Houthis had stormed Sanaa and sent Hadi fleeing south, effectively toppling the government.

The Houthi takeover was a major setback to efforts to stabilize Yemen. Hadi had failed to unify the country, and his officials were now scattered, most of them living in Saudi Arabia at the kingdom's expense. Meanwhile, scruffy militants wearing flip-flops and wielding Kalashnikovs ran the capital, with little idea how to provide basic services.

Saudi Arabia had long distrusted the Houthis, whose homeland abutted the kingdom's southern border. In the run-up to the Houthi takeover, Saudi officials had told the Americans about their fears that the Houthis were installing missiles that threatened the kingdom's security. The Houthi takeover amplified those fears by giving the rebels access to more territory and to Yemeni military stockpiles. The rebels also opened up regular flights to Tehran, making it clear which side of the regional Cold War they were on.

MBS responded by pulling together a coalition that included the United Arab Emirates and launching a military campaign aimed at ousting the Houthis and restoring Hadi's government. It was all done in great haste, and the Saudis presented the idea to the Americans at the last minute, effectively asking, "Are you with us or not?" recalled Lisa Monaco, Obama's top counterterrorism adviser at the time.

The war posed a dilemma for the Obama administration. On one hand, it was reluctant to get involved in another Middle Eastern war, especially one that few officials expected would go well and that had no direct bearing on the security of the American homeland. On the other hand, the United States had a long-standing commitment to Saudi Arabia's security, and some officials felt that standing with the kingdom on Yemen could assuage its anger over the Iran deal.

So the Obama administration agreed to provide Saudi Arabia with limited assistance, focused on supporting its military and securing its border, but not to participate in combat. Embedded in the decision was the hope that being involved would give the United States some leverage over the intervention. That hope would turn out to be ill-founded, as the United States ended up not being involved enough to guide the campaign, but just enough to share the blame for its momentous mistakes.

Inside Saudi Arabia, there was little debate about the war or whether MBS, the new 29-year-old defense minister, had the know-how to lead it. Nor was much thought given to the history of Yemen, which had given a bloody nose to every foreign power that had tried to use military means to change its internal politics. Over the centuries, the Romans, the Ottomans, the British, the Egyptians, and even the Saudis had sent troops to Yemen and ended up limping away after failing to achieve their goals. Yemen was the Afghanistan of the Arabian Peninsula. Still, Saudi officials in Washington and Riyadh told their American counterparts the war would be over in a matter of weeks.

But more experienced members of the royal family had misgivings. The kingdom had two main security services besides the military, both run by princes, and MBS launched the war without fully coordinating among them. MBN, the interior minister, worried that it would create chaos that Yemen's formidable Al Qaeda branch would exploit. Prince Mutib bin Abdullah, the head of the Saudi National Guard, learned that the intervention had begun only after the first bombs had fallen. He had just arrived for a visit to the UAE, and rushed home. His forces would soon be manning much of the Saudi-Yemeni border.

"It was a one-man show," a senior National Guard officer told me later. He suspected that the decision to launch the war was less about protecting the kingdom than burnishing MBS's reputation as a tough leader.

"Do you want to do something for yourself or for your country?" the officer asked. "If it is for your country, then everyone will be with you."

The initial intervention ousted the Houthis from the southern city of Aden and other parts of southern Yemen, a win for the Saudi-led coalition. But the war soon settled into a stalemate, and it became clear that the Saudi military was not only incapable of breaking the impasse, but also had trouble selecting targets. Since the start of the war, reports had rolled in about deadly strikes on apartment buildings, schools, and other civilian sites. A strike on a wedding in 2015 had killed dozens of people. An attack on a hospital shortly before I arrived had killed fifteen.

The mounting civilian toll cast a grim shadow over the United States' long alliance with Saudi Arabia, which had been solidified, in large part, by tens of billions of dollars in weapons sales. It is difficult to overstate the importance of the United States to the Saudi military. Most of its hardware—from jets to trucks to tanks—is American-made; many of its cadres have been trained by Americans; and the bulk of its 500-pound bombs are made in the USA.

For decades, American administrations had pushed the deals through based on the presumption that the Saudis would not use the weapons. The Yemen war put the lie to that idea, as Yemeni civilians digging through the rubble of Saudi strikes easily found parts of American bombs. In most cases, they could safely assume that the bombs had been dropped from American-made jets that had been refueled in midair by the U.S. Air Force and flown by U.S.-trained pilots.

Arms sales not only continued, but accelerated under Obama, even after the campaign's civilian toll became clear. In November 2015, Obama approved a massive weapons sale worth $1.29 billion. Over his two terms, the United States would approve deals worth $65 billion, more than under any previous president.

None of that assistance appeared to make the Saudis more effective in Yemen. A year into the campaign, a Saudi official acknowledged that the campaign was not progressing as planned.

"We hoped at the beginning it would be a quick thing, and that the Houthis would come to their senses that attacking Saudi Arabia has no purposes for Yemenis," Adel al-Toraifi, the kingdom's information minister at the time, said during a talk in Washington.

Now, he added, "there is no endgame."

• • •

BY THE TIME Tyler Hicks and I arrived, Yemenis had figured out the American role in the destruction of their country. At many sites I visited, locals ran over with the remains of bombs, pointing to codes indicating their American origin. On a wall in Sanaa, a large mural declared: "America is killing the Yemeni people."

On the edge of town stood the most recent example of the war's cost, and of the Saudis' disregard for civilian life. The Great Hall had been a towering hangar with red carpets and couches under a high tin roof that had hosted countless social events for the capital's elite. A month earlier, hundreds of people had crowded in on a hot Saturday afternoon for the funeral of the father of a local politician. The guests sported the light wraparound skirts worn by Yemeni men, with large curved daggers in their belts. As the Quran played on loudspeakers, they lounged on chairs and couches, chewing *qat*, a mild stimulant, and talking.

Suddenly, a roar shook the hall, knocking guests to the floor and enveloping the room in fire and smoke. Those who could rushed for the exits, while others were crushed by the collapsing roof or burned to death as the couches, rugs, and curtains went up in flames.

The explosion resounded across the capital, and ambulances and civilians rushed to evacuate the wounded. But a second bomb barreled through the roof shortly after they arrived, killing some who had been wounded by the first bomb and incinerating medics who had come to help.

The two strikes reduced the hall to an inferno, even igniting the cars in the underground garage. The carnage was overwhelming: More than 140 people were killed, many of their bodies so damaged that they could not be identified. Hundreds more were wounded, including two dozen children. The medics were overwhelmed, and radio stations broadcast pleas from the Health Ministry for off-duty doctors. Outside the city's hospitals, desperate families beseeched passersby to donate blood for their loved ones.

A United Nations report later deemed the attack "effectively a double-tap," and Human Rights Watch called it "an apparent war crime." United Nations officials gave me photos of munitions scraps found at the site that pointed to at least one American-made 500-pound laser-guided bomb.

The bombing was so gruesome, and so clearly of a non-military target that it prompted a rare public rebuke from the United States. A spokesman for the National Security Council said the United States would conduct an "immediate review" of its support for the Saudi-led coalition and possibly make adjustments "to better align with U.S. principles, values, and interests."

The Saudis initially dodged responsibility. Maj. Gen. Ahmed Asiri, the spokesman for the Saudi-led coalition, said Saudi officials were aware of the reported strikes but suggested that the blasts could have had other causes. Al-Arabiya, a Saudi-owned television network, reported that the coalition had not carried out any strikes in the area, and General Asiri told me the report was accurate.

It wasn't.

The next day, the kingdom announced an investigation into "reports about the regrettable and painful bombing."

The strikes killed a number of prominent officials, including the mayor of Sanaa, Abdulqader Hilal. He had chosen to remain in the capital after the takeover by the Houthis but had not joined their movement. Diplomats and analysts who tracked the conflict saw him as a rare figure who maintained enough credibility with both sides to help end the war. Now he was gone.

The attack marked a watershed in the war, and gutted the personal networks of many of the capital's residents.

"Every hour that goes by, I learn that someone I knew was either killed or wounded," said Ali al-Shabani, a Yemeni journalist who had fled the hall after the first strike and watched the second from nearby. "That was like our little Hiroshima."

IN HIS PUBLIC statements about the war, MBS remained upbeat.

"We believe that we are closer than ever to a political solution," he said in April 2016. "But if things relapse, we are ready."

In later interviews, he defended the war as necessary to root out militants who had toppled the government, threatened international navigation off Yemen's coast, and exacerbated the terrorist threat to the kingdom.

"If we had waited a little bit, threats would have been more complicated and there would have been threats inside Saudi Arabia and in regional countries and on international borders and crossings," he said in May 2017. "We had no other choice."

The Houthis were no angels. They had stormed the capital because they objected to the share of power they had been allotted in a plan to help the country move on from its uprising. Once in control of Sanaa, they had set up their own security state, putting their people in charge of key facilities such as hospitals, even if they had zero experience. They took control of what remained of the government, and their agents harassed and sometimes disappeared Yemenis who criticized them or were suspected of collaborating with the Houthis' many enemies. Over time, they established an elaborate war economy, charging fees at checkpoints and taxes on goods while rerouting humanitarian aid.

Ironically, Saudi Arabia's missionary zeal had contributed to the Houthis' evolution into a threatening force. The group, formally known as Ansar Allah, or the Partisans of God, had begun as a religious revival movement in the 1990s among Zaydi Muslims, a religious minority in northern Yemen, to push back against Saudi efforts to spread Wahhabism. The group's name came from its founder, Hussein Badr Eddin al-Houthi, whom Yemeni forces killed in 2004, sparking an insurgency among his followers. That led to six civil wars with the state that never got the Houthis what they wanted, but turned them into seasoned guerrillas, with skills they would put to use against the Saudis.

That revivalist, militant background instilled in them the idea that they were "revolutionaries" in the mold of Hezbollah in Lebanon or Hamas in Gaza, and their stated cause was to cleanse the country of corrupt leaders who were beholden to foreign powers.

Inside an Officers' Club in Sanaa that the Houthis had taken over, I met a fighter who had dropped out of university to join the rebels when they entered the capital.

"I saw that they stood with justice and the oppressed," he told me. "The goal was not to take control, but to help the oppressed and the weak."

The Saudis insisted that the Houthis were a dangerous proxy force that Iran was using to expand its influence and that the war was necessary to prevent the Houthis from threatening Saudi Arabia in the way that Hezbollah threatened Israel.

But analysts and diplomats who tracked the conflict said the reality was more complicated. Historically, there had been limited links between the Houthis and Iran, whose religious establishment looked down on their Zaydi beliefs. But once the war started and the Houthis found themselves up against a significantly stronger force, they welcomed Iranian help to fight back. The link between the Houthis and Iran would grow through the war, making the Iranian threat to Saudi Arabia from Yemen at least partly a self-fulfilling prophecy.

WHEN I WAS in the country in late 2016, the most recent round of peace talks had fallen apart and the combatants had returned to seeking an advantage on the battlefield. The Houthis had created a political council to govern their areas. Hadi, the exiled president, had moved the central bank from Sanaa to Aden. In the process, it stopped paying salaries to many of the country's 1.2 million civil servants, leaving Yemenis struggling to feed their families.

The bombing campaign had exacerbated the humanitarian crisis. Cholera was spreading, millions of people struggled to get enough food, and malnourished babies were overwhelming hospitals. Few targets seemed to escape the Saudis' bombs. They and their allies had struck schools and taken out bridges that connected communities separated by deep valleys. They had blown up power stations, poultry farms, and factories that produced yogurt, tea, tissues, and Coca-Cola.

The year before, the coalition had bombed the main port on Yemen's west coast, damaging the cranes needed to unload ships. That was a major problem because 90 percent of Yemen's food, fuel, and medicine was imported, and now those supplies could barely make it in. Jamie McGoldrick, the top United Nations official in the country at the time, told me that the pattern of airstrikes suggested a deliberate effort to dismantle Yemen's economy as a way of forcing the Houthis to surrender.

"It is an all-encompassing, applied economic suppression and strangulation that is causing everyone here to feel it," he said. "It is all consistent—the port, the bridges, the factories—they are getting dismantled and it is to put pressure on the politics."

One afternoon, I visited a family-run factory that had produced some of Yemen's most popular snacks. When it had opened more than thirty years before, it was the first of its kind in the country, and its treats have been part of childhood for generations of Yemeni children. It produced potato chips in salt, cheese, vinegar, and ketchup flavors, as well as corn curls with a picture of Ernie from *Sesame Street* on the wrapper. Mustafa Elaghil, the accountant who gave me a tour, said his family name was so closely associated with the brand that whenever he met other Yemenis, they would ask, "Are you the ones who make the potato chips?"

His grandfather had bought the land for the factory in the late 1970s, and the Yemeni government later built a military base next door. The family had not expected that to be a problem, but once the war began, the Saudis bombed the base. But even that had reassured the family, who concluded that the Saudis would differentiate between the factory and the base.

They didn't.

A few months before my visit, Saudi Arabia had bombed the factory in the middle of a shift, collapsing the roof, setting the place on fire, and trapping twenty-five employees inside. Firemen came to extinguish the flames, but ten workers ended up dead. When the owners finally got in, they found their employees' charred bodies at their workstations. One man had worked there since the place opened and planned to retire soon. His body was so badly burned that his daughter identified him by his gold tooth.

Elaghil estimated that the damage would cost $3 million to fix, money the family would struggle to get together.

"This is the product," he said, tearing open a charred package and letting its chips fall to the ground. "It was everything for us."

In the town of Amran, I visited a state-owned cement factory that had employed hundreds of people before being put out of commission by a series of strikes that killed fifteen people. The workers acknowledged that the Houthis had taken over the area, but said the militants had not interfered at the plant. They took me into an office where they had collected the remains of munitions used on the factory. Most were jagged pieces of shrapnel or twisted metal, but one was clearly a part of a cluster bomb unit manufactured in Rhode Island.

Elsewhere, I visited two brothers who ran their family's business selling agricultural equipment. Their grandfather had founded the company six decades before; his black-and-white photo still hung in their office. They imported tractors, generators, and other equipment, and ran a factory to produce water pumps in cooperation with an Italian firm. Before the war started, they had collaborated with another Italian company to build a pipe factory and were waiting for its technicians to install the software so it could start working.

But when the unrest began, the Italians postponed their trip, and the factory sat idle.

Then the Saudis bombed both factories—twice.

"They completely destroyed everything," Khalid Alsonidar, who managed the pump factory, told me as we walked through the wreckage. He estimated the losses at more than $50 million.

His brother, Abdullah, had worked for years to open the pipe factory and said he felt that "eight years of my life disappeared into thin air."

The brothers had both earned degrees from Seattle Pacific University in Washington state before returning to Yemen to work in the family business. Their fond memories of the United States made their loss to American-made bombs all the more painful.

"I know why the United States is cooperating with Saudi Arabia," Abdullah Alsonidar told me. "They have to look to their own benefit, and I don't think the U.S. has a strong interest in not letting Saudi Arabia do what it wants to do."

But he wished that Americans could see the price of that cooperation.

"Selling weapons to Saudi Arabia helps the economy in the U.S., but there should be a moral reason to stop selling the weapons once they see how they're used," he said. "We're not talking about something useless. We're talking about infrastructure and people's lives. Strikes like this can bring a family to the ground."

I sent photos of the remains of the munitions used on the factories to a colleague, who identified them as American-made guidance kits that were attached to 500- and 1,000-pound bombs to improve their accuracy.

After my trip, I asked the Saudis about the sites I had visited, and the coalition spokesman, General Asiri, told me the kingdom had "accurate intelligence" that the Houthis had used some of the sites to store weapons or as command-and-control centers. But he did not say which sites nor provide evidence.

After the story about my trip was published, I got an angry call from General Asiri, who asked why I had written that the Saudis were dismantling Yemen's economy when he had told me that they were not.

Soon after, the Saudis banned journalists from taking the U.N. flights to Yemen.

SO-CALLED ALLIES

In April 2016, *The Atlantic* magazine published a mammoth article based on extensive interviews with Barack Obama and his advisers spelling out how the president viewed the United States' relationship with the world. "The Obama Doctrine" was not kind to Saudi Arabia.

In it, Obama complained to Australian prime minister Malcolm Turnbull about how cash from Saudi Arabia and other Gulf nations had hardened Islam in Indonesia, where Obama had lived as a child.

"Aren't the Saudis your friends?" Turnbull asked.

"It's complicated," Obama said.

Obama criticized Saudi Arabia's treatment of women, saying "a country cannot function in the modern world when it is repressing half of its population." Most troubling to Saudi ears, he suggested that the kingdom "share" the Middle East with Iran in order to calm the proxy wars in Syria, Iraq, and Yemen. The United States should not endorse the Saudi view that Iran was the source of all the region's problems, which would only perpetuate conflicts and invite American military intervention.

"That would be in the interest neither of the United States nor of the Middle East," Obama said.

The rub was that for Saudi Arabia, Iran *was* the source of the region's ills, so much so that Mohammed bin Salman grew fond of comparing Iran's Supreme Leader to Adolf Hitler. So Riyadh took Obama's putting them in the same basket as an insult.

It *was* complicated, and as 2016 progressed, MBS's view of the

Obama administration got worse. They continued to cooperate on weighty issues, with the United States backing the Saudi campaign in Yemen and Saudi Arabia participating in the coalition against the Islamic State in Iraq and Syria. But the Saudis felt a deep sense of betrayal over the Iran deal and Obama's reticence to intervene against President Bashar al-Assad in Syria. Meanwhile, anti-Saudi momentum was building in the United States. Congress was pressing for the declassification of twenty-eight pages from the congressional report about the September 11 attacks that were said to implicate Saudi officials. It was also preparing to vote on the Justice Against Sponsors of Terrorism Act, or JASTA, a law that would allow Americans to sue Saudi Arabia for its alleged role in the attacks.

Those issues hung in the air when Obama flew to Riyadh in April 2016 for his final presidential visit to the kingdom. The Saudis made their displeasure clear from the moment he arrived. King Salman did not meet him at the airport, nor did MBN, the crown prince, nor MBS. Instead, while Saudi state television aired footage of the king warmly receiving a stream of Arab leaders, Obama was welcomed by the governor of Riyadh, clearly a snub, even though both sides denied it.

Word got around that MBS was ticked off at Ben Rhodes, Obama's deputy national security adviser, for comments he had made in a podcast about Saudi support for extremism. Rhodes had said that before September 11, it had not been official Saudi policy to fund terrorist groups like Al Qaeda, but that wealthy Saudis had bankrolled them anyway. That was far from an unconventional view among American officials, but MBS was insulted.

"It did not show a degree of self-assurance and self-awareness," Rhodes told me. "It showed a guy who was, on top of everything else, thin-skinned."

Obama's meeting with the king that day was in a cavernous, ornate room, its two dozen participants split between Americans and Saudis, with the president and the king in armchairs at one end, the flags of their respective countries behind them. As they spoke, the Americans noticed the king's iPad, perched before him on a coffee table adorned with lime green flowers and dishes of candy. The elderly monarch paid close attention to it when he spoke. During previous meetings, some of the officials had also seen MBS, or one of his aides, sitting elsewhere in the room and typing on another iPad, presumably dictating talking points to the king. The only place that system did not work was in the Oval Office, where foreign guests could not bring electronics, so there, MBS had resorted to conspicuously passing handwritten notes.

American officials had a long history of raising human rights concerns with Saudi leaders, but the exercise was usually perfunctory, an item to be crossed off the list amid the more substantive business of arms deals, oil, and counterterrorism. But this time, Obama laid out an elaborate argument for why the kingdom needed to provide more rights to its people, including women and journalists. Beheading prominent Shiites had not helped alleviate sectarian tensions and made it harder for the administration to defend the Saudis in Washington, Obama said. And giving citizens more rights was not only the right thing to do, it was necessary for the Saudis to achieve their goals.

The king pushed back, but Obama continued.

Then, MBS stood and raised his voice. Addressing the room, he argued that Obama did not understand the Saudi justice system, the pushback Saudi leaders faced from conservative parts of society, nor the population's desire for vengeance against criminals. He could arrange a briefing if the president wanted to learn more, he said.

The meeting grew more acrimonious from there. The Saudis brought up the *Atlantic* article, and Obama complained about how often he saw comments from anonymous Gulf officials in articles criticizing his foreign policy, implying that they came from Foreign Minister Adel al-Jubeir, who was in attendance.

"It was probably the most honest meeting we had with the Saudis," Ben Rhodes said later.

Subsequent meetings were held to try to patch things up, but the image that stuck with the Americans was that of a 30-year-old prince rising to his feet to lecture the president of the United States. They had never seen anything like it.

• • •

DESPITE HIS DISTASTE for Obama, MBS loved the United States and considered a deep relationship with it key to all he wanted to achieve. In June, he came to visit, an effort both to court powerful Americans for involvement in his reforms and to brand himself as the future of the kingdom.

His trip raised protocol questions at the White House. He was not head of state, or crown prince, so was it appropriate for him to meet the president? The day after he arrived in Washington, his name was not on the White House schedule, although he dined with John Kerry and met with lawmakers and the director of the Central Intelligence Agency.

MBS did end up meeting Obama, and the administration pulled together its top economic minds to talk about Vision 2030. They watched a PowerPoint presentation about the proposed reforms and peppered the Saudis with questions. How would Aramco meet the transparency requirements for an IPO? What was the business model for tourism, or mining?

The Vision got mixed reviews. Some felt the Saudis had trouble when pushed beyond their talking points and dismissed the plan as "more sizzle than steak." Others appreciated MBS's rapport with his aides, many of whom had impressive résumés. MBS was deeply invested in the process, but also seemed to think that that alone would make the reforms succeed when they had failed so often in the past. It seemed inconceivable to him that changes a leader wanted could not come to pass because of barriers in society. And those barriers were many. MBS had skilled aides and ministers, but the level of talent dropped off substantially a level or two below them. And some government bodies would need substantial overhauls. Courts run by clerics, for example, did not reassure foreign investors.

After Washington, MBS set off for Silicon Valley to meet his tech heroes and to try to get them as excited about Saudi Arabia as he was about them. The American media lightly covered the trip, but the Saudi news media tracked MBS's every move, trumpeting each nonbinding agreement and implying that America's tech giants loved

Vision 2030. The CEO of Six Flags said his company would look into opening a theme park in Saudi Arabia. Cisco Systems signed a preliminary agreement to upgrade the kingdom's digital infrastructure. Microsoft signed on to a program to train young Saudis. Dow Chemical received a license, billed as the first ever, allowing it to operate in the kingdom without a Saudi partner. MBS got sit-downs with Tim Cook of Apple and Mark Zuckerberg of Facebook. Photos of the young prince in jeans and a sport coat trying out a virtual reality headset at Facebook headquarters zinged around the kingdom, convincing many young Saudis that this prince was indeed different from the others. In his meetings, MBS pitched a bright future for Saudi Arabia and argued that authoritarianism would help bring it about.

"There is an advantage to quickness of decision-making, the kind of fast change that an absolute monarch can do in one step that would take a traditional democracy ten steps," he said during one Silicon Valley meeting.

He concluded his trip in New York, where his visit to the United Nations was clouded by an annual U.N. report that had blacklisted Saudi Arabia and its allies for killing children in Yemen. The report was hugely embarrassing, and Riyadh had threatened to suspend its funding of U.N. programs, forcing Secretary General Ban Ki-moon to remove the kingdom from the list. In New York, MBS showed up forty-five minutes late for his meeting with Ban, muddling the schedule of the world's top diplomat for the rest of the day and flustering his aides. Ban told the prince during their meeting that he stood by the report's original findings. MBS just smiled.

Later that year, a $1.15 billion weapons deal that Obama had pushed for survived an effort to block it in the Senate. Soon after, Congress overrode President Obama's veto of JASTA, the law allowing Americans to sue Saudi Arabia over the September 11 attacks. The contradiction between the two initiatives gave some lawmakers whiplash.

"This body voted unanimously to let the 9/11 victims sue them, and now this body wants to give them weapons?" Republican Senator Rand Paul of Kentucky asked while lobbying against the arms deal. "Does no one sense the irony?"

One month before Obama left office, and largely in response to the disastrous bombing of the Great Hall in Sanaa, the administration blocked the delivery of precision-guided bombs to Saudi Arabia, citing "systematic, endemic" problems with Saudi targeting.

But a remarkable presidential election had just concluded in the United States, and the Saudis were already looking to the next administration, hoping it would give them a better deal.

A TRUE FRIEND IN
THE WHITE HOUSE

I N MARCH 2016, as the U.S. presidential campaign heated up, Donald Trump, the New York real estate developer and reality television star, voiced his opinion of Islam in an interview on CNN.

"I think Islam hates us," he said. "There's tremendous hatred there. We've got to get to the bottom of it."

The interviewer gave him an opportunity to differentiate between terrorists seeking to attack the United States and law-abiding Muslims, but he declined to take it.

"It is very hard to separate, because you don't know who's who."

Earlier on, Trump had called for a "total and complete shutdown of Muslims entering the United States." Over time, his demand for a "Muslim ban" became part of his platform, with its implication that practicing the Muslim faith alone made people suspect.

In a debate with his Democratic rival, Hillary Rodham Clinton, he resurrected the term "radical Islamic terrorism," which Obama had avoided so as not to exacerbate Islamophobia. At other events, Trump spoke of attacks carried out by the Islamic State in the United States and Europe, vowing to establish a database to track Muslims and calling for surveillance of mosques.

"We're having problems with the Muslims, and we're having problems with Muslims coming into the country," he said. "You need surveillance. You have to deal with the mosques, whether you like it or not. These attacks are not done by Swedish people."

If such talk was not alarming enough for a kingdom that defined itself as "the heartland of Islam" and considered the Quran its constitution, Trump also made clear that he felt no fondness for Saudi Arabia.

"These are people who push gays off buildings," he told Clinton during another debate, criticizing the Clinton Foundation for accepting funds from Gulf states. "These are people that kill women and treat women horribly, and yet you take their money."

Perhaps most alarmingly for the kingdom, Trump claimed—twice in one day—that Saudi Arabia was behind the 9/11 attacks.

"Who blew up the World Trade Center? It wasn't the Iraqis. It was Saudi. Take a look at Saudi Arabia," he said.

But Trump did not call for abandoning the kingdom. Instead, he portrayed it as a helpless, wealthy place that needed the United States to protect it from Iran—and should pay handsomely for the service.

"Frankly, the Saudis don't survive without us," he said. "The question is, at what point do we get involved and how much will Saudi Arabia pay us to save them?"

(Trump was hardly popular in Saudi Arabia. One poll before the election found that 68 percent of Saudis wanted Clinton to win. Six percent favored Trump.)

Of the many ironies of the Trump era, one of the greatest was that Trump, after demeaning Saudi Arabia and its faith throughout the campaign, would, in the course of a few months, anoint Saudi Arabia a preferred American partner and the lynchpin of his Middle East policy.

That unlikely relationship, which few saw coming at the time, grew out of strategic, long-term shifts in the region and the outlook of Saudi Arabia's new driving force, Mohammed bin Salman. Raised in a different era than previous Saudi leaders, the young prince cared less about the kingdom's traditional priorities, such as the exportation of Wahhabism and support for the Palestinians, and more about confronting Iran and the Muslim Brotherhood. That realignment pushed MBS away from some of the kingdom's historic regional allies and toward onetime foes, like Israel and its right-wing prime minister, Benjamin Netanyahu.

Early on, the Saudis identified the Trump administration's approach to foreign-policy as transactional, run by deal-makers looking out for the bottom line, not by diplomats focused on long-term interests or even, at times, values. Trump's game was one the Saudis knew how to play.

At the nuts-and-bolts level, the relationship rested on frequent chats between two political novices who disregarded the conventional wisdom about the region: MBS, and Jared Kushner, Trump's son-in-law and senior adviser. Over time, the partnership between the Trump administration and Saudi Arabia would shift the rules of the U.S.-Saudi partnership in ways that would reverberate across the Middle East.

LIKE MBS, KUSHNER owed his standing to a family empire, albeit one that was not old and royal, but had been built by his father through savvy and sometimes crime-tinged dealings in New Jersey real estate. A grandson of Holocaust survivors, Kushner grew up in a tight-knit, Orthodox Jewish home that was dominated by his father, Charles. The elder Kushner had made hundreds of millions of dollars buying and developing properties and setting up his own children for elite lives of their own.

Jared was tall, thin, and well-mannered, with straight hair and a boyish grin. He grew up steeped in his father's world, and the wealth Kushner senior had built swung open doors that otherwise would have remained shut. Jared's high school record was not stellar, but he still got into Harvard, surprising school officials familiar with his credentials.

"His GPA did not warrant it, his SAT scores did not warrant it. We thought for sure, there was no way this was going to happen. Then, lo and behold, Jared was accepted," one recalled. Years later, it came out that his father had pledged $2.5 million to the university. He had also donated smaller amounts to Princeton and Cornell. (A spokeswoman for Kushner Companies said "the allegation" that Charles Kushner's gift had helped Jared get into Harvard "is and always has been false.")

After college, Kushner got a joint business and law degree from New York University and began working for the family business,

Kushner Companies. But the Kushner empire was shaken in 2004, when the elder Kushner pleaded guilty to eighteen counts of illegal campaign donations, tax evasion, and tampering with witnesses. He had paid a prostitute to sleep with his brother-in-law so he could mail a tape of the encounter to his sister. He was sentenced to two years in a federal prison in Montgomery, Alabama. Jared flew down to see him most weekends.

But there was still a large family business to run, and who better to fill in for the incarcerated patriarch than his elder son, despite being only in his mid-twenties and having limited business experience. It was like a monarchy, but New Jersey–style.

Like another young man granted great power at a young age, Kushner opened with big moves. In July 2006, he bought the New York *Observer* for $10 million, making himself the publisher of the weekly Manhattan newspaper. Before the year was over, he oversaw Kushner Companies' purchase of a 41-story office tower at 666 Fifth Avenue for $1.8 billion, at the time the highest price ever paid for a single property in the United States. Shortly after, the real estate market tanked, and the company would spend years looking for investors and seeking innovative ways to cover its debt.

Those two acquisitions put Kushner's name on the social and financial map of New York, a position he solidified by dating the statuesque daughter of one of the city's biggest real estate personalities, Donald Trump. His courtship of Ivanka, a Gentile, caused so much handwringing among the Kushners that the couple broke up for a while, but later reunited and married after Ivanka converted to Judaism. That brought Kushner into the high-profile Trump clan, and when its brash patriarch moved from reality television into the presidential campaign, Kushner helped out. Trump appreciated his service, and brought Kushner into the White House when he won, giving his son-in-law oversight of the Middle East file.

Kushner had little experience with the broader Middle East, but knew a lot about Israel. His relatives had donated to Jewish causes, and when he was young, his father had paid Benjamin Netanyahu to speak in New Jersey a number of times. The longtime Israeli prime minister was so close with the Kushners, in fact, that Jared once gave up his bedroom so Netanyahu could sleep in his bed. Jared's experience with the Arabs was less intimate and was limited to the world of high-end real estate. He and his father had unsuccessfully courted funds from the Abu Dhabi Investment Authority, and a former foreign minister of Qatar had considered investing $500 million in 666 Fifth Avenue. But as the American election heated up and Trump evolved from an unlikely outsider into a top contender, the Qatari pulled out.

Kushner had no significant history of political involvement, and many suspected that he and Ivanka were less interested in moving into the White House to do policy than in using America's highest office to boost their profiles and expand their business networks. Some who worked with Kushner in the White House described him as smart and praised him for playing a calming role in an often chaotic administration. Others who knew him were less impressed, attributing his power not to intelligence and hard work, but to inherited wealth and the successful deployment of its trappings. Aaron Gell, who worked under Kushner as an editor at the *Observer*, later wrote that Kushner often didn't seem to know what he was doing, but got away with it because he was rich and powerful.

"The trick is not complicated," Gell wrote. "If you look the part and keep your mouth shut, people will occasionally confuse your money with intellect. They will tend to project virtues onto you that you might not really possess. Eventually, you might even come to believe that what they're seeing is the truth."

After he entered the White House, Kushner found a kindred spirit in MBS, another young inheritor of great wealth and power who wanted to do big things.

IF TRUMP'S VICTORY set off any alarm bells in Riyadh, the Saudis kept it to themselves and went to work courting the new administration. Some of the groundwork was laid during the campaign, by businessmen close to the Trumps and officials from the United Arab Emirates who backed MBS. These efforts focused on Kushner, based on the correct presumption that he would play a large role in Trump's Middle East policy.

During the campaign, Tom Barrack, a Lebanese-American businessman and friend of the Trumps, had put Kushner in touch with contacts in the Middle East who he thought could be valuable.

"You will love him and he agrees with our agenda!" Mr. Barrack wrote in May 2016 to Yusuf Otaiba, the Emirati ambassador to Washington. Kushner and Otaiba struck up a friendship that allowed Otaiba to pass along the Emirati view of the Middle East, which saw Iran and the Muslim Brotherhood as the main sources of trouble—and MBS as the future of Saudi Arabia.

"MBS is incredibly impressive," Otaiba wrote to Barrack in June 2016 as the two men worked to arrange meetings between MBS and the Trump team.

The new administration heard the same message from the Emiratis. After Trump was elected, Rick Gerson, a hedge fund manager who had ties to the Trumps and the Middle East, helped set up a meeting in New York between Kushner and Mohammed bin Zayed, the de facto ruler of the UAE. In December, MBZ flew to New York without informing the Obama administration, an unusual violation of diplomatic protocol, for talks with Kushner about the Israeli-Palestinian peace process. He also put in a good word for MBS.

"I promise you this will be the start of a special and historic relationship," Gerson texted to the Emirati prince after the meeting.

He wrote again on the eve of Trump's inauguration.

"You have a true friend in the White House," Gerson said.

The Saudis also reached out to the incoming administration. After Trump's victory, a delegation of Saudi officials flew to New York to gather insights from politicians, businessmen, and former officials who knew Trump. They brought along a proposal of their own for a "strategic partnership" that would bring about unprecedented cooperation between the United States and Saudi Arabia on security, military, economic, and energy issues. Versions of some of the initiatives had been proposed to the Obama administration, which deemed them overly ambitious, so the Saudis recast the plan to appeal to Trump.

It called for the creation of a military coalition of Islamic countries that would have tens of thousands of troops "ready when the president-elect wishes to deploy them." It offered an American trade zone and a military base on Saudi Arabia's Red Sea coast; the open-

ing of a joint U.S.-Saudi center to fight extremism; and Saudi intelligence help with the process of "extreme vetting" that Trump had
promised to institute to screen immigrants.

The Saudis also laid out ways that their projects—and money—
could help Trump achieve his campaign promises. They offered to
spend $50 billion over four years on American defense contracts; to
increase Saudi investment in the United States to $200 billion; and
to invest up to $100 billion with other Gulf states in American infra-
structure. These investments could create 25 million jobs over 10
years, the plan suggested, without explaining how such an unlikely
figure was calculated.

The plan concluded with an invitation for the president to come
to Saudi Arabia to launch the new initiatives with "a historic welcome celebration." The administration did not adopt the strategic
partnership proposal wholesale, but a number of its initiatives would
surface in different forms in the coming years.

Upon their return to Riyadh, the delegation put their findings in
a report for the Royal Court about how Trump's team differed from
its predecessors.

"They are deal-makers, lack familiarity with political customs
and deep institutions, and support Jared Kushner," it said.

It spelled out the administration's interests in the Middle East: to
drum up investment for the American economy, defeat the Islamic
State, and combat extremism. This, the report noted, was seen as a
greater threat than Iran. But in general, the delegation found, the
administration had only vague notions about the Middle East outside of the Holy Land.

Some of the delegation's findings were not encouraging for the
Saudis. Many Americans they met said the kingdom had a bad reputation for its association with terrorism, and that its restrictions on
women played poorly in the United States. Members of the delegation had met with Kushner, and the report contained a profile of
him with a smiling photo and text boxes outlining his positions.
Kushner had shown "little enthusiasm" for the Saudis' proposed investment program, it noted, and had not known much at all about
Saudi Arabia.

"Kushner made clear his lack of familiarity with the history of

Saudi-American relations and he asked about its support for terror-ism," the report said. "After the discussion, he made clear his ap-preciation of what was mentioned about the Saudi role in fighting terrorism and its ability to ally in fighting extreme Islam."

But Kushner's overwhelming interest was the Israeli-Palestinian conflict.

"The Palestinian issue first," it said. "There is still no clear plan for the American administration toward the Middle East except that the central interest is finding a historic solution to support the sta-bility of Israel and solve the Israeli-Palestinian conflict."

The report helped MBS craft his approach to the new adminis-tration, which was to offer help on the issues that meant the most to Trump and Kushner. The tactic would succeed tremendously.

THE TWO PRINCELINGS—AN Arab from central Arabia and a Jew from New Jersey—had more in common than was immediately ap-parent. They were both in their thirties and scions of wealthy fami-lies who had been chosen by older relatives to wield great power. They both lacked extensive experience in government, and saw little need to be bound by its strictures. During Kushner's visits to the kingdom, they dispensed with official sit-downs with note-takers and met at MBS's desert camp, telling few others what they dis-cussed. Instead of secure calls with official translators, they swapped emojis on WhatsApp and other messaging platforms.

Once Trump moved into the White House, the Saudis consid-ered his administration a breath of fresh air. After eight years of sparring with Obama over human rights, the Iran deal, and the war in Yemen, they found a path forward with the new president. He sought to overturn the Iran deal and shared their view of Iran as the root of the region's problems. He hated political Islamists like the Muslim Brotherhood, and was sympathetic to the wealthy, espe-cially if he thought he could bring their money to the United States. He liked selling arms, regardless of how they were used. And he was not concerned about human rights, making it clear that America's Arab allies could rule as they saw fit.

The relationship between MBS and Kushner bloomed because

both came to believe that the other could advance issues they held dear. Kushner saw in MBS someone who could fund American military activities in the Middle East and serve as the skeleton key to unlock peace between Israel and the Arabs. For his part, MBS expected Kushner to push the United States to champion Vision 2030, stand up to Iran, and support him in his rivalry with Mohammed bin Nayef to become the kingdom's crown prince.

The depth of the relationship was already clear by March 2017, when MBS made a visit to Washington that other White House staffers said was largely coordinated with Kushner over WhatsApp, leaving them in the dark through much of the planning.

As with MBS's previous visit, his impending arrival sparked protocol discussions about the reception he should receive since he was neither head of state nor crown prince. Kushner argued that since MBS was the rising son of the king, he should be received as such. MBS also got lucky. A snowstorm clobbered the East Coast, delaying the arrival of Chancellor Angela Merkel of Germany, who had been scheduled to meet with Trump. Her time went to MBS, who got a sit-down with Trump in the Oval Office and a lunch in the State Dining Room. Kushner joined as well.

That visit appears to have been the first time the two young men met in person, but Kushner surprised others in the White House by telling them he and MBS had already spoken several times.

During the visit, Trump convened his economic experts for a discussion about Vision 2030, just as Obama had done the year before. The Saudis laid out their plans and the Americans peppered them with questions, many coming away with the same conclusion Obama's experts had: The intentions were good, but the plan was shallow. But Kushner's enthusiasm for the young prince was clear.

By May, Kushner was advocating for the Saudis in Washington. During a meeting with a Saudi delegation to discuss a proposed arms deal worth more than $100 billion, Kushner gave a strategic overview of the Saudi-American partnership.

"Let's get this done today," he said of the deal.

The two sides reviewed the list of proposed jets, ships, and bombs, and an American official suggested that the Saudis also buy a radar system from Lockheed Martin to shoot down ballistic missiles.

Kushner liked the idea, and to the amazement of others in the room, he picked up the phone and called Marillyn A. Hewson, the company's CEO, and asked for a discount for his Saudi friends. Hewson said she would look into it.

The request was not illegal, but highly unconventional, as American officials usually lobbied on behalf of American companies, not on behalf of their foreign customers.

As time went on, officials in the State Department and Central Intelligence Agency, as well as others in the White House, grew concerned about the direct relationship between Kushner and MBS, much of which was conducted through private channels and not reported to other parts of the government. Was Kushner mixing private interests with government affairs? Was MBS swaying him in ways that were detrimental to U.S. interests? No one could be sure, so efforts were made to restore White House protocols and have other staffers on calls with foreign leaders.

At one point, Kushner asked an intelligence official how the United States could influence the succession process in Saudi Arabia to give MBS a leg up over his cousin. That set off alarm bells among diplomats and spies who felt that the United States needed to stay out of the politics of the royal family. (White House spokespeople insisted Kushner had always followed the proper protocols when communicating with foreign leaders and that he had not asked about influencing the Saudi succession process.)

In any case, the new tone in Washington impressed MBS, who told an interviewer that he was "very optimistic" that Trump was "a president who will bring America back to the right track."

"Trump has not yet completed 100 days, and he has restored all the alliances of the U.S. with its conventional allies," he said.

AS THE ADMINISTRATION's relationship with Saudi Arabia was improving, mine was getting worse. When I had obtained my last visa—five years, multi-entry, nonrenewable—around the launch of Vision 2030, it had felt like winning the lottery. With that, I could come and go as I pleased, and that's what I did, for about a year.

But in 2016, my colleagues and I at *The New York Times* published a series of articles called "Secrets of the Kingdom" that delved into Saudi Arabia's ideological ties to extremism, the finances of the royal family, and MBS himself. Given that I was spending the most time in the kingdom, I played a large role in many of the stories. One, a profile of MBS with Mark Mazzetti, broke the news that MBS had bought the superyacht *Serene*. Those charged with protecting MBS's reputation tried to cast doubt on the story. No one from the Saudi government complained directly to me, but a while later, I got an email from an official I had never heard of, canceling my visa.

I texted my contact at the Information Ministry, and he said my visa had been issued to cover "a specific event." I asked which event that was and why I had been given five years to cover it.

"I am in a meeting and overseas right now," he responded. "U can get in touch with the embassy."

Who would have guessed that my next visit to Saudi Arabia would be thanks to Donald Trump?

But it was.

At Kushner's urging, Trump made the first foreign visit of his presidency to Saudi Arabia, and the Saudis were so overjoyed that they wanted all the journalists they could find to cover it, including me.

So I got a new visa—two weeks, single entry, nonrenewable.

I landed in Riyadh in May 2017 to find the city transformed. It was a sweltering 107 degrees, and there were welcome crews at the airport to pick up journalists and dignitaries. On highways throughout the city, alternating Saudi and American flags hung from lampposts, creating rivers of red, white, blue, and green for miles on end. Seemingly everywhere, billboards declared "Together We Prevail" with photos of Trump and King Salman. The same slogan appeared on the badges required to access official events, and on state television, even during the broadcast of Friday prayers from Mecca.

To entice Trump to choose them for his first overseas visit, the Saudis had offered more than a run-of-the-mill bilateral meeting. They had internationalized the event, branding it "The Arab Islamic American Summit" and inviting dozens of heads of state and other top officials from across the Muslim world.

In addition to the official meetings, the kingdom organized an array of events to showcase MBS's push to make Saudi life more fun and to show that the kingdom and the United States were not as different as they appeared. There was a classic car show. Skydivers parachuted into drag races. The Harlem Globetrotters performed. So did country music star Toby Keith, to an all-male audience, replacing some of his hits, such as "Beer for My Horses," with classics like "Johnny B. Goode." The Saudis wanted their American guests to feel at home, but within limits. The visit's official website advised men to wear pants and long-sleeved shirts, and told women it was "required to wear an abaya."

After I checked into my hotel, I learned that a Harley-Davidson rally was under way and ordered an Uber to go see it. A 27-year-old Saudi guy picked me up in a silver Dodge Charger, with a red interior and hip hop bouncing on the stereo. I told him I wanted to catch the rally.

"Fasten your seatbelt for some real driving," he said.

On the way, he told me he had been raised in Riyadh but had spent six years in Monterey, California, while his father was in university. Since his return to the kingdom, he had worked in banking, invested in food trucks, and was now trying Uber because he liked to drive. There were many people in Saudi Arabia resistant to change, he said, but life was changing nonetheless.

"It used to be weird for a Saudi family to ride with a Saudi. But now they like to help out young guys," he said. "That's different— and better."

I caught up with the rally and found hundreds of Saudi bikers cruising the city's highways on American machines, many adorned with American and Saudi flags. Some riders turned out to be pro-Trump, and I found them surprisingly willing to dismiss his anti-Muslim rhetoric as cheap campaign talk. One rider who managed a retail company told me Saudis found his style familiar.

"In the Arab world, in Saudi Arabia, the leader always has much stronger moves," he said. "There is a Parliament, but at the end of the day, the king says what goes, so what Trump does is similar in tactics to what the Arab leaders do. That's why some of the Americans are against him. 'He did this! He fired the head of the FBI!' This is how we do it here."

"I love America," another rider told me, volunteering that he had forty-three siblings, from his father's six wives.

He had moved to the United States at 18, studying English near Los Angeles before moving to Miami to study economics.

"Most Americans don't know much about Saudi Arabia," he said, recalling an American teacher asking if he had an oil pump at his house. He, too, liked Trump.

"Businessmen know how to make things work," he said.

He argued that American women would be happy not to drive if their husbands paid for drivers, as they did in the kingdom.

"You can just stay home, raise kids, and you don't have to work hard," he said.

The rally ended at Al-Imam Muhammad Ibn Saud Islamic University, one of the main institutions charged with steeping young students, clerics, and judges in Wahhabism, and thus an unlikely spot for a biker rally. The riders hung out on the grass, drinking Diet Pepsi and lining up to face Mecca when the call to prayer sounded. In some ways, it resembled any biker event: roaring machines, surging testosterone, ripped jeans, and black leather jackets. But there was no booze—or any women.

Nearby, young Saudis in a soccer stadium watched American and Saudi drivers compete in a drag race. Food trucks selling burgers and burritos did swift business, and the event opened with the Saudi national anthem and "The Star-Spangled Banner."

An American driver won, by a hair.

WHEN DONALD TRUMP descended from *Air Force One* in Riyadh, King Salman, who had snubbed Barack Obama during his last visit to the kingdom, was waiting on a long red carpet flanked by royal guards to welcome the new president. When Trump pulled up at the Riyadh Ritz-Carlton, where much of the American delegation stayed, he could see Saudi and American flags projected on its façade. But Trump didn't have to stay there. The Saudis put him up in a palace.

During the visit, there was a range of meetings and side meetings, but the main event was Trump's keynote address to the gathered dignitaries. For a public figure with a long record of straying from his prepared remarks and making nasty comments about Muslims, Trump performed well, sticking to his text and laying out his vision for the U.S. relationship with the Islamic world.

He honored his hosts, calling Islam "one of the world's great faiths," and appealed for respect between religions. But he mostly focused on terrorism.

"This is not a battle between different faiths, different sects, or different civilizations," he said. "This is a battle between barbaric criminals who seek to obliterate human life and decent people, all in the name of religion. . . . This is a battle between good and evil."

He called on the assembled leaders to step up their fight against "wicked ideology" and to purge the "foot soldiers of evil" from their societies.

"A better future is only possible if your nations drive out the terrorists and extremists," he said. "Drive them out. Drive them out of your places of worship. Drive them out of your communities. Drive them out of your holy land. Drive them out of this earth."

He singled out Iran for offering terrorists "safe harbor, financial backing, and the social standing needed for recruitment" and blamed it for "so much instability in the region."

But from the nations represented, he wanted "partners, not perfection," suggesting they could run their countries as they wished.

"We are not here to lecture. We are not here to tell other people how to live, what to do, who to be, or how to worship," he said. "Instead, we are here to offer partnership—based on shared interests and values—to pursue a better future for us all."

The audience gave him repeated standing ovations.

In the run-up to the visit, the White House had told the Saudis that for Trump to make Riyadh his first foreign destination, they needed to offer "deliverables" to be unveiled during the visit. The most significant was an arms deal worth $110 billion, which pointedly included the precision-guided bombs whose delivery Obama had blocked over civilian deaths in Yemen. Trump approved the deal and said it would bring "hundreds of billions of dollars of investments into the United States and jobs, jobs, jobs."

After Trump's speech, the Saudis hosted him for the unveiling of their new Global Center for Combating Extremist Ideology, or Etidal, another "deliverable." The center was in a large, domed building inside a military complex, and its interior looked like a spaceship command center from a science fiction movie. Massive screens on high walls flashed videos, graphs, and statistics, while hundreds of Saudi men in identical outfits manned banks of computers. For the unveiling, Trump, King Salman, and President Abdel-Fattah el-Sisi of Egypt laid their hands on a glowing orb, creating an image that swiftly went viral. Some lampooned it as a potential promo for a *Lord of the Rings* movie or an Al Qaeda recruitment poster, given how it seemed to cast the three leaders as masters of the universe.

The visit was packed with other hilarity, and the mixing of the Trump clan with the Saudi elite gave the event the feel of a cross-cultural wedding, bringing together two families from different backgrounds to celebrate their new bond. Although Trump's heavy reliance on his daughter and son-in-law bothered many Americans, that was business-as-usual for the Saudis. Hadn't the king conferred massive power on his own son? And while American watchdogs sought to make sure that Trump and his family were not using his presidency to benefit their businesses, that didn't bother the Saudis. Their whole country bore the name of the royal family, and there had never been a clear line between family and state funds anyway.

At one point, Steve Bannon, a Trump adviser who had run the Breitbart News Network, a website that often published anti-Muslim views, was caught chatting with a bearded cleric who happened to be the Minister of Islamic Affairs. A video spread online of a senior prince teaching Ivanka to jiggle her coffee cup so that the servers would stop refilling it, a Saudi tradition. The Saudi authorities intervened to stop a Saudi father from naming his daughter Ivanka, based on a statute banning baby names that "contradicted the culture or religion of the kingdom, or were foreign or inappropriate." Instead, the man named her Luma, meaning dark- or crimson-colored lips. He would call her Ivanka at home.

The enthusiasm for the Trump administration was not limited to the Saudis. El-Sisi, the Egyptian president who had come to power in a military coup after his forces had gunned down hundreds of protesters, told Trump: "You have a unique personality that is capable of doing the impossible."

"I agree!" Trump replied, spreading laughter through the hall.

He went on to declare that the administration had a "fantastic relationship with Egypt," and even complimented el-Sisi's fashion sense.

"Love your shoes," he said. "Boy, those shoes. Man!"

The Saudis sent Trump home with more than eighty gifts, including a substantial Saudi wardrobe, featuring an "orange and gold wool robe lined with cheetah fur," a "blue and silver wool robe lined with white tiger fur," a number of colored shirts with ammunition belts and holsters, and two books on "traditional Saudi Arabian costume." He also got boxes of cologne, children's books, wool blankets, a copy of the Kuwaiti constitution, three daggers, three swords, eleven pairs of leather sandals, and "artwork featuring [a] picture of president Trump."

One night, he joined his Saudi hosts for a folk dance known as the *Ardah*. They clasped hands, held swords and canes aloft, smiled broadly, and stepped back and forth together to the drums and chants.

A STAB IN THE BACK

O N MAY 23, 2017, a strange report appeared on the state news agency of Qatar, Saudi Arabia's tiny, rich, Persian Gulf neighbor. Qatar's emir, it said, had made some striking comments about the Middle East and the United States while addressing a graduation ceremony for the country's National Guard.

"It is impossible to disregard the regional and Islamic prominence of Iran, and unwise to escalate the conflict with it," the emir was quoted as saying.

He supposedly referenced "certain governments that created terrorism by adopting an extremist form of Islam," a veiled jab at Saudi Arabia, and spoke positively of the Muslim Brotherhood, Hezbollah, and Hamas, the last two of which the United States considered terrorist organizations. Hamas, in particular, the emir reportedly called "the legitimate representative of the Palestinian people" and said that he hoped to broker peace between it and Israel, a highly unlikely scenario.

As for the United States, he called its military base in Qatar "a Qatari stronghold that defends this country against the greed of some of its neighbors" and "America's only chance to have military influence in the region," a grandiose claim by the head of a state with only 300,000 citizens.

"Relations between Qatar and the Trump administration are strained," he was also quoted as saying, before suggesting that Trump's legal woes could cut short his stay in the White House.

The comments, as reported, were incendiary, both to Qatar's neighbors and to its American partners, but diplomats working in the region smelled a rat. The emir had indeed attended the graduation ceremony, as he always did, but he had not spoken, because the British military attaché had been in the audience and would have noticed.

The statements were also baffling, not least to the emir himself, 36-year-old Sheikh Tamim bin Hamad Al Thani. He was roused from his sleep with the news and scrambled his ministers to get it taken down. Within a half hour, it was gone, along with the references to it on state social media accounts and the ticker of the state television channel. The government denied the report, explaining that its news agency had been hacked, and hoped the incident would swiftly blow over.

It did not.

Media outlets owned by Saudi Arabia and the United Arab Emirates pounced on the news, reporting it as fact with heavy indignation that the head of a purported ally would say such things. They threw the comments on television in broad type over horror movie music. They added other accusations, that Qatar supported Al Qaeda, the Taliban, and the Islamic State, and lined up commentators to spell out how the incident had exposed the evil agenda of a puny country that overestimated its importance.

"Qatar has become accustomed to treating the problems of the region's countries as if it had political weight and influence or made decisions," a commentator in a Saudi newspaper wrote.

A headline in the same paper blared, "Qatari Emir Stabs His Neighbors with Iranian Dagger!!"

Qatari journalists fought back, accusing their Saudi colleagues of "media prostitution," and expressing the country's sense of betrayal.

"A treacherous stab in the back is always deadly, especially when it comes from those closest to us, from one of our brethren," a Qatari columnist wrote.

American intelligence agencies determined that the hack had been orchestrated by the United Arab Emirates, and the swift Saudi reaction made it clear that the kingdom was on board. (The UAE has denied it was involved in the hack.)

The feud escalated rapidly, and on June 5, Saudi Arabia, the United Arab Emirates, Egypt, and Bahrain announced that they were severing diplomatic ties with Qatar and pulling their citizens out of the country. They imposed a strict air and sea boycott, snarling shipping lanes and forcing the Qatari national airline to redraw its map of the world. Saudi Arabia also shut its border, Qatar's only land crossing, and evicted twelve thousand camels, five thousand sheep, and the Qatari herders who had long pastured their beasts in the kingdom's eastern desert.

THE INCIDENT THAT would come to be known as the Gulf Crisis was a perfect twenty-first century storm of hackers, fake news, feuding princes, shattered alliances, and Donald Trump. It would drive a wedge through the group of Gulf monarchies that had been considered a pillar of regional stability and put the United States in a bind, since it had partners on both sides who hosted the American military and had bought tens of billions of dollars' worth of American arms.

It also marked a serious escalation in Mohammed bin Salman's aggressive approach to foreign policy. No more would Saudi Arabia seek to solve conflicts behind closed doors. Going forward, the kingdom would do so openly, marshaling the full apparatus of the state to demonize its foes and rally its population against them. Many of the kingdom's smaller, poorer neighbors took note, fearing that if it could happen to Qatar, it could happen to them, too.

The boycott was a shock for Qatar, a sandy peninsula jutting into the Persian Gulf whose tremendous reserves of natural gas gave its citizens the highest per capita income in the world: $127,700 dollars per year before the crisis. Its leaders had used that wealth to punch above their weight. They funded Al Jazeera, the Arab world's most watched news network, which regularly gave headaches to the region's rulers. They had championed the Arab Spring uprisings, and the Islamists who had gotten involved to gain power and spread their views. Along the way, Qatari money had sloshed around the region, some of it reaching militants and extremists in Libya, Syria, and elsewhere. Qatar had also won the bid to host the 2022 World Cup, a golden opportunity for the tiny country to play host and showman to the world, further incensing its neighbors.

"They don't like our independence," the emir said. "They see it as a threat."

The United States, however, often found Qatar's maverick streak useful, and had long treated Doha, the Qatari capital, as a sort of hot, sandy Middle Eastern Switzerland where it could keep an eye on, and quietly talk to, American enemies. Qatar maintained ties with an array of armed groups, which proved useful for hostage negotiations. Khaled Meshaal, the political leader of Hamas, moved there from Syria in 2012. The Afghan Taliban had opened an office there that would help with the release of Bowe Bergdahl, an American soldier they had captured, as well as in peace talks aimed at ending the Afghan war. And while Qatar maintained relations with Iran, they had less to do with politics than with the massive gas field under the Persian Gulf that the two countries shared, the source of Qatar's wealth.

But as the feud escalated, Washington's primary concern was the Al Udeid Air Base, one of the largest American military facilities in the region. Qatar hosted the Americans—up to thirteen thousand forces—as an investment in its own security and spent $8 billion in support of American and allied operations coordinated out of Al Udeid between 2002 and 2019, including in Afghanistan, Iraq, and Syria. Members of the Trump administration who understood the base's importance were immediately alarmed, including Defense Secretary James Mattis and Secretary of State Rex Tillerson.

But Trump endorsed the Saudi and Emirati view of the rift, lauding the isolation of Qatar as a salvo in the battle against extremism he had called for in Riyadh.

"During my recent trip to the Middle East I stated that there can no longer be funding of Radical Ideology. Leaders pointed to Qatar—look!" he wrote on Twitter. "Perhaps this will be the beginning of the end to the horror of terrorism!"

The tensions between Qatar and its neighbors were not new. A previous flare-up in 2013 saw ambassadors withdrawn and redeployed only after the emir had vowed to change his country's ways. But the Qataris had been optimistic when King Salman came to the throne, hoping to turn a new page with a monarch seen as less hostile than his predecessor to political Islamists. Indeed, when Meshaal and other Hamas leaders performed the pilgrimage in Saudi Arabia in 2015, King Salman met them in Mecca, a move seen at the time as an effort to entice them away from Iran. The Qataris were further encouraged when Salman named Mohammed bin Nayef crown prince, since they knew and liked him.

But as MBS rose and increasingly absorbed Mohammed bin Zayed's view of the region, the Qataris felt a new chill. Other events accelerated the split. An Emirati dissident living in Doha published an op-ed with Al Jazeera about women's rights, and the Emiratis stepped up demands that she be sent home. Qatar refused. Then more than $300 million in Qatari cash landed in Iraq to secure the release of twenty-six Qatari falcon hunters, including nine members of the royal family, who had been kidnapped by a pro-Iranian militia. Qatar's foes saw it as yet another example of the emir's shipping cash to bad actors.

The emir himself had traveled to Riyadh for the Trump visit, where he had met the new president and come away thinking the meeting went well. But during a lunch with Tillerson and his regional counterparts, the Qatari foreign minister had been surprised to find himself seated near the kitchen, a deliberate snub.

Two days after the Qatari delegation returned home, the emir was roused from his sleep with news of the hack, leading to speculation that if MBS had not received explicit sign-off from the Trump administration, he at least believed it would support him.

Few other countries joined the boycott, not buying the allegations. A spokeswoman for the State Department said the United States was "mystified" that Qatar's foes had not released evidence to back up its allegations and questioned whether they were fueled by "long-simmering grievances."

Saudi Arabia and its allies presented Qatar with a list of thirteen demands, which included shutting down Al Jazeera, cutting ties with the Muslim Brotherhood, scaling back cooperation with Iran and Turkey, and submitting to monthly compliance checks. Together, they would have reduced Qatar to a vassal state. The demands were later boiled down to a set of principles Qatar was supposed to abide by, but the split lived on, undermining the strategic bonds between the United States' Gulf allies just months after Trump had called on them to unite against Iran.

MBS never questioned the boycott's wisdom, instead arguing that it was up to Qatar to come crawling back.

"It has to happen, one day," he said. "We hope they learn fast. It depends on them."

TRUMP WAS NOT the first official in the new administration to make Riyadh his first foreign destination. In February 2017, after being sworn in as the director of the Central Intelligence Agency, Mike Pompeo flew to Saudi Arabia to see the agency's old friend, Crown Prince Mohammed bin Nayef. In an official ceremony, he gave the prince the CIA's George Tenet medal to honor his counterterrorism work, and perhaps to make it clear that the embattled prince still had friends in Washington. But if the Saudi spy chief's American supporters had hoped to give him a boost in his rivalry with his young cousin, it was too late. MBN had failed to match MBS's energy. He had also opposed the boycott of Qatar, partly because of his relationship with its emir, and felt that the war in Yemen had diluted counterterrorism efforts, policy differences MBS considered unacceptable.

As summer set in and the holy month of Ramadan began, when Muslims fast from dawn to dusk and government work in Saudi Arabia slows to a trickle, MBS and his team kept working for his advancement. In mid-June, MBS contacted Saad al-Jabri, MBN's former deputy who had been fired in 2015, to offer him a new job if he returned to Saudi Arabia. Al-Jabri, who had left the kingdom earlier that year, feared trouble and distrusted MBS, so he declined, saying he was tied up with medical treatment. Al-Jabri informed MBN's aides about the call, suspecting that the young prince was making plans.

He was right.

On the night of June 20, many of the royals were in Mecca, where they traditionally spent the final days of Ramadan near the holy sites. The Council of Political and Security Affairs, which MBN headed, was scheduled to meet that night, after the fast had been broken and the evening prayers performed. But before it began, MBN was informed that the king wanted to see him.

So he flew to the monarch's Safa Palace in a helicopter with his security detail, and entered with two guards. They got in the elevator to go up, and when the doors opened, a team of royal guards rushed in, stripped them of their guns and cellphones, and led MBN to an adjacent room.

There, he would spend the night, unable to leave and under pressure from MBS's aides to abdicate as crown prince.

MBN refused to abdicate, and the pressure increased. His captors insulted him as a drug addict and threated to publicize his medical problems. But they could not simply shove him aside. When he had become crown prince, members of the royal family and the top clerics had pledged allegiance to him, an act with religious significance from the earliest days of Islam. That allegiance could usually be broken only by death or abdication. MBS's aides sought to secure the latter, by force.

Years before, King Abdullah had created a body called the Allegiance Council, which was supposed to institutionalize the succession process. The council's members were princes representing the lines of the founding king's sons, and they were supposed to approve changes to the royal lineup. The body had never quite worked as intended, given that kings, including Abdullah himself, preferred to choose their own successors.

That night, while MBN remained incommunicado in the palace, Royal Court officials called the council's members, informing them that the king had decided to make MBS crown prince and asking if they agreed. Most would have hesitated to voice their opposition to the king's wishes, so thirty-one of the council's thirty-four members agreed. Some of those calls were recorded and played for MBN to show how many of his relatives had turned on him, a royal checkmate.

As the night wore on, MBN's captors refused to give him food or his diabetes medication, and he grew tired. Sometime around dawn, he gave in, probably signing a document giving up his post. Once that was done, he was escorted to a nearby room, where he was surprised to find guards, men with cameras, and MBS. The young prince greeted him warmly, with a show of great deference, kissing him on the hand and kneeling to kiss the hem of his thobe.

MBN muttered a barely audible pledge of allegiance to Saudi Arabia's new crown prince.

"We will never dispense with your instructions and advice," MBS said.

"Good luck, God willing," MBN replied.

A black cape known as a *bisht* was draped over MBN's shoulders to signal his departure. A video of the encounter was widely distributed on social media and broadcast on Saudi television as proof of an amicable handover. But MBN left the room to find that his personal guards were gone, and a motorcade of royal guards drove him to his palace on the waterfront in Jeddah, where he was put under house arrest by guards who answered to MBS.

MBN was also removed as interior minister, and replaced by a nephew, a confidant of MBS. Soon after, the ministry was stripped of its most important counterterrorism and security duties, which were moved to a new security body that reported to MBS.

In a response to questions from *The New York Times*, the Royal Court told a different story about that night, saying that MBN had been removed by the Allegiance Council in "the best interest of the nation" and for reasons that were "classified and cannot be revealed."

"This decision was a guarantee for the nation's future, stability, and consistent advancement," it said, adding that MBN had been the first to pledge allegiance to MBS and that he had insisted that it be filmed and broadcast. The former crown prince, it continued, was staying at his palace in Jeddah and receiving guests daily.

"It is impossible for anyone who knows the kingdom and its values and understands the nature of the relationships among members of the royal family to believe that Prince Mohammed bin Nayef has experienced any pressure or disrespect," it said, dismissing allegations to the contrary as "baseless claims."

Later, MBS would tell an interviewer that it was the king's right to choose his crown prince and that the vote approving his appointment was the highest in Saudi history.

"Historically, I made a record in approval votes among the royal family," he said. "And their roles end when they vote."

A month later, an anonymous "Saudi source" told journalists from Reuters that the king had chosen to remove MBN because he had been "incapacitated by morphine and cocaine addiction."

Later that year, his bank accounts were frozen.

The next Ramadan, many of his assets were taken away.

The restrictions on MBN were later loosened and he made occasional appearances at family functions. But he mostly remained in his seaside palace in Jeddah, his communications and movements monitored. He never spoke publicly about what happened, or about his feelings for MBS.

About a year after his ouster, a princess who visited his wife told me, "She is depressed and she wants to die."

A JOURNALIST AT WORK

Y ou are the journalists, the prince had said after the launch of Vision 2030. If you want to write about it, go ahead.

So Jamal Khashoggi did, considering the prince's words a mandate. He had no reason to suspect that the rules for a Saudi media figure had changed, so he did what he had been doing for decades: communicating the kingdom's policies in his work and offering soft-gloved critiques along the way.

But privately, he had misgivings about the new direction. He told me in 2015, before Vision 2030 had launched, that he supported its goals of diversifying the economy, bringing young Saudis into the labor market, and loosening social restrictions; he had, in fact, been calling for such moves for years. But he felt that MBS's approach did not allow for feedback from the citizens who would be most affected.

"Saudi Arabia wants to be a modern country without democracy. Can we do that? We want to employ Saudis. We want the flourishes. We want the country to be entertaining, so that people will stay here. . . . We want to improve the performance of the government and local authorities, but without checks and balances," he told me.

MBS, on the other hand, was going for "a corporate-like administration where you set goals and review them," he said. "Will that make Saudi Arabia better? I don't know."

The Saudi news media marketed Vision 2030 breathlessly, but Khashoggi took a different approach. In a series of columns for *Al Hayat*, he laid out what he called "The Saudi Citizen's Vision 2030," suggesting needed changes not from the point of view of the Royal

Court and its foreign consultants, but from that of a citizen going about his daily life. He was approaching 60, he wrote, and so would write about his family's experiences, with a focus on "quality of life," which he was glad to see emphasized in the Vision.

He started with jobs. The abundance of foreign laborers had distorted the Saudi job market, he argued, suggesting that the government create more work for Saudis. He called for competitive education that involved parents and recalled a teacher saying she did not believe in dinosaurs because they were not mentioned in the Quran.

He asked for better health care, asking why, if proper care was provided by the state, citizens scrambled to get their relatives into private hospitals. He asked the municipal authorities for "a sidewalk to walk on," arguing that the absence of them in Saudi cities was emblematic of poor urban planning. He called for more parking, better zoning between residential and commercial properties, more soccer fields, more parks, and more trees.

His suggestions were charming in their modesty, simple steps the government could take to improve life. Only a few had a whiff of politics. He called for citizens to have a role in local decision-making and for free access to information. These were necessary, he said, for the leadership to achieve its goals. If everyone agreed that corruption was bad, why not allow citizens to see how public money was spent to ensure accountability? He, for one, would ask the Jeddah municipality how much its paving program had cost, which companies had received the contracts, and why they had made the sidewalks a half-meter tall. Why didn't the mayor hold a monthly press conference to explain his plans? Journalism could hold officials accountable, while giving citizens a way to raise grievances without going to court.

"If this system were provided, it would lead to a revolution in journalism and return the citizen's trust in it, and officials would benefit from the news and reports," he wrote.

The columns were published during the presidential campaign in the United States, and when Trump won, Khashoggi struggled to make sense of it. He joked to me that after a meeting with Barack Obama, someone in Riyadh had asked God for a change in the White House.

"And God answered his prayer—literally," he said.

But Khashoggi didn't know what to expect. Trump had bashed Muslims and said Saudi Arabia needed to pay for American security. But Trump was also a businessman, who could increase economic cooperation to help the kingdom create jobs.

"He has to make himself clear now that he is the president so that we will know how to deal with him," he told me.

He published a column telling Saudis not to fear Trump, but to prepare for him. He reassured them that, despite the rhetoric, Trump was unlikely to wage war on the region, chase Muslims from the United States, or send Saudi Arabia a bill for its protection. But he called Trump an "extremist, right-wing populist who sees the countries of the Arabian Gulf as mere oil wells." But this gave Saudi Arabia an opportunity: to be a true friend to the United States in the region and show Trump that "Saudi Arabia is more than an oil well."

He was blunter in other forums. On Twitter, he criticized Trump's style, and he said during an event in Washington that the Saudis were deceiving themselves if they expected Trump the president to act differently from Trump the candidate. The kingdom needed to expect surprises, including insults, from the administration.

His critical take was not welcomed in Riyadh. A few weeks after Trump's win, a powerful deputy to MBS named Saud al-Qahtani called Khashoggi to tell him that he was banned from tweeting, writing, and speaking to the news media. Other Saudi journalists criticized him, and the foreign ministry issued a statement saying that Khashoggi's positions "only represent his personal views, not that of the Kingdom of Saudi Arabia."

The ban was a shock for a man who had been counted on for decades to telegraph the kingdom's views. And he had not even criticized the kingdom, but expressed doubts about an Islamophobe, a position that would not have caused trouble before.

Khashoggi texted an old American friend, Maggie Mitchell Salem, to complain about the new restrictions.

KHASHOGGI: I been told not to tweet, not to write, not speak to foreign media, and a writer in *Okaz* called to arrest and put me on trial!!

MITCHELL SALEM: What?!?! SERIOUSLY?!? That's
ridiculous!!!

He had not tweeted in two days, but he asked her to be discreet
so as not to exacerbate the situation. Mitchell Salem agreed, but
volunteered to ask friends in Washington to tweet about how
Khashoggi had been uncharacteristically quiet.

KHASHOGGI: Ya, it might help.
MITCHELL SALEM: Done.

It was a first, tiny collaboration in a working friendship that would
grow over time.

A few weeks later, he wrote again.

KHASHOGGI: Merry Christmas to you and your lovely kids. I
hope you are having a great holiday.
MITCHELL SALEM: We are! . . . Have been thinking of you. Are
you ok?
KHASHOGGI: I'm OK. Bored and worried.

Unable to work, Khashoggi traveled to London to see his old
friend Azzam Tamimi, with whom he had campaigned for democracy in Algeria decades before. They discussed the possibility—
which they had never previously discussed—that Khashoggi could
get arrested. Tamimi asked whom he should call if that happened,
and Khashoggi said to call his wife, Alaa Nasief. But the prospect
still seemed remote, so Khashoggi returned to Jeddah and kept a
low profile, hoping the trouble would blow over.

It did not.

By February 2017, it was clear that Alarab, the new television
channel he was supposed to lead, was never going to launch and he
was looking for alternatives.

KHASHOGGI: I'm officially jobless and I don't like it.
MITCHELL SALEM: I don't know how best to help. If you think
of a way, let me know.

KHASHOGGI: I'm exploring many possibilities, including settling out of the kingdom. It's frustrating to be silenced and to worry about your freedom all the time.

Mitchell Salem suggested he ask his previous patrons, Prince Turki al-Faisal, his former boss at the embassies in London and Washington, and Prince Alwaleed bin Talal, who had funded the channel, whether they would sponsor a think tank job for him somewhere. But he rejected the idea, fearing that being associated with him could harm them. He considered seeking a job at Al Jazeera, the Qatari satellite channel, as a way of going abroad.

KHASHOGGI: I want to write and be free. That won't happen if I stay.

After Trump's visit to Riyadh, Khashoggi's situation got worse. The Saudi news media and prominent figures on social media praised the elevation of MBS and the Qatar blockade, and other Saudis were expected to join the chorus, especially those with profiles as high as Khashoggi's. He did not, resisting the new with-us-or-against-us tone, and his friends inside the government warned that he could be banned from travel or arrested if he did not get on board.

In June, Mitchell Salem asked how he was.

KHASHOGGI: Not good. Suffocating.
MITCHELL SALEM: I wish I could help you.
KHASHOGGI: It's turning to stupid McCarthyism here. It's crazy. Thank goodness I'm not an editor of a paper now. I would be ashamed to do what the others are doing.
MITCHELL SALEM: Can you get out?
KHASHOGGI: Of course, but to do what? I'm free to travel now, but with this craziness, I can't guarantee that.

Soon after, he left for America.

KHASHOGGI: Hello, dear. On my way to the States. It's suffocating at home!! I'll be in L.A. for a week, maybe later in

D.C. I'm just looking for anything to do that keeps me away.
It's so SAD what's happening.

By July, he knew it was risky to go home.

KHASHOGGI: I spoke to my lawyer. I think I should stay and go
to London. If I was a drinker, I would've gone to the bar. I hate
planning for my life.
I'll go and smoke a cigar.
Bye.

LORD OF THE FLIES

———————

IN 2012, AN amateur hacker and poet with an interest in bitcoin, bots, and online video games got in touch with Hacking Team, an Italian company that sold cyber tools to governments to allow them to hack cellphones and other devices.

> Dear Sir, We need people visit us in Hosted by the Saudi governmen that have high technical knowledge and high Authority in order to provide an integrated display and explain the solutions you offer and training and costs. we Will bear all the costs of the trip from a-z. please send to me all the info you need to manage that.
> Regards saud

An account manager replied that he would need confirmation that the query was from a government.

"we are from the royal court of Saudi Arabia, the king office," the customer replied.

The company received the required assurances, and the men planned for two Hacking Team technicians to travel to Riyadh. Their host said they would be "vip guests for the Royal Court."

A few years before, a user with the same email address had become well-known on Hack Forums, an online meet-up for cybercriminals, aspiring hackers, and those who preyed on them. During his more than six years on the forum, the user made hundreds of posts and donated more than $10,000 to the site, earning awards from its administrators and being described in its wiki as "one of the most known Hack Forums users." He had a reputation for inquiring about surveillance technologies, offering high sums for simple services, and requesting help with specific targets.

"IS THERE ANY RAT THAT CAN INFECT MAC PC?" he asked in March 2014, referring to a remote access Trojan, which can commandeer targeted devices.

His banking details showed that he lived Saudi Arabia.

His name was Saud al-Qahtani, and he would become one of MBS's most feared and powerful deputies—and eventually his Achilles' heel.

BRANCHES OF THE Saudi government had been dealing with Hacking Team since at least 2013. The Ministries of Interior and Defense had brought its technicians to Riyadh to train Saudis, but the technicians were not always impressed. One wrote after a course that most of the participants had not paid attention, acted unprofessionally, or failed to show up.

"I feel that 90% of them are not up to it," the trainer wrote.

Al-Qahtani would up the Saudi hackers' game, after a rough start in the online world. He was from a big tribe and had been a top student in the Saudi capital before earning a law degree. He attended a training course with the Saudi Air Force, graduating with the rank of sergeant, and got a master's degree in criminal justice. In 2008, he was recruited to the Royal Court to do media monitoring under King Abdullah.

He appeared on Hack Forums the next year, and was almost immediately hacked. He bought malware from another user, soon realizing that his computer had been infected by the very software he had purchased. He found it hard to believe that a hacker had hacked him.

"i think he is a very good man and look trusted!!!" he wrote.

That was the first of at least four times that the hackers whose services al-Qahtani sought tricked him. He later paid $150 to restore control of his Hotmail account, and lost $3,000 in Bitcoin. In 2015, someone hacked his account on the forum itself. Two weeks later, he returned and implored its other members to secure their accounts.

But his skills improved. At one point, he promised $500 to anyone who could hack Hotmail accounts, but soon rescinded the offer when he did it himself. On rare occasions, he posted personal comments, praising President Obama in 2010 as a "realy humanity leader for the earth," and arguing that the American president needed to use hard, soft, and smart power against Iran. Three times, he acknowledged posting while drunk.

"im on party and drunk and now im really happy," he wrote. "will go to drink tackila and dance lol."

He also expressed a recurrent interest in macro techniques to manipulate social media by boosting the popularity of content on YouTube and Facebook, getting Twitter accounts banned, and setting up servers to dispatch malware.

Those skills saved him from being purged in 2015 when Salman became king and MBS took over the Royal Court. American officials who watched al-Qahtani's rise say he quickly recognized that MBS feared plots by a range of enemies and rivals and convinced the prince that his knowledge of the dark electronic arts could help him prevail. In 2015, al-Qahtani was named an adviser at the court with the rank of minister and put in charge of a media office. Soon after, he got back in touch with Hacking Team, writing directly to its CEO from a Royal Court email address:

Dear David
Considering your esteemed reputation and professionalism, we here at the Center for Media Monitoring and Analysis at the Saudi Royal Court (THE King Office) would like to be in productive cooperation with you and develop a long and strategic partnership.

I would like you to be so kind as to send us the complete list of services that your esteemed company offers, in addition to their prices, all explained in detail, as soon as possible please.

An account manager said he would send the company's nondisclosure agreement so the men could talk business.

"great waiting for it so i sign it and we can go to the next step,"
al-Qahtani replied. "im sdure your nda will be very profisional and
will protect our privacy."

The account manager told his boss the guy seemed paranoid.

AL-QAHTANI'S OUTREACH TO Hacking Team was one of many projects he pursued as the head of the Center for Studies and Media
Affairs at the Royal Court, building it over time into an empire
whose activities would belie its seemingly banal name. CSMARC, as
it was known, did deal with the media. Al-Qahtani oversaw MBS's
interviews with foreign journalists, often dictating what was on or
off record. He also oversaw more covert operations aimed at shaping the conversation around MBS and crushing dissenting voices at
home and abroad.

Saudi Arabia had never been a democracy, but more of a soft-
gloved autocracy. Citizens were expected to keep up appearances in
public, but the authorities cared little what they did or said in private, as long as they were not Shiites planning protests or jihadists
plotting attacks. And some public criticism appeared in the newspapers, as long as it did not target the royal family or get too specific
about corruption.

That would change under MBS, and leading the charge were al-
Qahtani and a brash commoner named Turki al-Sheikh, a rotund
former security officer with an unruly beard who had won MBS's
friendship years before when Salman was the governor of Riyadh.
Al-Sheikh had married the daughter of one of Salman's advisers,
solidifying his place in the future king's circle and impressing MBS
with what the prince valued most: fierce loyalty. Over time, al-
Sheikh would become one of MBS's key fixers, counted on for his
willingness to wade in to solve the prince's problems. Dennis Horak,
the Canadian ambassador expelled from Saudi Arabia in 2018 over
his government's tweets, described the pair as "not so much good
cop/bad cop, more bad cop and lesser bad cop."

As MBS's power increased, so did theirs, and by the time MBS
had become crown prince, al-Qahtani had evolved into the prince's
media czar and fiercest protector. In a few years, he would build

Saudi Arabia into a laboratory for a new kind of electronic authoritarianism, with al-Qahtani as its chief scientist.

At the time, new technologies had given authoritarian governments from Russia to China new tools to pry into citizens' lives. No longer did they need to dispatch agents to shadow dissidents or tap their landlines. Instead, powerful technologies put them inside people's devices, allowing them to track their movements and eavesdrop on their communications. Saudi Arabia lacked the expertise to develop its own technologies, but it had the cash to buy the best off-the-shelf products available abroad.

The spread of social media, and its emergence as a primary source of news and information, provided further opportunities. If a government could manipulate the information its subjects saw online, it could shape their perception of reality, a technique one researcher called "pro-active thought authoritarianism." It was Big Brother, but instead of the state forcing it into people's living rooms, the people invited it into their own pockets with their cellphones.

MBS recognized the power of these technologies and deputized al-Qahtani to deploy them. His primary domain was Twitter, the social network that had come to play a massive role in Saudi social life. In a kingdom with a few outlets for public expression but where many citizens carried multiple cellphones, had free time, and were among the world's highest consumers of YouTube, Twitter provided an open space to share information and debate hot topics. It was an online town square of sorts, albeit one full of masks, since many Saudis used fake names.

Wielding a Twitter account with more than a million followers, al-Qahtani emerged as a major force on the platform, celebrating his boss's every move while marshaling attacks on enemies, from foreign news organizations, to Iran, Qatar, and Saudis who were insufficiently supportive of the prince. Al-Qahtani's attacks spurred offensives by hundreds of sympathetic accounts that critics referred to as "electronic flies" because of how they swarmed their targets. His detractors called him "Saudi Arabia's Steve Bannon" and the "Lord of the Flies."

After the Qatar boycott, al-Qahtani turned up the heat, spearheading a frenzied online McCarthyism. He announced an official hashtag, #The_Black_List, and called on his followers to suggest names for it.

"Saudi Arabia and its brothers do what they say. This is a promise," he wrote. "Add every name you think should be included on the #The_Black_List using the hashtag. They will be sorted and tracked, starting now."

Those on the list would be punished or prosecuted, he said, adding that hiding behind fake identities would not protect people because the state could unmask them. Al-Qahtani made clear whose authority he acted on.

"Do you think I act as I wish with no direction?" he wrote. "I am an employee and faithful implementer of the orders of my lord the king and his highness the faithful crown prince."

His techniques varied. To control the output of traditional media, he ran a WhatsApp group for the kingdom's editors to guide their coverage. On Twitter, he realized that even on topics involving millions of tweets, a few hundred accounts could shift the conversation. In addition to running armies of automated accounts, or bots, he oversaw hundreds of Saudis employed in "troll farms" in and around Riyadh. Most were recruited through social media, realizing the nature of the work only after they had been hired. Earning around $3,000 a month, they worked full-time to police online activity about the kingdom, attacking critical voices, shaping online conversations, and boosting messages that the government wanted delivered.

The workers received daily guidance on WhatsApp or Telegram. Homing in on conversations about the war in Yemen, the Qatar blockade, or women's rights, they would flood trending hashtags with pro-government views. Other times, they would report critical conversations as offensive, prompting Twitter to take them offline. By 2018, manipulation of the platform in Saudi Arabia was so great it was hard to determine what was real human activity. One researcher called the Saudi Twittersphere "a wasteland."

Al-Qahtani's targets were not all virtual. He pursued people in the real world too, even for small criticisms. In 2017, Saudi journalist Turki al-Roqi heard that a man had been arrested after complaining online that a train had been late. This was the kind of complaint Saudis had previously been able to make without trouble, and so al-Roqi criticized the arrest in a series of tweets.

Al-Qahtani called al-Roqi's online news site to order that the tweets be deleted, and insisted that al-Roqi claim his account had been hacked and write an apology to the king. To avoid endangering his colleagues, al-Roqi resigned from the site and wrote the letter. But al-Qahtani then told him to join a Twitter campaign against a cleric who had just been arrested. Al-Roqi refused.

"Am I talking about an adviser and a minister in the highest establishment in the state, or a teenager specialized in defamation and hacking?" al-Roqi wrote of al-Qahtani in an article he posted online about the incident.

Saudi Arabia also tried to get inside the tech companies themselves. In late 2015, Western intelligence agencies warned Twitter that the kingdom had cultivated a Saudi employee in hopes that he could get information about the owners of dissident accounts. Ali Alzabarah had been working at Twitter since 2013 and been promoted into an engineering job where he could access account information, including IP addresses, phone numbers, and other details that could identify users.

Twitter put him on leave and investigated the case, finding no evidence that he had passed sensitive data to the Saudi government. Shortly after Alzabarah left Twitter, and he returned to the kingdom to work for the government.

All along, the kingdom had been tapping outside expertise to understand the online world. After MBS reduced subsidies on utilities in 2015, causing a spike in prices, McKinsey & Company, the consulting firm, produced a nine-page study on how the measures were being received. The report found that the online reaction was profoundly negative and identified three Twitter personalities who had played an outsized role in the conversation: a writer named Khalid al-Alkami; an anonymous parody account named Ahmad; and a Saudi dissident in Canada, Omar Abdulaziz. Al-Alkami, the report said, "wrote multiple negative tweets regarding austerity," while Abdulaziz "has a multitude of negative tweets on topics such as austerity and the royal decrees."

In mid-2017, al-Alkami was arrested and the parody account was taken down. The Saudis would go after Abdulaziz later.

When asked about the report by my colleagues at *The New York Times*, McKinsey expressed outrage.

"We are horrified by the possibility, however remote, that it could have been misused," the company said. "We have seen no evidence to suggest that it was misused, but we are urgently investigating how and with whom the document was shared."

IN THE YEAR after Salman became king, three Saudi princes who had criticized the government were kidnapped abroad and returned to the kingdom. A year and a half into Salman's reign, a Saudi businessman named Tarek Obaid was arrested when he got off a plane in Beijing on suspicions that he was a terrorist financer. He was soon released, after the Chinese realized the Saudis had given them false information in order to have Obaid extradited.

A year later, a little-known Saudi prince was arrested in Morocco and flown home. That same month, a Saudi businessman named Salem al-Muzaini was arrested in Dubai and flown to Saudi Arabia, where he was jailed without charge. Al-Muzaini was not a prominent dissident, but ran a private jet charter service called Sky Prime. Most of its jets were owned by Mohammed bin Nayef, the deposed crown prince. Both lost their stakes in the company after al-Muzaini's arrest.

Thought control was one thing; pursuing dissidents in the real world was another. Sometime early in his father's reign, it was reported that MBS had ordered al-Qahtani and his organization "to target his opponents domestically and abroad," according to a classified assessment by the Central Intelligence Agency that was leaked to the *New York Times* and other publications (the CIA declined to comment when asked for official confirmation). The Saudi intelligence service issued a standing order to bring home dissidents from abroad, but without spelling out how to do it. Figuring that out fell to a team of operatives that al-Qahtani oversaw, called the "Rapid Intervention Group." Over time, it would engage in surveillance, harassment, and kidnapping of Saudi citizens overseas, as well as their detention and sometimes torture inside palaces belonging to MBS and his father.

Early on, most members of the team came from the military, which al-Qahtani could tap freely since his boss was the minister of defense. After MBN was removed as crown prince and interior minister, al-Qahtani tapped a wider pool of talent, pulling agents from the intelligence service. That was when his group really took off.

In the fall of 2017, a wave of arrests across the kingdom swept up about eighty men. Most were prominent clerics, both ultraconservatives and Islamists associated with the Muslim Brotherhood. The rest were campaigners who had called for political reforms years before and mostly remained quiet since, or individuals who had annoyed MBS and his aides in some way or another. One was an economist who had questioned the wisdom of privatizing Aramco. Another was a poet who had called on journalists to avoid harsh language in the dispute with Qatar.

The government did not release the detainees' names, but said the authorities had uncovered "intelligence activities for the benefit of foreign parties" and accused the men of "espionage activities and having contacts with external entities including the Muslim Brotherhood." Some would later get prison terms. Others would languish in detention without charge.

Among those picked up was a 62-year-old cleric named Salman al-Awda. He had long been a giant in the Saudi religious sphere, a renowned scholar with followers across the Islamic world.

Al-Awda had endorsed extremist views during his younger years and done substantial jail time for questioning the religious legitimacy of the royal family and participating in calls for reform. But he had mellowed with age. His books were widely read, he had hosted popular religious programs on television and YouTube, and he had more than 13 million followers on Twitter. Many of his fans also followed him on Snapchat, where the now-grandfatherly scholar had rebranded himself as a cleric of the people and sent out sunny dispatches about Islam in daily life. He had spoken fondly of the idea of constitutional monarchy and encouraged the kingdom's leaders to cater to their subjects' needs to avoid an Arab Spring–style uprising. As the dispute with Qatar escalated, al-Awda tweeted a prayer for the region's leaders: "May God harmonize their hearts for the good of their peoples."

A few hours later, security officials in civilian clothes showed up at his house and took him away, telling his family he would return soon.

He did not.

A few days later, his brother, an education professor, criticized the arrest on Twitter.

"The size of the demagoguery that we enjoy has been revealed, unfortunately," he wrote. Within hours, he, too, was arrested.

MBS rewrote the rules for public discussion in Saudi Arabia, scaling back the types of comments and criticisms that were permitted while greatly upping the price Saudis would pay for crossing the new red lines. Saud al-Qahtani was the primary enforcer of the new order, and the trajectory of Sheikh al-Awda was a telling barometer. Five years before, he had had 1.6 million followers on Twitter and had praised the spread of social media for facilitating communication between Saudis and their leaders.

"Twitter has revealed a great frustration and a popular refusal of the current situation," he said. "There is a complete gap between the rulers and the ruled. . . . Even those who are in charge of security do not know what the people really think, and this is not good."

At the time of his arrest, he had more than 10 million followers. A year later, the kingdom would put him on trial for thirty-seven charges, including inciting public discord, disrespecting the rulers, and "spreading corruption on Earth," a harsh accusation under Sharia law. The prosecutors would seek the death penalty.

AN INSIDER IN EXILE

IN LATE SUMMER 2017, Jamal Khashoggi landed in Washington, D.C., a silenced, saddened journalist who feared that the gates of his homeland were closing on him. The government's ban on his media appearances and use of Twitter had dragged on for eight months, preventing him from blasting updates to his millions of followers. When he did go online, the bots and trolls commanded by Saud al-Qahtani filled his account with hate. The pressures on him had spread to his family and his marriage, exacerbating his loneliness. For a writer and commentator who over the decades had grown used to being *in*, he was suddenly, decidedly *out*—and he didn't like it.

During the cloying Washington summer, he moved with his two suitcases back into the condo in Tysons Corner that he had bought years before while at the Saudi Embassy. He was depressed, often in tears, living in a country that was not his own, and struggling to figure out what to do with his life.

His religious and political views had broadened over the years, and he was often an ideological chameleon, giving whomever he was talking to the impression he agreed with them. He kept in touch with friends from the Muslim Brotherhood, who considered him a fellow traveler, while also mixing with a much wider circle of intellectuals from across the Arab world, Turkey, Britain, and the United States. Many of them were secularists with whom he would smoke cigars or enjoy a glass of wine. At times, he laughed at memories of his younger self, once recalling being in a restaurant in Peshawar during the Afghan jihad when a member of his group had huffily pulled shut the curtain of their room to separate them from the infidel drinkers at the bar.

But he remained devout, praying regularly and fasting for Ramadan. In Washington, he carried a little rug with him and would drop by the office of his old friend Maggie Mitchell Salem to pray before going on his way.

Mitchell Salem was a former American diplomat who had left government to do communications for a think tank and had worked at times for the Saudis. She had met Khashoggi at an event a decade and a half before and had put in substantial practice to correctly pronounce his name (Kha-SHOG-gi). They bonded over their shared passion for the Middle East and kept in touch over the years.

By the time Khashoggi returned to Washington, Mitchell Salem was 49, a twice-divorced mother of four who maintained a busy social calendar that kept her plugged in with the capital's Middle East crowd. She threw or attended frequent dinners and seemed to know every former official or big-name journalist who had ever been involved with the region. She worried deeply about her newly exiled friend, making it her job to check in on him every day and look out for his mental and emotional health.

The complicating factor in their relationship, however, was that Mitchell Salem now worked for Qatar, which the Saudis had deemed a state enemy a few months before. She wasn't a registered lobbyist, but was the executive director of Qatar Foundation International, which did educational and cultural programs. That meant she was paid by Qatar, which had responded to the boycott by Saudi Arabia and its allies by mobilizing its media to fight back. Khashoggi's relationship with Mitchell Salem, and her employment by Qatar, would later give ammunition to his detractors.

But as summer gave way to fall, it was unclear which way Khashoggi's relationship with his government would go. In August, the Saudi information minister called to tell him that MBS said hello and wanted him to come home. Khashoggi said he could not, because he was in the process of securing a long-term visa to the United States. But he asked if he could start writing again and the minister said yes. So Khashoggi thanked the minister and MBS in a Twitter post, ending his nine-month hiatus.

"May no free pen be broken and no tweep silenced," he wrote.

The minister proposed deeper cooperation, asking Khashoggi to write a proposal for up to $2 million in funding for a Saudi think tank in Washington that would help Riyadh "regain its positive role and image." Khashoggi was intrigued, so his wife helped him write up a proposal and send it to Riyadh.

But he still woke most mornings to find the kingdom's online armies assaulting him as a traitor or declaring that he was not a "real" Saudi because of his light skin. They blasted him for statements he had made that appeared to support the Muslim Brotherhood. On September 8, he published his last column in *Al Hayat*, "I Am Saudi but Different," arguing that "the right to disagree" was necessary for society to progress.

The breaking point, however, were the arrests that fall which netted a number of Khashoggi's friends, including Essam al-Zamil, an economist and entrepreneur who had questioned MBS's economic plans. Before his arrest, al-Zamil had been in Washington with a Saudi delegation. Khashoggi had sensed that the mood was turning and warned his friend not to go home. But the economist went anyway and was detained after he arrived.

When I asked Khashoggi about the arrests, he was irate, and dismissed the government's accusations that the detainees had been plotting against the country.

"It is absurd," he said. "There were no conspiracies."

What the detainees shared was that they had not joined the condemnations of Qatar.

"They are the silent or the people who refused to jump in the wagon with the government in its campaign against Qatar," he said.

He was clearer about what it meant for him with close friends.

"That's it. I can't go back," he told Azzam Tamimi. "If this is what they do to Essam, what do you think they'll do to me?"

In September, MBS complained to al-Qahtani that Khashoggi had become too influential and was damaging the crown prince's image. Al-Qahtani warned that a move against such a prominent figure could cause an uproar, but MBS said the kingdom should not care what others thought about how it dealt with its citizens and that he did not believe in half-measures.

Shortly after, another MBS confidant suggested that they lure Khashoggi home with a job at a Saudi-owned television network. MBS doubted that the plan would work and said Khashoggi should be forced home.

It was not clear whether the prince was speaking literally, but the message to his aides was clear: Khashoggi was a problem that needed to be taken care of.

As WORD SPREAD in Washington that Khashoggi was in town, an editor from *The Washington Post* asked him to write an opinion piece about the arrests. He was excited about it, and so was Mitchell Salem, who began working behind the scenes to help him find his footing as a respected U.S.-based Arab voice. He did not know the city well and was self-conscious about his English writing, so she helped him out in more ways than were clear at the time. She commissioned a programmer to build him a website, jamalkhashoggi .com, to feature his articles in English and Arabic and pressed him to send her a head shot and photos of himself with members of the royal family to show that he had "long been a trusted adviser."

Their friendship predated the Saudi rift with Qatar by more than a decade, but they realized that under MBS and his aggressive approach to the kingdom's tiny neighbor, the rules had changed and they had to be careful.

"I'm going to try and do this without fingerprints," Mitchell Salem texted Khashoggi about the website. "It's going to be one way we push you online."

Later, she emailed an editor at *The New York Times* to inquire about Khashoggi writing an op-ed, and Khashoggi told her to watch out.

> KHASHOGGI: We should keep our relationship discreet. When you write to the NYT and they Google you to find that you work for Qatar! It could hurt. We have to be strategic, not impulsive.

Mitchell Salem worried that the Saudis would hack his computer, so she got him a Mac laptop to replace his PC and told him to have his condo swept for listening devices.

KHASHOGGI: Now you are being dramatic!!
MITCHELL SALEM: I AM NOT BEING DRAMATIC!! You are taking on the leadership. Actually, they have identified you as a problem. So you need to take that seriously. I'm not kidding.

Khashoggi demurred, joking that someday over dinner and a cigar he would tell MBS how nice he had been to him in his writing. "He is mean," he wrote. "He has done ugly things."

He sent Mitchell Salem a draft of his op-ed to review before submitting it to *The Washington Post*.

IN MID-SEPTEMBER, MITCHELL Salem and Khashoggi went to the Brookings U.S.-Islamic World Forum in New York, an annual event for the East Coast foreign policy crowd that was co-hosted by Qatar. Mitchell Salem, Khashoggi, and some friends piled into Mitchell Salem's Volkswagen Touareg to head for New York City. They stopped on the on-ramp so Khashoggi could do a phone interview with the BBC, then took off up Interstate 95, talking about his column for the *Post*, which was still a work in progress. Mitchell Salem encouraged him to write more about himself and to express more emotion, but Khashoggi resisted, arguing that he wanted to write like David Ignatius, the *Post*'s veteran foreign affairs columnist.

"You have something that David Ignatius doesn't have," she told him. "You have to put something in this about you. Believe it or not, most people have no idea who you are."

In New York, they realized that Khashoggi, who had left Washington wearing khakis, running shoes, and a baseball cap, had no professional clothes for the event. Mitchell Salem suggested they go to Saks Fifth Avenue, but they ended up at Men's Wearhouse, where Khashoggi identified the salesman as Egyptian and chatted with him about politics. There was a sale on, offering a discount on a second item if you bought the first at full price, but Khashoggi declined.

"Maggie, I'm a minimalist," he said. "You should not have more than you need."

At the forum, Khashoggi was welcomed all around and burst into tears when he ran into an old friend who asked how he was. He was the only Saudi in attendance, and many of the participants knew him or his work and had heard about his flight to Washington. They came by to greet him and chat about Saudi Arabia, positive attention that took the edge off the attacks from home.

During the forum, *The Washington Post* published his column, entitled "Saudi Arabia wasn't always this repressive. Now it's unbearable."

"When I speak of the fear, intimidation, arrests, and public shaming of intellectuals and religious leaders who dare to speak their minds, and then I tell you that I'm from Saudi Arabia, are you surprised?" he began. He contrasted MBS's desire to spearhead reforms with the arrests of "intellectuals and religious leaders who dare to express opinions contrary to those of my country's leadership."

He had taken Mitchell Salem's advice and wrote about himself, describing his anguish in speaking to other Saudis who had fled the country, wondering if they would form "the core of a Saudi diaspora." The "climate of fear and intimidation" that MBS had created was unnecessary "when a young, charismatic leader is promising long-awaited reforms to spur economic growth and diversify our economy." He explained his own decision to speak out:

> It was painful for me several years ago when several friends were arrested. I said nothing. I didn't want to lose my job or my freedom. I worried about my family. I have made a different choice now. I have left my home, my family and my job, and I am raising my voice. To do otherwise would betray those who languish in prison. I can speak when so many cannot. I want you to know that Saudi Arabia has not always been as it is now. We Saudis deserve better.

They would become the most famous words he ever wrote.

• • •

As WINTER APPROACHED, his friends kept him busy, inviting him to dinners and events, introducing him to people, and working to occupy his mind. His column for the *Post* had not been well received in Saudi Arabia, icing his proposed think tank and driving the last nail into the coffin of his marriage. His wife, Alaa Nasief, who had warned him that being outspoken would blow back on the family, asked for a divorce. Many of Khashoggi's friends suspected that the Saudi government had forced her to do so.

He returned as a regular commentator on Arabic and Western television channels and filled his Twitter feed with thoughts, articles, and responses to what was happening back home. Being engaged with ideas he cared about made him feel better. He was well known to the Saudis in Washington and even kept in touch with those on the government's good side. At one point, he lost his passport and had to go to the Saudi Embassy to apply for a replacement. Mitchell Salem worried about him and told him to text her when he went in and out.

KHASHOGGI: Embassy time.
MITCHELL SALEM: Good. Get a damn ID.

A few hours later:

MITCHELL SALEM: Hey, you ok? Let me know when you're out of the Embassy.
KHASHOGGI: Went well. They were very nice.

He returned two days later and was taken to a surprise meeting with the ambassador, Prince Khalid bin Salman, a younger brother of MBS.

MITCHELL SALEM: Let me know when you get out!
KHASHOGGI: I'm out.
MITCHELL SALEM: Rejoicing begins!!
KHASHOGGI: I even met the Ambassador. He was really nice.

MITCHELL SALEM: Captain on the Death Star. They are on a charm offensive to quiet you. WHAT ABOUT THOSE JAILED? SILENCED?!
KHASHOGGI: I know what they are doing. We had a frank discussion. I even brought up Qatar and the Brotherhood.

A few days later:

KHASHOGGI: I'm going to the Embassy.
MITCHELL SALEM: Ok. I really think we need to install a tracking device on you!!

An hour and a half later:

KHASHOGGI: I'm out of the Embassy but will return after 12.
MITCHELL SALEM: Good.

Three hours later:

KHASHOGGI: Done with embassy, coming to your office.

During that time, Khashoggi set out to reacquaint himself with the city that had once been his home and that now looked like it might become so again, all the while sending dispatches to his followers back home.

An Egyptian-American friend, Mohamed Soltan, gave him an informal tour of the local Muslim community and the two men prayed in different mosques on Fridays and discussed the sermons. Khashoggi visited Congress and was moved to find a prayer space inside for people of any faith.

"Under this dome of Congress there is a prayer space," he wrote on Twitter with a photo of himself in front of the building. "I prayed in it today, Friday. To pass through these grandiose halls full of history and arrive at a prayer hall for the workers here means a lot."

He posted a smiling photo of himself at *The Washington Post*.

"Today I visited *The Washington Post* newspaper and met with the opinion editing team and other colleagues," he wrote. "I am grateful for their invitation to write for them regularly, and I'll do it."

More columns soon appeared.

Mitchell Salem kept him busy, inviting him to Thanksgiving at her father's house and to a "Friendsgiving" the next day in Washington. It was buffet-style in an old house that had been stripped down to its original stone. There was crowding in the kitchen, an array of dishes, and a large dining table with sunflowers in glass vases, scattered fall gourds, candles, china, and bottles of red wine.

The attendees were not Middle East wonks and many had no idea who Khashoggi was, but he relished the holiday mood and tried to fit in. Once the turkey was carved, he filled his plate with meat and yams, took his place, and tucked in. He was struck when the guests went around the table and spoke of what they were thankful for.

Another guest took a picture of him in a white sweater at the table, looking up at the camera through his glasses. Saudis would attack him online the next day for eating at a table where alcohol was served, but he was elated that night to share his experience.

"Today is Thanksgiving, an occasion celebrated by Americans regardless of their religion," he wrote. "They have a tradition that every invitee mentions what makes him grateful this year. In my turn, I said, 'Because I have become free and I can write freely.'"

A FEW WEEKS later, he returned to the Saudi Embassy.

KHASHOGGI: I'm going now to the Saudi Embassy. Will text you when I'm out.
MITCHELL SALEM: God be with you!!

Twenty minutes later:

KHASHOGGI: I'm out.

DRIVING A LIFE

In September 2017, I received a message from a well-connected Saudi friend.

"Make sure you're around a computer/tv/twitter after 9:30 pm tonight," he wrote.

"Can you give me a hint?" I asked.

"All I know is that something is up. Could be anything."

I had two guesses. For weeks, there had been rampant speculation that King Salman was going to abdicate the throne and name Mohammed bin Salman the new Saudi king. My other guess was that the kingdom was going to lift the ban on women driving. So I got to work, writing up two news stories that anticipated how each change would likely be announced. I saved them both in the system at the *Times* and they were edited and ready to be published. I sat in front of the TV and waited.

Sure enough, at about 9:30, a newsreader on state television announced that in June 2018 the kingdom would lift its longtime ban on women driving.

It would be a watershed moment in a kingdom that had long been one of the world's most restrictive environments for women, a place where they were deprived of fundamental rights, kept out of sight, and seen primarily as bearers of children and cookers of meals. The restrictions had their roots in traditional Arabian culture, where the honor of an entire family was wrapped up in its ability to protect its women's virtue. Those traditions had been turbocharged by the Wahhabi tenet that when in doubt, it was best to go with stricter rules to decrease the potential for sin. If letting women out of the house increased the chance that they would engage in premarital sex or infidelity, it was better to keep them at home. And if allowing women to drive increased the chance that they would mingle with unrelated men, it was better to keep them grounded.

These attitudes affected all aspects of women's lives, to the extent that much of Saudi society opposed sending girls to school until the 1960s. When King Faisal first proposed the concept then, the clerics mounted such a battle against it that he won their assent only by putting it under their control, instead of under the Education Ministry. The opposition to opening the first girls' school in the city of Buraidah, northwest of Riyadh, was so fierce that the king sent armed guards to prevent attacks on students.

The kingdom's restrictions on women shocked even women from other conservative Arab countries. In 1969, a Sudanese consultant for UNESCO visited the kingdom to inspect the state of girls' education and was baffled by what she found.

"An iron curtain is drawn on women," she wrote. "No respectable Saudi woman walks in Riyadh streets alone without the company of another woman, or a man who should either be her husband, her brother, her father, or even her son or child." When women did appear in public, the religious police would confront those whose dress was deemed insufficiently modest, sometimes with the "famous white cane." To avoid contact with strange men, women avoided shopping, and no women appeared on television other than in cooking shows, where "cameras are only directed to the hands of a woman doing some cookery."

A woman's objective in life was to become a good, devout housewife.

"She should know how to cook well and produce as many children as possible," the consultant wrote, noting that polygamy and marriage with girls as young as 14 were encouraged as necessary to prevent "debauchery," which could be punished by public execution.

Nevertheless, the consultant noted some progress on girls' education. In 1960, there had been only sixteen girls' elementary schools and 5,200 female pupils in the kingdom, whose population was about 7 million. By 1969, there were more than 350 girls' schools with nearly 116,000 students. She found the students "intelligent and industrious," but described school life as "dull and monotonous." The teaching was poor, questions and discussions were frowned upon, and recreation nonexistent.

"This made the Saudi pupil very serious and deprived her of the cheerfulness and joy of childhood. I tried to convince them to give the children a brighter school atmosphere by allowing some game, but it seems it is going to take some time to do this. Singing, music, and picnics are out of the question," she wrote.

Even after girls' education took off, there were terrible mishaps. In 2002, a fire broke out in a girls' school in Mecca, and the religious police refused to let the students flee because they were not properly covered. Fifteen students died. The tragedy so angered King Abdullah that he transferred the authority over girls' education from the clerics to the Education Ministry.

Much had changed by 2017, but the ban on women driving remained the most potent symbol of the kingdom's oppression of women, and the issue remained a key battleground in the culture war between Saudi liberals and conservatives. The liberals saw ending the ban as a first step toward loosening other constraints. The conservatives saw it as a dangerous crack in the dam that could open a wider breach, allowing the forces of liberalism, Westernization, and secularism to flood in.

Soon after the announcement that the ban would end, I returned to Saudi Arabia to meet the first women who had defied it, twenty-seven years before.

IN 1990, WHEN MBS was four years old, Iraqi strongman Saddam Hussein invaded Kuwait and set off a panic in Saudi Arabia. Many feared that after Kuwait, he would send his forces after the kingdom's oil wealth, so Saudi Arabia invited in American troops, a move so controversial that it required a special dispensation from the clerics, who disapproved of "infidel" forces on Saudi soil. Among those troops were American servicewomen, who wore fatigues, showed their hair, and drove military vehicles.

Some Saudi women took note.

At the time, Nourah Alghanem was a 34-year-old mother of four who taught at a girls' elementary school in Riyadh. She was not an activist nor involved in politics, but an educated, working woman who saw no reason why women couldn't drive.

"I saw that we as Saudi women were powerless," she told me. "We didn't have anything in this country. We were confined, so what could we do?"

She invited a group of women over for tea and suggested that they defy the ban. Those women contacted others, a series of meetings were held, and the idea spread, resonating with a small group of professional women whose prospects had been hampered by the kingdom's restrictions.

One of them was Madeha Alajroush, the photographer and psychoanalyst I had interviewed after the driving protest in 2013 when she and her friend had given the yellow toy car to the men who were following them. As the daughter of a Saudi diplomat, she had spent time in New York in the 1960s, where she saw American feminists up close. She sympathized with their goals, but still got married young because her father would not have let her out of the house otherwise. Life in Saudi Arabia limited her. She worked as a photographer, but lacked the opportunities her male counterparts had.

"My male colleagues were able to open studios and get big projects and I wasn't, so it was natural to be frustrated," she said.

Another woman in the group, Fawziya al-Bakr, had recently finished her PhD in education at the University of London and had been appointed as an assistant lecturer at a Riyadh university. She, too, found herself constrained. Her husband was working in another Saudi city and her foreign driver had fled the country because of the war, so she was stuck at home with two children and a British driver's license that she could not use.

"What if something happens?" she asked. "I went to the meeting and I thought, 'Oh, this is a good idea,' because I was furious."

The women chose a date and time for their protest and sent a letter to Prince Salman, the future king who was then the governor of Riyadh, informing him of their plans. They received no response, which they interpreted, perhaps naïvely, as permission.

Before dusk on November 6, 1990, forty-seven women met up in a supermarket parking lot, piled into a dozen cars with women in the drivers' seats, and took to the roads. Some had been dropped off by supportive brothers or husbands. Others defied their families to take part. At the time, there was no law explicitly barring women from driving, only a social convention enforced by the authorities, so the group made sure that all the drivers had valid foreign licenses so the government could not accuse them of breaking the law.

If the protest had a whiff of Rosa Parks, the women were more Elizabeth Cady Stanton. Many hailed from elite families and had been educated abroad, where they had gotten used to living without Saudi strictures and learned to drive. Most were working professionals, with jobs as teachers, administrators, and university instructors. One was a social worker. Another was a dentist. Most were also mothers. One was breastfeeding. At least one was pregnant. One woman heard about the protest after it had kicked off and drove over with her two daughters to join in. All the women had covered their hair, and some covered their faces. The organizers had discouraged single women from taking part for fear it would damage their marriage prospects, but a few came anyway.

The women's convoy went mostly unnoticed during its first loop around Riyadh. But eventually, the police pulled them over, confused. Were the women from Kuwait, where women drove? No, the women told them. We are Saudis, and we expect you to arrest us. There was no social media at the time and the women could not count on coverage by government-controlled news outlets, so they calculated that getting arrested was the best way to draw notice.

The situation grew more tense when the religious police showed up with the "volunteers" who often accompanied them, and an argument broke out over whether women driving was a traffic violation, to be handled by the police, or a moral violation, to be handled by the clerics. The conservatives made it clear that they considered the women's action a grave affront, and some surrounded the cars, banging on their windows and insulting the women. Seared into the memory of al-Bakr, the education professor, was the image of a man in sandals running in circles and screaming.

"I want to dig a hole and bury you all!" she recalled him yelling. "They were thinking that we were going to destroy this country."

"What made them really angry was our demeanor and that we did not care for them," recalled another participant, Monera Alnahedh. Years later, she lit up at the memory. "It was the highest point in my life."

Later, some of the women credited Salman with making sure the police handled the issue, not the clerics, because he feared for the women's safety. At the police station, the women were divided up and questioned: Who were the organizers? Did they have foreign backing? Had Saddam Hussein encouraged them in order to destabilize the kingdom?

No, they said. We just want to drive.

Before dawn, they were released, after they and their male relatives had signed pledges that the women would not drive again. For a few hours, it appeared that was that.

Then the attacks began.

One participant went home, changed clothes, and went to the school where she worked, where she overheard colleagues gossiping about a group of women who had reportedly burned their abayas to reveal bikinis and danced in the street.

"That was a shock," recalled Asma Alaboudi. "Who defamed the issue in that way?"

It got worse from there as the kingdom's conservatives mounted a full-scale attack, wielding television stations, radio programs, and mosque pulpits to vilify the women as a grave threat to society. A list of their names was distributed as "fallen women" and "advocates of vice." The king suspended them from their jobs, and some were denounced by their tribes and relatives.

Alghanem, who had hosted the original tea party, said she had expected that the women could go to jail, but had not anticipated the social blowback.

"The society was hard, fierce, savage," she recalled.

After Alajroush, the photographer, was released, officers from the Interior Ministry came to her home to confiscate and burn all her negatives—fifteen years of work.

"I was a freelancer, so that was a way of punishing me," she said.

Alnahedh was fired from her job as an assistant university professor and her father quit praying at the mosque near their home after he heard the imam say that the women had each been inseminated by ten men.

The attacks were so harsh that they drove the issue underground for many years.

"It was a very heavy blow on the women who drove, and it was actually perceived by the society as a heavy blow," Alnahedh said. "There was a decade of silence, a decade of no action."

A few years later, a princess intervened with King Fahd and he returned most of the women to their jobs and paid some of their back wages. Over time, some of the women pursued advanced degrees abroad or had families and focused on private life. Others worked in education and social work, permissible ways to help girls and women. But the stigma of having been "drivers" stuck with them, preventing many from getting promotions they felt they deserved. For a while after the protest, they would meet up on its anniversary to reminisce. After a few years, that stopped, too.

THE BAN REMAINED in place, but slowly, the kingdom changed. It went on a university building spree that brought higher education to far-flung areas and enrollment for both women and men rose. In 2005, King Abdullah created a scholarship program that sent hundreds of thousands of young Saudis, including women, abroad, to the United States, Britain, France, China, Japan, and elsewhere. Many came home with new perspectives on women's roles. He also added a contingent of women to the Shura Council, the appointed body that advised the king, and the spread of satellite television showed many Saudis how out of step the kingdom was. Social media and the Internet broke the Saudi clerics' monopoly on religious interpretation, allowing curious citizens to seek out the views of clerics from more open societies.

King Abdullah also changed regulations to allow women to work in jobs they had been barred from, such as retail. That raised the question of how these women were supposed to get to work. Many spent large portions of their salaries on drivers. Driving themselves would cost less.

Younger activists picked up the baton. In 2011, Manal al-Sharif, frustrated with the restrictions on her movement while working at Saudi Aramco, posted a video on YouTube of herself driving. She was jailed and pilloried in the media, but she revived the issue. And in 2014, Loujain Al-Hathloul, whose father had filmed her driving home from the airport during my first visit to Saudi Arabia a year earlier, attempted to drive her car into Saudi Arabia from the United Arab Emirates and was jailed for seventy-three days. She, too, was attacked by conservatives.

The 1990s drivers played no role in the new protests, but admired their younger sisters. Alajroush, the photographer, called the jailing of Al-Hathloul a breakthrough.

"We could not sleep all night, every night while she was in prison," Alajroush told me. "But inside of me, I thought it was a big step forward because finally we were taken seriously."

Meanwhile, women advanced in other fields. In 2015, they were allowed for the first time to vote and run for seats on municipal councils, and some won. In 2017, public schools began offering physical education for girls, in defiance of clerics who argued that exercise could harm their femininity.

On the night the decision to lift the ban was announced, Alghanem, who had instigated the original protest seventeen years before, was playing cards with her sisters when all of their phones rang. She picked up to hear her husband yelling, "Congrats! Congrats!"

When I met her a week later, she was still elated.

"What we are seeing today, I never thought I'd see. I thought that maybe I'd die before I saw it. But it's good for our daughters, our granddaughters," she told me. "What's important is that our kingdom entered the twenty-first century. Finally!"

The Saudi government expected a public relations boost from the lifting of the ban, and the Saudi ambassador to Washington, MBS's younger brother, held a rare press conference, but skirted questions about why the ban had lasted so long.

There was "no wrong time to do the right thing," he said.

But the government was determined not to credit the women for forcing the issue. They were never thanked publicly, and there is not and will probably never be a monument commemorating the first women who defied the ban. In fact, the government's defenders fought the idea that the women had played any role at all.

"It is natural that they are happy that they have been given their legal right that they had previously asked for," a prince wrote on Twitter. But attributing the change to their actions was "a great fantasy."

The women didn't care.

"Among themselves, they know," Alghanem said. "But they don't want to admit it."

THE ORIGINAL DRIVING protest shaped its participants' later lives. Alajroush still worked in Riyadh as a psychoanalyst and photographer. When I visited her, she showed me a photo book of petroglyphs of women from around the kingdom, her way of showing that women had been active in Arabia for a long, long time. She was then working with other women to open a shelter for abused women and girls.

After losing her job at the university, Alnahedh had pursued a successful career in international development. Now a grandmother, she was impressed by the younger generation of Saudi women, whose approach to feminism was active, not theoretical.

"They are more intent on what they can get and how they fight for their space professionally," she told me. "Saudi women act like immigrants and minorities in Western societies. They close ranks and they absolutely concentrate on how to develop themselves."

When I visited Alaboudi, who had heard her colleagues gossiping at school, she had retired after decades as a social worker at a girls' school. Along the way, she had pursued her interest in culture and literature, publishing interviews in a Saudi newspaper and becoming the first female announcer at the Riyadh Book Fair. People had been shocked the first time they heard her voice over the loudspeakers. But eventually they got used to it.

A bowl of Hershey's Kisses sat on the coffee table in her modest living room and she told me that on the day of the protest, she had put three bags of them in her purse, not knowing what was going to happen. When the women were at the police station, she distributed the Kisses, she told me, laughing at the memory of the ladies munching on chocolate while the authorities were determining their fate. She has kept the candies in her house ever since.

Like the other women, she mourned the years that had been lost to the driving ban. She did not have family wealth, had separated from her husband, and at one point had held down three jobs to support her children, so paying for drivers had always sapped her finances. Lifting the ban, she said, would change women's lives in drastic ways.

"I drive a car and the car remains a vehicle, but that I am driving means that I know where I'm going, when I'm coming back, what I'm doing," she said. "It's not just driving a car, it's driving a life."

A HOLOGRAM FOR THE
CROWN PRINCE, PART ONE

IN SEPTEMBER 2017, Richard Branson, the British entrepreneur who had founded Virgin Records and built it into a business empire that included music stores, an airline, hotel chains, and civilian space travel, came to Saudi Arabia. It was an unlikely destination for the floppy-haired icon whose life was entwined with rock and roll and Western pop culture, forces that had long been inimical to everything the kingdom stood for. But Branson spent a few days traveling around and was amazed by what he saw.

In the western desert, he inspected tombs carved into solid rock by a pre-Islamic civilization and suggested launching Virgin hot air balloons for a better view. Donning a red-and-white Arab headdress with his orange T-shirt and khakis, he posed for a photo next to a restored locomotive he said had been blown up by Lawrence of Arabia, his childhood hero.

A helicopter ferried him to the kingdom's Red Sea coast, and he found its azure waters so alluring that he stripped down to his swimsuit before the aircraft had even touched down. He visited a string of fifty nearly untouched islands, where he watched dugongs and eagle rays cruise by while turtles climbed out of the water to lay eggs.

"It is a truly unspoilt ocean environment, possibly one of the last marine wonders of the world," he wrote, praising Mohammed bin Salman for his commitment "to moving his country into the modern world, and bringing its citizens with him."

Branson's visit so surprised my Saudi friends that they could barely believe it was happening. But his trip was merely a teaser for the massive investment conference that MBS hosted a few weeks later to amplify his message that Saudi Arabia was open for international investors.

At the time, the vast economic transformation MBS had proposed the year before with the launch of Vision 2030 had yet to gain much traction. A sudden hike in water prices had caused grumbling, and earlier that year the king had restored pay cuts to civil servants. Saudi officials said the reforms had to be implemented gradually, but the broader economic challenges remained. How to cut generous subsidies on electricity and water without killing the businesses built on them or cutting into family budgets? How to get young Saudis to compete for jobs in the private sector instead of angling for cushy government positions?

The fate of the Aramco IPO was also unclear. It had been proposed as the centerpiece of the proposed makeover, a way to give the state oodles of cash for non-oil investments, but no one knew when it would happen. MBS had said it would occur in 2018, but by the fall of 2017, the kingdom had yet to determine whether it would sell shares on its domestic stock exchange, in New York, London, or some combination thereof. A week before the conference, *The Economist* magazine called the IPO plans "a mess," saying MBS's micromanagement and uncertainty had caused "delay and confusion." When he had launched the idea, the magazine said, MBS had underappreciated the threat of 9/11-related lawsuits in New York and the complexity of meeting the listing requirements in London.

"His attitude so far suggests too little faith in the market forces that he wants to unleash," it said.

MBS insisted that the IPO was still in the works and his aides argued that it was too early to judge a long-term reform process that had barely begun. In any case, the investment conference aimed to put wind in its sails. It was called the Future Investment Initiative and was hosted by the Public Investment Fund as a dramatic display of MBS's lofty ambitions aimed at convincing global investors to bring their capital to Saudi Arabia. As with the Trump visit earlier that year, the kingdom wanted maximum news coverage of the so-called "Davos in the Desert." My visa for the Trump visit had expired, but I got a new visa for the conference—three months, multi-entry, nonrenewable.

The three-day event unfolded in a sprawling conference center next to the Riyadh Ritz-Carlton, and its 3,500 attendees included big-name money managers, corporate CEOs, investment bankers, and government officials from dozens of countries, making it a veritable Who's Who of the global business elite. The center was filled with virtual rollercoasters, spherical holograms featuring roaring lions, and interactive robots. The kingdom used the event to announce three new megacities meant to represent its new direction.

The first was a sprawling entertainment complex called Qiddiya to be built near Riyadh that would bring together movie theaters, concert venues, theme parks, and perhaps a space tourism site. The second was a sprawling eco-tourism project on the very islands that Branson had visited a few weeks before. The third and most ambitious would be unveiled by MBS himself—when he finally showed up.

According to the schedule, the prince was supposed to open the event, and the guests packed into the same conference hall where Donald Trump had spoken to see him. But MBS didn't show. Instead, the head of the Public Investment Fund greeted the guests and launched into a panel with no apology and no explanation for why the man of the hour had stood up his thousands of guests.

He did show up that afternoon, when he took to the stage to announce NEOM, the $500 billion business and technology hub that would rise from a patch of virgin earth near the Red Sea coast and be run on sustainable energy and staffed by robots. A video introducing the city flashed shiny images of women wearing virtual reality headsets, families frolicking on expanses of grass, a painter working on a canvas, and a ballerina spinning in a white tutu. NEOM, the video said, was "the world's most ambitious project" and "a chance to design a better way of life, with a blueprint for sustainable living." NEOM was not merely a city, but "a roadmap for the future of civilization."

MBS, overflowing with enthusiasm, spelled out what the site had to offer: untouched nature, with islands, coastline, and mountains near key shipping lanes. The city was to grow on a site of more than ten thousand square miles that spanned into Egypt and Jordan, where businessmen would write the regulations to foster growth and innovation.

"All the elements for success are present to create something big and great inside the kingdom of Saudi Arabia," MBS said. To make his point about how different NEOM would be from the world's current cities, he pulled two cellphones from his pockets—an old, "dumb" phone and a new iPhone.

"Like the difference between this phone and this phone," he said, holding the handsets aloft. "This is what we will do inside NEOM."

The Royal Court distributed fact sheets packed with terms plucked from technology magazines and consulting reports. NEOM would have disruptive solutions, passenger drones, online education, e-government, and net-zero carbon houses, a combination that would "allow for a new way of life to emerge." MBS later explained that the name combined neo, Latin for "new," with *mustaqbal*, meaning "future" in Arabic. But since *neo-mustaqbal* was unwieldy, he shrank the name to NEOM.

"NEOM gives you the sense that this is a name of the future," he said. "You feel like NEOM is a name from outer space."

The overall picture was of an Arabian Xanadu, where the weather was pleasant, everyone was rich and smart, and residents lived an idealized life of luxury and leisure—like the Jetsons, but better— a far cry from the reality of other Saudi cities. By all accounts, reforming the Saudi Arabia that actually existed would be tough, and I suspected that MBS found NEOM enticing because it promised a fresh start, an urban *tabula rasa*, where stuffy clerics, entitled citizens, and groaning infrastructure would not stand in the way of a new dreamland of drones, biotech, and artificial intelligence.

Saudi Arabia was already dotted with the Ozymandian remains of grand plans launched by previous leaders. Ten years earlier, the kingdom had announced the creation of six "economic cities" to encourage foreign investment and boost the economy. Most had never taken off, and only one was seriously developed, but it fell far short of its projected scale. And if the conference's attendees had paid attention during their drive from the airport, they would have seen another: a planned $10 billion financial district that remained unfinished and largely vacant.

But if the prince's guests had doubts about the feasibility of NEOM, they kept them to themselves, applauding when a Chinese-built robot named Sophia, who was modeled on Audrey Hepburn, was granted Saudi citizenship, yet another gimmick to re-brand the kingdom as forward-looking. Few concrete deals were signed during the conference, but many investors went home intrigued by the kingdom's new tone, if not quite yet ready to lay their money down. Others were happy to accept Saudi cash for their own projects. Branson, for one, said he would consider building some hotels in the proposed cities and that the kingdom planned to invest $1 billion in his space companies.

DURING HIS TALK about NEOM, MBS made a parenthetical yet remarkable statement, a forceful public vow to stamp out extremism for the good of the kingdom's young people.

"We will not waste thirty years of our lives dealing with any extremist ideas," he said. "We will destroy them today. Immediately."

The crowd paused as his words sunk in and then erupted in applause. MBS then laid out an argument that he would flesh out over time that extremism and intolerance were foreign to Saudi society and had taken root in recent decades only because of outside forces.

"We were not like this in the past," he said. "We are only returning to what we were, moderate, balanced Islam that is open to the world and to all religions and to all traditions and peoples."

He would continue to make the argument in future interviews and it was picked up by his boosters in the West. It revolved around the year 1979, when two monumental events altered the trajectory of the Middle East. The first was the Islamic Revolution in Iran, which toppled the shah and put in its place a system of rule by Shiite clerics who sought to implement their vision of an Islamic society at home while exporting their "revolution" abroad. The second was the armed takeover of the Grand Mosque in Mecca by apocalyptic Saudi militants who accused the royal family and the clerics of losing their legitimacy to corruption and Westernization.

Before 1979, Saudi Arabia's ideological competitors in the region had mostly been Arab nationalists and socialists inspired by the Soviet Union. But the Iranian Revolution created a regime that competed with the Saudis at their own game of basing their rule on a claim to Islamic orthodoxy.

The more immediate threat to the kingdom came from the domestic militants, who accused the Al Saud of forsaking the very rules they said they stood for. It took two weeks, special forces from abroad, countless bullets, and lots of tear gas to flush out the militants and restore control of the holy site. But the seizure had long-lasting consequences for Saudi society. Fearing that other Saudis would endorse the militants' accusations, the kingdom doubled down on Wahhabism. It shuttered its few movie theaters, formalized restrictions on women, and opened floodgates of cash for religious organizations, deepening their power in society at home and fueling their drive to spread Wahhabism abroad.

Other challenges to the royals' religious legitimacy would arise from Saudi society over the years, most notably after American troops flooded into the kingdom with Saddam Hussein's invasion of Kuwait. The presence of "infidel" troops on Saudi soil inflamed the tempers of conservative clerics belonging to a movement known as the *Sahwa*, or "awakening." They, too, accused the royals of corruption and religious laxity, and the state again tried to blunt the accusations by boosting its conservative credentials. Instead of fighting extremism with less religion, they fought it with more.

These were the forces that had built the international religious infrastructure I had read about in the Saudi Wikileaks cables and that created the highly restricted society I found during my early visits to the kingdom.

Now MBS wanted to dismantle this web of social restrictions. He argued that he was not creating anything new and harkened back to the pre-'79 era in interviews with Western journalists. He told *New York Times* columnist Thomas Friedman, "Do not write that we are 'reinterpreting' Islam—we are 'restoring' Islam to its origins." That meant imitating the practices of the Prophet Muhammad and in Saudi Arabia "before 1979," he said.

"This is not the real Saudi Arabia," he told *60 Minutes* a few months later. "We were living a very normal life like the rest of the Gulf countries. Women were driving cars. There were movie theaters in Saudi Arabia. Women worked everywhere. We were just normal people developing like any other country in the world until the events of 1979."

It was a powerful narrative that allowed Saudis to believe that the new direction flowed from their heritage while eliding the history of Wahhabism and the royal family's historic patronage of its more extreme elements. MBS's argument was at best an oversimplification and at worst revisionist history that allowed him to blame the kingdom's problems on someone else.

Saudi rulers had made use of extremism since the founding of the first Saudi state in the mid-1700s, when Mohammed Ibn Saud rallied ideological fighters who branded those who resisted their rule "infidels" and put them to the sword. The Islamic State took the same approach in the twenty-first century, but with social media and global ambitions. In 1802, Saudi forces sacked the Shiite holy city of Karbala in Iraq and massacred thousands of people, including women and children, while destroying ancient tombs whose veneration they considered blasphemous. They carried out another massacre in the Saudi city of Taif later that year. Mecca was subjected to a similar religious cleansing after they took it the next year and destroyed tombs, installed Wahhabi religious leaders, and barred Muslims who did not accept their doctrine from performing the pilgrimage.

In the early twentieth century, King Abdulaziz, MBS's grandfather, resurrected the alliance with the clerics, weaponizing their ideological zeal to build the state that would become Saudi Arabia. He later turned on some of them, crushing forces known as the *Ikhwan*, who refused to renounce expansionary jihad. But the clerics maintained power over Saudi social life throughout the twentieth century—and before 1979. Saudi Arabia saw a continuous push and pull between the royals, the clerics, and society itself, but few outsiders would have called the result "very normal life" as MBS did.

Slavery persisted until 1962, when King Faisal decreed its end among reforms promised to President John F. Kennedy. Before then, Saudi delegates to the United Nations had staunchly denied that the practice existed. The introduction of television in the 1960s

Mohammed bin Salman enters the main hall during the first edition of his international investment conference, the Future Investment Initiative, in October 2017. From the stage, he vowed to crush extremism and build NEOM, a $500 billion business and technology hub staffed by robots near the Red Sea.

King Abdulaziz, the founder of Saudi Arabia and MBS's grandfather, speaks with President Franklin Delano Roosevelt during their secret wartime meeting in February 1945 aboard the USS *Quincy*. The two leaders reached a lasting agreement that guaranteed American access to Saudi oil in exchange for American protection from foreign attacks, an arrangement that would underpin American policy in the Middle East.

MBS's father, King Salman, who served for nearly five decades as the governor of Riyadh Province as Saudi Arabia's capital city grew from an isolated desert outpost into a sprawling metropolis.

King Abdullah, whose death in January 2015 led to the coronation of his half brother, Salman, and the rise of MBS.

Mohammed bin Nayef, who led the campaign against Al Qaeda in Saudi Arabia and was named crown prince in 2015. MBS disarmed him over time before replacing him as next in line to the throne and putting him under house arrest in June 2017.

Sheikh Ahmed al-Ghamdi, the onetime head of the Committee for the Promotion of Virtue and the Prevention of Vice in Mecca Province. He became a pariah to the kingdom's religious establishment after challenging its deep conservatism about gender segregation by going on a television talk show with his wife.

Jamal Khashoggi, who lived through Saudi Arabia's most important social and political trends and became one of its best-known media figures at home and abroad.

President Barack Obama meets in the Oval Office with Crown Prince Mohammed bin Nayef and Deputy Crown Prince Mohammed bin Salman in May 2015. As the rivalry between the two princes grew, Obama tried to keep the United States out of it, saying America should not get involved in the politics of the Saudi royal family.

President Donald Trump walks with MBS and an aide along a White House colonnade. The Trump administration quickly embraced MBS as a key partner in its plans for the Middle East.

MBS with Jared Kushner, Ivanka Trump, Commerce Secretary Wilbur Ross, Secretary of State Rex Tillerson, and Chief of Staff Reince Priebus during the Arab Islamic American Summit in Riyadh in May 2017. MBS would build a close bond with Kushner, who would remain his staunchest defender in the White House.

Nourah Alghanem, who held a tea party that led to the 1990 women's driving protest, at her home in Riyadh after the end of the driving ban was announced in 2017. "What's important is that our kingdom entered the twenty-first century. Finally!" she said.

Lebanese Prime Minister Saad Hariri disembarks from a jet in Beirut after being summoned to Riyadh and forced to tender his resignation on television.

Prince Alwaleed bin Talal, who was Saudi Arabia's most famous investor and one of its best-known personalities abroad. Above, surrounded by paperwork in his desert camp near Riyadh. Below, during an interview after MBS locked him and hundreds of others in the Riyadh Ritz-Carlton as part of a purported anti-corruption drive.

Trump brandishes a poster detailing U.S. weapons sales to Saudi Arabia, during an MBS visit to the White House in March 2018. "Saudi Arabia is a very wealthy nation, and they're going to give the United States some of that wealth, hopefully," Trump said.

MBS in London at the outset of his 2018 charm offensive across the U.K. and U.S.

Loujain Al-Hathloul, a women's rights activist and social media figure. She was detained in May 2018 before the lifting of the ban on women driving and later told relatives that she was tortured in prison.

Jamal Khashoggi at a 2017 "Friendsgiving" in Washington, D.C. When his turn came to say what he was grateful for, he said, "I have become free and I can write freely."

Hatice Cengiz, Jamal Khashoggi's Turkish fiancée. He went to the Saudi consulate in Istanbul in order to get their marriage paperwork.

Surveillance camera footage of Maher Mutrib, a Saudi intelligence agent involved in the murder of Jamal Khashoggi, in front of the residence of the Saudi consul in Istanbul.

spurred outrage and may have played a role in the assassination of King Faisal. The introduction of girls' education sparked riots.

Many Saudis argue that the society was conservative, not the Al Saud, and that the royals could move only so fast without provoking pushback from their people. That may have been true, but the result was often royal support for archconservatives. For 16 years until his death in 1969, Muhammad ibn Ibrahim al-Sheikh served as the kingdom's Grand Mufti, issuing volumes of fatwas that forbade, among other things, toy dolls, photography, gender mixing, shaking hands with non-Muslims, the adornment of camels, and the celebration of Saudi National Day. Since the mufti was appointed by the king, the king could have removed him if he disapproved.

In some parts of the kingdom, foreign and elite Saudi women did wear skirts and short sleeves in public before 1979, but ultraconservatism still coursed through daily life. Sandra Mackey, who worked undercover as a journalist in the kingdom during that time, described arriving from abroad at a Saudi airport and facing what was probably "the most tyrannical customs organization in the world." Customs agents rummaged through all arriving luggage, seizing not only pork, alcohol, and pornography, but anything else that offended their religious sensibilities. Museum guides with pictures of the *Venus de Milo* and the *Mona Lisa* were destroyed, as was Mackey's book of knitting patterns, because its models were deemed too immodest. Bibles and crucifixes were contraband, as were books by Jewish authors—or even authors the Saudis suspected of being Jewish, like James Michener. Mackey saw one family lose its Christmas tree, watching while customs agents crushed its ornaments under their sandals. Distraught little girls sometimes saw their dolls, which the agents considered idols, torn limb from limb.

That conservatism—many would say extremism—was more formalized after 1979, but that was due to state support, a reinvestment in the alliance with the clerics that went back to the origins of the state.

But for MBS, Wahhabism didn't exist.

"What's Wahhabist? You've got to explain what's Wahhabist. Because there is nothing called Wahhabist," he said in one interview.

Wahhabism was an idea that extremists had linked to the kingdom after 1979, "to let the Saudis be part of something that they are not part of."

In MBS's telling, the kingdom was blameless. The ills afflicting the Arab world—in Iraq, Yemen, Syria, and Lebanon—all flowed from Iran.

"Saudi doesn't spread any extremist ideology. Saudi Arabia is the biggest victim of the extremist ideology," he said. "If you see any problem in the Middle East, you will find Iran."

But MBS struggled to compete with Iran's deftness at turning the Arab world's dysfunction to its advantage. Some of his efforts to push back would be more successful than others.

WE HAVE REASON TO BELIEVE
OUR PRIME MINISTER HAS BEEN
KIDNAPPED BY SAUDI ARABIA

A FEW DAYS AFTER the attendees of the investment conference left Riyadh, Saad Hariri, the prime minister of Lebanon, returned home from his own trip to the kingdom in a good mood. For one of the top politicians in Lebanon, a small, turbulent, and dysfunctional country sandwiched between Israel and Syria on the Mediterranean coast, few things were more important than his relationship with the kingdom. Business dealings with Saudi Arabia had made his family rich, and the Saudis were the main patrons of his political party, funding its campaigns and helping it hold ground against rivals backed by Syria and Iran. Hariri was also seen as the political guardian of the country's Sunni Muslims, many of whom saw him as a bridge to the wealthy Sunni kingdom.

As he disembarked from his private jet, he bore good news for his government in Beirut. He had met with Mohammed bin Salman and came away thinking that an expansion of Saudi-Lebanese cooperation was on the way. There had been talk of new trade deals and the restoration of $3 billion in aid for the Lebanese army that the Saudis had promised and later canceled. Hariri felt that he had convinced MBS, who had been making belligerent vows to confront Iran across the region, not to do so in Lebanon. Hezbollah, which was backed by Iran, was the most powerful political and military force in the country, where it used its clout to menace Israel and frustrate American and Saudi plans. It was also the most formidable rival to Hariri's party, but he worried that any confrontation could tip the country into economic crisis or civil war.

Hariri left the airport, climbed into his motorcade, and threw himself into activities fit for a head of government. His first stop was to inaugurate a new training center for the Lebanese national airline. Wearing a dark suit and a red tie, with his black hair slicked back, the 47-year-old politician strolled down a red carpet and cut a ribbon before smiling for photos with other dignitaries. Beirut's airport was named for his father, Rafic Hariri, a former prime minister and towering figure in Lebanese politics who had been assassinated with a car bomb on Beirut's seafront in 2005. As was his custom during his public appearances, the younger Hariri wore a pin on his lapel bearing his father's picture.

The next day, he briefed his cabinet about the good news from Saudi Arabia and said he planned to return to Riyadh in a few days to see King Salman and finalize the new agreements. That night, he received a call from MBS's protocol office inviting him to return to the kingdom to spend the weekend in the desert with the crown prince. He accepted.

SAAD HARIRI WAS the scion of a unique kind of Lebanese dynasty. While officially a democratic republic, Lebanon was governed according to a complex sectarian political system that had been formalized near the end of the country's disastrous fifteen-year civil war that ended in 1990. During the war, warlords representing the country's myriad sects had carved out pieces of the economy to enrich themselves and fund their militias. After the war, many of those warlords became politicians and ended up in parliament, where they granted themselves amnesty and continued to loot the country. The prolonged occupation of Lebanon by Syrian forces further entrenched a culture of corruption.

Rafic Hariri had spent most of the war abroad making money, but after it ended, he returned and as prime minister tapped his business know-how and deep-pocketed friends in the Gulf to help rebuild the country. At the time, his son Saad was out of politics and spent most of his time doing business with Saudi princes. That gave him a status in the kingdom like that of a well-liked cousin, and he often showed up at royal family functions.

Everything changed when the elder Hariri was assassinated and the Hariri family chose Saad to pick up his father's mantle. Many in Lebanon felt that Saad lacked his father's charisma and political savvy, but he was appointed prime minister twice. In the decades after the civil war, through politics, threats, and assassinations, Hezbollah expanded its power, building a formidable militia to threaten Israel and dispatching operatives to support its allies in Syria, Iraq, and Yemen. Hariri proved unable to counter Hezbollah and Syria, whom many in Lebanon accused of assassinating his father, and often spent time in Paris for fear that he, too, could be blown up in Beirut.

But by 2017, Hariri's party and Hezbollah had reached a détente. Each held portfolios in a power-sharing government that allowed Lebanon to maintain a veneer of normalcy. The day after he received the invitation to the desert trip with MBS, Hariri had a full schedule. He met Ali Akbar Vilayati, a senior adviser to Iran's Supreme Leader, who was in Beirut; chaired a meeting about upcoming elections; and met the French minister of culture, who was also in town. Before lunch, he excused himself to fly back to Saudi Arabia.

After he landed in Riyadh that evening, a royal protocol team drove him to his residence in a motorcade befitting his position. He was told to wait for instructions on when to meet the prince, but none came. After 1 A.M., he received a call telling him news would come the next day.

The call came the next morning before 8 A.M., an early hour for business involving Saudi royals. Hariri was told to come to MBS's residence, and he wore sneakers, jeans, and a casual shirt since they were supposed to go to the desert. But when he arrived, royal guards surrounded his motorcade and made Hariri's entourage stay in their cars. He and two of his guards were taken into the building, and all were stripped of their cellphones, weapons, and belts and made to go through a scanner. Then Hariri was taken into another room alone, where he was confronted by two state officials.

They and other Saudi officials insulted, belittled, and roughed up Hariri, making it clear the treatment would get worse if he did not go along with their plan that he stand down as prime minister. (Hariri's aides insist he was never mistreated.) Hariri eventually gave in and a member of his entourage was sent to his house to get a suit. He was given a statement to read, and on the afternoon of November 4, 2017, he suddenly appeared on television, looking haggard at a desk next to a Lebanese flag and reading from a piece of paper.

Addressing "my brothers and the cherished sons of the great Lebanese people," he called Lebanon a "lighthouse of science, knowledge, and democracy" that had been infiltrated by hostile powers. He fingered Iran, saying it "does not enter a place without planting discord, destruction, and ruin in it" and blasted Hezbollah for using its arms to threaten the region. Iran's interventions would fail, he declared, vowing that the Arab world would rise up and "cut off the hands that reach out to it in evil."

Then he resigned his post, saying that it would make Lebanon "stronger, independent and free, with no sultan on it other than its great people."

The statement sent shock waves through Lebanon and through the Western capitals that worked to keep Lebanon stable and saw Hariri as an ally in that effort. His aides had not known the resignation was coming and were baffled by their boss's rhetoric. In his many years in public life, Hariri had never used such language against Iran and Hezbollah, and at times tripped over the highly formal language in the text, making it clear that he had not written it. And if his goal was to assert Lebanese sovereignty, why was he resigning from a foreign country?

In Beirut, the cellphone of Nader Hariri, Saad's cousin and the head of his office, exploded with calls asking what had happened. Nader didn't know, so he called Saad in Riyadh, who had recuperated his cellphone and said he had fled an assassination attempt in Lebanon. Nader didn't buy it.

"May God protect you," he told Saad and hung up.

As NADER WAS fielding calls, he spoke to the heads of Lebanon's security agencies and found that no one had information about an assassination plot. But what to do, say that the prime minister had lied? Yes, they decided, and rolled out a series of statements denying evidence of a plot.

After Hariri announced his resignation, he was transferred from MBS's residence to a guesthouse near the Riyadh Ritz-Carlton, where many of MBS's high-profile guests had stayed during the investment conference. Hariri's wife visited him that evening, and called his aides in Beirut, telling them he was being held against his will. The Saudis also allowed one of Hariri's guards to return to Beirut to visit his ailing mother, and he flew home to tell the team what had happened.

The resignation had been an earthquake for Hariri's political party, the Future Movement, and many of its members feared their political foes would seize the opportunity to appoint a prime minister more to their liking. But President Michel Aoun, too, realized that something strange was afoot and said he would accept Hariri's resignation only in person.

During his detention, Hariri was able to respond to calls and messages, but his aides decided not to call too much, suspecting that he could not speak freely. As the days passed, Lebanese officials realized that the reality of what was happening had not sunk in abroad, so they spread the word. One flew to Egypt. The head of General Security, Gen. Abbas Ibrahim, went to foreign ambassadors in Beirut with a message they had never expected to hear: "We have reason to believe that our prime minister has been kidnapped by Saudi Arabia."

When some expressed skepticism, the general explained how it worked: "It's simple. I could bring two soldiers and put you on TV saying you hate your country."

Hariri's allies said little in public for fear of exacerbating the situation. Their foes were less cautious. *Al Akhbar*, a Lebanese daily that often attacked Hariri, ran a picture of him on its front page under a banner headline reading: "The Hostage."

In an attempt to show that Hariri was free to travel, the Saudis put Hariri on a plane and flew him to the United Arab Emirates to meet Mohammed bin Zayed. Although MBZ was MBS's closest ally in the region, even he felt that the young prince had gone too far.

Gradually, the details of the Saudi plot came out. They were cra-
zier than anyone expected. By forcing Hariri to resign, the Saudis
had hoped to spark civil strife between Lebanese Sunnis and Hezbollah that would force Hezbollah to withdraw its fighters from
Yemen, where the Saudis believed they were helping the Houthis.
The Saudis had even reached out to militants in Lebanon's Palestinian refugee camps to see if they would join the fight. They thought
the idea was dangerous and said no.

Saudi officials also invited the members of the Hariri family to
Riyadh for consultations. But the family found out that the Saudis
wanted them to anoint Saad's older brother Baha as their new leader,
believing that he would take a harder line on Iran. So they refused
to go. Lebanon's interior minister, an ally of Saad's, shot the idea
down publicly.

"We are not herds of sheep, nor a plot of land whose ownership
can be moved from one person to another," he said. "In Lebanon,
things happen through elections, not pledges of allegiance."

If there was one thing that *l'affair Hariri* made clear, it was that as
vulnerable to interference and upheaval as Lebanese politics was,
the system belonged to Lebanon, and some kinds of foreign meddling were too much for anyone to stand for.

Hariri returned from Abu Dhabi to Riyadh, and was allowed to
move back into his residence. While his aides in Beirut avoided calling him for fear that the Saudis had hacked his phone or bugged his
house, they managed to set up a secret communications channel
with him to plot their next moves.

First, they asked foreign ambassadors in Riyadh to visit the prime
minister, knowing that the Saudis could not deny such requests
while insisting that Hariri was a free man. Then they informed the
diplomats of seemingly benign phrases that Hariri would utter during their visits to indicate that he needed help. The plan worked,
and cables zipped back to foreign capitals sounding the alarm. When
the French ambassador, François Gouyette, went to see Hariri, the
guards surrounding the residence insisted on searching his car—
a grave breach of diplomatic protocol—even making him open the
trunk, as if they suspected him of trying to smuggle out Lebanon's
prime minister.

The plot fell apart. The Saudi official who had dreamed it up was chewed out at the State Department in Washington, and an effort by the Saudi ambassador in Beirut to rally the country's "tribes" went awry when the heads of big families called for the return of their prime minister. So the Saudis cooked up another plan to convince the world that Hariri was indeed a free man: a live television interview.

IN HER DECADES-LONG career as a journalist, Paula Yacoubian, a tall woman with a smoky voice from Lebanon's Armenian minority, had navigated the country's entangled worlds of fashion, politics, and media to make herself a household name. In her work as a news presenter and talk show host, she had interviewed Rafic Hariri, President George W. Bush, and Libyan dictator Moammar al-Qadaffi. On the day Hariri resigned, she was associated with his political party and had an interview show on its TV station.

She was at a bank filming a commercial when she got a surprise call telling her that Hariri was resigning. No one at the bank believed it, so they turned on the television and saw the prime minister, looking grave and attacking Iran and Hezbollah. That set off a panic, as clients rang up the bank to send their money abroad, fearing a new crisis.

Yacoubian herself knew the importance of Saudi Arabia to Lebanon. Her father, who had escaped the Armenian genocide, had died when she was young, so a brother-in-law who worked in the kingdom had supported her while she was growing up in Beirut. She didn't like Hezbollah, but found the idea that the Lebanese could rise up against it unrealistic.

"This is more than we can handle, the talk that Hezbollah should be destroyed," she told me. "This is an issue that Netanyahu and Trump and the whole universe is not able to deal with. Am I going to go with my aunt and a few Lebanese who are broke to deal with 150,000 of Hezbollah's missiles and a militia that is like an army?"

She called Hariri to ask him to go on TV, but he said no. A few days later, he called her back, sounding depressed, and asked her to come to Riyadh to do an interview.

"Are you sure?" she asked.

"Yes, I'm sure," he said.

The next day was the annual Beirut Marathon, which was taken over by the caper of the missing prime minister. Posters bearing Hariri's face lined the streets, and organizers passed out yellow caps reading "We want our PM back!"

Yacoubian flew to Riyadh, and a Filipino driver took her to Hariri's residence. But instead of the meeting in the main house, she was shown into a nearby building where Hariri's guards hung out and where a Saudi television crew was setting up to film the interview.

Back in Beirut, Hariri's team had heard about the interview and worked behind the scenes to turn it to their advantage. Using their secret communications channel, they gave Hariri instructions: Don't speak openly about what happened so as not to antagonize the Saudis, but drink lots of water, talk about being tired, express concern for your family, and don't wear your father's pin on your lapel. Together, those signals would make it clear that something was amiss.

The interview was a blockbuster TV event in Lebanon and across the region, even though President Aoun asked Lebanese channels not to air it, like a hostage video that could play into the captors' hands. Hariri sat hunched at a table, with his hands clasped in front of him, bags under his eyes, and without his father's pin. Across the table, Yacoubian, in a black blazer over a white shirt, leaned in, pleading with him, at times more like a concerned friend than a journalist.

Hariri repeated that he had resigned for the good of Lebanon, but Yacoubian dismissed the possibility.

"Every word you say raises more than one question," she said. "The predominate belief of most people is that Prime Minister Hariri, every word he said has no value, and the president of the Republic has said this more than once. . . . Even I am being accused now of participating in a piece of theater. What I have seen so far, I am not sure of anything."

Hariri said his resignation was intended as "a positive shock for the Lebanese, so that we know how dangerous of a place we're in," and denied that he was constrained.

"Let me tell you something: I am free here in the kingdom, and if I want to travel tomorrow, I travel, but I want to . . . and I have my family. It is my right to protect my family."

To prove that the interview was live, Yacoubian mentioned breaking news of an earthquake in Iran. Hariri kept drinking water, speaking in an exhausted voice, and choked up.

"We have to always think, 'Lebanon first.' We have to put Lebanon in our hearts. I sometimes go to other countries and I see that they care about Lebanon more than the Lebanese. Why? Why do we Lebanese want to torture ourselves?" he said.

"I'll give you a chance to rest a bit," Yacoubian said and cut to a commercial.

If anyone in Riyadh had hoped that the interview would end doubts about Hariri's status, that idea was dead by the time the interview concluded. Yacoubian bid Hariri goodbye, slept at a fancy hotel, and called the Filipino driver to take her to the airport. He said he couldn't, so one of Hariri's guys dropped her off. She never saw MBS or other Saudi officials, but assumed the crown prince had not appreciated her interview.

"Is he crazy enough to shoot down my plane?" she thought as she took off.

By the time Yacoubian landed in Beirut, Lebanon's politicians were reacting and President Aoun said Hariri's interview did not "reflect the truth" due to his "ambiguous situation" in Saudi Arabia.

The French got involved. When the Louvre Abu Dhabi opened on November 11, Mohammed bin Zayed suggested to French president Emmanuel Macron that he stop in Riyadh on his way home to see MBS and help Hariri. Before he was elected president, Macron had become friends with Hariri during a visit to Beirut, so he took the advice and invited Hariri to Paris. On the day Hariri was supposed to leave, Macron's staff called the Royal Court repeatedly to make sure that Hariri got on the plane.

He finally did. He flew first to Paris for a few days before stopping in Egypt and Cyprus on his way back to Lebanon. Around midnight, seventeen days after his resignation, he landed in Beirut and was driven to Martyrs' Square downtown to pray at his father's tomb.

A senior foreign diplomat in Beirut who met Hariri soon after his return avoided asking about what had happened, but told me he got the feeling it had been terrible, leaving Hariri "a broken man."

"Physically, you could feel that he was completely shaken. He sounded as if he was here without being here," the official said. "I think he was still trying to understand what happened."

The official had never seen anything like it in his decades of diplomacy.

"Do you know of any other head of state who has been arrested or detained or held against his will?" he said. "It is the super script of a Hollywood movie."

THE DAY AFTER Hariri's return, Lebanon celebrated its Independence Day, which turned into a festival for the returned prime minister. Hariri dressed casually, in jeans and a blue jacket, and television cameras followed him as he greeted flag-waving fans and waded into crowds to take selfies.

He was back, but the experience had damaged his relationship with Saudi Arabia, and with it, Lebanon's relationship with the kingdom. Over the next few weeks, he rescinded his resignation and the government limply recommitted the country to avoiding regional conflicts, an empty pledge since Hezbollah still had thousands of fighters in Syria, Iraq, and Yemen.

A few months later, Hariri returned to Riyadh and posted a selfie of himself with MBS and his younger brother Khalid bin Salman, the Saudi ambassador to Washington. At the time, MBS was planning an extensive trip to the United States and many in Lebanon speculated that the selfie sought to prevent questions about what the kingdom had just done to Hariri.

The Lebanese went to the polls later that year to elect a new parliament and Hariri's party lost seats. That led to a drawn-out process of government formation in which Hezbollah and its allies increased their role. Saudi Arabia did little to help Hariri, but he couldn't complain because he had nowhere else to go for support.

"What are we supposed to do?" one of his political allies asked me. "Go to Iran?"

In public, the kingdom continued to insist that Hariri had never been anything less than a honored guest in the kingdom and a brother to MBS. A year later, the two men appeared onstage at a conference in Riyadh and MBS addressed the crowd with a grin.

"I'd like to conclude by saying something: Prime Minister Saad is staying in Saudi for two days, so I hope no rumors go out that he has been kidnapped."

The audience gasped, then laughed, then applauded.

Hariri laughed, too, raising an arm to the crowd.

"Of my own free will!" he said.

GUESTS OF THE KING

BEFORE DAWN ON November 4, 2017, the same day that Saad Hariri appeared on television and shocked the world with his resignation as prime minister, Prince Alwaleed bin Talal was woken up by a surprise phone call. As he did on many weekends, the prince had escaped the city with his family to a desert camp outside Riyadh, where he liked to ride horses, admire falcons, and enjoy a luxury version of the desert life his people had mostly left behind since the discovery of oil. Even when seated on the ground and reclining on a cushion, he kept a big-screen TV nearby so he could follow the financial markets—royal glamping at its best.

At the time, Alwaleed was the kingdom's most famous investor and its best-known personality abroad. His reputation for eye-popping investments and flamboyant living frequently landed his face—usually wearing sunglasses, with a trademark mole on his right cheek—in the news. He was a scion of not one, but two political dynasties. His mother's father was the first prime minister of Lebanon. His father's father was King Abdulaziz, the founder of Saudi Arabia, which granted him automatic standing in the royal family. But he was still a black sheep. His father, Prince Talal, who had served as finance minister in the early 1960s, later dabbled in opposition politics, convincing his relatives to keep him from power.

Alwaleed embraced his outsider status by championing unbridled capitalism. In his own telling, after his parents divorced he spent part of his childhood in Beirut, where he sometimes ran away from home and slept in unlocked cars. His father dragged him back to Riyadh and enrolled him in a military academy, which Alwaleed says taught him hard work and discipline. He studied at Menlo College in California and Syracuse University in New York before returning to Saudi Arabia to launch his business career with a $30,000 gift and a $300,000 loan from his father.

He exploded onto the global financial scene in the early 1990s by plowing more than $700 million into Citicorp after its share price had tanked. Within a few years, its price had rocketed, making the prince a fortune and earning him comparisons with Warren Buffett, which he loved. Further investments followed, in 21st Century Fox, Apple, Twitter, and other multinational firms, and he snapped up high-class hotels in London, Paris, and elsewhere.

He was a billionaire and lived like one, with a royal twist. He traveled on a 747 complete with a throne. He bought a 282-foot yacht from Donald Trump. In a kingdom that was notoriously media shy, he courted journalists to build his brand. But bling often trumped content. His aides gave reporters stacks of glossy magazines with the prince on the cover under headlines such as "The World's Shrewdest Businessman." But the magazines were fake, with covers made by his staff. In the photo on the back of his authorized biography, Alwaleed stands in front of George W. Bush and a group of Arab leaders, including King Abdullah of Jordan. But the photo has been doctored. In the original, King Abdullah stood in front and Alwaleed in the back.

He once spent a week showing off his wealth to a reporter from *Forbes*. She wandered through his 420-room palace, with indoor swimming pools, a tennis court—and many, many pictures of Alwaleed. In the marble hallway near his bedroom, he showed off a jewelry collection he said was worth more than $700 million. Outside of town, she saw his 120-acre "farm and resort," with a zoo, artificial lakes, expanses of green grass, and a mini–Grand Canyon.

But his eccentricities never really diminished his standing. He socialized with everyone from the Clintons to Prince Charles to Michael Jackson. In Riyadh, he built the Kingdom Tower, the capital's tallest building when it was completed, and put his office in the penthouse. He ran an entertainment company that pumped out seductive music videos. He spoke openly against the ban on women driving and employed large numbers of women when most Saudi businesses had no women at all. He kept them stylishly dressed with twice-yearly clothing bonuses of $10,000. He also kept a group of dwarves in his entourage because he thought they were funny.

Despite his cultivated glitz, he maintained the trappings of an Arabian prince, inviting journalists to the desert where he held court, receiving long lines of Bedouins asking for help buying homes or clearing debts. In 2017, months before he got the call that jolted him from his sleep, *Forbes* had estimated his net worth at $18.7 billion.

That pre-dawn call was from the Royal Court and the caller told Alwaleed that the king wanted to see him. It was a strange request for such an hour, but the prince had no reason to suspect he was in trouble, so he got dressed, climbed into his motorcade, and headed for the city.

THE DAY BEFORE, another billionaire, Waleed al-Ibrahim, had received a similar call. While he was not a royal himself, royal money and power had defined his life. Years before, his sister had married King Fahd, who had given al-Ibrahim seed money to found MBC, a satellite television channel that he had expanded into the largest media company in the Arab world. It offered a range of channels that were among the most watched in the Middle East, bringing hit shows like *Arabs Got Talent*, *The Voice*, and *Oprah* into tens of millions of homes.

The caller, also from the Royal Court, reached al-Ibrahim in Dubai, where the company was headquartered, and invited him to Riyadh to see Mohammed bin Salman. The prince had expressed interest in buying MBC after his father became king in 2015, but the two men had failed to come to terms. International auditors were brought in to assess the company's value, but the deal had not gone through. Perhaps it would now, al-Ibrahim thought as he flew to Riyadh on his private jet and checked into a luxury suite at the Al Faisaliah Hotel downtown to await his meeting.

Others got calls too.

Prince Mutib bin Abdullah, a son of the late King Abdullah who headed the National Guard, was told that a missile from Yemen had struck near Riyadh and that he needed to attend an urgent meeting to plan the response. The prince had heard nothing of the attack, but he, too, had little reason to be suspicious and rushed off. Other sons of the late king were summoned as well.

Calls also came for prominent businessmen: a shopping mall magnate who held the kingdom's Zara and Gap franchises; three brothers from the bin Laden family who ran the construction conglomerate that had built much of the kingdom's infrastructure; and a Saudi-Ethiopian man *Forbes* had called "the richest black person in the world." When an elderly billionaire from Jeddah asked if he could come the next day because he was on his way to a funeral, he was told, "Come now or we'll come get you." He flew to Riyadh that night.

Over the course of a few days, hundreds of men got similar calls from the Royal Court, inviting them to dinners, meetings, or other private audiences with the king or MBS. The invitations were not only impossible to turn down, they were actually welcome, dripping with the possibility that the kingdom's leaders wanted the men for important business. When the men turned up, however, security agents took their phones and wallets, dismissed their security details, drove them to the Riyadh Ritz-Carlton, and checked them in.

The Ritz-Carlton had long served as the de facto royal hotel, providing world-class lodging for businessmen, consultants, U.S. presidents, and other guests of the government. Not long before, attendees of MBS's investment conference had mingled in its vaulted marble lobby and chatted over coffee under its bronze statues of rearing stallions. But as the kingdom's switchboards had lit up with calls to the Saudi elite, the Ritz had informed its guests that standing reservations had been canceled and that current guests needed to move out. Meanwhile, the kingdom's airports froze private plane traffic.

By that evening, it was clear that something major was afoot. Social media accounts close to the government reported the arrests of prominent princes, businessmen, and government officials, including some who had been close to MBS up to the moment of their detention. MBS's aides distributed the news, amplifying the charge against the detainees: corruption.

That night, the government announced that King Salman had created a new anti-corruption committee and empowered it to log crimes, investigate cases, freeze accounts, and issue travel bans and arrest warrants in order to "combat corruption at all levels." The campaign, it said, aimed at "tackling a persistent problem that has hindered development efforts in the Kingdom in recent decades." The committee included the public prosecutor and top security officials and was led by MBS.

The kingdom already had an anti-corruption organization, but it had always been seen as a joke for never taking on serious cases. The new committee was no joke.

THE ROYAL DECREE that created the committee was correct that corruption had long been a problem. What it did not make clear was how deeply it was baked into the kingdom's economy and into the relationship between the people, the government, and the royal family.

Saudi Arabia's tremendous oil wealth pumped great capital into the family and the state budget. From there, it fueled a "waterfall economy" in which cash gushed from the top while society jockeyed below to catch as much as it could. At the very top was the royal family, whose thousands of princes and princesses received monthly stipends that allowed them to employ cadres of cooks, housekeepers, nurses, fashion designers, hairdressers, interior decorators, horse trainers, and other hangers-on. Below them was the government, which employed most working Saudis and powered most of the private sector with contracts often laced with kickbacks.

That system allowed princes and prominent businessmen to siphon money from the government's coffers in myriad ways. Their schemes were rarely exposed, because Saudi journalists knew to steer clear of such topics, as did domestic law enforcement. But foreigners in the kingdom witnessed blatant looting.

"Saudi princes and princesses, of whom there are thousands, are known for the stories of their fabulous wealth—and tendency to squander it," an American diplomat wrote in 1996.

He explained common schemes. Royals often "borrowed" money from Saudi banks and never paid it back, a practice so common that many refused to loan to royals who lacked track records. The exception was the National Commercial Bank, long considered the royals' bank, which had reportedly been saved by a $2 billion bailout from King Fahd to keep it from going bust due to unpaid loans.

Princes often used their clout to become the agents of foreign companies, earning commissions and kickbacks, and to appropriate land, especially if it was in the path of an upcoming construction project, like an airport or a military base. Once the building started, they would sell the land to the government at a tremendous profit. Another scheme involved "sponsoring" foreign workers who would survive in the local economy and pay their bosses a monthly commission for the privilege of working in Saudi Arabia. If a prince sponsored 100 such workers and each paid $100 per month, he could earn $10,000 dollars per month for next to zero work.

The diplomat also revealed that five or six senior princes controlled the revenue from 1 million barrels of oil per day, one-eighth of the kingdom's daily production, for "off budget" programs that provided huge opportunities for "royal rake-offs."

It was all terrible for the economy, the diplomat concluded.

"It is our assessment that of the priority issues the country faces, getting a grip on royal family excesses is at the top," he wrote. But little was likely to change as long as the royal family viewed the country as "Al Saud Inc."

Eleven years later, another American diplomat credited King Abdullah with cleaning up some royal excesses, causing "the most widespread source of discontent in the ruling family." The king cut free mobile phone service for thousands of royals; kicked them out of hotel suites they had booked year-round; prohibited them from getting unlimited free tickets on the national airline, knowing that they often sold the extras for cash; and curtailed the passing of government land to private citizens.

When royals talked about corruption, which was rare, they argued that it was nobody's business. In an interview in 2001, Prince Bandar bin Sultan, then the Saudi ambassador to Washington, said that if the kingdom had spent $400 billion on development and lost $50 billion to corruption along the way, it had been worth it.

"What I'm trying to tell you is, so what?" he said. "We did not invent corruption, nor did those dissidents who are so genius discover it. This happened since Adam and Eve."

There was little reason to believe that corruption had become rare by the time King Salman came to power. To the contrary, a decade of high oil prices had boosted the kingdom's finances, giving the leadership little motivation to crack down, and King Abdullah's illness had weakened oversight, fueling a bonanza.

A few months before the calls from the Royal Court went out, MBS told an interviewer that the kingdom had not taken the fight against corruption seriously enough, but would soon.

"If fighting corruption is not on the top of the agenda, it means the fight is not succeeding and attempts being made to do so will not succeed no matter what you do," he said. "I reiterate that anyone who is involved in corruption will not be spared, whether he is a minister, a prince, or whoever he is."

The statement drew little notice at the time.

Once the crackdown was underway and more than 350 men, including at least eleven princes, former government ministers, and some of the kingdom's best-known businessmen had been detained in the Ritz and other facilities, Saudi officials hailed it as transformational. The minister of finance said it would "consolidate the principles of governance, accountability, and justice" and create "a fair and transparent investment environment based on merit, not nepotism or favoritism." The public prosecutor said the accused would face an "independent judicial process" and that "everyone's legal rights will be preserved." Top clerics praised the move as serving "the public interest."

The campaign received another ringing endorsement—from the United States.

"I have great confidence in King Salman and the Crown Prince of Saudi Arabia, they know exactly what they are doing," President Trump wrote on Twitter. "Some of those they are harshly treating have been 'milking' their country for years!"

Trump had history with at least one detainee. He and Alwaleed had sparred publicly for years. After Trump entered the presidential race, the prince called him "a disgrace not only to the GOP but to all America" and told him to withdraw. Trump responded by calling the prince "dopey" and accused him of trying to "control our U.S. politicians with daddy's money." (After the election, Alwaleed congratulated Trump on his win.)

There was little doubt that to guarantee a sound financial future, the kingdom had to root out corruption, especially with the war in Yemen sapping its finances and a large youth population looking for jobs. The question was whether locking a bunch of men in a luxury hotel was the best way to go about it.

LATER, I TRACKED down a Saudi professional who had been detained in the Ritz and he agreed to tell me about it on the condition that I not identify him, so as not to endanger him or his family. He was an older man, near retirement, who had worked both in government and the private sector and had even traveled with Salman's entourage.

When he had received his call from the Royal Court inviting him to meet the king, he was at home in Jeddah and was told a plane ticket was waiting for him at the airport. When he got there, he found others who had received similar calls and they flew to Riyadh together. Once they arrived, security officers took their phones, put them in separate cars, and drove them to the Ritz. As he was checked in, his wallet, pens, and bag of clothing were also taken. A team of medics looked him over, and he was put in a room by himself.

"In the name of the king, I welcome you to this place," he was told.

There were guards in the hallways, he couldn't close his door, and he was ordered not to leave. The room was lavish, with comfy armchairs, pillows piled high on the bed, and thick curtains over the windows. The hotel offered same-day laundry service and in-room dining. At night, a food cart came down the hall offering Saudi treats. The television worked, and like many of the detainees, he spent much of his time following the caper of Saad Hariri. But as he settled in, he realized that the drinking glasses, pens, razors, curtain cords, and glass shower doors—anything a guest could use to harm himself—had been removed.

On the morning of his second day, a tailor showed up to take his measurements and he soon received a new custom wardrobe: twelve T-shirts, twelve pairs of underwear, twelve pairs of pants, some traditional Saudi headgear, a pair of shoes, a pair of flip-flops, some socks, three thobes, and three short-sleeved gowns to sleep in.

"When I saw all that, I knew the issue was going to take a while," he said.

Then the real business began. Officials from the Royal Court took the men elsewhere in the hotel for investigation, interrogating them about corrupt deals they were accused of having been part of or privy to and confronting them with documents said to show their complicity. Some of the detainees were handed proposed "supplements," listing specific assets the committee had deemed ill-gotten and had to be returned to the state. Others were told to pay enormous lump sums as a sort of opening bid for a lengthy negotiation. At least one was forced to sign a blank document that the government could fill in later as it chose.

Meanwhile, the crackdown accelerated. The government froze 1,200 bank accounts to keep wealthy Saudis from moving their money abroad, and added 500 more accounts a few days later. New people were brought in, including the most powerful businessman in Jordan, who was held for a few days with no explanation.

As questions mounted abroad about what was going on, Saudi officials compared the process to a plea bargain for white-collar criminals in the West, saying the detainees could consult their lawyers and challenge the accusations against them.

In an interview at the time, MBS said that roughly 10 percent of the government's yearly spending was lost to corruption, which had led his father to launch an investigation into the issue after he became king. The settlements could eventually total about $100 billion, he said, while the crackdown would shock corruption out of the system.

"You have to send a signal, and the signal going forward now is, 'You will not escape,'" he said. He dismissed the idea that the campaign was a power grab as "ludicrous."

Saudi Arabia had never seen such an operation, and it spread terror among the detainees' relatives, employees, and business partners, who were not allowed to visit; the detainees' lawyers were not allowed in either. The denizens of the Ritz were allowed brief phone calls, but they were routed through the hotel switchboard, monitored, and sometimes cut off in the middle if the conversation strayed beyond basic greetings.

As the detainees' relatives panicked and the managers of their businesses struggled to keep them running, a number of them quietly reached out to me, at great risk to themselves. Using encrypted messaging apps and agreeing to meet only outside the kingdom, they passed along whatever information they could gather.

There was little doubt that many of the detainees had been involved in corruption, and that their associates were unlikely to tell me about it. Prince Turki bin Nasser had been implicated in the al-Yamamah scandal, a corrupt arms deal that had become a scandal in Britain, though no charges were ever brought against him. And the fact that Saad Hariri had been forced to resign on the same day the others were thrown in the Ritz led many to suspect that at least part of his ordeal was financial. Perhaps MBS wanted to take away his premiership so he could throw Hariri in the Ritz, too. All that was possible, but the government refused to comment on specific cases, leaving the entire process murky.

The detainees' relatives argued that if there had been mass corruption, it had been with the complicity of the authorities. The kingdom's businessmen had merely operated in the environment created by the royal family.

"Saudi Arabia is the safest place in the world!" one detainee had always argued, a relative told me later. In the Ritz, however, he had signed away everything, including the house the relative lived in.

"It is piracy," she said, accusing MBS of using the allegation of corruption to cut down anyone who might outshine him. "Anyone who has money in this country, he wants it. Anyone who has a good reputation in this country, he wants to destroy it."

Others questioned why some princes widely seen as notoriously corrupt had not gone to the Ritz. Had he given them a pass, or an opportunity to strike a private deal beforehand? It was never clear.

MBS also faced an optics problem. He had never explained where he got the money to buy his yacht. Less than two weeks into the campaign, a mystery buyer at Christie's auction house in New York laid down $450.3 million for Leonardo da Vinci's *Salvator Mundi*. That was more than three times what the painting's previous owner had paid and it shattered the record for the highest price ever paid for a piece of art at auction. A little-known Saudi prince was soon revealed to be the mystery buyer, and American intelligence agencies confirmed that he was a proxy for MBS. (MBS later denied that he had bought the painting, but said that "any human with good taste must admire art.")

A short time later, "The World's Most Expensive Home," which MBS had bought for more than $300 million two years earlier, was also unearthed. These did not appear to be the shopping habits of a man committed to curbing royal excesses, but many of my Saudi friends cheered on the crackdown nevertheless, taking pleasure in seeing figures who had flown so high brought so low.

Over time, information trickled out casting the operation in a harsher light. Princes who had dodged the first round of arrests but complained about them were arrested. Some of the detainees were welcomed with beatings and other physical abuse, sending a number to a nearby hospital. One ended up dead, a man named Ali al-Qahtani, who had been a sidekick to one of King Abdullah's sons. When his boss was arrested, al-Qahtani was taken, too, and died in custody. When his body reached the hospital, his neck was twisted and his body bruised as if he had been given electrical shocks. His family buried him quietly and was told not to speak about what had happened.

When the detainees were later released, or let out briefly to attend family funerals, some told relatives of sleep deprivation, beatings, and lengthy interrogations with their heads covered. One had wounds on his legs. Another had black fingernails. They spoke of the role played by MBS's enforcers, who were frequently in the hotel.

An American citizen received some of the worst treatment. Walid Fitaihi had been born in Saudi Arabia but had become an American while studying medicine on the East Coast. He returned to the kingdom to open a private hospital and build a career as a motivational speaker. He, too, was scooped up in the crackdown and after about a week in the hotel, guards dragged him into another room, where they slapped and blindfolded him, stripped him down to his underwear, tied him to a chair, and electrocuted him.

The Saudi government vehemently denied that any detainees were abused. But no American, Western, or Arab official I have spoken with since has cast doubt on the allegations, although it remains unclear how widespread the abuse was.

The Saudi professional I interviewed who was in the Ritz said he had not been physically abused, but his detention had soured him on his homeland.

"There was certainly corruption that spread, but the government was part of it and so was the royal family," he told me. "I was mistreated and I couldn't find anyone to give me justice, because there is no one you can go to, and that has weakened my loyalty to my country."

NEARLY THREE MONTHS after the first arrests, the BBC aired an explosive report about the Ritz. In it, a mysterious Canadian businessman named Alan Bender said he had been flown to Riyadh, where officials from the Royal Court had put him on a video call with Alwaleed, who appeared to have been taken from a cell. Bender said the officials gave him a list of allegations to read to the prince that appeared to have been taken from private conversations the government had intercepted. Bender guessed that the idea had been to demoralize the prince to give the government leverage in negotiating his "settlement."

I interviewed Bender at length, but could never determine whether his story was true. He clearly had an anti-Saudi agenda and could provide no proof that he had been in Riyadh when he claimed. But Saudi officials found the BBC report so alarming that they invited a reporter from Reuters to interview Alwaleed inside the Ritz to rebut the accusations.

The reporter, Katie Paul, was shepherded into the Ritz by Saudi officials and taken to the prince's 4,575-square-foot royal suite, room 628, where he welcomed her. He was wearing sunglasses, appeared to have lost weight, and sported an uncharacteristic salt-and-pepper beard. He gave her a tour of his accommodations, pointing out his living room, dining room, office, and kitchen. He drew her attention to tiny jars of ketchup and mustard, held up a Diet Pepsi, and took a swig. Then he sat at a desk, with a mug bearing his face before him, and told his visitor that everything was totally normal.

"There are no charges," he said, squirming in his chair and never removing his sunglasses. "Rest assured this is a clean operation that we have, and we're just in discussion with the government on various matters that I cannot divulge right now. But rest assured we are at the end of the whole story. And I'm very comfortable because I'm in my country, I'm in my city, so I feel at home. It's no problem at all. Everything's fine."

He dismissed the BBC report as "all lies," saying that during his time in the Ritz, he had been given good food and was able to walk, swim, and follow the news.

"It's like home," he said, skirting questions about why he was in the hotel in the first place. "I can only say I'm supporting the king and crown prince in all the efforts they're doing to really have a new Saudi Arabia."

A number of people who had worked for Alwaleed later told me he was fastidious about his diet and avoided ketchup. I was also shown instructions his team had sent to a hotel a few years before where he was planning a vacation. It stipulated that his room have a firm mattress and blackout curtains, that all booze be removed from the minibar, and that pornography and cartoons be excised from the television offerings for his whole entourage. The first line of the section about food read: "HRH no longer drinks Diet Pepsi," referring to "His Royal Highness." That raised the question of whether his conspicuous wielding of the soda can had been a message, like a hostage blinking in a ransom video. Or perhaps he had merely slacked on his diet while in detention.

In any case, it appeared that he had said whatever was expected of him, and he was released that night and returned home to be watched over by guards who answered to MBS. Other detainees also began leaving the hotel, and the government announced that the campaign had recouped $106 billion, most of it in real estate, companies, stocks, and other illiquid assets. Of the 381 people who had been summoned—some as suspects and some as witnesses—only 56 remained who had not yet settled, the government said.

But who knew for sure? None of the detainees wanted to acknowledge that they had been corrupt or had surrendered assets, and the government never spelled out who had paid what, why, or how the amounts had been calculated. In mid-February, the Ritz officially reopened, and the foreign consultants who had scrambled to find rooms elsewhere moved back in. And so the crackdown ended.

SORT OF.

The government had let the detainees out of the Ritz, but in many cases it had sent the Ritz home with them, in the form of electronic ankle bracelets that tracked their movements. Many of the former detainees suspected that the devices had microphones to eavesdrop on them, so they avoided discussing what had happened, even with relatives. One took to wrapping pillows around his anklet when he wanted to chat. Another played loud music. The devices were monitored remotely, and the men had to keep them charged or the government would call to tell them to plug them in. A number of detainees were not released, but moved to other facilities where they were held without charge, some for more than a year.

The Ritz was an economic earthquake that shook the pillars of the kingdom's economy and rattled its major figures. But its effect on investor confidence and on the fates of the men targeted would become clear only over time.

The Saudi Binladin Group, which had been the royals' primary contractor for decades, would end up effectively controlled by the government. According to an investigation by Reuters, MBS had told the company's chairman in 2015 that he wanted to become a partner and that the company should sell shares in an IPO. The brothers who ran the firm resisted, and at least three of them ended up in the Ritz. As part of their "settlements," the authorities seized the deeds to their homes as well as private jets, jewelry, cash, and one brother's $90 million car collection. Another member of the family had his Maserati showroom cleaned out.

The 36.2 percent of the company held by the three brothers was transferred to the state, and the government set up a five-man committee to oversee its operations. Other family members retained their shares, and two were given oversight roles.

The company still had 93 projects on deck, but most of its work was put on hold so it could focus on NEOM, MBS's dream city on the Red Sea coast. The first buildings were palaces, including a replica of the one the company had built for King Salman in Morocco. The construction was so rushed to meet a tight opening deadline that the grass had not had time to grow and was replaced with artificial turf.

"It was a shitty experience," one of the brothers said of his time in the Ritz.

MBC, the Arab world's largest media company, met a similar fate. After al-Ibrahim, its chairman, had turned down MBS's offer to buy the firm, a team from the international accounting firm PwC had been brought in to vet the company's books. The next month, al-Ibrahim and most of the company's board members were thrown in the Ritz. A few days later, the PwC accountants visited the company's headquarters in Dubai to finish their report as if nothing had happened. The British law firm Clifford Chance was then tasked with drafting the paperwork to transfer shares of the company to the Saudi government. Neither firm publicly objected to facilitating a transaction for a buyer who had locked up the seller.

Al-Ibrahim left the Ritz in late January and later returned to Dubai, where he retained a 40 percent stake in the company. The remaining 60 percent was transferred to a mysterious new body in the Ministry of Finance called "Istidama," which MBS said managed companies and properties seized in the Ritz. Over time, the channel's operations shifted to jibe with MBS's policies. Under orders from the Royal Court, for example, it canceled six popular Turkish drama series to protest the Turks' closeness to Qatar, costing the company about $25 million.

Alwaleed continued to run Kingdom Holding, on paper at least, but appeared to be no longer master of his fate. Before his release, *The Wall Street Journal* quoted "people familiar with the matter" saying the government wanted $6 billion from him. After he got out, he acknowledged having reached "a confirmed understanding" that was "secret and confidential" with the government, but insisted that life was back to normal and praised MBS.

"He's establishing a new era in Saudi Arabia," he said. "Any person who does not support what Mohammed bin Salman is doing right now, I say, is a traitor."

A foreign money manager who saw Alwaleed after his release told me: "Even the prince doesn't know what happened to him."

Long afterward, Saudi watchers would swap rumors they had picked up about who had lost what in the Ritz, but confirmed details remained elusive. If there were any documents, they were locked away somewhere in the Royal Court, hidden from scrutiny.

But the greater result was clear. After the removal of Mohammed bin Nayef as crown prince, a few princes had remained in positions where they could wield power to challenge MBS. After the Ritz, none were left. Gone were the days when the kingdom had relatively independent power centers with lucrative businesses and rich tycoons linked to them. Now they all answered to MBS, who could marshal their resources as he saw fit in service of his plans. The old elites may have hated him for it, but there was little they could do. MBS now ruled the Saudi economy.

"No one can talk about what happened in the Ritz," an employee of a prince who had been in the Ritz told me. "In the end, they all have to live in Saudi Arabia."

A NIGHT AT THE OPERA

_____

JAMAL KHASHOGGI WAS blunt when I asked him about the Ritz. "It's just like playing Monopoly with a bunch of guys, but you are in charge of everything and you can change the rules," he said. "But everyone has to stay at the table and play with you."

He took up the issue in *The Washington Post*, calling the day of the arrests the "Night of the Long Knives," a reference to Adolf Hitler's purge to consolidate power in Nazi Germany, arguing that Mohammed bin Salman's goal was to centralize "all power within his position as crown prince." He lauded the idea of fighting corruption, and listed corrupt schemes he had seen himself, including a sewer project in Jeddah that consisted of manhole covers with no pipes underneath.

"I, as the editor of a major paper at the time, can say that we all knew, and we never reported on it," he wrote. "So yes, I, as a Saudi citizen, am eager to see this scourge end."

But he accused MBS of dealing with foes in the style of Vladimir Putin of Russia and enforcing selective justice. Hadn't MBS bought a half-billion-dollar yacht?

"The buck stops at the leader's door. He is not above the standard he is now setting for the rest of his family, and for the country."

As he settled into life in exile in late 2017, Khashoggi reacted to events back home in his writings. He criticized the recent fall's arrest campaign, saying that while some of those detained had espoused hard-line views, others supported positions that jibed with MBS's reforms while also calling "mildly for political rights."

"Can we really present a compelling image of a modern society, complete with robots, foreigners, and tourists, when Saudis, many miles from NEOM, are silenced?" he asked.

He called on Saudi Arabia to push for peace talks to end the Yemen war and blasted its move against Saad Hariri, blaming it on the same impulsiveness that sparked the Qatar boycott.

He and Maggie Mitchell Salem met frequently and texted constantly, sharing thoughts, feelings, and articles as she helped him relaunch his career from Washington. She connected him with powerful people, booked him hotels, and paid airline change fees so he could make important meetings. She offered to get him a researcher, arranged translators so his articles could be simultaneously published in Arabic, and helped with his writings for *The Washington Post* and other publications. The pair brainstormed ideas and Mitchell Salem edited drafts or wrote sections to get Khashoggi going. To make his work more accessible to American readers, she adjusted his language. Once, she added a quote from the Dave Eggers novel *A Hologram for the King* that Khashoggi didn't understand.

> KHASHOGGI: There were people in the world for whom the world and its people were subjects on which to cast spells. I didn't get this! What do you mean?
> MITCHELL SALEM: Alluding to MBS.

The line was published in a column about the Ritz.

Other times, she would ask him for information about Saudi Arabia—such as the names of media magnates locked in the Ritz—and work it in while editing.

> MITCHELL SALEM: Not a bad team, you and me! Despite all the pain & suffering you have to endure!!
> KHASHOGGI: Yes, we are.

They often argued about tone, with Mitchell Salem pushing him to take a harder line. He resisted.

> MITCHELL SALEM: I'm tired of saying this. And I will do it again. Your favorite Crown Prince has enough people making nice for him. Stop pulling your punches. . . .

KHASHOGGI: Let strategy move you, not anger.

MITCHELL SALEM: The strategy I thought we were employing is advice and a reminder of what NOT to do, and a bit of heart—you can't go home because you would be them. So they cannot be forgotten.

KHASHOGGI: I'm not planning to go home. I'm not kissing asses. This independent, rational voice of mine has more effect than being angry.

Theirs was a deep and complicated relationship. They had known each other for years and he trusted her, telling her after he landed in Washington that she was "the best friend I have." She worried about him and felt that the best way to combat his sense of helplessness was to keep him engaged in issues he cared about. They had been talking about the Middle East for years, but the rise of MBS had substantially raised the stakes. They were no longer just two friends arguing about regional politics. Khashoggi was now a prominent writer challenging his country's crown prince from the capital of Saudi Arabia's most important ally, and Mitchell Salem was serving as his de facto agent, adviser, and editor while on the payroll of a country the Saudis considered an enemy. It is unclear what role, if any, Mitchell Salem's work for Qatar played in her interactions with Khashoggi, and there is no evidence that he ever published words he disagreed with. But for Saudi Arabia, the arrangement could hardly have looked worse.

Khashoggi knew that the more he wrote, the less chance there was that he would return to the kingdom.

KHASHOGGI: I don't feel good. I'm safe now, but don't feel good.

MITCHELL SALEM: Why?!?!?

KHASHOGGI: It's a declaration that I'm away, maybe for good, from home.

But he kept publishing. He was alarmed by Saudi Arabia's new with-us-or-against-us rhetoric and criticized Saud al-Qahtani, the media czar, for fueling attacks on anyone who strayed from the official line.

"Writers like me, whose criticism is offered respectfully, seem to be considered more dangerous than the more strident Saudi opposition based in London," he wrote. The government had rounded up clerics and intellectuals, while "compliant journalists are rewarded with money and access to senior officials." Average citizens could seek out dissenting views online, but "just think twice about sharing or liking whatever isn't fully in line with the official government groupthink."

Mitchell Salem worried that the Saudis would come after him, so she insisted that he check in whenever he went to the Saudi Embassy.

In February:

KHASHOGGI: I'm on my way to the embassy to pick up the power of attorney I asked them to do for me.
MITCHELL SALEM: Let me know when you're out.

Eleven minutes later:

KHASHOGGI: Out.

He knew his writings had made him toxic to other Saudis, and did not call a Saudi friend who was passing through Washington, in case the friend wanted to keep his distance.

KHASHOGGI: I'm too much of a pariah for him. I hate it):
MITCHELL SALEM: Everyone is scared.
KHASHOGGI: I'm going to the Saudi embassy now.

Seventeen minutes later:

KHASHOGGI: I'm out.

DURING MY LAST trip to Saudi Arabia, I went to the opera. I arrived late for the show, in a cavernous concert hall with plush red seats at a women's university, and entered just as the houselights dimmed. A conductor in a tuxedo emerged to applause from the nearly full house. He raised his baton, the music swelled, and the stage lights went up.

"My love, speak to me in a poem," the female lead sang, opening *Antar and Abla*, an Arabic opera about racism, love, and war.

The show, packed with swordfights, dramatic deaths, and actors in historic garb, was part of the push by MBS to make life more enjoyable in the kingdom while building a domestic entertainment industry. The initiative had picked up speed since the religious police had lost their powers, and the kingdom was suddenly hosting comic book festivals, professional wrestling matches, dance performances, and monster truck rallies. The American rapper Nelly performed for an all-male audience. New Age music guru Yanni wowed the kingdom, twice. Mariah Carey and the Backstreet Boys came later.

There had been quiet grumbling about the changes in conservative parts of society, but there was nothing but enthusiasm in the opera hall that night. During the intermission, I saw a Saudi ambassador I knew with his daughter.

"Are you an opera fan?" I asked.

"Yes," he said. "As of today."

The intrigue resumed onstage, and after more rousing numbers and a huge battle, big Saudi flags appeared and the crowd rose for a standing ovation.

After the show, I asked three Saudi men in their early twenties what they would have done on a weekend night two years before. They shrugged.

"Before, the only entertainment in Saudi was food," one said. "We'd get together to decide what to do and we'd go eat. No concerts, no shows. Now we can plan events on the weekend."

The entertainment push played multiple roles in MBS's plans. He knew that young Saudis were bored out of their minds since they lacked the diversions that their foreign peers had, even in other Islamic countries. And this boredom drove them abroad. The money-eyed classes jetted off to Paris and London; others spent weekends in Dubai or Bahrain, where they could catch a movie, women could drive, and those who chose to could have a beer—or three. MBS's goal was to keep them—and the $20 billion the government said they spent on entertainment abroad each year—at home, to fuel the economy and create jobs.

In a historical sense, the idea that entertainment was not only permitted but beneficial was revolutionary. The best-known early encounter of a Saudi royal with film was in 1945, when American sailors treated MBS's grandfather to a screening of a documentary called *The Fighting Lady*, about an aircraft carrier. The king was impressed, but did not want such diversions in his kingdom.

"I doubt whether my people should have moving pictures even like this wonderful film because it would give them an appetite for entertainment which might distract them from their religious duties," he said.

(Unbeknownst to the king, two of his sons joined the American sailors late one night to watch Lucille Ball run wild in a male dormitory and get her dress torn off. The princes loved it.)

Previous royals had legitimized their rule by burnishing their religious credentials, to which cinema was seen as antithetical. But MBS was building a new model. He had cut down the traditional pillars of power—the clerics, the business elite, the wider royal family—and sought to build a new constituency among the kingdom's young people. It was a royal populist appeal, made through music, movies, and pro wrestling.

In 2016, MBS created the General Entertainment Authority to foster the new sector. Around the time I went to the opera, the GEA invited me to a flashy event to lay out its plans for 2018. It opened with a light show and a performance by an illusionist with a Rubik's Cube, followed by a talk by the authority's chairman. The GEA was going to double the number of events it oversaw to more than 4,000, he said, and was launching a new website and app to host its schedule.

"It is wrong that we who love happiness go to look for it in neighboring countries," he said.

He ran through a dizzying array of upcoming initiatives: an opera house, street festivals, and the entertainment city that MBS had announced during the investment conference.

"We have a long road in front of us. We know what we want to do, God willing. We have unlimited support from the leadership, and we will carry it out with your help."

It felt a bit Soviet to have a government body oversee entertainment, but the idea was that decades of conservatism had baked so many restrictions into the bureaucracy that only a powerful commission backed by the crown prince could break through. But the kingdom was starting from scratch. Its few movie theaters had been shut down after 1979. Shops sold musical instruments, but schools did not teach music, theater, or other arts. The country's experience with entertainment was limited to private consumption of content from Egypt, Syria, Lebanon, Hollywood, and Bollywood.

The head of the GEA acknowledged this, saying that a young Saudi girl who wanted to learn ballet would struggle to find a teacher. Recorded music for a recent National Day celebration had been produced in Lebanon because the kingdom lacked studios with enough expertise. The kingdom had budgeted $64 billion over the coming decade to give birth to the new sector.

The change was a boon for those who had battled the old system. Ameera al-Taweel, the ex-wife of Prince Alwaleed bin Talal, was the chairwoman of Time Entertainment in Saudi Arabia. She told me she had started the company in 2012 to tap the kingdom's youth market, but planning events had required huge effort to secure permits from the police and a range of ministries. That process often took nine months, so the company had done only a few events per year. Now the GEA obtained permits in a few weeks and the company had planned twenty-eight events for 2018, including Cirque du Soleil, Saudi Fashion Week, a jazz festival, and the opera I had attended.

The government vetted content, and shows were modified for local sensibilities. Cirque du Soleil was going to be less racy, and al-Taweel had been surprised to receive approval for a dance performance called *Shadowland*, which featured men and women together. A performer in a short dress had been required to wear leggings, and an image evoking Darwin's theory of evolution was removed.

"Because in Islam, we don't believe in it," al-Taweel said.

But her company struggled to find Saudi acts.

"The problem is not that we don't have talent," she told me. "It is just that we don't have the educational structure to turn that talent into professional working talent. We don't have art academies or music academies. They are the ones who can create an orchestra or make an opera. Those are the ones who can create a band that can perform at festivals. Other than that, they have to learn on their own, either from YouTube, festivals, gatherings in houses, or being underground. I feel that now we are in a stage where, thankfully, the country said, 'Hey come out. You don't have to hide anymore.'"

There were hiccups along the way. A video of boys and girls dancing together at a comic book convention in Jeddah went viral, causing outrage among those who felt that the kingdom was sacrificing its Islamic identity. But people adjusted, and it became normal to hear music at public functions.

I spent another evening at an outdoor event called "The Gathering." Fast food stands and picnic tables stood in the grassy courtyard of a downtown hotel. Hip hop played quietly on big speakers, strings of lights hung overhead, and young men and women lined up to order burgers and french fries. It was a scene that would not have drawn a glance elsewhere in the world, but for the kingdom's socially parched youth, it was a drink of cool water.

I met two women in their mid-twenties who had dropped by after work, and they walked me through the before-and-after social scenarios for women their age. Before MBS, they had gathered in homes or at restaurants, where they sat with their girlfriends in the family section and didn't mix with men. When they ventured further afield, the religious police harassed them, despite their modest dress.

"They would walk behind you and say: 'Cover your face, cover your face,'" one woman told me.

Now they could move freely and rarely saw the bearded enforcers. On weekends, they would check the entertainment authority's calendar for stuff to do, and they planned to get their driver's licenses when the ban was lifted.

The other woman hoped to be able to travel without the permission of a male "guardian," and said she had once almost missed a flight because her father had forgotten to give her permission. Her brother had had to drive to the airport to sign for her to leave. She worked, was not from an elite family, and *loved* that MBS had thrown rich people in the Ritz.

"Before, a prince could do anything—steal, seize properties. Afterward, everyone will walk on the straight path," she said, praising MBS for the changes. "I love him. He came as a young man who thought more like us."

MANY OF THE kingdom's conservatives had trouble keeping up, including top clerics. In 2017, a caller on the live television show of the Grand Mufti, the man who had beseeched me to become a Muslim the year before, asked for the blind cleric's position on cinemas and concerts.

"We know that singing concerts and cinemas are a depravity," he said. Cinemas "might show movies that are libertine, lewd, immoral, and atheist, because they rely on films imported to change our culture." And there was "nothing good" in concerts because they were "a call for mixing between sexes." He foresaw a slippery slope.

"At the beginning, they will assign areas for women, but then both men and women will end up in one area. This corrupts morals and destroys values," he said.

Since that ran against where MBS was taking the kingdom, a prominent journalist close to the crown prince wrote that the mufti had not outright banned cinemas or concerts, but merely said they should not spread "debauchery and atheism." The head of the entertainment authority visited the mufti to reassure him that there were no plans to open cinemas "at the current time," a hugely misleading statement. The mufti's live call-in show soon ended. Henceforth, his program would be prerecorded so that such condemnations would not slip through.

The kingdom introduced a law criminalizing sexual harassment, "in order to preserve the individual's privacy, dignity, and freedom." Perpetrators could face up to two years in prison or a fine of up to $26,000 for first-time offenders, or both. The move was seen as an effort to keep men in line at the new events, so it was a shock when the first person it ensnared was a woman. At a concert by an Iraqi-Saudi singer, a fan wearing a full face veil ran onstage and gave him a hug. The ladies in the audience cheered, and bouncers rushed in to pull her away. The police arrested the woman, and local media suggested she had fallen victim to a dangerous dare by her girl-friends. Her name was never released, and it was unclear whether she was charged with a crime.

I was deeply curious about how conservative parts of society were receiving the changes. The struggle for the kingdom's social future had been raging for years, and now MBS was handing a firm win to the liberalizers. How did the other side feel, especially since the kingdom's leaders had spent decades preaching that what set Saudi Arabia apart was its strict adherence to rigid Islamic codes?

My friend the *salafi* and fan of *The Da Vinci Code* said it was a mixed bag. He had no religious objections to women driving, work-ing, or going to university, as long as they were segregated from men. He didn't love the idea of cinemas, but didn't oppose them either.

"Everyone has a cinema in their pocket anyway," he said, holding up his iPhone.

Concerts were a problem, especially when they encouraged men and women to dance together, but his deeper grievance was less with the changes and more with the sense that the conservatives had been shafted. He, for one, had *not* cheered when MBS had vowed at the investment conference "to destroy extremist ideas." My friend had no sympathy for jihadists, but worried that the state would dis-mantle its religious foundations.

"Why all this talk of destruction?" he asked. "The whole message is, 'You are with me or you are with me. There is no way to be against me or to disagree with me.'"

He had been particularly incensed when the head of the enter-tainment authority said that Saudis who objected to the new events could just stay home.

"Stay home! Why should we stay home?" he said.

But he did not oppose the government, or entertainment per se. If the authority organized events with no music or gender mixing, where prayer times were respected, he would have happily taken his whole family.

I traveled to Buraidah, a deeply conservative city northwest of Riyadh, to see some clerics I had met a few years before while reporting an article about Sharia law and the death penalty. Then, the clerics I had met, all government employees, had been confident that there was no daylight between them and the state. Now MBS's reforms had thrown that into question.

"For sure, it doesn't make me comfortable," one told me of the new direction. "Anything that has sin in it, anything that angers the Almighty, it's a problem."

I asked why there had been so little response to the decision to lift the ban on women driving.

"They did a preemptive strike," he said. "All those who thought about saying no to the government got arrested."

The city was so conservative that the entertainment authority had scarcely planned anything there, so women driving was the main issue on people's minds. He acknowledged that there was no clear theological reason for the ban, but said many locals feared the behaviors it could incite: men sabotaging women's cars to assault them; men climbing into cars after women to feel the warmth left by their bodies; daring plots by assertive young women to rendezvous with strange men. He recalled being shocked after giving a religious talk at a mall when young women had come up afterward to take selfies with him.

"The problem here is that the girls are daring and hysterical," he said. "If you give them the space, they'll go crazy."

Another cleric launched into a diatribe against the liberals who he said were corrupting Saudi society through its women.

"They want her to dance. They want her to go to the cinema. They want her to uncover her face. They want her to show her legs and thighs. That is liberal thought," he said. "It is a corrupting ideology."

But his position on women driving was complex, reflecting the competing forces pulling conservatives between loyalty to the state, adherence to their creed, and concerns about their own families. In public, he said the state had allowed women to drive, so he supported it. Personally, he also backed the decision. But privately, he would not let his wife or daughters drive (he claimed they did not want to, but I couldn't ask them myself).

In the end, however, he acknowledged the long history of conservatives rejecting innovations they later accepted—radios, televisions, girls' education, cellphones—and said the same could happen with women driving.

"Society in general at this time is very scared," he said. "It will take time, but people will get used to it."

MBS DID NOT wait for the conservatives to catch up, and continued to demolish old constraints. The government instituted physical education classes for girls, which clerics had argued could damage their femininity. It allowed women to attend public soccer games, seating them in family sections with male relatives. During one of my visits, I attended a reception at the Lebanese Embassy, where the Patriarch of the Maronite Church, dressed in his full regalia, greeted Christians living in the kingdom. Many who came to see him had spent years in Saudi Arabia keeping their faith to themselves and were overwhelmed that the leader of their flock had been allowed to visit. MBS would name a Shiite to his cabinet and another as the CEO of NEOM, positions that would have gone to Sunnis in the past.

In his push for change, MBS had an advantage embedded in Wahhabism itself. Along with its quest for religious purity was an injunction to obey the ruler, even if he was unjust, as long as he did not hinder the practice of Islam. MBS was well aware of that tenet and leveraged it against the clerics, who mostly kept their grumbling to themselves.

Some of the conservatives I spoke with worried that pushing society too fast would drive extremists underground, where they could resort to violence. The 1979 seizure of the Grand Mosque in Mecca and Osama bin Laden's invectives against the kingdom selling out Islam were scary precedents, and it was impossible to predict whether a similar challenge would arise. It didn't take more than a small band of crazies to do serious damage.

Some foreign writers argued that MBS's effort to tame Wahhabism was among the most significant parts of his reform package. If the kingdom's vast international campaign to spread its intolerant creed had hardened the character of global Islam, they argued, a change in the other direction would have the opposite effect. It was an argument put forward by *New York Times* columnist Thomas Friedman after he interviewed MBS in 2017.

"If this virus of an antipluralistic, misogynistic Islam that came out of Saudi Arabia in 1979 can be reversed by Saudi Arabia, it would drive moderation across the Muslim world and surely be welcomed here where 65 percent of the population is under 30," he wrote.

My take was more restrained. Taming the nastier aspects of Wahhabism was a net benefit, because diminishing intolerance anywhere was a win. And I didn't doubt that many of the kingdom's youth would welcome the change. But I doubted that it would echo abroad in the way Friedman suggested. The kingdom no longer invested in foreign missionary activity as it had in the past, and it no longer held the same prominence in global Islam. Salafism, the hyperconservative trend to which Wahhabism belongs, was alive and well in many Islamic countries with little connection to Saudi Arabia. And the continued ferocity of Al Qaeda and the Islamic State, which had borrowed from Wahhabism before going their own way, showed they could thrive without it.

The topic reminded me of a young cleric I had met at a dinner in Jeddah who worked for the security services. He was privately critical of the deep conservatism in the religious establishment and said it had impeded the country's development. One of his jobs was to give religious lectures to security officers, and he was saddened by how often they asked whether wearing uniforms was forbidden, based on a Wahhabi injunction against "resembling infidels."

Wearing a uniform was fine, he said, but the prevalence of the question among those trusted to defend the kingdom showed that Saudi Arabia had lost control of the effects of its own teachings.

"It's like in those American movies when they invent a robot and then they lose control and it attacks them and the remote control stops working," he said.

MBS was taking charge of the remote, but the robot had already gone its own way.

CHARM TOURS

_____

After President Donald Trump concluded his visit to Saudi Arabia, an unusual accessory showed up in a hallway at the U.S. Embassy in Riyadh: one orb, slightly used. The Saudis had noticed that Americans visiting their new counter-extremism center loved taking pictures with their hands on the glowing ball. So they let them have it. It sat in an embassy hallway for a number of days, where diplomats passing by would pose for photos. Someone apparently worried that the photos would make their way online and cause a scandal, so the orb was hidden away in embassy storage.

Trump's visit to Riyadh had laid the foundations for a strong relationship with MBS that won the young prince American support for his initiatives, kept alive by the administration's hopes that he would back its policies in the Middle East and pipe Saudi cash into the American economy. Trump also grew fond of the idea that the United States' Arab allies, led by Saudi Arabia, could bankroll American military activities in the Middle East. The thinking was that the United States was keeping them safe, so shouldn't they pay for it?

At one point, Trump tasked members of his National Security Council with calculating the cost of the U.S. military presence in Syria so he could pass Saudi Arabia and its neighbors the bill. They came back with an estimate of about $4 billion. When the White House presented its plan, the Gulf countries avoided committing the funds, and State Department officials instead pushed for money to stabilize parts of Syria liberated from the Islamic State. That money did eventually come through—$100 million from Saudi Arabia and $50 million from the UAE. But Trump's multibillion-dollar ask eventually faded away.

The hope for assistance went both ways. MBS was looking to the West for help with the Vision, and in the spring of 2018 set off on two ambitious tours to pitch his plans—and himself—as the future of Saudi Arabia.

He landed first in the United Kingdom, where Saud al-Qahtani, his media czar, had paid millions of pounds to plaster the crown prince's face on billboards, highway overpasses, and the sides of black taxi cabs, next to inspiring messages: "He is creating a new, vibrant Saudi Arabia," "He is opening Saudi Arabia to the world," and "He is empowering Saudi Arabian women." The Brits, unaccustomed to such cults of personality, groaned.

He sat for an interview with *The Telegraph* newspaper, which called him "the epitome of a human dynamo," and he ran through talking points he would hit repeatedly during his travels.

"We believe that Saudi Arabia needs to be part of the global economy," he said, adding that after Britain's exit from the European Union, or Brexit, it would have "huge opportunities" thanks to Vision 2030.

He spoke of the special bond between the two kingdoms, recalling the British army captain William Shakespear, who had befriended MBS's grandfather. He acknowledged that Saudi Arabia could improve its human rights record.

"We do not have the best human rights record in the world, but we are getting better, and we have come a long way in a short time," he said.

In London, he had private meetings with the heads of MI5 and MI6 and attended a meeting of the National Security Council—a rare honor for a foreign visitor. He even met the Queen, and his aides distributed photos of MBS in an Arabian headdress and brown cloak towering over Queen Elizabeth II, in a purple dress with a pearl necklace and diamond brooch. The trip lasted only a few days, but the Saudis signed about $2.1 billion worth of deals, including for oil and fighter jets.

Soon after, MBS touched down in Washington in a 747 with the phrase "God Bless You" written on the nose. His three-week visit to the United States was so sweeping in ambition that Saudi watchers had to go back decades to find another event that even came close. Despite Saudi Arabia's long relationship with the United States, the kingdom was not popular with most Americans. Fifty-five percent of respondents to a recent Gallup poll viewed it unfavorably, as compared to 41 percent who expressed favorable views.

But MBS's team found no shortage of powerful Americans willing to fit the crown prince into their schedules as he traveled to five states and the District of Columbia, meeting with giants of government, finance, technology, and entertainment. It was a remarkable tour that took him to the White House, Wall Street, Harvard, MIT, Lockheed Martin, Google, and Facebook and got him sit-downs with three former American presidents, Henry Kissinger, and Oprah Winfrey.

His team apparently realized that their billboard campaign in the UK had flopped, so they changed approach, pushing MBS in the American media. His face appeared on the cover of *TIME* magazine, and a headline on its website asked, "Should We Believe Him?" *60 Minutes* got exclusive access inside the kingdom for a glowing segment in which reporter Norah O'Donnell chatted with women at a driving school and let MBS make his case to American viewers.

O'Donnell asked whether women and men were equal, and MBS said, "Absolutely. We are all human beings. There is no difference."

He defended the Ritz crackdown as a necessarily harsh measure to stamp out corruption and acknowledged his personal wealth.

"I am a rich person. I am not a poor person. I am not Gandhi or Mandela," he said.

O'Donnell was impressed and asked if he planned to become king and rule for the next five decades. For the first time in public, he said yes.

"Only God knows how long one will live, if one would live fifty years or not," he said. "But if things go their normal ways, then that is to be expected."

Only "death" could stop him.

The segment aired during prime time on Sunday night at the start of his visit—a coup for MBS and his team. But the complexities of Saudi Arabia lurked below the fanfare. While in Riyadh, a female producer had been accosted by the religious police, who yelled at her through a megaphone to cover her hair. An aide to MBS called it progress.

"About three years ago, you probably would have been arrested," he said.

In Washington, President Trump brought reporters into the Oval Office to introduce MBS as "a very great friend and a big purchaser of equipment and lots of other things."

To brief the president before the visit, officials had prepared posters with photos of military equipment the Saudis planned to buy and their price tags. The posters had not been intended for public display, and one administration official told me they looked like "a middle school science project." But Trump liked them so much that he pulled them out for MBS in front of the TV cameras. Lifting a blue poster, he read off the price tags: $3 billion for fighter jets; $533 million for helicopters; $525 million for surveillance equipment.

"That's peanuts for you," Trump said. "Should have increased it."

MBS laughed and shook his head.

Trump continued: $880 million for tanks; $645 million for missiles; $6 billion for frigates; $889 million for another kind of missiles; $63 million for artillery.

Then Trump picked up a second, yellow poster and kept going: $13 billion for a Thaad missiles defense system; $3.8 billion for Hercules airplanes; $1.2 billion for Bradley Fighting Vehicles; $1.4 billion for Poseidon aircraft.

"We understand each other," Trump said. "Saudi Arabia is a very wealthy nation, and they're going to give the United States some of that wealth, hopefully, in the form of jobs, in the form of the purchase of the finest military equipment anywhere in the world."

MBS headed to New York, where the Saudi delegation spent millions of dollars to rent out the Plaza Hotel near Central Park and hang a massive Saudi flag over the entrance. He met with former Secretary of State John Kerry, the secretary general of the United Nations, reporters and editors at *The New York Times* and *The Wall Street Journal*, and had coffee at Starbucks with former New York mayor and fellow billionaire Mike Bloomberg.

He flew to Seattle to meet Bill Gates and Jeff Bezos, two of the world's richest men, then to Silicon Valley, where his entourage rented out the Four Seasons in Palo Alto and he visited Facebook, Apple, and Google.

In Los Angeles, his entourage took over yet another Four Seasons while MBS slept at a mansion nearby. The kingdom sponsored a film festival in a theater owned by the Academy of Motion Picture Arts and Sciences, where guests sipped virgin cocktails and ate dates from the Saudi desert.

There were scattered protests, including at the Beverly Hills office of the William Morris Endeavor talent agency, which was expecting a $400 million investment from Saudi Arabia. Mayor Eric Garcetti of Los Angeles expressed concerns over human rights and the humanitarian crisis in Yemen. But few others raised such matters with MBS.

Richard Branson of the Virgin Group discussed space travel with MBS in the California desert. Movie and television producer Brian Grazer hosted a glitzy dinner in the prince's honor attended by Amazon's Jeff Bezos, Snapchat's Evan Spiegel, and Disney's Bob Iger. Another evening, Rupert Murdoch hosted him in Bel-Air with other film and TV executives, directors James Cameron and Ridley Scott, and actors Michael Douglas, Morgan Freeman, and Dwayne "The Rock" Johnson.

Johnson later wrote that it had been "a fun night and great to hear his deep rooted, yet modern views on the world and certainly the positive growth of his country." Johnson planned to visit Saudi Arabia and "bring my finest tequila to share with his Royal Highness and family."

Then it was off to Texas, where MBS saw oil executives and wrote a message in marker on a piece of a Saudi satellite that was to be blasted into space. He also, with no explanation, showed up two hours late for lunch with *not one* former president George Bush, but *two*—the elder of whom was 93, in a wheelchair, and would pass away seven months later.

The three-week trip was many things: a visual tour of American power; a branding coup that introduced powerful Americans to MBS; and a Saudi plea for broad American engagement in the kingdom's future. Despite the impressive itinerary, only one major deal was inked—a joint venture with Japan's SoftBank on solar power—but MBS generated enthusiasm in Washington and among other elites, opening possibilities for future collaboration.

The trip made clear MBS's deep admiration for the United States and its role in Saudi Arabia.

"We have been influenced by you in the U.S. a lot," he had said the year before. "Not because anybody exerted pressure on us—if anyone puts pressure on us, we go the other way. But if you put a movie in the cinema and I watch it, I will be influenced." Without that American influence, he said, "we would have ended up like North Korea."

The warm welcome MBS received also showed that the disturbing events that occurred under his regime on the other side of the planet—the Yemen intervention, the arrest campaigns, the coerced resignation of Saad Hariri, the Ritz crackdown—had not affected how powerful Americans viewed him.

At least not yet.

WHILE IN THE United States, MBS spoke with Jeffrey Goldberg of *The Atlantic* magazine, the same journalist to whom President Obama had criticized Saudi religious influence abroad. Goldberg, an American Jew who served in the Israeli army, asked about Israel and the prince answered that both Palestinians and Israelis "have the right to their own land."

He said the Saudis had no religious problem with Jews and expressed surprising admiration for the Jewish State.

"Israel is a big economy compared to their size, and it's a growing economy, and of course there are a lot of interests we share with Israel," he said. "If there is peace, there would be a lot of interest between Israel and the Gulf Cooperation Council countries and countries like Egypt and Jordan."

Years before, Saudi Arabia had endorsed the two-state solution to the Israeli-Palestinian conflict, but when its leaders spoke about Israel at all, it was to blast its treatment of the Palestinians, not to imagine the Jewish state's possible political and economic relations with its Arab neighbors.

Saudi animosity toward the Zionist project in Palestine dated back to MBS's grandfather, whose help President Franklin D. Roosevelt sought in 1945 for the creation of a Jewish homeland. King Abdulaziz rejected the argument that the Jews needed a country in the Middle East because of their treatment by the Nazis.

"Make the enemy and the oppressor pay; that is how we Arabs wage war," the king told FDR. "What injury have Arabs done to the Jews of Europe? It is the 'Christian' Germans who stole their homes and lives. Let the Germans pay."

After the founding of Israel in 1948, the Saudis consistently stood with the Palestinians and against Israel, doling out aid to Palestinian groups and joining the OPEC oil embargo in 1973 to pressure Israel's allies during the Yom Kippur War. That sent fuel prices in the United States soaring and caused a crisis in the relationship with Saudi Arabia.

In 1967, King Faisal created a committee to raise money for Palestinians fighting against Israel. Its budget grew over the years, from $5 million dollars in 1968 to $45 million in 1982. To head it, he named his half brother, Salman, MBS's father and the future king.

Despite his father's long involvement in the Palestinian cause, it became clear that MBS viewed Israel and its conflict with the Palestinians differently, for a number of reasons. He was younger, his political outlook shaped more by the Arab Spring than by the Arab-Israeli wars and the Palestinian intifadas. When he rose to power and looked around the region, he saw three threats, and Israel was not among them. The first were the jihadists of Al Qaeda and the Islamic State. The second was the Muslim Brotherhood, the transnational Islamist movement whose members had sought to gain power during the Arab Spring. The third was Iran, which MBS talked about constantly. It, too, had benefited from the chaos of the Arab Spring by using militias and proxy forces to increase its influence in Yemen, Syria, Iraq, and Lebanon. MBS's hostility toward Iran was political, ideological, and religious, which he said made dialogue impossible.

"What interests are there between me and them? How do I reach an understanding with them?" he said in another interview. "Where are the meeting points where I can reach an understanding with this regime? They are almost nonexistent."

Seeking to hit home the Iranian threat, MBS compared it to that of the Nazis, telling Goldberg, "I believe the Iranian Supreme Leader makes Hitler look good."

The comparison surprised Goldberg, but MBS stuck to it. Hitler tried to conquer Europe, he said, "but the Supreme Leader is trying to conquer the world. He believes he owns the world. They are both evil guys. He is the Hitler of the Middle East."

In other interviews, MBS accused Iran of seeking to take over Mecca.

"We are an essential target of the Iranian regime," he said. "We will not wait until the battle is in Saudi Arabia. Instead, we'll work so that the battle is for them in Iran."

So when MBS looked for other regional powers who shared his view, he found Israel, setting in motion a major regional shift.

"MBS comes from a generation of Saudi leaders that doesn't have a visceral, emotional attachment to the Palestinian cause," said Rob Malley, a senior White House official in the Obama administration who continued to meet with the prince afterward. MBS, Malley said, considered the Israel-Palestinian conflict "an annoying irritant—a problem to be overcome rather than a conflict to be fairly resolved."

MBS found other things to admire in Israel: its economy, its military, and its intelligence services. Looking to the future, given the proximity of NEOM to Israel and its dynamic technology sector, it was hard to imagine that MBS had not considered an eventual role for the Jewish State in his planned city's future. Also pushing MBS toward Israel was his interest in pleasing not only Trump, but Kushner, who was working on a plan to break the Israeli-Palestinian impasse and counting on Saudi help to do so.

While in New York, MBS had an off-the-books meeting with pro-Israel American Jewish leaders. The Americans were sworn to silence over the discussion, but a number of leaks suggested that MBS surprised them by bashing the Palestinian leadership. One credible report cited him criticizing them for rejecting previous peace offers, saying they should "agree to come to the table or shut up and stop complaining."

Later that year, he welcomed a delegation of American evangelicals in his palace in Riyadh that was led by Joel C. Rosenberg, a Jewish author who also holds Israeli citizenship and whose sons served in the Israeli army. One of them, in fact, was the delegation's note taker. Such a meeting would have been unthinkable for previous Saudi leaders. The only portion of their two-hour talk that MBS asked his guests to keep private was about Israel and the peace process.

"He was quite candid, quite surprising in some of the things he said," Rosenberg told me. "But he asked that that not be for public consumption."

In public, MBS was more guarded, and his father, King Salman, reiterated the kingdom's traditional support for the Palestinians. MBS and his aides have said that any future moves with Israel depend on a peace agreement, and MBS called the Trump administration's recognition of Jerusalem as Israel's capital "painful." But the fact that the likely next ruler of Saudi Arabia sees Israel not as a foe, but as a legitimate neighbor with shared political and economic interests could lead to a lasting realignment of the Middle East.

BLACK PANTHER

―――――――――

"OKAY. COME DRIVE now," a driving instructor told the architecture student.

"Oh my God," the student replied.

She climbed into the driver's seat of a car, pulled the seatbelt across her abaya, found the pedals, eased off the hand brake, and put the car in drive. She took a breath, lifted her foot from the brake, and her eyes widened as the car crept forward.

"Is this okay?" asked the student, Rahaf Alzahrani.

"Yes, it's okay," the instructor said.

As the end of the driving ban approached, the kingdom and its women prepared for a sea change in Saudi society. Women's universities planned to open driving schools, and Ford, Nissan, and Jaguar launched ads targeting what they hoped would be a flood of women drivers (and car buyers). According to one estimate, car sales would grow by 9 percent each year through 2025 and 20 percent of Saudi women would be driving by 2020. The ride-hailing company Uber planned to recruit women, and dealerships set aside women-only shopping hours.

The lifting of the ban would change Saudi society in myriad ways in the years ahead, facilitating women's entry into the workforce and giving them greater control over their social, economic, and even romantic lives. But first, most needed to learn to drive.

On my last visit to Saudi Arabia in the spring of 2018, I spent a day at a women's university in Jeddah where the Ford Motor Company Fund was giving a drivers' safety workshop. For many students, it was their first chance to get behind the wheel.

The excitement was tangible. The young women, dressed in abayas with personal fashion touches such as white tennis shoes or colored trim, sat through a talk on safety, with warnings about how many car accidents were caused by texting at the wheel. Then they broke up for hands-on experiences. At one station, they wore goggles that blurred their vision to simulate drowsiness from medication or booze, the latter not much of a problem in Saudi Arabia because of the alcohol ban.

But the real action was in the parking lot, where the cars were. Groups of students piled in and the instructors explained the features: the gear shift, the gas and brake pedals, the turn signals, the windshield wipers. One student accidentally sprayed the windshield, startling herself and making her friends laugh. The instructor told her to hold down the brake pedal and fire the ignition. The car roared to life.

"All right!" the student said. Her friends clapped.

The issue of women driving had divided Saudi Arabia for decades, but the young women in the workshop were busy looking forward and had set their sights on specific cars. One wanted a Mercedes, "like my dad." Another wanted an Audi, "a strong car." They said driving would allow them to get to school and back without depending on Indian or Pakistani drivers or coordinating transport with male relatives.

"I don't want to drive just to drive," one student told me. "I want to be able to do my daily routine."

She hated waiting for someone to drop her off at the gym in the morning. The best part of driving would be "feeling more freedom."

Most of the students planned to get licenses as soon as possible, while a few would wait to see how the first women fared. Saudi Arabia had notoriously dangerous roads. One report said that car accidents had killed over nine thousand people in 2016. But the women were undeterred. Alzahrani, the architecture student, had ridden Jet Skis in the Red Sea and motorcycles in the desert, but had never driven a car.

"I don't know where the brake is and where the gas is," she told me.

But she managed to weave through a series of cones before hitting the brakes hard at a stop sign, jolting her passengers. Then she let up on the brakes again and finished the course, arriving at the end with a graceful stop.

"Yay me!" she said.

Her friends applauded.

She was smitten.

"It was so amazing. I loved it!" she said. "It felt good to be behind the wheel."

AROUND THAT TIME, another major change was coming soon: the opening of commercial cinemas. The kingdom's few theaters had been shut down after 1979, and while most Saudis had satellite television and could watch whatever they wanted at home, movie consumption remained private. Now movie theaters were to open in the kingdom's malls and cities, bringing public entertainment to the masses.

Like the rest of the entertainment push, the move was cultural and economic. The government predicted that movie theaters would contribute more than $24 billion to the economy and create thirty thousand jobs by 2030, when the kingdom planned to have three hundred cinemas and two thousand screens.

To mark the new era, the government held a glitzy opening for the first commercial movie house in Riyadh. In a hastily converted hall in the capital's half-built financial district, the screening was by invitation only, with government ministers, Saudi social media figures, and at least one princess. The organizers sought to give the event a sense of Hollywood glamour, with red carpets, a jazz band, concession stands selling popcorn and soda, and mimes snapping photos with antique cameras.

The featured movie could not have been more appropriate: *Black Panther*, the Marvel blockbuster about a young prince who takes charge of an isolated kingdom dependent on a valuable natural resource. During the movie, the hero, T'Challa, tangles with international arms dealers and fends off a challenge for the throne from a relative, Erik Killmonger, before opening up his kingdom for the good of the world. The plot, in many ways, sounded familiar.

AMC Entertainment put on the screening, and its CEO, Adam Aron, told me he had decided to bring the company to Saudi Arabia after meeting Mohammed bin Salman in his palace. The company was aiming to open a hundred movie theaters in ten years.

I was dying to know whether MBS had seen *Black Panther* or chosen it for the inaugural screening, given its similarities to his own story, but Aron dodged the question.

"It's a great movie, very popular with audiences, and we thought it would make everyone happy," he said. "What movie would you have picked?"

MBS CLEARLY WANTED to be Saudi Arabia's T'Challa, but his deputies were increasingly acting like Erik Killmonger. While the prince was off charming Hollywood and Silicon Valley, his team had ramped up their activities against those they perceived as threats to the kingdom—and to MBS. The coordinated social media attacks continued, and the team unmasked and arrested Saudis who ran sarcastic Twitter accounts, just as they had promised to do. The team went after people in the real world, too, and the hammer fell particularly hard on one charismatic couple who had been otherwise well placed to benefit from the kingdom's new direction.

Since 2013, I had followed Loujain Al-Hathloul, the young, self-declared feminist and driving activist whose father had filmed her driving home from the airport during my first trip to the kingdom. Her reputation in the kingdom had grown since.

She was the fourth of six siblings and had been raised in Jeddah before spending a few years in France and returning to Riyadh for high school. Later, while studying in Canada on a government scholarship, she began posting videos online criticizing the kingdom's social restrictions. Her complaints about the religious police and her refusal to cover her hair made her a lightning rod back home. Liberals cheered her frankness, conservatives found her dangerous, but they all followed her. After she graduated and moved to the United Arab Emirates to work for a media company, her profile grew.

Along the way, a funny Saudi man who had lived in Texas and was trying to launch a career as a comedian caught her eye. Nicknamed the "Seinfeld of Saudi Arabia," Fahad Albutairi did stand-up comedy and appeared in YouTube videos while developing a large following on social media. As it turned out, I had come across him during my first visit to the kingdom as well. He had been one of the crooners in the "No Woman, No Drive" video.

Al-Hathloul liked his style and got in touch with him through social media. They began chatting, fell in love, and got married in 2014. A week later, the Saudi authorities arrested Al-Hathloul as she tried to drive her car into the kingdom from the United Arab Emirates to protest the driving ban. She was jailed for seventy-three days and referred to a court that normally handled national security cases. Her husband stood by her, and she was finally released without charge the month after Salman became king.

MBS's talk about opening up the kingdom had initially made her optimistic about the future, and she and her husband lived a rare public Saudi love story, both proudly declaring themselves the other's spouse in their bios on Twitter, where they had hundreds of thousands of followers.

Al-Hathloul remained an outspoken, controversial voice, and her detention gave her an international profile. A photo of her with former president Mary Robinson of Ireland and the actress Meghan Markle, who would marry into the British royal family, was published in *Vanity Fair*. Three years in a row, *Arabian Business* magazine included her in its rankings of the hundred most powerful Arab women, giving her spot number three in 2015.

Foreign journalists sought her out, and in 2016 she appeared in a documentary by PBS's *Frontline* called "Saudi Arabia Uncovered" that was widely criticized by Saudis as misrepresenting the kingdom. Al-Hathloul regretted taking part, feeling that the program had cherry-picked her comments, and was so heavily attacked online that she posted a declaration of loyalty to the kingdom on her website. Responding to those who accused her of seeking fame or political asylum abroad, she said she had turned down a job in Canada to live in the Gulf region, even though her activist reputation had hindered prospects for both her and her husband.

She enrolled in a master's program at the Abu Dhabi branch of the Sorbonne and was working to start a talent agency to help Arab artists like her husband pursue international opportunities. But the authorities arrested her at the airport when she arrived home for a visit in 2017. During her interrogation, they asked why she always criticized the kingdom. She took it as a message that they wanted her to shut up.

But when Saudi Arabia announced in the fall of 2017 that it would lift the driving ban and that cinemas were on the way, she and her husband were overjoyed.

"She was so enthusiastic about it at the time," her sister Lina told me. "She was saying, '2018 will be a very nice year for us. It will be our year.'"

She kept campaigning. Once the driving ban was on its way out, she and other activists redoubled their efforts on another target, the kingdom's so-called "guardianship laws," which gave women legal rights similar to those of minors. Every Saudi woman had to have a male "guardian"—a father, a husband, a brother, or sometimes even a son—whose permission was needed for the woman to get a passport, travel abroad, work, or do certain medical procedures. Al-Hathloul joined online campaigns to promote the issue, and she was invited to observe a United Nations review of Saudi Arabia's efforts to eliminate discrimination against women.

At the U.N. conference, the Saudi government delegation said the kingdom was fulfilling its responsibilities. Al-Hathloul felt they were sugarcoating reality and posted videos of their statements on Twitter, showing the Saudi delegates denying the existence of guardianship and claiming that Saudi women were free to choose their spouses, cancel their marriage contracts, and live and work where they chose. In one video, a delegate said citizens could use cyberspace "in a very free manner to express their criticism, advice, or views to government agencies."

A month later, she was driving to the university in Abu Dhabi when her car was surrounded by police. She was handcuffed, blindfolded, arrested, and flown back to Saudi Arabia, where the authorities held her incommunicado. Around that time, her husband was in Jordan acting in a new project when security forces showed up at his hotel room, arrested him, and flew him back to Saudi Arabia, where he, too, was detained.

The couple were released a few days later but banned from travel. Albutairi, as one of Saudi Arabia's best known entertainers, was invited to the screening of *Black Panther*, where he hung out at a bar that served virgin cocktails. He told few people what had happened to him, but one night, Al-Hathloul told a gathering of female friends about her ordeal, suspecting that she might be detained again. She worried about the stress her activism put on her husband, who had never set out to challenge the government.

"He is not used to this," she told them. "I am."

Her premonition was correct. A few weeks before the driving ban was lifted, security forces banged on the door at her family's home in Riyadh, found her in her room, and took her away like a criminal.

At the time, the government was working to prevent activists who had campaigned against the ban from taking credit for its end. Security officers ordered them not to speak to journalists or to comment about the issue on social media. Before the big day, more than a dozen people had been arrested. They included women who had defied the ban, men who had supported them, and three women who had participated in the 1990 driving protest, including Madeha Alajroush, the photographer whose photo archive had been torched decades before. It was unclear why those activists were arrested while others were not, but some of the detainees had been working to open a shelter for abused women and girls. Some were released with travel bans, while the Saudi news media set out to destroy the reputations of the others.

When the Saudi government did not want to release the names of people it had detained, such as those held in the Ritz, it cited privacy rules and Sharia law's injunction on defamation. The activists were not afforded those protections. Their names and photos were published with red stamps branding them "traitors." One newspaper quoted anonymous "analysts" saying that seven of them were being tried on charges that could carry prison terms of up to twenty years or even the death penalty.

The new wave of arrests, on top of those the year before, spread fear among Saudis who had pushed for change in the past, and those who had avoided detention mostly clammed up, hoping it would blow over. A Saudi cartoonist captured the mood with a drawing of two men in prison.

"I'm jailed for armed robbery. You?" one said.

"WhatsApp," the other replied.

During her detention, Al-Hathloul's marriage to Albutairi collapsed. He had deleted the Twitter account where he had identified himself as her "proud husband" and disappeared from view, an entertainment pioneer who vanished from public life just as Saudi entertainment was taking off.

The arrests cast a cloud over the end of the driving ban, and more arrests followed. During a trip to Riyadh, *New York Times* columnist Roger Cohen interviewed Hatoon al-Fassi, a scholar of women's history who had long been a go-to source about the status of Saudi women. She told him that the government had ordered her not to publicly celebrate the ban's end because it did not want to show that activism worked.

Cohen summarized her take on MBS like this: "The crown prince is genuine. He's put his finger on what is keeping Saudi Arabia back. He lacks wisdom, especially on Qatar. There are lots of red lines, new and old, constant censorship, calls to blacklist any 'anti-Saudi' media. The centralization of power is alarming. Changes have occurred but have not been framed in law, which makes them vulnerable."

"I am hopeful," al-Fassi told Cohen. "Hopeful that ten years from now, we will have a public sphere that is more humane and safe for women, freed of the guardianship's abuses, and that will be good for the Saudi economy."

She was arrested soon afterward.

THREE WEEKS BEFORE the driving ban was lifted, the kingdom issued the first driver's licenses to women. The government distributed a short video showing a woman named Ahlam Al Thunayan wearing a black abaya and receiving her license from a uniformed police officer. Nine other women also received licenses that day, and the kingdom sent a press release hailing it as a "historic moment."

On June 24, 2018, the ban was officially lifted, as promised.

"Finally!" Prince Alwaleed bin Talal wrote on Twitter with a video of him during a drive around town with his daughter and granddaughters at 12:01 A.M. His movements had been restricted since the Ritz, but he had nothing but praise for MBS.

"There is no doubt that the thoughts of my brother Mohammed bin Salman led to this great result," he said. "Women have now taken off, gotten their freedom."

The kingdom worked to get credit for the change while heading off broader discussions of women's rights. In France, a Saudi woman race car driver did a lap at the French Grand Prix. A few days before, she had received her Saudi license, and journalists watched her take an inaugural lap in Riyadh, although they were told that she would not comment on women's rights. A visiting American journalist realized that the driving students she was interviewing were in fact the instructors who were acting like students. Once the ruse was uncovered, the instructors pressed students into taking their first lesson so the journalists could follow along.

In any case, the dam against women driving had broken, and future battles over the issue would not be fought with the government, but between women and their male relatives—or neighbors. Saudi newspapers covered the ordeal of a woman who had received a license and begun driving her late father's car to work while enduring insults from guys in the neighborhood. One morning, she found her car on fire outside her house. The police opened an arson case and arrested two suspects, and a municipal official gave the woman a car to replace the one she had lost.

But such incidents were rare. If significant opposition to women driving remained in Saudi society, it did not immediately surface.

MEANWHILE, LIFE GOT worse for the detained activists. After her arrest, Al-Hathloul was transferred to the Dhahban Prison in Jeddah, but a few days later, a group of men came at night, put her in the trunk of a car, and drove her to an unknown facility nearby. There, she and at least two other women were held by members of the Rapid Intervention Group.

The women were kept in small rooms whose windows had been covered. They were taken downstairs frequently for interrogation and torture by men who seemed more interested in humiliating them than in getting information. They were hit, sexually harassed, and given electric shocks. When Al-Hathloul screamed, they poured water over her mouth. Sometimes, members oversaw her torture, threatening to rape her, kill her, and throw her body in the sewer, where it would never be found. If she did not end up dead, they told her, she would go to prison for twenty years for treason.

During Ramadan, the Muslim holy month, men tortured her through the night, forcing Al-Hathloul to eat after the sun came up and the mandatory fast began. She asked if they would keep eating all day.

"No one is above us, not even God," one of the men told her.

Another prisoner was Aziza al-Yousef, a 60-year-old retired computer science professor and rights activist who had been arrested at her home by armed security agents and told her family she would return in a few hours. She did not. She, too, was beaten and electrocuted, and an associate who saw her later was shocked by how much weight she had lost. She twitched and had black bruises on her legs.

With them as well was Eman Al Nafjan, the linguistics professor and blogger who in 2013 had laughed with me about her Bangladeshi driver. She had spent the subsequent years campaigning against the driving ban, and described the moment the government had announced its end as bittersweet. She recalled the "unnecessary sacrifices" of so many men and women to defy it over the decades, but was so happy it was gone that she laughed at jokes about the havoc women drivers would cause on the roads. Still, she concluded, only ending the guardianship system would make Saudi women truly equal.

Her treatment during her detention was so harsh that she tried to kill herself, and her captors had to summon medics to treat her.

For weeks, Al-Hathloul's family had no idea where she was. Then she called and told them she was in a "hotel." Everything was fine and the place was nice, she said, but she skirted their questions, so they didn't know what to believe. Maybe the government just wanted the activists out of sight to manage media coverage as the driving ban was lifted, they thought.

After about a month, the women were moved back to Dhahban Prison, where the abuse stopped and their families could visit. The first time Al-Hathloul's family saw her, they noticed that she had trouble walking and was shaking uncontrollably. When they asked, she blamed the air-conditioning. They bought her a croissant and realized that she could barely lift it to her mouth. They asked if she was hurt and she snapped back, "I'm okay. Do you want me to show you my body so that you believe me?"

During a later visit, after the first reports of abuse in the Ritz, her family pressed her for information and she broke down, telling them what had happened and showing them the black marks on her thighs that she said were from electric shocks. The government would later charge her with a number of crimes and deny that she had ever been mistreated.

OH CANADA

BEFORE MOHAMMED BIN Salman's official visit to the United Kingdom, Jamal Khashoggi published a column in *The Washington Post* with an old friend, the writer and historian Robert Lacey, about what the young prince could learn from the British monarchy (limit royal privilege, accept criticism, listen to the people). The pair published a second piece while MBS was in the United States, suggesting that MBS visit Detroit to see the value of investing in existing cities over building new ones, like NEOM.

In another column, Khashoggi dismissed MBS's claim that there had been no extremism in Saudi Arabia before 1979 as "revisionist history." MBS was right to go after "ultra-conservative religious forces," but was wrong to replace them with a "new radicalism" that "is just as intolerant of dissent."

He sent the column to his American friend, Maggie Mitchell Salem, to review before he submitted it to the *Post*. She accused him of letting MBS off easy.

KHASHOGGI: I feel like I'm a bipolar. One moment, I feel I should go for it. Another, I think of family and say, 'Is it worth it?'
MITCHELL SALEM: You are doing nothing more than stating facts. . . . And that nonsense you added to try and send a message that you're with him?! The paragraph on the new radicalism—I'm cutting it. . . .
KHASHOGGI: Please don't. It's a balancing act.

MITCHELL SALEM: You are balanced. This is all in your head. You are trying to have a conversation with a man who issues orders and jails your friends. #insane.

KHASHOGGI: It's also for my readers who like my balanced criticism.

Khashoggi won. The line stayed in.

In yet another column, he attacked the arrests of the driving activists, saying they sought to show Saudis that "activism of any sort has to be within the government" and that "everyone must stick to the party line." The social reforms could not come "at the expense of the public space once available to us for discussion and debate."

But he was confronting the pains of exile. He had friends, but was far from relatives. He missed the familiar streets of Jeddah and Medina, the social gatherings with fellow Saudis, his aunt's cooking. The online onslaughts continued and thoughts of his friends in prison haunted him. He had nightmares, "full of their voices and silhouettes."

KHASHOGGI: 2 of my closest friends were arrested.
MITCHELL SALEM: WHAT?!? MORE?!?
KHASHOGGI: More and more.
MITCHELL SALEM: WTF!?!?
KHASHOGGI: He can't control himself.

She told him to channel his anger into his writing.

KHASHOGGI: And what would happen? Anyone care?
MITCHELL SALEM: STOP!! Many do. And NOT writing means he wins. Sigh.
KHASHOGGI: I'm so down.

During trips to Istanbul, another old friend, Ayman Nour, who had run for president in Egypt years before and fled the country after President Abdel-Fattah el-Sisi came to power, tried to convince Khashoggi that he was a dissident, a term Khashoggi rejected. "A person who is not fixable cannot be fixed," Nour told him of

MBS. Khashoggi disagreed, saying it was his job to point out the young leader's mistakes.

Khashoggi resisted the dissident label with others, too, arguing that he supported MBS but wanted the freedom of expression that existed in monarchies such as Jordan and Kuwait.

"I think it's reasonable," Khashoggi said. "I'm not an extremist. And I disagree with Saudis who are calling for regime change and stuff like that. It's just ridiculous. We don't need that in Saudi Arabia. I believe in the system—I just want a reformed system."

Over time, Khashoggi visualized a new path to push for the changes he wanted to see in the Arab world from abroad. He felt that few Arab intellectuals understood how their countries' economies worked, so one idea was a website that would publish Western economic reports translated into Arabic. He planned to found an organization called Democracy for the Arab World Now, or DAWN, that would press for political reform. As of June 2018, he was refining the concept and looking for funding.

His writings drew the attention of other thinkers from the Middle East, and the Center for the Study of Islam and Democracy, a think tank in Washington, gave him its Muslim Democrat of the Year award. In his award speech, he said democracy was under attack in the Arab world, not just by radical Islamists, but also by so-called liberals who supported dictators.

He called on Arab writers, intellectuals, and politicians to stand up for democracy when speaking with foreign powers who he feared had begun to believe the "racist" idea that "Arabs are not ready for democracy."

He was not a revolutionary, arguing instead that democracy would improve governance. The region's monarchies, such as Saudi Arabia, Morocco, and Jordan, needed accountability to ensure wise decision-making, while the republics, such as Egypt, Yemen, Iraq, and Syria, needed democracy to stop conflicts by balancing power between tribes, sects, and political parties.

Someone asked about MBS, and Khashoggi said he wished the crown prince well, but felt he needed checks on his power.

"The prevailing thought that is leading authoritarian regimes today is that 'We are able to lead, we don't need the hindrance of a parliament, the hindrance of committees, we know what is good for the people,'" Khashoggi said. "If it succeeds, we the people will say, 'Thank you.' If they fail, we'll just go quiet."

ON JUNE 21, 2018, I received a text message on my phone that read, in Arabic, "Ben Hubbard and the story of the Saudi royal family." It contained a link to the website arabnews365.com and struck me as fishy. I searched the Web for an article with that title and found nothing. I asked the editor of *Arab News* if his newspaper had sent it. No, he said. It was not their website. The website, in fact, didn't exist.

Had I clicked on the link, it could have let in a proverbial Trojan horse, giving the hackers full access to my phone—my contacts, chat histories, passwords, microphone, and camera, allowing them to spy on me and eavesdrop on my conversations. It was a terrifying prospect. I didn't click on the link, and so didn't think the hackers were inside my phone, but the mere attempt suggested that the stakes of reporting on Saudi Arabia and MBS had gone up.

At least four others were targeted around the same time: two prominent Saudi dissidents in London, a researcher for Amnesty International, and a Saudi activist in Canada named Omar Abdulaziz. Technology researchers with a group called "Citizen Lab" at the University of Toronto concluded that hackers linked to Saudi Arabia had launched the attacks with software from NSO Group, an Israeli company. Some of the targets had fallen into the trap, including Abdulaziz, who had recently struck up a friendship with Khashoggi. (A spokesperson for NSO Group said the company did not comment on specific cases but that its product was "not a tool to target journalists for doing their job or to silence critics.")

Abdulaziz was in his late twenties and had moved to Canada years before on a Saudi government scholarship. While there, he had earned notoriety in the Saudi Twittersphere for his sarcastic posts about the kingdom. The government had canceled his scholarship, so he applied for and received political asylum. Then the gloves came off, and Abdulaziz grew into a one-man opposition news network, posting frequent videos of his bearded face glaring into his phone and making fun of whatever Saudi Arabia or MBS did.

Abdulaziz differed from the older Saudi dissidents who had long operated out of London. He was younger, more Web savvy, and his biting wit attracted young viewers. After Khashoggi fled the kingdom, the older dissidents kept their distance, doubting that such a well-known member of the establishment had truly cut his ties. But Abdulaziz reached out to Khashoggi, and they became friends. Like a concerned uncle, Khashoggi questioned Abdulaziz about skipping classes or keeping erratic hours. In return, Abdulaziz soaked up the journalist's experience and tried to connect him with a younger audience. Once, he told Khashoggi that speaking at Washington think tanks was "elitist" and suggested that he, too, make online videos. Abdulaziz clearly admired his older colleague, and they texted frequently.

ABDULAZIZ: You are today a nation unto yourself.
KHASHOGGI: Not to that degree, but you put a smile on my face.
ABDULAZIZ: May God make it permanent.

The two men discussed their plans. Abdulaziz asked for Khashoggi's advice on a website he planned to launch about Saudi detainees, and Khashoggi wired him $500 to pay the programmer. He told Abdulaziz about DAWN, his planned pro-democracy organization, and asked if Abdulaziz's friends could build its website. Khashoggi told Abdulaziz that it pleased him to have a younger friend who valued his work.

KHASHOGGI: I am happy that you agree with me. Your opinion is important to me as a young person because I am old and life has tired me out and I was scared that they would say that I had betrayed the youth. But as you said, where is the force for change? Sometimes I think of withdrawing to the side, waiting for God's fate to pass, and enjoying private life.

The detentions of the women's rights activists left both men struggling to make sense of MBS's actions.

KHASHOGGI: The arrests are unjustified and they do not help him (that's what logic says). But autocracy does not have a logic, but instead loves power and violence and needs to show it. He's like a beastly creature. Pacman. The more victims he eats, the more he wants. . . .

ABDULAZIZ: It's amazing. Is there a possibility that after he becomes king he will release them all? As a move to show amnesty and mercy?

KHASHOGGI: That is logical, but I no longer believe in analyzing the man's mentality.

Abdulaziz's online commentaries provoked the Royal Court, and in mid-2018, two envoys who said they represented MBS and had been sent by Saud al-Qahtani flew to Canada to see him, bringing with them one of Abdulaziz's brothers to entice him to meet. During meetings in Montreal cafés, the men encouraged him to come home, telling him the kingdom could benefit from his high online profile. If he refused, they said, he could get arrested at the airport and go to jail. But Abdulaziz didn't trust them and refused to go.

In the meantime, he had developed an idea to respond to Saud al-Qahtani's pro-government "flies" with an online force of his own, the "Bees Army." He would distribute American and Canadian SIM cards to Saudis who would use them to set up social media accounts to fight al-Qahtani's "flies." In June, he sent Khashoggi a plan so the journalist could help find funding.

ABDULAZIZ: I sent you a brief thought on the nature of the electronic army. By email.

KHASHOGGI: Great report. I will try to come up with the amount. We need to do something. You know sometimes I am affected by their attacks and I hate tweeting.

ABDULAZIZ: Sometimes they are three or four attacking your account and you feel that all of Saudi Arabia is against you.

Khashoggi later wired him $5,000 to get the project going.

That summer, the government briefly detained two of Abdulaziz's brothers, a move he assumed aimed to silence him. After their release, one brother asked Abdulaziz to tone down his criticism and warned that the government was watching him closely.

"They know everything about you," the brother told him.

DURING THE HOTTER months of 2018, MBS spent increasingly lengthy stretches on his superyacht in the Red Sea, near where he hoped NEOM would rise from the sands. When President Donald Trump needed to talk to him, someone from a U.S. diplomatic mission flew out with a secure call kit to connect the prince with the White House, leading to jockeying among American diplomats over who got to see the big boat.

MBS held other meetings in the area as well, flying out consultants, foreign officials, and businessmen he was courting for projects or investments. Some guests got custom white slippers with S's on the toes for *Serene*, as if the yacht were a hotel. Others came away from those and other meetings baffled by topics the prince had raised. He told some visitors of his interest in neuro-linguistic programming, a pseudoscientific technique aimed at mobilizing the subconscious to increase human potential. He spoke to others about his hopes for biotech, suggesting that in a few decades science would create a pill that would use artificial intelligence to find and fix whatever was wrong with the human body from the inside. His guests left wondering whether the prince was pondering eternal life.

MBS was an imaginative futurist, with a virtually unlimited budget and an army of consultants who were well paid to try to make his dreams come true. His plans for NEOM got bigger and stranger. To cut the desert heat, cloud seeding could make it rain. Scientists could modify the human genome to make people smarter and stronger. Mechanical dinosaurs could populate a Jurassic Park–like attraction. Robotic gladiators could spar for entertainment. At night, a fleet of drones would hoist a giant, artificial moon into the sky. A beach would feature glow-in-the-dark sand.

MBS's authoritarian outlook fueled the vision for NEOM as well. Its plans called for drones and facial recognition technology to track residents at all times.

"This should be an automated city where we can watch everything," wrote the city's board, which MBS headed.

How often consultants or anyone else tried to steer MBS away from his more fanciful ideas was unclear. But he once snapped at a foreign adviser who suggested they lay out a street plan for the city.

"I don't want any roads or pavements," MBS said. "We are going to have flying cars in 2030!"

Sometime that year, his mother, who had been under a form of house arrest since at least 2015, began showing up again at family functions. Other royals noted her presence, but did not dare ask her where she had been, or why. Whatever her situation had been, it appeared that her constraints had been loosened, perhaps because too many people had begun gossiping about what the crown prince had done with his mother.

Princess Fahda was not the only close relative of MBS to run into trouble. The French authorities briefly detained his older half sister, Princess Hassa bint Salman, after a dust-up with a plumber working in her mansion on Avenue Foch in Paris's upscale 16th Arrondissement. The plumber told police she had seen him taking a photo inside the residence and ordered her bodyguard to stop him, yelling, "You must kill him, this dog. He doesn't deserve to live."

The plumber argued that he always took photos so he could put the furniture back when he was done; the princess suspected he planned to sell the images to the tabloids. The bodyguard punched the plumber in the temple, bound his hands, forced him to kiss the princess's feet, and held him for four hours. The princess soon fled to Saudi Arabia, missing her trial in France and staying out of sight, prompting speculation that MBS had put her under house arrest, too. One of his younger brothers, Bandar, was also reported to be under house arrest, but no one was sure why.

THE INTERNATIONAL RESPONSE to the arrest of the driving activists had been muted, but in late summer, the Saudi authorities arrested more women, including a well-known campaigner named Samar Badawi. She was the ex-wife of a lawyer who had been sentenced to prison for setting up a human rights organization and the older sister of Raif Badawi, a blogger who had been sentenced to ten years in prison and a thousand blows with a cane for running a liberal website. He had received his first installment of fifty blows in front of a mosque in Jeddah in 2015, but a video of his caning sparked such outrage that the next installment never happened.

Badawi herself had many international contacts and had received the State Department's International Women of Courage Award in 2012, given to her by Hillary Clinton and Michelle Obama. It was unclear why she was arrested in 2018, given that she had kept a low profile, but once news of her detention got out, the Canadian government spoke up.

"Very alarmed to learn that Samar Badawi, Raif Badawi's sister, has been imprisoned in Saudi Arabia," Foreign Minister Chrystia Freeland wrote on Twitter. "Canada stands together with the Badawi family in this difficult time, and we continue to strongly call for the release of both Raif and Samar Badawi."

The Canadian Embassy in Riyadh issued its own tweet in Arabic calling for the activists to be released.

These appeals were similar to those Western governments had made in the past, which the Saudis usually just ignored. But this time, the response was massive.

The Saudi Foreign Ministry accused Canada of "blatant interference in the internal affairs" of Saudi Arabia, gave the Canadian ambassador to Riyadh twenty-four hours to leave, and threatened to freeze trade and investment. It canceled flights by the Saudi national airline to Canada; pulled the Saudi ambassador from Ottawa; and announced the withdrawal of Saudi students from Canadian universities. That upended the lives of thousands of students, including about eight hundred doing medical residencies at Canadian hospitals. The Saudi Foreign Ministry even raised the specter of a tit-for-tat response, saying that further criticism would give the kingdom the right to interfere in Canada's domestic affairs.

The kingdom rallied its media to demonize Canadians, hosting commentators on air who claimed that Canada persecuted women and airing a montage about "the worst Canadian prisons," saying they had terrible food and medical care, and that 75 percent of prisoners had died before trial between 2015 and 2017, a hugely dubious claim. Some Saudis suddenly voiced support for Quebecois separatists. Others took up the plight of indigenous Canadians.

"They are poor, they are killed, they are displaced," one TV commentator said. "Canada is a racist country."

A Twitter feed that posted infographics about Saudi Arabia caused a stir with a post that read, "He who interferes with what doesn't concern him finds what doesn't please him." The accompanying image showed an airplane flying toward Toronto's landmark CN Tower, reminding many who saw it of the 9/11 attacks. Saudi officials pulled the account down and apologized, but the demonization of Canada continued.

"The Kingdom Is Immune to Conspiracies," blared a headline in one newspaper. Its lead article quoted "experts" accusing Canada of exploiting human rights to shelter "terrorists" and pursue "malicious goals." Next to the article was an image of a man's bare legs wearing red socks and black shoes with a maple leaf falling between his knees.

"The fig leaf has fallen," the caption read.

THE CANADA FLAP baffled nearly everyone outside of Saudi Arabia, including members of the Trump administration, one of whom compared it to "poking a teddy bear." But it was a boon for Abdulaziz, who had been given refuge by the kingdom's new enemy and now stood up for it with a series of sarcastic videos. Police in Saudi Arabia rearrested his brothers and several of his friends, which he took as increased pressure to shut up.

Soon, he learned that his brother's earlier warning about the kingdom watching him had been more correct than either of them realized at the time. In August, researchers from Citizen Lab inspected his phone and found the suspicious text message he had received in June, the same day I had received mine. It looked like a tracking notification from DHL, but contained a link to a website called sunday-deals.com. Abdulaziz had clicked on the link, letting the kingdom's hackers into his phone—and presumably into his chats with Khashoggi. As soon as Citizen Lab confirmed the hack, Abdulaziz warned Khashoggi that the kingdom could have inter-

cepted all their communications—about MBS, about DAWN, about
the electronic bees.

> **KHASHOGGI:** How did they know about the bees? May your
> family stay safe.
> **ABDULAZIZ:** I started making groups.
> I started working and for sure there was a gap.
> Such work has to involve tens of people.
> Imagine, my brother told me, 'Omar, don't tweet about
> Canada, don't continue with the bees.'
> !
> Or he'll go to prison. . . .
> **KHASHOGGI:** God help us.

LOOKING FOR LOVE

F THE MANY joys that exile tore from the life of Jamal Khashoggi—respect of the state he had loyally served, financial security, frequent gatherings with relatives and friends, familiar food cooked by loved ones—the lack of female companionship was particularly painful. He liked women, and his prominence meant he had rarely been alone. His first wife had borne him four children. He had married two others, one of them twice, leaving even his close friends disagreeing about the exact chronology. In any case, before he fled to Washington he had settled down with a successful businesswoman, Alaa Nasief. By all accounts, he loved her dearly.

But she had been irate when he continued to criticize the government after fleeing the kingdom, fearing that his family would pay the price. She was right. One of his adult sons, Salah, went to the airport for a business trip to learn that he was banned from travel. Nasief was, too, even though she had filed for a divorce after Khashoggi's first column appeared in *The Washington Post*. The void hurt.

"I begin to grow tired of those dinners and trips to D.C.," Khashoggi wrote to Maggie Mitchell Salem. "Would much rather be at home with someone, have a good dinner, watch TV, and go to bed. La la land. This mood will make me fall in love with the 1st woman who smiles at my face:)."

She suggested he get a dog.

He dated. His Egyptian-American friend, Mohamed Soltan, kept an eye out for candidates in the local Arab community.

"What do I do, message her and say I'd like to talk about democracy?" Khashoggi asked about one prospect.

Khashoggi traveled to Boston to meet one woman, but it didn't stick. He flew to Italy for another, but couldn't get his mind off his ex-wife.

"I hate Alaa. She is still everywhere in my thoughts," he wrote. "Will I ever find a women who will free me from her?"

He reached out to other women he knew, including an Egyptian who lived in Dubai and worked as a flight attendant for Emirates airline. Hanan al-Atr was just shy of 50, never married, and the oldest of six siblings she had raised after her father died. She had met Khashoggi at an event years before, and they had messaged now and then. But when he reached out to her from an American number, he seemed warmer.

In March, she flew to Washington for work, and he took her to a dinner his friends threw for his fifty-ninth birthday. They grew closer as he confided in her about his depression, and he asked her to marry him. She said yes.

But after she returned to the United Arab Emirates, she was arrested, stripped of her tablet, phone, and passport, and held for seventeen hours before being released with a travel ban. It pained Khashoggi to think the government had targeted her because of him, but he saw no way out.

"She can come and stay with me, but I'm sure she will return because of her family and job," he wrote to Mitchell Salem. "This is the weakness of every Arab under an oppressive regime. How can I live abroad? What about my family?"

Mitchell Salem asked what they could do. Write about it? Use his website to publicize such cases?

"Nothing," he wrote. "There are thousands like her."

Al-Atr got her passport back and traveled to Washington to see Khashoggi, who met her at Dulles airport and put a ring on her finger. They married in a private, religious ceremony in Virginia on June 2, 2018. She wore a white dress and red lipstick; he wore a blue sport coat and khakis, no tie. Photos taken that day show him kissing her on the cheek, and her riding shotgun in a sedan on a drizzly Virginia day, grinning with a white bouquet in her lap.

In their haste to tie the knot, they had not figured out how the relationship would work, instead leaving it to fate. Her job would bring her to Washington to see him, she figured, and he spoke wistfully of introducing her to his relatives in Medina. Perhaps he would reconcile with the Saudi government, and the couple would live together somewhere in the Arab world. In the meantime, she suggested they not legally register the marriage for fear it would cause further problems for her and her family.

She returned to Dubai, but helped him battle his sadness from afar, using the time difference to make sure he was up and moving at 7 A.M.

"What you are doing is right, Jamal," she would tell him. "Stand up and don't feel bad. What you did is right, to have freedom and say your opinion."

In early September 2018, al-Atr flew to New York for work and Khashoggi met her in her hotel, the Sheraton near Times Square. They spent the night together, but he seemed different.

"Hanan, don't hate me," he told her.

Is there another woman? she asked.

He said no.

He left the next morning.

It was the last time she saw him.

A few weeks later, he called. When he learned she was in Miami, he told her to go to Disney World.

She said no. They would go together, someday.

On September 30, he called again, but missed her because she was on a flight. When she landed, she found two messages from him, wishing her a happy birthday.

AMONG THE THINGS that Khashoggi never told al-Atr was that the month before their marriage in Virginia, he had met a 36-year-old Turkish researcher at a conference in Istanbul. Hatice Cengiz was the second of five siblings from a conservative, middle-class family who had run a bakery. After the family moved to Istanbul, her father had opened a successful cookware shop that allowed him to support his daughter's academic ambitions.

Cengiz loved history and literature and had considered becoming an investigative reporter before pursuing international affairs and studying Arabic in Cairo. Her father funded her graduate research in Oman, and when Khashoggi met her, she was a sharp, serious woman who spoke both Turkish and Arabic with a lisp and was publishing her first book. As a scholar of the Persian Gulf, she had followed Khashoggi's work, looked forward to hearing him speak at the conference, and asked him for an interview. But they had only a short time to talk, and she wrote to him later to apologize for not publishing the interview.

They met again when he returned to Istanbul in July and the meeting turned personal quickly, as Khashoggi asked Cengiz about herself and confided that he was unhappy and needed someone in his life. He later told her that he had liked her from the moment they met, and they were soon talking about marriage, not as starry-eyed romantics, but as mature adults planning intertwined lives.

She called him "Mr. Jamal."

He never mentioned his Egyptian wife.

Khashoggi kept writing about Saudi Arabia. When the spat with Canada broke out, his editor at *The Washington Post* asked for a column and he reached out to Mitchell Salem.

KHASHOGGI: How about you write something and I'll take it from there. But you are too busy.
MITCHELL SALEM: What are you willing to say?

They argued about the approach, but the resulting column said the hyper-nationalism of the campaign risked isolating the Western partners MBS needed and had worked so hard to court. Canada's stance, on the other hand, restored hope among freedom-seeking Arabs that "someone out there does indeed still care."

"They're going to hang me when it comes out," he wrote to Mitchell Salem.

He had spent years fighting accusations that he was an agent of the Muslim Brotherhood, and he joked that he should post a photo of himself with a glass of wine on the Internet to put the suspicions to rest. But he considered the Brotherhood an organic part of Arab states and believed that democracy could work only if Islamists participated.

"The only way to prevent political Islam from playing a role in Arab politics is to abolish democracy, which essentially deprives citizens of their basic right to choose their political representatives," he wrote.

He was pleased to have spoken his mind.

KHASHOGGI: If I retire after this op-ed, I'll be happy.
MITCHELL SALEM: The night is young, *habibi*!! The fight is just beginning.
KHASHOGGI: Next one on Yemen. I'll start working on it tonight.

The war in Yemen had dragged on for more than three years, churning out increasingly grim manifestations of human suffering: a widespread cholera epidemic; an increase in child marriage and child soldiers; mass hunger. In April 2018, the United Nations deemed Yemen "the world's worst humanitarian crisis." More than three-quarters of its people needed humanitarian aid; more than one million suffered from watery diarrhea or cholera; half of the country's medical facilities had closed; and a child younger than 5 died every ten minutes from a preventable cause.

The Saudis' mass-casualty airstrikes had grown less frequent, but in August, the kingdom bombed a bus full of students on a field trip, killing fifty-four people, including forty-four children. It was horrific, its human cost made even more visceral by a cellphone video found in the rubble that one of the children had filmed earlier in the day of his young colleagues dressed up for the occasion and chatting excitedly on the bus.

The strike showed that more than three years into the war, Saudi efforts to avoid killing civilians still fell far short. The continuously high civilian toll, often caused by American-made bombs, was fueling calls from members of Congress to stop American support and investigate whether it exposed American military personnel to war crimes charges.

Khashoggi had supported the intervention at the start, but changed his mind as the war ground on, calling on Saudi Arabia to end the conflict in order to restore the kingdom's dignity.

More bad news came from home. The trial opened of Salman al-Awda, the famous cleric who had been pulled from his home by security forces the year before. Prosecutors pressed thirty-seven charges and sought the death penalty. Soon after, Khashoggi's economist friend, Essam al-Zamil, who had been arrested after his trip to Washington, was put on trial for charges that included joining a terrorist organization and providing information to diplomats.

That fall, Khashoggi and Cengiz attended an event in Istanbul, where he suffered a bronchitis attack and she took him to the hospital. A nurse gave him an IV and Cengiz sat next to him as he rested, feeling close. A nurse asked how she was related.

"Next of kin," she said.

She covered him with a blanket and watched over him as he slept. She didn't know his family, so in the taxi after he was discharged, she asked him whom to call if anything happened to him. He told her to call his friend Yasin Aktay, a ranking member of Turkey's Justice and Development Party and an adviser to President Recep Tayyip Erdogan.

He'll know what to do, Khashoggi told her.

She saved Aktay's number in her phone.

They visualized a life together. Khashoggi would write and work on his new projects from Washington and travel frequently to Turkey. Cengiz's father stipulated that he had to buy her an apartment, so he did, planning to register it in her name after their marriage. They shopped for housewares and furniture.

"The most beautiful period of my life begins," he told her. "No woman that I married understood me like you do."

On September 28, a Friday, the couple took a taxi to the marriage office in the Fatih district of Istanbul to do the bureaucracy of matrimony. They were told that Khashoggi needed a document confirming that he was legally divorced, which he could get from the Saudi consulate. They left the clerk's desk after less than five minutes, and walked out holding hands.

That afternoon, he went to the consulate. Even though he had visited the Saudi Embassy in Washington numerous times, he was nervous because his relationship with the kingdom had deteriorated. But the consular staff recognized him and treated him well. It would take a few days to prepare the document, so he was told to return in four days, on Tuesday.

He flew to London that afternoon and spoke at an event the next day. On Sunday, he had the flu, and on Monday, he met his old friend Azzam Tamimi for lunch at Nando's. Khashoggi seemed happy. They discussed his plans, the economics website and the pro-democracy organization, and joked about his new marriage. He told Tamimi about going to the consulate, remarking that the staff were "just ordinary Saudis, and the ordinary Saudis are good people."

Khashoggi returned to Istanbul on a red-eye flight, arriving just after 4 A.M. on October 2, and met Cengiz at their apartment. She had taken the day off from the university, and around noon, they took a taxi to the Saudi consulate. On the way, they chatted about the future. They'd buy appliances that afternoon. They'd celebrate over dinner that night with friends and family. Their furniture would arrive the next day. But Cengiz was uneasy, fearing it had been a bad idea to set the appointment in advance. Khashoggi told her not to worry. The Saudis would not harm him in Turkey.

At the barricades blocking the street in front of the consulate, he gave her his cellphones, said he'd be back soon, and got patted down by a guard. At 1:14 P.M., a Turkish surveillance camera outside filmed the portly, bearded, middle-aged man in a navy blue blazer, gray slacks, and black shoes as he crossed the street, stepped up the curb, and walked through the consulate's heavy gray door.

Outside, Cengiz waited.

And waited.

And waited.

The consulate closed at 4 P.M.

Khashoggi did not return.

She asked the guards.

They said no one was inside.

She got worried, and started making calls.

. . .

UNBEKNOWNST TO THE couple, Khashoggi's first, surprise visit to the consulate on September 28 had set in motion a chain of events that would destroy their lives and batter the political fortunes of Mohammed bin Salman.

Before Khashoggi had caught his plane to London that afternoon, a spy working in the consulate spoke to an intelligence officer in Riyadh. The spy said the consular staff had been shocked when Khashoggi came in, and that the journalist was supposed to return on October 2.

"There isn't anything official, but it's known that he is one of the people sought," the spy said.

That evening, another official told the Saudi consul general in Istanbul to choose a member of his staff for a "top secret" mission. The next day, September 29, two security officers from the consulate flew to Riyadh and returned to Istanbul on October 1 with three Saudi agents. Not long after Khashoggi's lunch with his friend in London, the three agents spent a few hours in the consulate and returned to sleep at their hotel. Also that evening, a member of the consular staff called a travel agency about hotel options close by and booked three suites and seven rooms for three days. That night, there was talk in the consulate about a group coming from Saudi Arabia the next day who had "something to do in the consulate" near the consul's office.

In the early hours of October 2, three more Saudi agents landed in Istanbul on a flight from Cairo and checked into a hotel near the consulate. Shortly after, and less than an hour before Khashoggi returned to Istanbul on his red-eye flight from London, nine more Saudi agents arrived on a private jet with diplomatic clearance. They checked into another hotel.

As the sun rose and Khashoggi spent the morning with his fiancée, the consul told his local staff not to come to work, to go home at noon, or to remain in their offices because of important visitors. The staff at his residence, a short drive from the consulate, were told not to go in or out of the property because of repair work.

After 10 A.M., the fifteen agents split into two groups. Five went to the consul's residence. The other ten entered the consulate, where the hard drives had been removed from the security cameras so they could not record.

HE'LL KNOW WHAT to do, Khashoggi had told Cengiz of Yasin Aktay, his Turkish friend. She found his number in her phone and called.

When Aktay's phone rang at 4:41 P.M., he was in his office in Ankara and on deadline for a newspaper column. So he missed the call.

Aktay, a short, soft-spoken academic with glasses and a mustache, spoke Arabic and helped manage his political party's relations with the Arab world. He knew Khashoggi well and had met Cengiz, but did not know of their engagement.

She called again and he answered, hearing the worry in her voice. She told him what had happened, but Aktay did not immediately see cause for concern. He told her to wait where she was and called a Saudi friend who knew Khashoggi to ask what he thought.

The friend got angry, asking, "Why did he go?"

Aktay called the Saudi ambassador to Ankara, who said he had not heard anything about Khashoggi, but would check and call back.

Then he stopped taking Aktay's calls.

Cengiz waited on the curb outside the consulate until after midnight, fielding calls from officials and journalists as the news spread, then went home and returned the next morning. Khashoggi's friends feared that he had been detained in the consulate or even kidnapped. Later in the day, Saudi Arabia said Khashoggi had left the consulate shortly after he arrived, but the Turks insisted he was still inside. That night in Riyadh, MBS gave an interview about his social and economic reforms, the arrested activists, and the delayed IPO of Aramco.

The reporters asked about Khashoggi.

"We hear the rumors about what happened. He's a Saudi citizen and we are very keen to know what happened to him," MBS said. "My understanding is he entered and he got out after a few minutes or one hour. I'm not sure. We are investigating this through the foreign ministry to see exactly what happened at that time."

He deflected a question about whether Khashoggi faced charges in Saudi Arabia, saying that the kingdom needed to know where he was first.

"If he's in Saudi Arabia, I would know that," MBS said, adding that the Turks were free to search the consulate.

"We have nothing to hide."

That failed to stop the mounting questions. *The Washington Post* published a blank column it said should have been an op-ed from the missing journalist. *The New York Times* editorial board called for Khashoggi to be found. In Istanbul, a crowd gathered in front of the consulate holding his photo and chanting, "Free Jamal Khashoggi!"

So the Saudis invited reporters from Reuters to tour the consulate. They walked from room to room as the consul opened cupboards, filing cabinets, and air conditioners to show that Khashoggi was not inside. Nor was he in the basement prayer room, the kitchen, the storeroom, or the ladies' restroom.

"I would like to confirm that Jamal is not at the consulate nor in the Kingdom of Saudi Arabia, and the consulate and the embassy are working to search for him," the consul said. "The idea of kidnapping a Saudi citizen by a diplomatic mission is something that should not be put forward in the media."

When asked about the consulate's security system, he said its cameras provided only live surveillance but did not record, meaning the Saudis did not have footage of Khashoggi leaving the building.

Nobody bought it, especially not the Turks.

Aktay's phone calls had led him to believe that Khashoggi's disappearance could be a serious issue, so he sounded the alarm. He told the head of Turkish intelligence. He, too, asked, "Why did he go?" Aktay called the president's secretary, who interrupted a meeting to pass Erdogan a note alerting him. The president emerged and made his own calls, and the Turkish state mobilized.

At the time, relations between Saudi Arabia and Turkey were functional but cold. Turkey's ruling party was affiliated with the Muslim Brotherhood, and Turkey had supported many of the Arab Spring uprisings that the Saudis had worked to put down. Turkey was also close to Qatar, and had stood up for it after the boycott.

The issue was personal as well. Erdogan was an Islamist leader, proud of his country's Ottoman heritage, which he felt made it a natural leader in the Islamic world, as it had been for centuries before MBS's grandfather had founded Saudi Arabia. Erdogan did not feel that Saudi control of the holy sites gave the kingdom a monopoly on Islam, and he considered MBS a dangerous upstart.

But the Turks realized the delicacy of the situation and wanted to avoid the full-fledged blowout that an official condemnation would likely provoke. So the president's office devised a strategy of leaking details of its investigation into what happened to Khashoggi that would reveal what it knew without putting accusations in the mouths of specific Turkish officials. The Turks' hope was that by revealing what they knew, they could push the Saudis to come clean. When the Saudis did not, the goal became to damage MBS.

So the leaks began—first as a trickle, then as a flood—cited to unnamed Turkish officials: Khashoggi had been killed inside the consulate in a premeditated murder and his body taken offsite. A team of fifteen Saudi agents had flown into Turkey before the murder and left soon after. Turkey opened a criminal investigation, and a Turkish friend of Khashoggi's added a grim new detail: Khashoggi's body had been dismembered.

But who knew what to believe? Critics pointed out that Erdogan was no champion of journalistic freedom; Turkey itself was a prodigious jailer of journalists. Indeed, many of the Turkish papers that published the leaks had dubious records for accuracy and histories of poorly sourced hit jobs on the president's foes. It was a confusing time, and my colleagues and I worked to see which leaks we could confirm with our own sources. But since most of the information came from anonymous Turks, it left room for doubt. Perhaps Khashoggi was locked up in the consulate and would emerge unharmed, or suddenly pop up in Riyadh, pledging allegiance to MBS.

The Saudis tried to shift the narrative. Prince Khalid bin Salman, the Saudi ambassador to Washington and MBS's younger brother, wrote that he was "gravely concerned" about Khashoggi, whom he considered a "friend."

"I assure you that the reports that suggest that Jamal Khashoggi went missing in the consulate in Istanbul or that the Kingdom's authorities have detained him or killed him are absolutely false," he said.

But each day brought new, explosive revelations, as the Turks mobilized the media to humiliate the Saudis. The same day that Prince Khalid called Khashoggi a "friend," it was reported that Khashoggi had been dismembered with a bone saw. The Turks said they had audio and video to support their accusations and they released the names of the fifteen Saudis who had flown into Turkey in the hours before Khashoggi disappeared, publishing photos of them looking into cameras at passport control or checking into hotels.

Internet sleuths went to work on the names, and so did I and my colleagues, searching for information about the men's backgrounds. One, Maher Mutrib, was an intelligence agent who had worked at the Saudi Embassy in London at the same time as Khashoggi. He was tall and thin, with a stern mouth and droopy eyes. We took to calling him "Jaws," for his resemblance to the metal-toothed villain from the Roger Moore–era James Bond films.

Three others were members of the Royal Guard, and one had been promoted the year before to the rank of lieutenant for bravery during an attack on MBS's palace in Jeddah.

A fifth was a forensic doctor with high positions at a Saudi medical school and in the Interior Ministry. Dr. Salah al-Tubaigy had studied at the University of Glasgow in Scotland, spent time at a forensic institute in Australia, and published academic papers on mobile autopsies and dissection.

Of the fifteen, we established that at least nine were connected to the Saudi security services, and a number had served in MBS's security detail, traveling with him on foreign trips. Jaws, for example, had shown up with the crown prince abroad, following him off airplanes in Paris and Madrid, and standing guard while MBS made appearances in Houston, Boston, and at the United Nations in New York. It would later come out that he had accompanied MBS when he visited MIT and had spoken with university officials.

One member of the team appeared out of place. He was a portly, middle-aged man identified online as an engineer. His presence in the group was a mystery at first.

The revelations were humiliating for Saudi Arabia, not just because so many of its agents had been caught on film while traveling under their real names, but because they were linked to powerful parts of the government. The Saudi government say that those involved in the murder were acting of their own volition.

Seventeen days after Khashoggi disappeared—and after repeated denials from a range of Saudi officials—the kingdom acknowledged that the Turks were right: Khashoggi had been killed inside the consulate by a team from Riyadh. But the details of the Saudi narrative differed from that of the Turks.

The operation had been launched based on a standing order from Saudi intelligence to bring dissidents home, a Saudi official told me. After Khashoggi's initial visit to the consulate, Saud al-Qahtani had organized the operation with Maj. Gen. Ahmed Asiri, the deputy head of Saudi intelligence (and, incidentally, the same general who had complained about my reporting from Yemen).*

The Saudis said that when Khashoggi had entered the consulate for his second visit on October 2, the agents had told him he was going back to Riyadh. He had resisted, a fistfight had broken out, and one of the agents had put Khashoggi in a chokehold, killing him. His body had been passed to a local collaborator to dispose of.

At no time was MBS aware of the operation, the Saudis insisted.

That confirmed that the Saudis had killed Khashoggi, but cast the operation as a kidnapping gone wrong. But questions remained. Why the autopsy doctor? What about the bone saw? And why was the middle-aged engineer on the team?

Turkey had the answer to that last question, and gave surveillance footage to CNN of a portly, bearded, middle-aged man in a navy blue blazer and gray slacks emerging from the consulate's back door on the afternoon of October 2. But instead of wearing black shoes as Khashoggi had, the man wore sneakers with white soles.

Accompanied by a younger man in a black hoodie carrying a plastic bag, the man hailed a cab, walked through a green gate into the courtyard of the Sultan Ahmet Mosque, one of Istanbul's prime attractions, and strolled through crowds of tourists. He entered a

---

* In December 2019, Saudi Arabia said that a court had ordered the release of Ahmed Asiri without charge and announced that al-Qahtani had not been tried because of lack of evidence.

public restroom and reappeared wearing a blue-and-white-plaid shirt and dark pants, with the same white-soled shoes but no beard.

It was not Khashoggi, but the purported engineer, who had been dispatched as a body double to leave a trail of false Khashoggi sightings around the city—and he had blown it.

DONALD TRUMP WAS not impressed by the body double.

"They had a very bad original concept, it was carried out poorly, and the cover-up was one of the worst in the history of cover-ups," he said. "Whoever thought of that idea, I think, is in big trouble, and they should be in big trouble."

Khashoggi's disappearance caught the administration flat-footed. Early on, it had doubted the Turkish reports, but as the evidence had leaked out, boxing in the Saudis, Trump and his aides realized that it was no joke—and a threat to their plans for the Middle East. Now the young prince's value as a partner was in jeopardy because of the botched murder of a journalist who was not even an American citizen.

But for weeks after Khashoggi disappeared, the United States knew little more than what the Turks were leaking. American intelligence officers who had worked with Saudi Arabia argued that such an amateurish gambit was out of character. Saudi operations were usually cleaner.

Meanwhile, the National Security Agency was combing through intercepted Saudi communications for clues. Among their findings were conversations between top Saudi officials about how to lure Khashoggi back to the kingdom and detain him.

Since he entered the White House, Trump had spoken with MBS and King Salman frequently, developing a casual rapport. Now, as the Turkish leaks increased, so did the calls.

MBS and his father continuously denied knowing anything.

Trump said later that Saudi officials called Khashoggi an "enemy of the state." On another call, MBS told Jared Kushner and John Bolton, Trump's national security adviser, that Khashoggi was a member of the Muslim Brotherhood, casting him as a dangerous Islamist.

The White House worried that leaks about the calls would embarrass its Saudi partners, so it first tightened distribution of their transcripts, then stopped producing transcripts at all, leaving officials in other parts of the government in the dark about what was said.

Trump repeatedly talked about Khashoggi in public, expressing concern over the killing and threatening consequences if Saudi culpability was confirmed.

"Well, it'll have to be very severe," he said. "I mean, it's bad, bad stuff."

But then he stepped back, acknowledging that the Saudis were obfuscating but reiterating how important he considered MBS.

The prince was "a person who can keep things under check," Trump said, and Saudi Arabia was better than Iran.

"I would love if he wasn't responsible," he said. "I think it's a very important ally for us. Especially when you have Iran doing so many bad things in the world, it's a good counterbalance to the world. Iran, they're as evil as it gets."

Questions mounted inside the American government for three weeks until Gina Haspel, the head of the CIA, flew to Ankara to see her Turkish counterparts. They laid out their evidence: reams of surveillance footage of the Saudi agents coming and going and hours of audio captured inside the consulate before, during, and after the killing. She returned to Washington and briefed Trump, leaving little doubt about what had been done. Saudi officials continued to insist that the decision to kill Khashoggi had not been ordered from Riyadh, but was made by the agents on the ground.

BEFORE KHASHOGGI ENTERED the consulate on October 2, the agents inside discussed his torso. Mutrib, the Jaws-like agent leading the operation, asked the forensic doctor if it would be "possible to put the trunk in a bag?"

"No. Too heavy," the doctor replied. Khashoggi was a big man.

The doctor said his boss didn't know what he was up to, and he worried he might get in trouble. It was the first time he would cut a body on the floor as opposed to on a table, but he hoped it would go smoothly.

"Joints will be separated. It is not a problem," he said. "If we take plastic bags and cut it into pieces, it will be finished. We will wrap each of them."

There was talk of cutting skin, and the doctor told his colleagues he usually put on headphones and listened to music while he worked.

"At the same time, I drink coffee and smoke," he said.

Mutreb asked whether "the sacrificial animal" had arrived.

"He has arrived," another agent said.

A minute later, a security camera caught Khashoggi stepping into the building.

Once inside, Khashoggi recognized Mutrib from their time together at the Saudi Embassy in London.

The men led Khashoggi upstairs near the consul's office.

There was talk of whether he would return to Saudi Arabia.

Khashoggi said he hoped to, someday.

"We will have to take you back," one agent said, adding that there was an Interpol notice out for his arrest. "We are coming to get you."

Khashoggi said there was no case against him.

His driver was waiting outside, he told them. Actually, it was his fiancée.

The men asked about his phones and told him to send a message to his son, Salah: "My son, I am in Istanbul. Don't worry if you don't hear from me for a while."

He refused.

They told him to take off his jacket.

"How could this happen in an embassy?" he asked. "Are you going to give me drugs?"

"We will anesthetize you," they told him.

A struggle began.

Khashoggi fought back but did not scream.

"I can't breathe, I can't breathe," he said.

Then he went quiet.

Among themselves, the agents said, "Did he sleep?" "Keep pushing," and "Don't remove your hand. Push it."

The Turks concluded that the agents gave him some sort of shot and suffocated him with a plastic bag. He may have been dead within ten minutes of entering the building.

"THERE WERE NO expressions of surprise or shock at his death among the Saudi officials present at the scene," a United Nations investigator who listened to audio from the consulate wrote later. "There were no sounds or words that suggested an attempt to resuscitate him."

Instead, there were sounds of movement and exertion.

The agents laid Khashoggi on plastic sheeting and removed his clothes. They may have drained his blood to avoid making a mess and dumped it in the sink or flushed it down the toilet.

There was a buzz that the Turks determined to be a saw.

At some point, Mutrib made a call telling someone to inform his superior that the job was done. It was reported to CNN that he was talking to Saud al-Qahtani about MBS.

At around 3 P.M., a black van pulled out of the consulate's driveway and drove a few blocks to the consul's residence. It parked in front, and Mutrib got out and entered the gate. The van pulled into the driveway, and Turkish surveillance cameras caught three men lugging five black suitcases from the van into the front door of the residence. One of the men then carried in what appeared to be two large black plastic bags.

The Turks suspected that the suitcases contained Khashoggi's body. They never saw it or the suitcases again.

A short time later, the body double emerged from the back door of the consulate wearing Khashoggi's clothes, a fake beard, and the sneakers with white soles. After he and his companion visited the mosque and he changed back into his own clothes, they stopped at Mesale Café, a tourist spot that offers coffee, tea, grilled meat, and live music. They returned to their hotel, ditching Khashoggi's clothes on the way.

If they felt any guilt, it did not show on their faces. Surveillance footage of the pair waiting for an elevator shows the body double laughing, then grinning as he looks around, like a man pleased with himself.

Over the next few hours, the operatives checked out of their hotels and went to the airport.

Six left on a private jet to Cairo.

Seven others took a private jet to Dubai.

After midnight, the body double and his companion boarded a commercial flight to Riyadh.

By the time the sun came up the next morning and Cengiz returned to the consulate to wait for Khashoggi to come out, the agents were all gone.

A HOLOGRAM FOR THE
CROWN PRINCE, PART TWO

N MID-OCTOBER, HUNDREDS of members of the Saudi royal family and the kingdom's elite gathered at the palace of a senior prince to celebrate the wedding of two of their own. As was customary, the women were in their own area, dressed in ball gowns and designer dresses with heavy makeup and ornate coiffures. After an elaborate buffet, they danced to Arabic music with a live singer. The men, in white robes, black or brown cloaks, and white or checkered headdresses, gathered elsewhere for food, coffee, and photos. Around midnight, it was announced that the groom was on his way, and some of the women covered their arms, hair, and faces. The groom swept in, a handsome prince from a secondary branch of the family, with the evening's host and the bride's grandfather, Prince Khalid al-Faisal.

Prince Khalid, in his late seventies, was a son of the late King Faisal and trusted by his uncle, King Salman. He had served for years as the governor of Mecca Province, home to Islam's most important sites, and was esteemed inside the family as measured and intelligent. That night, he had reason to be joyful, but as he greeted his guests, he also had reason to worry. Less than two weeks had passed since the murder of Jamal Khashoggi, and the king had tasked him with flying to Ankara to see the Turks about the expanding crisis.

Prince Khalid's branch of the family had long been Khashoggi's patron. It had owned the *Al Watan* newspaper that Khashoggi had been fired from, and when the death threats began, the prince's half brother, Turki al-Faisal, had taken Khashoggi to work for him at the embassy in London. Khashoggi had been close with both princes for years, serving as an unofficial adviser, although one said they had grown apart more recently.

The weekend of his granddaughter's wedding, Prince Khalid flew on a royal jet to Ankara to meet President Recep Tayyip Erdogan and other top officials. The Turks had hoped he would bring information about the murder and its perpetrators, but the prince seemed more interested in finding out how much the Turks knew. He stayed only a few hours and flew home disturbed.

"It is really difficult to get out of this one," he told relatives after his return.

Some commentators called Khashoggi's murder the kingdom's worst foreign affairs crisis since the terrorist attacks of September 11, 2001. But the two incidents were profoundly different. It was hard to compare anything with 9/11, which had killed thousands of Americans inside the United States. There was also the grimly personal nature of the murder, of a writer who had not called for violence or regime change. He had not even wanted to be called a dissident.

The scandal rippled through the royal family, whose thousands of members knew the importance of Saudi Arabia's relationship with the United States and its status as the guardian of the Islamic holy sites. Would the killing shake those pillars? What if the United States scaled back weapons sales? Would Muslims in, say, India or Indonesia still see Saudi Arabia as a champion of Islam after it had butchered a nonviolent writer?

But there was little they could do, because the royal family no longer functioned as it once had. Gone were the days when seniority reigned, elder princes divided the portfolios among themselves, and made decisions through consensus. MBS has destroyed that system, extending his control over the military, the oil industry, the intelligence services, the police, and the National Guard, replacing senior princes with younger ones who answered to him.

Other top princes had been thrown in the Ritz, sullying their reputations and depriving them of the money they needed to maintain their standing. When Khashoggi was killed, a number of them were still locked up. Others were stuck in the kingdom due to travel bans and lived in fear that their phones were tapped and that any negative comment could get them hauled in again. A smaller number were settling into new lives abroad and lying low, scared that MBS would send goons to drag them home.

The royal family had always been synonymous with the kingdom, so when the kingdom did something nasty, it reflected on the royals. That dilemma was clear when a group of protesters chanting against the war in Yemen and for the fall of the Al Saud ambushed Prince Ahmed, a younger brother of King Salman, on a street in London. Instead of ignoring them, he responded.

"What does this have to do with the Al Saud?" the prince asked. "Those responsible are the king and his crown prince."

The protesters asked about the war in Yemen and he said, "I hope the situation ends, whether in Yemen or elsewhere, today before tomorrow."

After the video spread online, Prince Ahmed said his comments had been misinterpreted and reaffirmed his allegiance to the king and MBS. A short time later, he returned to Riyadh and kept quiet.

MBS's rise had angered other royals, either because they saw his leadership as dangerous or because he had hurt them personally.

"Of course there are people who were affected," a princess who had had a relative in the Ritz told me. "They hate him, but what can they do? If you speak, they'll put you in jail, while other countries want to sell arms and buy oil."

But Khashoggi's killing was a problem the Saudis could not buy their way out of, and no other princes were willing or able to match MBS's Machiavellian tactics.

"They aren't a particularly draconian bunch," a longtime associate of the family told me. He described the philosophy of most princes as: "We just want to eat burgers and go on foreign holidays."

Some hoped that the gravity of the scandal would move King Salman to limit MBS's power, if not replace him with a less controversial crown prince. But the king was old, and MBS his gatekeeper. Senior princes who once had the king's ear now found him hard to reach. Some had discovered that they could no longer enter the

Royal Court if their names had not been placed at the door. That left few options. They could see the king at events, but the crowding at such occasions made it hard to raise sensitive topics. They could drop by at night when the king played *Belote*, his favorite card game, but that was also a bad time for serious talk.

Then there was the issue of the king's health. Saudi officials swore up and down that the 83-year-old monarch maintained his full mental capacities, but indications to the contrary slipped out. He had had at least one stroke. There was the iPad that American officials had noticed during their meetings. And at an international summit in Egypt in early 2019, the king lost his place while reading his opening remarks and froze for fifteen seconds until an aide told him where to continue. Less than two minutes later, he called for a Palestinian state on the "1937 borders," misreading his text and missing a landmark date by three decades.

As speculation mounted that the king would intervene, I messaged a friend who worked for a senior prince to ask if he expected any movement.

"The king has no capacity to handle it," he wrote. MBS's control was absolute.

"He is No. 1 and No. 2."

Advisers to MBS said he was shocked by the outrage over the killing, asking confidants why the death of one Saudi had caused such an uproar. He scrambled to mitigate the damage, creating a crisis committee with representatives from the intelligence services and the Foreign Ministry to give him frequent updates. But the kingdom flailed. It threatened to retaliate against measures taken against it, mentioning its "vital role in the global economy." An MBS confidant warned that sanctions against Saudi Arabia could push it and the entire Muslim world "into the arms of Iran."

When the kingdom finally acknowledged the murder, it laid out measures taken in response. The authorities had arrested eighteen men in connection to the case: the fifteen agents who had traveled to Istanbul, two consular workers, and a driver. A number of top officials were fired from the intelligence agency, and Saud al-Qahtani lost his position as an adviser to the Royal Court. To prevent such incidents in the future, the king decreed the creation of a high-level committee to restructure the intelligence service.

To lead it, he named Mohammed bin Salman.

ON OCTOBER 3, the day after Khashoggi was killed, the consular staff returned to work but were not allowed upstairs. The consul did not leave his residence all day, and smoke rose from the backyard of the consulate, where men burned documents in a barrel. That night and the next, a team stayed inside until dawn, cleaning. On the third day, a consular worker took the van that had carried the five black suitcases from the consulate to the residence to a car wash. It was thoroughly cleaned, inside and out.

New teams of Saudis arrived in Istanbul, allegedly to investigate the crime. When they met their Turkish counterparts, they asked repeatedly for Khashoggi's phones. The Turks refused to hand them over. Among the investigators were men the Turks identified as experts in toxicology and genetics. One team spent a full night in the consulate, returned two days later, and again that night, remaining inside until 4 A.M.

The next morning, October 15, a cleaning crew showed up and journalists waiting outside snapped photos of workers in white smocks entering the consulate with mops, buckets, and what appeared to be bleach. That night, thirteen days after the murder, the Turks were finally allowed in, where, accompanied by Saudi officials, they didn't find much. They spread luminol, a chemical that gives off a faint blue light when it reacts to blood. On a carpet near the consul's office, they found what appeared to be a path of drops in a curved line. But the luminol reacted less than expected in a facility where even Saudi Arabia would acknowledge that Khashoggi had been cut into pieces.

The next day, the investigators searched the consul's residence. Again, they found little. A sniffer dog drew them to a fridge, but samples turned up nothing. They found a well, but the Saudis barred them from searching it. They inspected the consulate's cars, but the

Saudis resisted, refusing to move the vehicles under cover when it rained.

That evening, the consul left the country.

Within a week, the Saudi technicians were gone, too.

A U.N. investigator later found credible evidence that the crime scene had been "thoroughly, even forensically cleaned." She concluded that the Saudi investigation had not been "conducted in good faith" and could qualify as obstruction of justice.

Meanwhile, the Turks pressed the Saudis for answers. President Recep Tayyip Erdogan took up the case, saying the murder had been ordered from the top of the Royal Court while praising King Salman (showing he did not think the king, at least, was responsible).

In Washington, the picture of what happened in Istanbul became clear after Director Gina Haspel of the Central Intelligence Agency returned from Ankara, but the White House struggled to respond. Jared Kushner continued to message directly with MBS in defiance of regulations on official communications and the sharing of information inside the U.S. government. (White House spokespeople denied this.)

But as the outrage grew, the administration felt pressed to react. A member of Trump's National Security Council met in Riyadh with Prince Khalid bin Salman, MBS's younger brother, to discuss measures the United States could take against the kingdom—a move not unlike talking with a criminal about how he will be punished. The White House saw MBS's position as inviolable, so sought measures that would encourage better behavior. They included sanctioning Saudis who were involved in the plot, shutting down al-Qahtani's media operation, and stopping the American aerial refueling of Saudi jets in Yemen. Prince Khalid agreed, but asked that the Saudis be allowed to announce that they no longer needed U.S. refueling, to save them the embarrassment. The White House agreed, but that part of the agreement was leaked to the news media.

Six weeks after the killing, a spokesman for the Saudi public prosecutor modified the kingdom's story once again, portraying the killing as the result of a last-minute decision by the team on the ground.

Khashoggi had been killed with a heavy dose of tranquilizer, he said, not by choking, as the kingdom had said before. And for the first time, the kingdom acknowledged that Khashoggi's body had been dismembered. Prosecutors would try eleven suspects, and seek the death penalty for five of them.

A few hours later, the U.S. Treasury Department announced sanctions for human rights violations on seventeen Saudis, some of them agreed upon with the White House. They included the fifteen agents, the consul, and Saud al-Qahtani, who was described as "part of the planning and execution of the operation."

Absent from the list was Maj. Gen. Ahmed Asiri, the deputy head of Saudi intelligence, whom the Saudis had portrayed as one of the masterminds of the intended extradition but not the killing. The United States left him off because it lacked proof that he had been involved and because it worried that sanctioning him could damage the relationship between intelligence services.

The White House, and Trump released an extraordinary statement to try to put the issue to rest.

"America First!" it began. "The world is a very dangerous place!"

It blasted Iran as "the world's leading sponsor of terror," and said Saudi Arabia would gladly leave Yemen if the Iranians did too. It praised the kingdom for agreeing to spend $450 billion in the United States, including $110 billion on arms. If the United States did not sell the Saudis those weapons, Trump said, Russia and China would. He called Khashoggi's killing "terrible" and said MBS and his father had denied involvement, but that it didn't really matter anyway.

"It could very well be that the Crown Prince had knowledge of this tragic event—maybe he did and maybe he didn't!" Trump said. But the United States' relationship with Saudi Arabia would stand, to protect Israel, fight Iran, combat terrorism, and maintain oil prices.

"The United States intends to remain a steadfast partner of Saudi Arabia to ensure the interests of our country," Trump said. "Very simply it is called America First!"

. . .

THE WHITE HOUSE had MBS's back, but what about everyone else he had charmed during his rise?

On a sunny California day, Richard Branson, who had once seen such promise in Saudi Arabia and given MBS a tour of his desert space station, stood on a red carpet on Hollywood Boulevard in jeans and a leather jacket for the unveiling of his star on the Walk of Fame. He posed for photos and spoke of Khashoggi.

"I think that people cannot go around killing and cutting up journalists in this day and age, and I think if they do, everybody in the world has to make a stance against that," he said.

His company, Virgin Group, told the Saudis to keep the $1 billion they had planned to invest in its space ventures, and Branson quit his roles in Saudi tourism projects and canceled his attendance at the second edition of MBS's investment conference, scheduled for late October.

Others did, too.

Amid the global headlines and lurid details about the Khashoggi killing, big names dropped out, including the CEOs of Blackstone Group and Uber, both of which had received large Saudi investments. The CEO of SoftBank, who had appeared onstage with MBS the year before for the announcement of NEOM, canceled.

Foreign officials stayed away, and U.S. Treasury Secretary Steven Mnuchin skipped the conference but met MBS privately in Riyadh. Media organizations that had signed up as official sponsors pulled out, including *The New York Times*, Bloomberg, and *Fox Business*. The Brookings Institution terminated a Saudi research grant, the Gates Foundation halted a partnership with MBS's foundation, and lobbyists hired to promote Saudi Arabia ran for the exits, fearing for their reputations.

As the conference approached, executives pleaded with MBS to postpone it, but he refused, not wanting to show weakness or imply culpability. So it went ahead, with an inauspicious start. Hackers defaced its website, posting a picture of MBS wielding a bloody sword over a kneeling Khashoggi. The World Economic Forum condemned the use of the "Davos" brand for unaffiliated events, threatening to "use all means" against "illicit appropriation"—clearly an effort to kill the "Davos in the Desert" comparisons. Once the conference began, Saudi speakers sought to express consternation while not dampening the kingdom's attractiveness for investment.

"The terrible acts reported in recent weeks are alien to our culture and our DNA," Lubna Olayan, a Saudi billionaire businesswoman, said at the opening. "I am sure we will grow and emerge stronger as a result of dealing with the crisis of the last few weeks."

In some ways, the conference resembled the inaugural event the year before. Businesspeople in dark suits coursed through the lobby of the Ritz-Carlton, sipping juice, chatting over coffee and dates, and arranging side meetings to talk business. The CEO of Total S.A., the French oil company, attended, and Lucid Motors, Inc., an electric car maker from California, showed off a prototype. The kingdom had promised it a $1 billion investment.

But the event felt smaller, diminished. Organizers said three thousand people attended, but repeat attendees noted fewer Americans and Europeans, and more Russians, Asians, and Arabs. Big Wall Street firms sent local representatives instead of top brass, and some hid their names behind their ties.

MBS made a surprise appearance in the lobby one night, drawing a crowd that scrambled for selfies and held their phones aloft to film him. Trailing behind him was Alwaleed bin Talal, once the kingdom's most famous investor, who had been locked up by his younger cousin in the same complex and now walked in his entourage.

The kingdom announced some new agreements. The energy minister said more than twenty-five deals, worth $56 billion, were signed, most with American companies. But $34 billon of those were with Saudi Aramco, suggesting that investors were sticking to what Saudi did best instead of buying into the new sectors it wanted to build. Other planned agreements failed to materialize. The day after Khashoggi disappeared, MBS had promised that "an amazing deal . . . far away from oil" would be unveiled at the conference. It was not, raising questions about what it was and whether other agreements had also fallen through.

The conference sought to court foreign capital, but ended up showing—yet again—how hard it would be for Saudi Arabia to shake its reputation as the world's ATM. As other foreign leaders canceled their trips, Prime Minister Imran Khan of Pakistan agreed to come. In an interview beforehand, he described Khashoggi's killing as "sad beyond belief," but said Pakistan had to seek Saudi loans because "right now we have the worst debt crisis in our history."

"We're desperate at the moment," he said.

He flew home with a $6 billion aid package.

King Abdullah II of Jordan also attended, months after Saudi Arabia and its Gulf neighbors had promised him $2.5 billion in economic support.

MBS's own formal appearance was a downgrade. The year before, he had shared the stage with a female foreign journalist and world-class businessmen to wow the crowd with a promise to crush extremism and build a $500 billion robot city. This year, the journalist stayed home and MBS sat on a panel with the crown prince of Bahrain, an island nation heavily dependent on Saudi Arabia, and Saad Hariri of Lebanon, whom he had detained the year before and whose country was hugely corrupt and struggling economically.

MBS spoke of Khashoggi without uttering his name.

"The event that happened was very painful for all Saudis, especially for the Saudi citizen, and I believe it is painful for any human in the world," he said, calling it "a terrible, unjustifiable event."

He vowed that justice would be done and said the reforms were going ahead.

"All our projects are proceeding, reform is proceeding, our war on extremism is proceeding, our war on terrorism is proceeding, developing the kingdom of Saudi Arabia is proceeding," he said. No challenge was too big for "the great Saudi people."

Since he had appeared on the world stage in 2015, MBS had been selling a dream—not what Saudi Arabia was, but what he hoped it would become—and he had spread enthusiasm for that dream among many who would not otherwise have paid the kingdom much mind. Of course, embracing that dream meant overlooking MBS's more reckless moves. But the dream's allure—of a diversified, egalitarian, moderate Saudi Arabia—was so strong that many had been happy to share the dream with the charismatic, young prince.

Khashoggi's killing was a wake-up call. In a few weeks, it flushed away much of the goodwill and excitement that MBS had spent the last four years generating. Sure, Khashoggi was only one man, but the contrast between his reasoned criticism and his gruesome end caught the world's attention. The Eiffel Tower went dark. *TIME* magazine named Khashoggi and other embattled journalists "Person of the Year." His murder crystalized, and made it harder to ignore, the ruthlessness of state officials in the MBS era: the uncounted deaths in Yemen; the detainment of a foreign prime minister; the lock-up at the Ritz; the arrests and torture of activists and clerics; and the harsh, new, with-us-or-against-us environment that considered those who did not cheer, or cheer loudly enough, enemies.

The conference went ahead anyway, a plea by MBS to keep his dream alive.

At the closing gala, guests mingled and exchanged contacts while filling their plates with grilled lamb and Peking duck. A rock band played onstage, encircled with flashing blue and green lights, and as the guests moved from dinner to dessert, the band eased into the Eagles' classic "Hotel California," a choice so pregnant with meaning that some guests laughed out loud. Was it a sly reference to the Ritz? Merely a reliable crowd-pleaser? Or a commentary on MBS's quest to pull the kingdom from its past?

"You can check out any time you like, but you can never leave."

B Y THE TIME he reached his 34th birthday, Mohammed bin Salman had done it: After emerging from the shadows only a few years before, he had eliminated his rivals, extended his control over the essential organs of the Saudi state, and solidified his position as the kingdom's undisputed center of power. Some of his rise was due to luck. Had his father, Salman, not outlived his own brothers, he would not have become king. Even after Salman ascended to the throne, he could have delegated power to anyone, but he chose MBS, despite his sixth son's youth, inferior résumé, and troublemaker reputation. An absolute monarchy is essentially a democracy of one, and MBS got his father's vote, the only one that mattered.

Once his father had chosen him, MBS's own attributes propelled his rise. He may never have studied abroad, run a company, or served in the military, but he made it clear that among the contenders for leadership of the kingdom, he was harder-working, more strategic, more willing to shatter traditions, and, at times, more brutal than anyone else—a truly Machiavellian prince. Now, unless some unforeseen and remarkable circumstance intervenes, MBS will become king after his father dies, at an age that could allow him to rule for decades to come.

What should the world expect from a Saudi Arabia ruled by Mohammed bin Salman?

His rise has been dominated by two simultaneous drives that will continue into the future. He has championed a vast social and economic overhaul in tandem with an extreme concentration of authoritarian power. MBS's Saudi Arabia is a place where women can drive and work and travel, but where campaigning for more rights can mean jail time. It is a place where young people can mingle and ride rollercoasters and launch start-ups, but where questioning the wisdom of government policies is considered treason. It is a place where young women can entertain dreams forbidden to their mothers and grandmothers, but where law-abiding citizens fear that talking to journalists or human rights groups could make them disappear.

MBS's efforts on the social front are groundbreaking, and he deserves credit for reading the kingdom's demographics and taking the risk to break old rules. It is unclear whether his rivals for the throne would have done the same, and the lives of young Saudis will be richer as a result, a gift from their young crown prince.

He should also be acknowledged for providing a wide-ranging diagnosis of the kingdom's economic challenges and putting momentum behind a plan to address them. But good intentions aside, the required changes are momentous. No country so heavily dependent on oil has yet succeeded in transitioning to a truly diversified economy, and there is little reason to expect that MBS will find the magic solution. Doing so would require overhauling the Saudi workforce, creating an unprecedented number of jobs, and building large new sectors in domains the kingdom has little or no experience with—all at a time when low oil prices have constricted state spending.

The initial public offering of stock in Saudi Aramco, the state oil monopoly, illustrated the gap between MBS's vaunted ambitions and real life. After MBS unveiled the idea of the IPO in 2016, he and his advisors pitched it as a watershed moment in global finance, suggesting the company would be valued at $2 trillion or more and its shares sold on a prominent global exchange, with foreign investors flocking to the deal.

But those goals were scaled back once planning began. The sale was repeatedly delayed before finally going ahead in December 2019 as more of a regional than a global event. Less than two percent of the company's shares were sold, and Aramco was listed only on Saudi Arabia's domestic stock market, because the kingdom had balked at the stringent reporting that a listing in New York or London required and because advisors had told the company that its pricing was too ambitious. The main buyers were wealthy Saudis, who were given incentives to buy, and who had learned the risks of not supporting MBS's initiatives from the lock-up at the Ritz.

The IPO earned Aramco the title of the world's most valuable company (until Apple surpassed it in July 2020), and its stock price rose, pushing its value above the desired $2 trillion mark soon after the sale, if only temporarily. The more than $25 billion the sale raised gave MBS more cash for his diversification plans, but less than the $100 billion he had hoped it would bring in. And the IPO failed to convince outside investors that the company's decision-making would be guided primarily by business, not politics, as was clear when the kingdom launched an oil price war with Russia in early 2020, crashing global prices as the coronavirus pandemic slashed demand.

The pandemic made the challenges of diversification and economic growth even greater, as the kingdom shut down civilian air traffic and imposed strict lockdowns, taking a toll on the economy. Even the annual Hajj pilgrimage, which had welcomed 2.5 million people the year before, was shrunk nearly beyond recognition. At most, a few thousand pilgrims from inside the kingdom took part, bringing in a tiny fraction of the billions of dollars the event earns the kingdom in normal years.

In the long run, MBS's greatest challenge could be the high expectations of his fellow young Saudis. Each year, hundreds of thousands of them enter the job market, and it remains unclear how MBS will create enough jobs not only to employ them, but to maintain the standard of living they grew up with. They may be excited now to go to the movies or dance to the Backstreet Boys, but their perspectives could darken over time as the government's budget tightens and they find themselves unemployed or working harder, and earning less money, than their parents did.

As for NEOM, who knows?

Through his rise, MBS has restructured the nature of power in Saudi Arabia. No longer is the royal family a broad body whose senior princes rule by consensus and maintain relatively independent power centers. Now all significant players, and their capital, answer to MBS. Countering centuries of Saudi history, he has begun un-

linking the clerics from the monarchy. Under MBS, the state's authority comes less from its claim to defending religious orthodoxy
than from a new sense of authoritarian nationalism. So far, MBS's
efforts to weaken the clerics have sparked no major blowback. But
given how long the kingdom has steeped its people in hyper-
conservative ideology, it is hard to imagine that the old ways will
simply fade away, yet difficult to predict how they might resurface.

Across the Middle East, Saudi Arabia has asserted itself in unprecedented ways, often prioritizing force over diplomacy and risky
gambits over thoughtful policies, as the people of Lebanon, Qatar,
and Yemen have witnessed. If this continues, the kingdom's neighbors and international partners could be in for a wild ride as MBS
seeks new ways to counter the Muslim Brotherhood and Iran.

The kingdom's vulnerabilities were laid bare in September 2019,
when surprise attacks with drones and guided cruise missiles put
two key Saudi oil facilities out of commission and filled the skies
above them with plumes of black smoke. The Houthis in Yemen
claimed responsibility for the attacks, but the technology used was
far beyond their capabilities. American and Saudi officials accused
Iran of orchestrating the assault, either directly or through its Arab
proxy militias.

The damage was quickly repaired, but the attacks raised grave
questions for the kingdom. The year before, it had been the world's
third biggest spender on military equipment, investing an estimated
$67.6 billion. So why had facilities of such import, not just to the
kingdom but to the global oil supply, remained so vulnerable to such
cheap weapons? And while President Trump vowed that the United
States was "locked and loaded," he leveraged no American military
might to respond, raising doubts about the United States' decades-
old commitment to ensuring the safety of its allies in the Persian
Gulf.

Saudi officials avoided voicing those concerns publicly, but there
were signs that MBS took them seriously enough to adjust his tactics. Instead of ordering attacks on Iran or its allies, he allowed for
indirect diplomacy through officials in Iraq and Pakistan aimed not
at reaching a formal détente between Iran and the kingdom but at
bringing down the temperature to avoid further violence.

In September 2020, the kingdom's closest regional allies, the United Arab Emirates and Bahrain, announced that they were establishing formal diplomatic relations with Israel, making them only the third and fourth Arab states to do so and the first of the Gulf monarchies. Saudi Arabia did not immediately follow, despite the softer tone MBS has taken toward the Jewish state. How close he will bring Saudi Arabia to Israel will only become clear over time, but there is little reason to expect that sympathy for the Palestinians will guide him as it did his elders. His quiet rapprochement with Israel could accelerate after his father dies.

If MBS deserves credit for the good, he must also accept responsibility for the bad. MBS appears no closer to victory in Yemen than he did years ago. In the meantime, his air force has continued to kill civilians as the country shatters into ever smaller pieces that may never fit back together. MBS did not start the war, and the Houthis are no peacemakers, but the Saudis' callous tactics and inability to change strategy in the face of failure have invited Iran in and fueled great suffering that will not soon be forgotten.

WHEN ASKED ABOUT the killing of Jamal Khashoggi, MBS and other Saudi officials have sought to write it off as an exceptional event, an unauthorized act by a small group of people out of step with the kingdom's policies and character.

I don't buy it.

During his rise, MBS sanctioned a harsh approach to his perceived enemies, allotting state resources to an escalating campaign of electronic attacks, arrests, prosecutions, kidnappings, and torture. Along the way, he and his deputies paid little or no price for any of it, either because their activities remained covert or because the alluring image of the liberalizing young prince overshadowed his harsher side. But by going after Khashoggi, his agents upped the ante and lost the bet, unleashing international condemnation.

Much ink has been spilled on the question of whether MBS ordered the operation, whether there is a "smoking gun" linking him to the killing. We may never know for sure, but that misses the point. Regardless of MBS's role in the murder, he fostered the environment in which fifteen government agents and a number of Saudi diplomats believed that butchering a nonviolent writer inside a consulate was the appropriate response to some newspaper columns. Even if he did not directly order the killing, as a crown prince with oversight of those agencies, it is hard to believe that he had no idea what they were planning.

MBS acknowledged some personal culpability for creating this atmosphere one month after Khashoggi's death.

"I may bear some guilt," he told a group of Americans. "But not because I authorized the heinous act, because I did not, but because I may have caused some of our people to love our kingdom too much and delegated authority in a way that made it too easy for them to think they would be pleasing us by taking matters into their own hands."

Was that really the problem? Or was it his failure to understand that citizens might question their leaders not because they hate their country, but because they love it?

Khashoggi's killing came to symbolize the harshest aspects of MBS's rule, leaving an ugly stain. It will fade over time, but it raises questions about how the United States and other Western nations will deal with Saudi Arabia going forward. Will future American presidents be as happy as Donald Trump to welcome MBS into the Oval Office? Anger has grown in other parts of the government, particularly in Congress. Senators emerged from a briefing on the killing by Director Gina Haspel of the Central Intelligence Agency in a rage. Lindsey Graham of South Carolina, who had been so impressed with MBS a few years before, called him "a wrecking ball."

"There is not a smoking gun, there's a smoking saw," Graham said. "You have to be willfully blind" to miss it.

The Senate passed a unanimous but symbolic resolution holding MBS "personally responsible" for Khashoggi's death, and legislators continued to wage battles with the administration over support for the war in Yemen.

The immediate, concrete effects on U.S.-Saudi relations were minimal, but the chill was significant. Arms and oil companies continued to do business, while many of MBS's heroes in Silicon Valley and Hollywood kept their distance. MBS may have to accept that doors across the United States will no longer swing open when he comes to town—and that protesters might show up outside, wielding saws.

But such reactions may be short-lived. The United States has a long and bipartisan history of working with authoritarians, and MBS is still young. If he succeeds his father and lives to be as old, he will lead an important American partner in a turbulent region into the 2060s.

As policy makers in Washington and other world capitals ponder that possibility, many wonder whether MBS is learning from his mistakes. Are his dangerous acts the youthful faults of an inexperienced ruler? Or do they spring from deep in his character and serve as harbingers of things to come? Will MBS mature into a wiser monarch, or will unpleasant surprises continue to punctuate his reign?

People who have met with him over the years say he now listens a bit more and talks a bit less. His spoken English has gone from nearly nonexistent to good enough to conduct meetings in, indicating that he is a quick study. He seems to enjoy having his ideas challenged, at least by foreigners. And he has finally stopped insisting that victory in Yemen is only three months away.

As the outrage spread over Khashoggi's death, foreign friends told MBS that to move on, he must accept responsibility and ensure justice. He promised to do so. But when the trial of the suspects in the killing opened in Riyadh, it was shrouded in secrecy and Saud al-Qahtani, MBS's "Lord of the Flies," was not among the accused. The trial wound its way through a series of closed sessions that resulted in five unnamed defendants being sentenced to death and three others to prison terms. But before the sentences were carried out, Khashoggi's son Salah announced that the family had pardoned the killers, taking the possibility of execution off the table. (Salah and his siblings received tens of thousands of dollars, as well as real estate worth millions, from the Saudi government after their father's murder in what was widely seen as compensation.) In September 2020, the court gave those eight men prison terms ranging from seven to twenty years, punishment the kingdom hoped would put the Khashoggi issue to rest. But human rights groups dismissed the trial as a farce for not holding accountable or even examining the possible culpability of senior officials, including MBS.

"The Saudi authorities are closing the case without the world knowing the truth of who is responsible for Jamal's murder," Hatice Cengiz, Khashoggi's fiancée, wrote. "Who planned it, who ordered it, where is his body?"

Only time will tell how long the stain of Khashoggi's killing will cling to MBS, and how the scandal might affect his decision-making in the future.

Perhaps it is lonely at the top. Perhaps as he moves through his days in his palaces, in the Royal Court, and on his yacht in the Red Sea overlooking the barren sands where he hopes NEOM will rise, he meets few people with the courage to blunt his more destructive impulses or an incentive to tell him that a beach with glow-in-the-dark sand is less crucial to Saudi Arabia's future than investments in peace, education, and the rule of law.

IN THE SUMMER of 2019, Saudi Arabia announced that women could obtain passports and travel without the permission of a male relative. The new regulations were significant blows to the kingdom's "guardianship" system, and marked another step forward for Saudi women.

Curious how these changes affected women I had met, I got back in touch with Rahaf Alzahrani, the architecture student whose inaugural drive I had witnessed at the women's university in Jeddah the year before. She was elated. Now 23, she had landed a scarce spot in a women's driving school and gotten her license. When I called, she had just taken a seven-hour road trip with her mom to the family's hometown. Along the way, other drivers had honked to show their support, and soldiers at checkpoints had smiled and waved her along. Driving through one village, she said, a young girl had spotted her in the driver's seat and flashed a thumbs-up.

"I was like, whoa, even young girls know about these things," Alzahrani said.

So much had changed in the lives of young Saudi women in such a short time that they were still making sense of it. Guardianship had never been a big barrier for her, but its erosion still empowered her. Her father had recently injured his hand, so she volunteered as his personal chauffeur. Her driving so impressed him that he gave her his Range Rover. The entertainment push had taken off in Jeddah, where she lived, and her friends had recently attended a show by the American DJ Marshmello.

"I never thought in a million years he would come to Jeddah," she said.

Thanks to MBS, when her generation had their own children, they would probably consider such events normal and find it funny that Saudi Arabia had once barred women from driving.

But Alzahrani was not thinking that far ahead yet. She would finish her degree in a year and a half and wanted to teach other aspiring architects to use design software. Later, she would practice architecture herself. She had always been fascinated by mosques and wanted one day to design her own.

"I am going to build a mosque," she told me. "I don't know when, but I'm going to do it."

ONE OF MY best friends in Saudi Arabia was a guy who worked in a bank. He was not political, but was thoughtful and curious about the world. Like many of the young Saudis I got to know, he was excited about MBS. Finally, he told me, the kingdom had a leader who understood young people and would not be cowed by the clerics.

But as MBS gained more power, my ability to speak with people like him, and the ability of people like him to speak their minds, waned. Waves of arrests spread fear among Saudis I knew. One fled the kingdom after the government put him on trial for some tweets. He is still abroad, struggling. Others sought out foreign jobs or study programs, planning to stay away until the situation calmed down. Some of those who had been jailed during MBS's rise were released, but shed their public profiles lest they get arrested again. Trials for some began, and well-known activists such as Loujain Al-Hathloul faced charges that included speaking to diplomats and journalists, making it clear that such activities were suspect, even criminal. The authorities later told Al-Hathloul that to get out of jail, she had to make a video denying she had been tortured. She refused, and remained in prison.

Even Saudis who avoided activism worried about the government eavesdropping on them or hacking their phones. Over time, people I enjoyed chatting with on the phone suggested we move to encrypted messaging apps. Later, some cut me off or blocked me, just to be safe. Others got in touch only while abroad. The braver ones switched to apps they thought were more secure, setting their messages to disappear in twelve hours, then six hours, then thirty minutes, then five minutes. After Jamal Khashoggi was killed, a friend I had known for years set his messages to disappear in thirty seconds. As I raced to read them, I realized that something fundamental had changed in Saudi Arabia.

Something fundamental had changed for me, too. Over my years of reporting on the kingdom, I had spent significant time there, made friends, and generally wished the place well. But my reporting on MBS and his activities got me cast as a hostile party. The visas grew scarce and then stopped altogether; my work was attacked on social media; and it appeared that the Saudis had tried at least once to hack my cellphone. When Jamal Khashoggi was killed, it became clear the old rules no longer applied. I was not a Saudi and so had no reason to think that MBS and his people felt the same sense of betrayal toward me that they did toward him, but here I was writing a book about the prince himself. I did wonder, while walking home late at night or drifting off to sleep, whether they might come after me as well.

Not long after Khashoggi's death, I messaged my friend who worked in the bank.

"It's you, Ben!!!" he responded. "Hiii!!"

He was glad I had gotten in touch, he wrote. There was something he needed to tell me. The situation in Saudi Arabia had changed since we met and he was now afraid of communicating with a journalist. If the messages were intercepted, he would be at the state's mercy, with little chance to defend himself.

He was breaking up with me.

He said not to take it personally and that having me as a friend had been "a real honor." I told him I understood and asked that he save my number so he could call me from abroad someday to say hi.

"I promise to do so," he wrote.

I haven't heard from him since.

Beirut
September 2020

ACKNOWLEDGMENTS

THIS BOOK WOULD not have happened had I not been lucky enough to work for *The New York Times*, which gave me the resources to do the reporting, skilled editors to polish my articles, and enough time away from the news to refine five years of notes into the work you hold in your hands. It was, first and foremost, the deep commitment of the Sulzberger family to international reporting that enabled me to spend so much time in Saudi Arabia so I could put my experiences into print.

I am particularly grateful to Michael Slackman, who directs the newspaper's international coverage, for recognizing—before any of us had heard of Mohammed bin Salman—that Saudi Arabia had a story worth telling, and sending me back to the kingdom again and again and again to tell it. His vision proved to be prescient and his dedication unshakable. I also received valuable support from Dean Baquet, Joe Kahn, Matt Purdy, Carolyn Ryan, Greg Winter, and Herbert Buschbaum. Too many other *Times* staffers and editors shared their skills and wisdom along the way to be mentioned here.

The reporting in these pages would be significantly thinner had I not had the privilege to work with and learn from a range of talented colleagues. David D. Kirkpatrick, Mark Mazzetti, and Nicholas Kulish proved to be trusted comrades who skillfully dug up troves of information. Carlotta Gall and Declan Walsh generously shared interviews they had conducted with main characters. Eric Schmitt, Peter Baker, Katie Benner, and Kate Kelly helped run down leads from Washington, D.C., and New York. Malachy Browne and the video investigations team brought our common work to life.

Mayy El Sheikh spent many hours digging through, organizing, and translating cables for the first section of "MBS's War," and Shuaib Almosawa provided on-the-ground reporting on events in Yemen outside of my visits. In Beirut, Anne Barnard and Thanassis Cambanis offered encouragement and companionship when the task felt insurmountable. Hwaida Saad and Karam Shoumali remained true friends throughout, while deftly juggling a range of tasks and offering insights.

Inside the kingdom, Tasneem Alsultan's unique eye and deep human sense helped me navigate during a number of trips. I always enjoyed sharing thoughts and meals with Stephen Kalin, Sarah Birke, and Vivian Nereim. Further afield, Hala Aldosary and Robert Lacey continually taught me new things about the kingdom. I am grateful to Maggie Mitchell Salem, who shared with me more than she realized at the time because she wanted to make sure that Jamal Khashoggi's words were preserved.

My greatest debt is to the many, many Saudis who shared their thoughts and stories with me inside Saudi Arabia and elsewhere over the years, but I will forgo naming them here so as not to jeopardize their status in the kingdom. They include friends and contacts in and outside of the government who welcomed me into their homes and offices for chats; took me out for breakfast; introduced me to their children and, sometimes, their wives; challenged my assumptions over drinks in Beirut; strolled with me through parks in London; fielded extended queries on encrypted messaging apps; and continued to take my calls long after many others had stopped. They know who they are, and I hope they will see their time with me reflected in these pages.

As for the many other Saudis whose paths I crossed, it is my sincere hope that they will tell their own stories of this momentous time in their country's history.

As this manuscript came together, Ryan Lucas, Abigail Hauslohner, and Sana; Karim Lebhour, Nicola Palmer, Léa and Lucian; and Ben C. Solomon helped me stay housed, fed, and entertained in Washington, D.C., and New York.

My agent, Larry Weissman, grasped the idea of this book before I did and skillfully guided me through the business side. My editor,

Tim Duggan, took a good book and made it much better. Pam Feinstein did a tight copyedit. Hilary McClellan did a thorough fact-check and helped me avoid errors. Ruth Fecych untangled sentences to make the text easier to read.

A number of friends agreed to enrich this work with their insights and expertise. Vivian Nereim, Emile Hokayem, and John Evans— a dear friend for two decades—each read the full text and offered invaluable guidance. Cole Bunzel and Stéphane LaCroix reviewed sections on Saudi history and religion; April Longley Alley ensured I got the war in Yemen right; Kristian Ulrichsen did the same for the Qatar blockade; and Carlotta Gall vetted sections on the events in Istanbul.

All mistakes, oversights, and omissions are my fault alone.

My parents have always done their utmost to support my career choices, even when they led me many time zones away. My mother, Pamela, is a model of how not to forget the most vulnerable. My father, Robert, showed me through years of scholarship that good things could be done through long hours at a computer. Matt, Danielle, and Elliott, thanks for all the fun.

In Beirut, the Choucair and Khodr clans—Naoum, Amira, Dimitri, Cynthia, George, Mada, and Bechara—welcomed me as one of their own and allowed me to stick around, no matter who won at cards. And I have nothing but love and gratitude for Sabine, the clown-in-chief, who put up with seemingly interminable hand-wringing and working weekends as this book progressed while valiantly battling the Middle East's doom and gloom with her bountiful laughter.

NOTES

ABBREVIATIONS

NYT *The New York Times*
WaPo *The Washington Post*
WSJ *The Wall Street Journal*
AP *The Associated Press*
SPA *Saudi Press Agency*
MMS-JK WhatsApp messages between Jamal Khashoggi and Maggie Mitchell Salem, provided by the latter.
OA-JK WhatsApp messages between Jamal Khashoggi and Omar Abdulaziz, provided by the latter.
(Ar.) Source language is Arabic.
(Tu.) Source language is Turkish.
(Fr.) Source language is French.

EPIGRAPH

vii *introduction of changes:* Translation by Ninian Hill Thomson.

INTRODUCTION

xiv *22 million: CIA World Factbook: Saudi Arabia.* Saudi Arabia's total population in 2017 was estimated at 33 million, about one-third of which were foreigners.
xvi *human inhabitants:* "Sun, Sea and Robots: Saudi Arabia's Sci-Fi City in the Desert," Bloomberg, Oct. 26, 2017.
xvi *place for "dreamers":* MBS onstage at the Future Investment Initiative, Oct. 24, 2017.
xvi *"leap for humanity":* "Saudi Arabia Crown Prince Details Plans for New City," Bloomberg, Oct. 26, 2017.

xvi *"of the whole world":* MBS onstage at the Future Investment Initiative, Oct. 24, 2017.

xvii *"learning from him":* Author interview, relative of Ritz detainee, Nov. 2017.

xviii *"so-called":* cited in "Obama, in an awkward twist, becomes Saudi Arabia's defender," *Politico*, Sept. 22, 2016.

THE KINGDOM

To paint a picture of MBS's life before 2015, I interviewed a range of Saudis and others who crossed paths with him in his youth, including members of the royal family, three of his classmates, diplomats who served in Saudi Arabia, members of the Saudi elite who socialized with his family, and others who spent time in the entourages of Salman and his sons. Most spoke on condition of anonymity for fear of jeopardizing their interests or relatives in Saudi Arabia. I also consulted published reports, cited below.

For the history of Saudi Arabia and Wahhabism, I benefited from the following works:

Robert Lacey, *The Kingdom: Arabia and the House of Saud* (New York: Avon Books, 1981).

Robert Lacey, *Inside the Kingdom: Kings, Clerics, Modernists, Terrorists, and the Struggle for Saudi Arabia* (New York: Penguin Books, 2009).

Michael Darlow and Barbara Bray, *Ibn Saud: The Desert Warrior Who Created the Kingdom of Saudi Arabia* (New York: Skyhorse Publishing, 2010).

Michael Crawford, *Ibn 'Abd Al-Wahhab* (London: Oneworld Publications, 2014).

Madawi Al-Rasheed, *A History of Saudi Arabia* (Cambridge, Cambridge University Press, 2010).

3 *one of his wives:* There is some confusion over whether MBS's mother is Salman's second or third wife. Karen Elliott House, in "Profile of a Prince" (Belfer Center for Science and International Affairs, 2019), says she is third, while a number of my own sources and Michael Field, *Tree of Al-Saud* (Arabian Charts, version 24.6), have her as second.

3 *for an English tutor:* Sekkai's story is from an author interview in March 2018 and "MBS: My strange experience of teaching the Saudi crown prince," BBC, Dec. 9, 2018. Quotes from each are noted as such.

3 *named Mohammed bin Salman:* "MBS: My strange experience of teaching the Saudi crown prince," BBC, Dec. 9, 2018.

4 *regale his siblings:* Ibid.

4 *surveillance cameras on the walls:* Ibid.

4 *family lavished on him:* Author interview, Rachid Sekkai, March 2018.

4 *"attention of everybody"*: Ibid.

5 *"prison at this moment"*: "How Stable Are the Saudis?," *The New York Times Magazine*, Nov. 8, 1981.

5 *"get back to work"*: Embassy Riyadh. "Crown Prince Sultan Backs the King in Family Disputes," Wikileaks cable: 07RIYADH296_a. Dated Feb. 12, 2007. https://wikileaks.org/plusd/cables/07RIYADH296_a.html

5 *in trade caravans:* Michael Darlow and Barbara Bray, *Ibn Saud.*

7 *twenty-seven daughters:* Michael Field, *Tree of Al-Saud*, Arabian Charts, version 24.6. Reports conflict on the number of King Abdulaziz's wives and children, so I have relied on Field's well-regarded research.

7 *more than $2 billion per year:* Embassy Riyadh. "Saudi Royal Wealth: Where Do They Get All That Money," Wikileaks cable: 96RIYAD H4784_a. Dated Nov. 20, 1996. https://wikileaks.org/plusd/cables/96 RIYADH4784_a.html

7 *feasts for his subjects:* Ibid.

7 *communities where they landed:* For example, about 1,500 guests showed up in Marbella, Spain, for the wedding of one of Salman's granddaughters to another royal in 2011. "Saudi royal wedding to bring welcome boost to local economy," *Sur in English*, June 17, 2011.

8 *of his father's thirty-six sons:* Michael Field, *Tree of Al-Saud*, Arabian Charts, version 24.6.

9 *cover the war:* "Prince Fahd ibn Salman dies at 46," *Arab News*, July 26, 2001.

9 *"were in the U.S.":* Embassy Riyadh. "Saudi Leadership Profiles: Prince Sultan bin Salman," Wikileaks cable: 10RIYADH31_a. Dated Jan. 5, 2010. https://wikileaks.org/plusd/cables/10RIYADH31_a.html

9 *family's media company:* "Prince Ahmed ibn Salman passes away," *Arab News*, Sept. 23. 2002.

9 *"member of Saudi royalty":* "A Charming Prince Is Lost," *Los Angeles Times*, July 23, 2002.

9 *her bodyguard to kill him:* "French Judge Has Issued Arrest Warrant for Saudi Princess," *NYT*, March 15, 2018.

10 *mother was harsh, too:* "The $2 Trillion Project to Get Saudi Arabia's Economy Off Oil," Bloomberg, April 21, 2016.

10 *"the mistakes we made":* Ibid.

10 *made him stronger:* Ibid.

11 *died suddenly at age 46:* "Prince Fahd ibn Salman dies at 46," *Arab News*, July 26, 2001.

11 *died, too, at age 44:* "Prince Ahmed ibn Salman passes away," *Arab News*, Sept. 23, 2002.

11 *near him at the mosque:* Author interviews, associates of the royal family, 2017–19.

12 *palace built by his brother:* "An Arabian manna from heaven for Marbella," *Sur in English*, August 12, 2016.

12 *family in Barcelona:* Author interviews, associates of the royal family, 2017–19, and Karen Elliott House, "Profile of a Prince," Belfer Center for Science and International Affairs, 2019.

12 *brought from home:* Author interviews, associates of the royal family, 2018–19.

12 *governor's son:* Author interviews, associates of the royal family, 2016–19.

12 *"a backward, crazy country":* Author interview, Joel C. Rosenberg, Nov. 2019.

13 *Alexander the Great:* Author interview, MBS classmate, Dec. 2018.

13 *"to be in the lead":* Author interview, Saudi prince, Sept. 2016.

13 *"system of Great Britain":* Ibid.

13 *"'like some criminal'":* Embassy Riyadh. "Ambassador's Farewell Call on Riyadh Provincial Governor Prince Salman," Wikileaks cable: 07 RIYADH651_a. Dated April 1, 2007. https://wikileaks.org/plusd/cables/07RIYADH651_a.html

13 *fourth in his class in 2007:* House, "Profile of a Prince," and "The $2 Trillion Project," Bloomberg.

13 *work for his father:* Ibid.

13 *ball in Riyadh:* "al-ameer salmaan yaHtafil b: zawaaj najlihi" (Ar.), *Al-Riyadh*, April 7, 2008.

13 *for their wives and daughters:* Author interviews, associates of the royal family, 2018–19.

14 *land near a casino:* Ibid.

14 *during a single shop visit:* "An Arabian manna from heaven for Marbella," *Sur in English*, August 12, 2016.

14 *pork, and all-night parties:* Ibid.

14 *"catwalks for fashion models":* Ibid.

14 *forty-one rooms for five months:* "The Saudi Princess and the Multi-Million Dollar Shopping Spree," *Vanity Fair*, April 2015.

14 *came to $19.5 million:* "Saudi prince forks out 15 mn euros at Paris Disneyland," *AFP*, June 3, 2013.

15 *"the governor's kid":* Author interview, retired Western diplomat, Sept. 2018.

15 *"when I was young":* "The $2 Trillion Project," Bloomberg.

15 *king later relented:* House and Ibid.

16 *cabinet-level position:* "Leadership's trust in me is my motivation—Muhammad," *The Saudi Gazette*, March 3, 2013.

16 *"psychology of his countrymen":* Lacey, *The Kingdom*, p. 230.

17 *father appreciated it:* Author interview, associate of the royal family, Aug. 2018.

17 *"I need a Bedouin":* Author interview, associate of the royal family, Nov. 2018.

17 *on a small pad:* All quotes from Joseph Westphal from author interview, Sept. 2018.

ARRIVALS

22 *covert church service:* "Christian prayer group arrested in Saudi Arabia," *Christian Today*, Sept. 15, 2014.

22 *"inappropriate dancing":* "Report: Saudi men arrested for dancing at party," *AP*, Feb. 22, 2015.

22 *James Dean era:* An excellent book about Riyadh and *tafheet* is Pascal Menoret, *Joyriding in Riyadh: Oil, Urbanism, and Road Revolt* (Cambridge: Cambridge University Press, 2014).

23 *"open the door to evil":* "DMTV #hash_khaliji . . . hamlet qiyaadat al mar'a lis-siyaaraat fi as-sa'udiya," YouTube video, Oct. 21, 2013. https://www .youtube.com/watch?v=NGb4JEwB1aE The cleric was Mohammed al-Nujaimi.

23 *"conspiracy of women driving":* "sheikh naaSir al-'omar fi ziyaarat ad-diwaan" (Ar.), YouTube, Oct. 22, 2013. https://www.youtube.com/watch ?v=6AuaxaGIwTM

23 *to weaken the kingdom:* The video, by David Keyes is available at "aS-Sahyuuni deefid keys yad'u ila qiyaadat al-mar'a fi as-sa'udiya" (Ar.), YouTube video, Oct. 23, 2011. https://www.youtube.com/watch?v =mYmq90ML90k

23 *"split and divide society":* Saudi Foreign Ministry statement, Oct. 24, 2013.

24 *"will laugh at this image":* "lujain al-hathluul tasuuq min maTaar ar-riyaaDH ila manziliha bi rifqat waalidiha" (Ar.), YouTube, Oct. 25, 2013. https://www.youtube.com/watch?v=9UHLm6_CGpU

24 *"not a revolution":* Author interview, Madeha Alajroush, Oct. 2013.

24 *"That's Saudi for you":* Author interview, Eman Al Nafjan, Oct. 2013.

25 *"no woman, no drive":* "No Woman, No Drive," YouTube, Oct. 26, 2013. https://www.youtube.com/watch?v=aZMbTFNp4wI

26 *"who this will be":* Embassy Riyadh. "Saudi Succession: Can the allegiance commission work?" Wikileaks cable: 09RIYADH1434_a. Dated Oct 28, 2009. https://wikileaks.org/plusd/cables/09RIYADH1434_a.html

CORONATION

For this and other sections dealing with the Obama administration, I interviewed and corresponded with nine members of the administration and spoke during my trips to the kingdom with a number of Saudi officials. The names of those who agreed to speak for attribution are in the text or noted below where relevant.

27 *left with Salman:* Author interview, associate of the royal family present at the time, Apr. 2019.

29 *having him around:* Author interview, Ford Fraker, 2015.

30 *the other for security:* Karen Elliott House, "Profile of a Prince," Belfer Center for Science and International Affairs, 2019.

30 *"entire government was restructured"*: "The $2 Trillion Project," Bloomberg.

30 *"a nervous breakdown"*: "The $2 Trillion Project to Get Saudi Arabia's Economy Off Oil," Bloomberg, April 21, 2016.

31 *$32 billion:* Author interview, John Sfakianakis, Feb. 2015.

32 *"believed to be about 30"*: "Germany Rebukes Its Own Intelligence Agency for Criticizing Saudi Policy," *NYT*, Dec. 3, 2015.

32 *"referred to as 'MbS'"*: "Obama smooths relations with Saudi rulers," *Politico*, May 13, 2015.

33 *an Arabic translator:* Author interviews, Obama administration officials, Sept. 2018, May 2019.

33 *advance women's rights in Saudi Arabia:* Ibid.

33 *MBS's strategic move:* Ibid.

33 *from his own father, the king:* The confinement of MBS's mother and the theories surrounding it are from author interviews with six U.S. officals with access to intelligence reports, September 2018 and May 2019, and with other members of the royal family and the Saudi elite, 2018–19.

33–34 *the king's wife highly offensive:* When *NBC News* first broke the story in "U.S. officials: Saudi crown prince has hidden his mother from his father, the king," *NBC News*, March 15, 2018, spokespeople at the Saudi Embassy in Washington offered to arrange a private meeting so she could refute the story. The reporters declined to accept a meeting that had to stay secret, and a Saudi spokesman declared their decision to publish "reckless."

"The story is absolutely false and highly offensive," the spokesman, Saud Kabli, wrote. "The Princess offered to meet with you privately to personally refute the story but you declined. Instead, you have chosen to rely entirely on unnamed and anonymous sources for your reporting. Thus, your viewers cannot judge your sources' motives or credibility."

NBC misspelled Kabli's name as Kabil.

YOUNG PRINCE RISING

36 *"used them to attack us"*: Embassy Riyadh. "Special Advisor Holbrooke's meeting with Saudi Assistant Interior Minister Prince Mohammed bin Nayef," Wikileaks cable: 09RIYADH670_a. Dated May 17, 2009. https://wikileaks.org/plusd/cables/09RIYADH670_a.html

36 *MBN said, "that's dumb"*: Ibid.

37 *United Kingdom and defused:* "U.S. Sees Complexity of Bombs as Link to Al Qaeda," *NYT*, Oct. 30, 2010.

37 *court into his own:* "Saudi king orders merging of royal courts," *AlArabiya*, May 1, 2015.

37 *inherit the kingdom:* Author interviews, former White House officials, Sept. 2018, July 2019.

37 *"believe the earth is flat"*: Embassy Abu Dhabi. "A Long Hot Summer for UAE-Saudi Relations," Wikileaks cable 09ABUDHABI981_a. Dated Oct. 15, 2009. https://wikileaks.org/plusd/cables/09ABUDHABI981_a .html

38 "Darwin was right": Embassy Abu Dhabi. "S/P Director Haass and Chief of Staff Muhammad bin Zayid Discuss Iraq, Iran and Saudi-U.S. Relations," Wikileaks cable: 03ABUDHABI237_a. Dated Jan. 15, 2003. https://wikileaks.org/plusd/cables/03ABUDHABI237_a.html

38 *the two could meet:* "Tiny, Wealthy Qatar Goes Its Own Way, and Pays for It," *NYT*, Jan. 22, 2018.

38 *deemed too old:* Author interviews, Obama administration officials, 2018–19.

39 *profits to his family:* "I Am the Mastermind": Mohammed bin Salman's Guide to Getting Rich, *WSJ*, May 16, 2018.

39 *vacation to the Maldives:* The vacation in the Maldives and some of its details are from author interviews with two service providers near the resort, Jan. 2017 and July 2019; a Maldivian official, July 2019; and four U.S. officials with access to intelligence reports.

39 *$30,000 per night:* Details and quotes about the resort and its amenities are from "Velaa Private Island: A Marvel In The Maldives," *Forbes*, March 31, 2014, unless otherwise noted.

40 *escorted to a seaplane:* "Saudi Prince Visiting Maldives For His $8m Private Party," *Maldives Finest*, June 11, 2015.

40 *"how long it would last"*: "Shakira Visits Maldives For The Private Party Of Saudi Prince," *Maldives Finest*, June 16, 2015.

40 *"forward to the next trip"*: Pitbull (@pitbull), "The Maldives is heaven like," Twitter post, June 15, 2015. https://twitter.com/pitbull/status /610446395699503104

40 *"sophistication and technology"*: "Scoop: Fincantieri delivers 134 metre superyacht Serene," *Superyacht Times*, August 5, 2011.

40 *feet of internal space:* Ibid.

40 *Grand Central Terminal:* Calculations by author.

40 *two dozen guests:* "Serene Yacht for Charter," YachtCharterFleet website, accessed May 2019. https://www.yachtcharterfleet.com/luxury-charter -yacht-23155/serene.htm

41 *after a tennis match:* "Thanks dad! Bill Gates treats his family to a Mediterranean vacation on board a 450-ft superyacht complete with a submarine, 12 state rooms and a helicopter to fly them to and from tennis," *The Daily Mail*, Aug. 7, 2014.

41 *done within hours:* "Rise of Saudi Prince Shatters Decades of Royal Tradition," *NYT*, Oct. 15, 2016.

41 *more than $456 million:* The *Serene* contract was first published in "Offshore Gurus Help Rich Avoid Taxes On Jets And Yachts," *International Consortium of Investigative Journalists*, November 6, 2017.

41 *his "inner circle"*: "Saudi king's French Riviera holiday provokes beach protest," Reuters, July 25, 2015.

41 *hundreds of luxury cars*: "King Salman's French holiday: A throne, motor-cades and a lift to the beach," BBC, July 27, 2015.

41 *an elevator for the king*: "Saudi king's French Riviera holiday provokes beach protest," Reuters, July 25, 2015.

41 *the negative media coverage*: "Saudi Arabian king leaves France after holiday controversy," Reuters, Aug. 2, 2015.

41 *villas, and a giant tent*: "Saudi Royal Family Is Still Spending in an Age of Austerity," *NYT*, Dec. 27, 2019.

41 *to hunt big game*: "How a South African hunting resort opened a window to Saudi crown prince's business empire," *amaBhungane*, May 9, 2019.

41 *"world's most expensive home"*: "This $301 Million Mansion is the World's Most Expensive Home," *Money*, Dec. 15. 2015.

41–42 *wedding to Kanye West*: Kim Kardashian (@kimkardashian), Instagram photo, Apr. 15, 2014.

42 *twenty-first-century technology*: "COGEMAD Redefines 'The Royal Touch' at Château Louis XIV," COGEMAD press release, April 18, 2014.

42 *"an exclusive royal touch"*: Ibid.

42 *"brand new for ghosts"*: MBS's château was first reported by Nicholas Kulish and Michael Forsythe in "World's Most Expensive Home? Another Bauble for a Saudi Prince," *NYT*, Dec. 16, 2017.

COURTING OBAMA

43 *"unclench your fist"*: President Barack Obama's Inaugural Address, White House transcript, Jan. 21, 2009.

44 *not understand Saudi society*: Author interviews, four Obama administration officials, 2018–19.

44 *"know what they meant"*: Author interview, Ben Rhodes, Feb. 2019.

44 *"he'll be out"*: Author interviews, three Obama administration officials, 2018–19.

45 *the prince's cockiness*: Ibid.

45 *have enough cash*: "Letter From Saudi Arabia," *NYT*, Nov. 25, 2015.

45 *"connecting to the top"*: Ibid.

45 *"decide to do something"*: Ibid.

46 *"family and the population"*: "Germany Rebukes Its Own Intelligence Agency for Criticizing Saudi Policy," *NYT*, Dec. 3, 2015.

46 *"player in local politics"*: Embassy Riyadh. "Meeting with controversial Shi'a Sheikh Nimr al-Nimr," Wikileaks cable: 08RIYADH1283_a. Dated Aug. 23, 2008.

47 *"his reward from God"*: "maatha qaala as-sheikh nimr an-nimr 'an suriya wa bashaar al-asad" (Ar.), YouTube, July 8, 2012. https://www.youtube.com/watch?v=iJyEETz2Mlo

47 *"want to remove them"*: "al-feedeo allathi sayo'dam bi sababihi as-sheikh nimr an-nimr" (Ar.), YouTube, Oct. 21, 2014. https://www.youtube.com /watch?v=l9C3DMGSXIU

49 *"a better Saudi Arabia"*: MBS's complete interview is "Transcript: Interview with Muhammad bin Salman," *The Economist*, Jan 6, 2016.

NO SUCH THING AS WAHHABISM

My understating of Saudi Arabia's modern religious and social history was enriched by Stéphane Lacroix, *Awakening Islam*, Cambridge: President and Fellows of Harvard College, 2011.

50 *and stopping bad:* Quran 3:104 says "Let there arise out of you a band of people inviting to all that is good, enjoining what is right, and forbidding what is wrong: They are the ones to attain felicity."

51 *"Filthy criminals"*: Author interview, Saudi businessman, Feb. 2015.

53 *"believe we have Wahhabism"*: "Saudi Crown Prince: Iran's Supreme Leader 'Makes Hitler Look Good,'" *The Atlantic*, April 2, 2018.

54 *"only true Islam"*: All details and quotes from Hisham al-Sheikh are from author interviews, 2016. His last name and that of his uncle, the Grand Mufti, is more correctly Al al-Sheikh, but I have opted for al-Sheikh to ease reading for the nonspecialist.

56 *final decision to wed:* All quotes from interview by Sheikha al-Dosary, from Meshael al-Sheikh, April 2016.

57 *death of Mickey Mouse:* "Saudi Cleric Muhammad Al Munajid Mickey Mouse Must Die," YouTube, Feb. 13, 2009. https://www.youtube.com /watch?v=j7IpMIhR6Yg

57 *and then backtracked:* "SALIH AL-MUNAJJID AND MICKEY MOUSE FATWA!! (BEWARE OF JEWS)," YouTube, July 23, 2011. https://www .youtube.com/watch?v=vIxR1NGZY3I

57 *all-you-can-eat buffets:* Sheikh Saleh al-Fawzan, "taktheeb shaa'ia," statement published by mu'asasat ad-da'wa al khayriya website, Mar. 18, 2014. https://web.archive.org/web/20140523231314/http://www.af.org.sa:80 /ar/node/3430

57 *"not with anything"*: "sheikh saaleh al-fawzaan HafaTHahu alla wa mata'na bihi, mooDat at-taSweer ma'a al-qiTaT" (Ar.) YouTube, Apr. 17, 2016. https://www.youtube.com/watch?v=OivAbgXf2LQ

57 *"sin and transgression"*: English Translations of Majmoo' al-Fatawa of the Permanent Committee for Scholarly Research and Ifta' of the Kingdom of Saudi Arabia, Second Collection, Vol. 11, p. 52. https://archive.org /stream/en_10_Majmoo_alFatawa_IFTAA_COLL02/en_11_Majmoo _alFatawa_IFTAA_COLL02_djvu.txt

57 *"destruction of societies"*: Fatwas of Ibn Baz, Vol. 1, Part 1, Pg. 418, Portal of the General Presidency of Scholarly Research and Ifta,' The Kingdom

of Saudi Arabia. https://web.archive.org/web/20180318061837/http://
alifta.com/Fatawa/fatawaChapters.aspx?languagename=en&View=Page
&PageID=75&PageNo=1&BookID=14&TopFatawa=true

57 *"from another door"*: English Translations of Majmoo' al-Fatawa of the
Permanent Committee for Scholarly Research and Iftaa' of the Kingdom
of Saudi Arabia, First Collection, Part 16, p. 572. https://archive.org
/stream/en_10_Majmoo_alFatawa_IFTAA_COLL02/en_16_Majmoo
_alFatawa_IFTAA_COLL01_djvu.txt

58 *"That is not permitted"*: Author interviews, Hisham al-Sheikh, 2016.

58 *"you must face God"*: Author interview, Abdulaziz al-Sheikh, 2016.

59 *forbade collecting duties:* All information about and quotes from Ahmed al-
Ghamdi are from author interviews over the course of 2016 unless otherwise noted.

61 *"its evil is great"*: "maqTa' kaamil as-sheikh sa'ad as-shathri 'an ikhtilaaT
jaami'at kaust" (Ar.) YouTube, Sept. 30, 2009. https://www.youtube.com
/watch?v=hMVWJsgAoos

61 Okaz *newspaper in 2009:* "al-ikhtilaaT muSTalaH jadeed wa al-adila ash-
shar'iya tarod bi quwa 'ala man yaHrimuhu" (Ar.), *Okaz*, Dec. 9, 2009;
and "al-qawl bi taHreem al-ikhtilaaT ifti'aat 'ala al-shar' wa ibtidaa' fi
ad-deen" (Ar.), *Okaz*, Dec. 10, 2009.

61 *early retirement:* Author interviews, al-Ghamdi, 2016.

61 *dusting of makeup:* Sheikh and Mrs. al-Ghamdi appeared on "Badria,"
MBC, Dec. 13, 2014.

61 *"summon and torture him"*: The cleric was Sheikh Saleh al-Luheidan. "aajil
'alaamat Saalih al-luHeidan yad'u ad-dawla ila ta'theeb wa ta'deeb as-
sheikh aHmad al-ghaamdi" (Ar.) YouTube, Dec. 16, 2014. https://www
.youtube.com/watch?v=mY35rIEFCO8

62 *"morals and values of society"*: "radd samaaHat al-mufti 'ala aHmad al-
ghaamdi Hawl aqwaalihi ash-shaatha" (Ar.), YouTube, Jan. 20, 2012.
https://www.youtube.com/watch?v=BxXin1ITQvM

62 *death threats on Twitter:* Author interviews, al-Ghamdi, 2016.

62 *"troubled and confused"*: "bayan min ahl al 'ilm min qabeelat ghaamid
'an maa saTarahu al-mad'u: aHmed qaasim al ghaamdi Howl mowDuu'
al ikhtilaaT allathi qaamat bi nashrihi SaHeefat 'okaaz bi tareekh 23-
23/12/1432," Tribal statement published on ar.islamway.net, April 9,
2010.

62 *called the police:* Author interviews, al-Ghamdi, 2016.

62 *stood by her brother:* Ibid.

62 *Ammar punched him:* Author interview, Ammar al-Ghamdi, 2016.

62 *character assassination:* The talk show host was Ali al-Oleyani.

63 *interactions with citizens:* "majlis al-wuzara' yuwaafiq 'ala tanTHeem ar-
ri'aasa al-'aama li hay'at al-amr bil-ma'roof wa an-nahi 'an al-munkar"
(Ar.), *SPA*, April 12, 2016. https://www.spa.gov.sa/viewstory.php?lang=ar
&newsid=1488836

GRAND VISIONS

My description of the consulting culture in Saudi Arabia is based on interviews with five current or former consultants working in the kingdom who had experience with McKinsey and Company, Boston Consulting Group, and other firms. I also benefited from: Calvert W. Jones, "All the King's Consultants: The Perils of Advising Authoritarians," *Foreign Affairs*, May/June 2019.

65 *"like a beauty pageant":* Author interview, consultant who had worked in Saudi Arabia, Oct. 2018.
65 *increased by double digits:* "The GCC Consulting Market in 2016," Source Global Research.
65 *more than $1 billion per year:* Source Global Research reports on the GCC consulting market 2017–19.
66 *"they were all-in":* Author interview, former McKinsey consultant, Oct. 2018.
67 *proposing a range of fixes:* "Saudi Arabia Beyond Oil: The Investment and Productivity Transformation," McKinsey Global Institute, Dec. 2015.
67 *"feel an immense pride":* Vision 2030 text, Vision.2030.gov.sa.
68 *"with our prosperous economy":* Ibid.
68 *"able to live without oil":* MBS interview with Turki Aldakhil, *AlArabiya*, April 25, 2016.
68 *"land crossing in the world":* Ibid.
68 *"achieve their personal goals":* Vision 2030.

A ROLE FOR JOURNALISM

I re-created MBS's meeting with the clerics and intellectuals from interviews with Adel Kalbani and Hisham al-Sheikh, May 2016, the latter of whom showed me photos from the event. I also consulted written mentions of it by attendees, including two by Jamal Khashoggi, cited below.

For Jamal Khashoggi's personal history, I read scores of his articles in English and Arabic going back several years; watched many of his television interviews on different subjects; interviewed more than a dozen people who knew him at various stages; and consulted the notes from my own interviews with him between 2014 and 2018.

70 *his luscious lips:* The clerics mentioned here were, in order, Saleh al-Maghamsi, Adel Kalbani, and Mohammed al-Arefe.
71 *association's U.S. national conference:* Author interview, Thomas Hegghammer, who interviewed Khashoggi about the Brotherhood and Afghanistan, Oct. 2019.
72 *from potential attacks:* Ibid.

72 *"the Communist forces"*: "Arab youth fight shoulder to shoulder with Mujahideen," *Arab News*, May 4, 1988.

73 *"praying to God Almighty"*: Ibid.

73 *"countries when they return"*: Ibid.

73 *"always talked about that"*: Author interview, former Khashoggi colleague, Oct. 2018.

73 *"surrendered to hatred and rage"*: Jamal Khashoggi (@JKhashoggi), "inhartu qabla qaleel Hasratan 'alayka abaa 'abd alla" (Ar.), Twitter post, May 2, 2011. https://twitter.com/JKhashoggi/status/65001683628986368

74 *realizing he was Saudi*: Author interview, Khashoggi colleague, Oct. 2018.

74 *behind the scenes*: Author interview, Azzam Tamimi, Feb. 2019.

74 *a hostile power*: Ibid.

75 *"coexistence that it preaches"*: quoted in "Jamal Khashoggi," Biographical Encyclopedia of the Modern Middle East (Farmington Hills, Mich.: Thompson/Gale, 2008).

75 *"called them* mujahideen*"*: quoted in "After the War: Riyadh; A Saudi Editor Who Offended Clerics Is Ousted From His Post," *NYT*, May 28, 2003.

75 *show the question's absurdity*: Embassy Riyadh. "Saudi Editor Laments Muslim Insensitivity to Violence," Wikileaks cable: 09RIYADH911_a. Dated July 12, 2009. https://wikileaks.org/plusd/cables/09RIYADH911 _a.html

76 *bicycle, then a donkey*: "Saudi Arabia's women can finally drive. But the crown prince needs to do much more," *WaPo*, June 25, 2018.

76 *Najib Razak of Malaysia*: "1MDB conspirators and the Khashoggi connection," *The Edge Malaysia Weekly*, Dec. 3, 2018.

77 *"who has brought them back"*: Author interview, Jamal Khashoggi, Dec. 2014.

77 *it was off the air*: "Channel in Bahrain Goes Silent After Giving Opposition Airtime," *NYT*, Feb. 2, 2015.

77 *threat posed by Iran*: "The Salman Doctrine," *AlArabiya*, April 1, 2015.

77 *"I am free to do so"*: "I want to think freely, and write freely," *AlArabiya*, Dec. 29, 2015.

78 *Pakistan, and Djibouti*: "Why Saudi Arabia's crown prince should be worried about Iran's protests," *WaPo*, Jan. 3, 2018.

78 *write about it, go ahead*: Author interview, Hisham al-Sheikh, May 2016.

78 *performed the last prayer of the day together*: Ibid.

78 *"journalists want that role"*: "ro'iyat al-muwaaTin 2030. al-Haq fi al-HuSuul 'ala ma'luuma" (Ar.), *Al Hayat*, Oct. 29, 2016.

THE TWO MOHAMMEDS

79 *older cousin's schedule:* Author interviews, four U.S. officials briefed on the event, Sept. 2018, May 2019. Westphal declined to comment.

80 *on a range of issues:* Embassy Riyadh. "MOI Underscores Need for Broad and Flexible Energy Facilities Security Cooperation," Wikileaks cable: 06RIYADH8989_a. Dated Dec. 4, 2006. https://wikileaks.org/plusd /cables/07RIYADH2474_a.html

80 *the king had fired al-Jabri:* "amr malaki bi-'ifaa' wazeer ad-dawla ad-doktoor sa'ad al-jabri min manSibihi" (Ar.), *Al-Sharq Al-Awsat*, Sept. 11, 2015.

80 *without his most trusted aide:* Author interviews, three associates of Mohammed bin Nayef, 2018–19.

80 *"parts of the Islamic world":* Mohammed bin Salman, press conference, Saudi state television (Ar.), Dec. 14, 2015.

81 *"and to good effect":* Author interview, Lisa Monaco, May 2019.

81 *one prince over the other:* Author interviews, Obama administration officials, 2018–19.

81 *"developing that relationship":* Author interview, Monaco.

81 *cross-dressing and homosexuality:* Author interviews, four U.S. officials with access to intelligence reports, 2018–19.

82 *"He won't be king":* Author interviews, U.S. officials with knowledge of the meeting, 2018–19.

82 *"more for the many":* Details and quotes about Graham's trip to Riyadh from "The $2 Trillion Project to Get Saudi Arabia's Economy Off Oil," *Bloomberg*, April 21, 2016.

83 *less than an hour:* The think tank trip was described in author interviews with Philip Gordon, Dennis Ross, and Michael Allen, 2018–19. All their quotes here are from those interviews.

83 *"head-of-state-like":* Author interview, Michael Allen, Feb. 2019.

85 *"got half of that right":* Author interview, Westphal.

MBS'S WAR

Mayy El Shiekh dedicated many hours to helping me digest and translate the Saudi Wikileaks cables. Shuaib Almosawa provided reporting from Yemen. C. J. Chivers helped identify munitions scraps. Many of the Wikileaks documents cited here were first reported in "Cables Released by Wikileaks Reveal Saudis' Checkbook Diplomacy," *NYT*, June 20, 2015, and "Wikileaks Shows a Saudi Obsession With Iran," *NYT*, July 16, 2015.

For background on the Houthis, I consulted "Regime and Periphery in Northern Yemen: the Huthi Phenomenon," *RAND Corporation*, 2010.

86 *pilgrimage to Mecca:* Saudi Foreign Ministry document, Wikileaks, Jan. 22, 2012. https://wikileaks.org/saudi-cables/pics/5357859a-e321-4088-9137-4b69e0a87f30.jpg

86 *hand out as he saw fit:* Saudi Foreign Ministry document, Wikileaks document: #80451. Undated. https://wikileaks.org/saudi-cables/doc80451.html

86 *"the kingdom asks of him":* Saudi diplomatic cable, Wikileaks document #53032. Dated Aug. 14, 2008. https://wikileaks.org/saudi-cables/doc53032.html

86 *"problems the agency is facing":* Cited in "Cables Released by Wikileaks Reveal Saudis' Checkbook Diplomacy," *NYT*, June 20, 2015.

87 *from going to prison:* Saudi diplomatic cable, Wikileaks document #72359. Undated. https://wikileaks.org/saudi-cables/doc72359.html

87 *preachers had been "prepared":* Reports on the website of the Saudi Ministry of Islamic Affairs, Endowment, Preaching, and Guidance, moia.gov.sa, accessed 2015, since removed.

87 *employed in Guinea:* Saudi Foreign Ministry document, Wikileaks. Dated Jan. 18, 2013. https://wikileaks.org/saudi-cables/pics/5a3363c8-a11e-4a5d-8b66-f39af6077f20.jpg

87 *twelve others in Tajikistan:* Saudi Foreign Ministry document, Wikileaks document 96427. Dated 2011. https://wikileaks.org/saudi-cables/doc96427.html. The Indian scholar was Sheikh Suhaib Hasan.

88 *Islamic association in India:* Saudi Supreme Council of Islamic Affairs document, Wikileaks. Dated Feb. 6, 2012. https://wikileaks.org/saudi-cables/pics/8770db3f-984c-4dda-8b78-96bd2853b063.jpg

88 *overwhelmingly Christian country:* Saudi Foreign Ministry document. Wikileaks document 112213. Dated Feb. 29, 2012. https://wikileaks.org/saudi-cables/doc112213.html

88 *"regional and international issues":* Cited in "Cables Released by Wikileaks Reveal Saudis' Checkbook Diplomacy," *NYT*, June 20, 2015.

90 *"Are you with us or not?":* Author interview, Lisa Monaco, May 2019.

91 *in a matter of weeks:* "Quiet Support for Saudis Entangles U.S. in Yemen," *NYT*, March 13, 2016.

91 *"everyone will be with you":* Author interview, Saudi National Guard officer, May 2016.

92 *killed dozens of people:* "Airstrikes in Yemen Hit Wedding Party, Killing Dozens," *NYT*, Sept. 28, 2015.

92 *had killed fifteen:* "Bombing of Doctors Without Borders Hospital in Yemen Kills at Least 15," *NYT*, Aug. 15, 2016.

92 *sale worth $1.29 billion:* "U.S. Approves $1.29 billion sale of smart bombs to Saudi Arabia," *Reuters*, Nov. 16, 2015.

92 *under any previous president:* "Saudi Arabia: Background and U.S. Relations," Congressional Research Service, Sept. 21, 2018.

92 *"there is no endgame":* "Quiet Support for Saudis Entangles U.S. in Yemen," *NYT*, March 13, 2016. Al-Toraifi was speaking at the Washington Institute for Near East Policy.

93 *father of a local politician:* The funeral was for the father of Galal al-Rawishan, an ally of the Houthis who was serving as interior minister.

93 *including two dozen children:* "Letter dated 27 January 2017 from the Panel of Experts on Yemen addressed to the President of the Security Council," United Nations Security Council, Jan. 31, 2017.

93 *"effectively a double-tap":* Ibid.

93–94 *"an apparent war crime":* "Yemen: Saudi-Led Funeral Attack Apparent War Crime," *Human Rights Watch*, Oct. 13, 2016.

94 *"principles, values, and interests":* "Statement by NSC Spokesperson Ned Price on Yemen," White House press release, Oct. 8, 2016.

94 *"regrettable and painful bombing":* cited in "A Roar at a Funeral, and Yemen's War Is Altered," *NYT*, Oct. 9, 2016.

94 *"our little Hiroshima":* Interview by Shuaib Almosawa, Oct. 2016.

94 *"we are ready":* "The $2 Trillion Project to Get Saudi Arabia's Economy Off Oil," *Bloomberg*, April 21, 2016.

95 *"We had no other choice":* "Watch & Read: Mohammed bin Salman's full interview," *AlArabiya*, May 3, 2017.

96 *"oppressed and the weak":* Author interview, Majid Ali, Oct. 2016.

97 *"to put pressure on the politics":* Author interview, Jamie McGoldrick, Oct. 2016.

97 *"who make the potato chips":* Author interview, Mustafa Elaghil, Oct. 2016.

97 *the factory and the base:* Ibid.

97 *by his gold tooth:* Ibid.

97 *"It was everything for us":* Ibid.

98 *more than $50 million:* Author interview, Khalid Alsonidar, Oct. 2016.

98 *"disappeared into thin air":* Author interview, Abdullah Alsonidar, Oct. 2016.

99 *"a family to the ground":* Ibid.

99 *command-and-control centers:* Author correspondence, Ahmed Asiri, Nov. 2016.

SO-CALLED ALLIES

100 *"It's complicated":* "The Obama Doctrine," *The Atlantic*, April 2016.

100 *"nor of the Middle East":* Ibid.

101 *Saudis had bankrolled them anyway:* "Episode 42," *The Axe Files with David Axelrod*, April 18, 2016. Rhodes said: "Basically there was, certainly, at least kind of an insufficient attention to where all this money was going over many years from the government apparatus."

101 *"everything else, thin-skinned":* Author interview, Ben Rhodes, Feb. 2019.

102 *passing handwritten notes:* Author interviews, Obama administration officials, 2018–19.

102 *who was in attendance:* Author interviews, Ben Rhodes and other Obama administration officials, 2018–19.

102 *"we had with the Saudis":* Author interview, Rhodes.

103 *the White House schedule:* "After U.S. Arrival, Saudi Prince Remains Off White House Schedule," *Foreign Policy*, June 14. 2016.

103 *model for tourism, or mining:* Author interviews, five U.S. officials who attended or were briefed on the meeting, Sept. 2018, May 2019.

103 *did not reassure foreign investors:* Ibid.

104 *theme park in Saudi Arabia:* "US theme park giant Six Flags to invest in Saudi Arabia," *AlArabiya*, June 20, 2016.

104 *kingdom's digital infrastructure:* "Saudi Arabia inks digital transformation plans with Cisco Systems," *AlArabiya*, June 21, 2016.

104 *to train young Saudis:* "Saudi Arabia and Microsoft ink plans to support Vision 2030," *AlArabiya*, June 22, 2016.

104 *"traditional democracy ten steps":* "A 30-year-old Saudi prince could jumpstart the kingdom—or drive it off a cliff," *WaPo*, June 28, 2016.

104 *MBS just smiled:* "Saudi deputy crown prince, U.N. chief talk protecting Yemen's children," Reuters, June 22, 2016.

104 *survived an effort to block it in the Senate:* "Senate clears way for $1.15 billion arms sale to Saudi Arabia," Reuters, Sept. 21, 2016.

104 *"sense the irony":* Congressional Record Volume 162, Number 143 (Wednesday, Sept. 21, 2016).

105 *problems with Saudi targeting:* "U.S. to halt some arms sales to Saudi, citing civilian deaths in Yemen campaign," Reuters, Dec. 13, 2016.

A TRUE FRIEND IN THE WHITE HOUSE

To write about Saudi Arabia's relationship with the Trump administration, I interviewed three former administration officials and more than a dozen officials from other branches of the U.S. government who were involved in Saudi policy as well as consulting public reports, cited below.

For Jared Kushner's personal and family background, I consulted Vicky Ward, *Kushner Inc.: Greed. Ambition. Corruption.* (New York: St. Martin's Press, 2019) ebook, and other sources cited below.

The leaked Saudi Strategic Partnership proposal was obtained by the Lebanese newspaper *Al-Akhbar* and shared with *NYT*.

106 *"don't know who's who":* Donald Trump on CNN, March 9, 2016. https://www.youtube.com/watch?v=C-ZjotfZY6o

106 *"Muslims entering the United States":* Donald J. Trump Statement on Preventing Muslim Immigration, press release, Dec. 7, 2015.

106 *calling for surveillance of mosques:* Trump during the presidential debate, Oct. 9, 2016.

106 *"not done by Swedish people"*: Trump on *Fox Business Network*, March 22, 2016.

106–107 *Quran its constitution*: "About Saudi Arabia," website of the Embassy of Saudi Arabia in Washington, D.C., accessed June 2019.

107 *"yet you take their money"*: Trump during presidential debate, Oct. 19, 2016.

107 *"Take a look at Saudi Arabia"*: "Donald Trump Suggested Saudi Arabia Was Behind 9/11 Multiple Times Wednesday," *New York*, Feb. 17, 2016.

107 *"pay us to save them"*: *The O'Reilly Factor*, Fox News, Jan. 4, 2016.

107 *Six percent favored Trump:* "Arab Public Opinion and the 2016 US Presidential Elections," The Arab Center, Washington, D.C., Nov. 1, 2016.

108 *officials familiar with his credentials:* Daniel Golden, *The Price of Admission: How America's Ruling Class Buys Its Way into Elite Colleges—And Who Gets Left Outside the Gates* (New York: Broadway Books, 2007).

108 *smaller amounts to Princeton and Cornell:* Ibid.

108 *"always has been false"*: "The Story Behind Jared Kushner's Curious Acceptance into Harvard," *ProPublica*, Nov. 18, 2016.

110 *was rich and powerful:* "Jared Kushner Was My Boss: What I learned about power, real and imagined, from Trump's 'senior adviser' and son-in-law," *GEN*, June 18, 2019.

110 *"what they're seeing is the truth"*: Ibid.

111 *future of Saudi Arabia:* The correspondence between Tom Barrack, Yusuf Otaiba, and Rick Gerson was reported in "The Wooing of Jared Kushner: How the Saudis Got a Friend in the White House," *NYT*, Dec. 8, 2018.

111 *MBS and the Trump team:* Ibid.

111 *violation of diplomatic protocol:* "Blackwater founder held secret Seychelles meeting to establish Trump-Putin back channel," *WaPo*, April 3, 2017.

111 *Emirati prince after the meeting:* "The Wooing of Jared Kushner."

111 *"true friend in the White House"*: Ibid.

113 *other messaging platforms:* Author interviews, two Trump administration officials and Saudis with knowledge of the relationship, 2018–19.

114 *Israel and the Arabs:* Author interviews, Trump administration and U.S. officials, 2018–19.

114 *through much of the planning:* Author interview, Trump administration official, Sept. 2018.

114 *Kushner joined as well:* "Trump Meets Saudi Prince as U.S. and Kingdom Seek Warmer Relations," *NYT*, March 14, 2017.

114 *had already spoken several times:* "The Wooing of Jared Kushner: How the Saudis Got a Friend in the White House," *NYT*, Dec. 8, 2018.

114 *the young prince was clear:* Author interview, two U.S. officials with knowledge of the meetings.

114 *"Let's get this done today"*: "$110 Billion Weapons Sale to Saudis Has Jared Kushner's Personal Touch," *NYT*, May 18, 2017.

115 *would look into it:* Ibid.

115 *calls with foreign leaders:* Author interviews, two Trump administration officials, Oct. 2018, May 2019.

115 *politics of the royal family:* After some of this information was published in *NYT*, White House officials denied that Kushner had inquired about how to influence the Saudi succession process and insisted that all of his communications with foreign leaders had respected established protocols. They declined, however, to describe those protocols.

115 *the Saudi succession process:* Author correspondence, White House spokespeople, July 2019.

115 *"the U.S. with its conventional allies":* "A young prince is reimagining Saudi Arabia. Can he make his vision come true?" *WaPo*, Apr. 20, 2017.

116 *had bought the superyacht* Serene: "Rise of Saudi Prince Shatters Decades of Royal Tradition," *NYT*, Oct. 15, 2016.

116 *cast doubt on the story:* Mazzetti and I originally reported that MBS had paid about €500 million for Serene. We later obtained the contract, which said he had paid €420 million.

117 *"That's different—and better":* Author interview, Mohanad Aljuaied, May 2018.

117 *"how we do it here":* Author interview, Eyad Alrumaih, May 2018.

118 *"don't have to work hard":* Author interview, Ahmad Aldubaikhi, May 2018.

119 *"a better future for us all":* "President Trump's Speech to the Arab Islamic American Summit," whitehouse.gov, May 21, 2017.

119 *unveiled during the visit:* Author interviews, U.S. officials, Oct. 2017.

119 *civilian deaths in Yemen:* "Trump to resume precision munitions deliveries to Saudis: officials," Reuters, June 13, 2017.

119 *"jobs, jobs, jobs":* "Saudis Welcome Trump's Rebuff of Obama's Mideast View," *NYT*, May 20, 2017.

120 *call her Ivanka at home:* "Saudi father forbidden from naming his daughter Ivanka," *Gulf News*, May 7, 2017.

121 *"picture of president Trump":* State Department document published in "The Insane Gifts Saudi Arabia Gave President Trump," *The Daily Beast*, Sept. 4, 2017.

A STAB IN THE BACK

122 *stay in the White House:* The quotes from the false report were taken from "Uproar In The Gulf Following Alleged Statements By Qatari Emir Condemning Gulf States, Praising Iran, Hizbullah, Muslim Brotherhood And Hamas," *MEMRI*, May 25, 2017, which also summarized regional writings in response, some of which are cited below.

123 *and would have noticed:* Author interviews, Qatar-based diplomats, July 2018.

123 *to get it taken down:* "Tiny, Wealthy Qatar Goes Its Own Way, and Pays for It," *NYT*, Jan. 22, 2018.

123 *"influence or made decisions":* Khalid Al-Malik in *Al-Jazirah*, cited in "Uproar In The Gulf."

123 *"from one of our brethren":* Muhammad Al-Ansari in *Al-Raya*, cited in "Uproar In The Gulf."

123 *the kingdom was on board:* "UAE orchestrated hacking of Qatari government sites, sparking regional upheaval, according to U.S. intelligence officials," *WaPo*, July 16, 2017.

123 *involved in the hack:* "Tiny, Wealthy Qatar Goes Its Own Way, and Pays for It," *NYT*, Jan. 22, 2018.

124 *kingdom's eastern desert:* "Gulf crisis: camels become casualties of Qatar blockade," *Al Jazeera*, June 21, 2017.

124 *dollars per year before the crisis:* 2016 estimate from "Qatar," The World Factbook, Central Intelligence Agency, accessed July 2019.

125 *"They see it as a threat":* "Tiny, Wealthy Qatar Goes Its Own Way, and Pays for It," *NYT*, Jan. 22, 2018.

125 *useful for hostage negotiations:* "Qatar: Governance, Security, and U.S. Policy," Congressional Research Service, June 13, 2019.

125 *Afghanistan, Iraq, and Syria:* Ibid.

125 *"pointed to Qatar—look!":* Donald Trump (@realDonaldTrump). "During my recent trip to the Middle East I stated that there can no longer be funding of Radical Ideology," Twitter, June 6, 2017. https://twitter.com/realDonaldTrump/status/872062159789985792

125 *"end to the horror of terrorism":* Donald Trump (@realDonaldTrump). ". . . extremism, and all reference was pointing to Qatar," Twitter, June 6, 2017.   https://twitter.com/realDonaldTrump/status/872086906804240384

126 *entice them away from Iran:* "King Salman of Saudi Arabia Meets With Hamas Leaders," *NYT*, July 17, 2015.

126 *Qatar refused:* "Tiny, Wealthy Qatar."

126 *shipping cash to bad actors:* "Kidnapped Royalty Become Pawns in Iran's Deadly Plot," *NYT*, March 14, 2018.

126 *near the kitchen:* Author interviews, Qatari and U.S. officials, July 2018.

126 *"long-simmering grievances":* State Department spokeswoman Heather Nauert, June 20, 2017.

126 *monthly compliance checks:* "Qatar given 10 days to meet 13 sweeping demands," *The Guardian*, June 23, 2017.

127 *"It depends on them":* "Saudi Crown Prince: Iran's Supreme Leader 'Makes Hitler Look Good,'" *The Atlantic*, April 2, 2018.

127 *to honor his counterterrorism work:* "Saudi crown prince receives CIA honor for anti-terror efforts," *Arab News*, February 12, 2017.

127 *diluted counterterrorism efforts:* Author interviews, U.S. officials, 2018–19.

127 *prince was making plans:* Author interview, associate of Saad al-Jabri, May
     2019.

128 *king wanted to see him:* To reconstruct the night of Mohammed bin Nayef's
     removal as crown prince, I interviewed three associates of the royal family
     and one of his relatives. I also consulted written reports about that night,
     including "How a Saudi prince unseated his cousin to become the King-
     dom's heir apparent," *WSJ*, July 19, 2017, and "Addiction and Intrigue:
     Inside the Saudi palace coup," Reuters, July 19, 2017, although my re-
     porting did not corroborate all their details.

129 *"Good luck, God willing":* Bader Al Asaker (@Badermasaker). "fideo: al
     amir moHammad bin nayef bin 'abd al 'aziz yubaya' al amir moHammed
     _bin_salman," Twitter, June 21, 2017. https://twitter.com/Badermasaker
     /status/877394629011939328

129 *answered to MBS:* Author interviews, associates and a relative of Moham-
     med bin Nayef, 2016–19.

129 *body that reported to MBS:* The new interior minister was Prince Abdulaziz
     bin Saud bin Nayef, and the new security body was the State Security
     Presidency.

129 *"baseless claims":* Royal Court response to questions from *NYT*, July 19,
     2017.

130 *"roles end when they vote":* "Saudi Arabian Crown Prince Mohammed bin
     Salman Interview," *TIME*, April 5, 2018.

130 *"morphine and cocaine addiction":* "Saudi source gives more detail on crown
     prince's dismissal," Reuters, July 21, 2017.

130 *accounts were frozen:* Author interviews with associates of Mohammed bin
     Nayef and "Saudi Authorities Freeze Former Crown Prince's Bank Ac-
     counts," *WSJ*, Nov. 8, 2017.

130 *assets were taken away:* Author interviews, associates of the royal family.

130 *at family functions:* Author interviews, members and associates of the royal
     family, 2018–19, and social media posts.

130 *"she wants to die":* Author interview, Saudi princess, June 2018.

A JOURNALIST AT WORK

In this and later sections about Jamal Khashoggi, I made use of thousands of
WhatsApp messages between him and Maggie Mitchell Salem between 2015
and 2018, which Mitchell Salem shared with me. Some have been edited for
grammar, spelling, and clarity.

131 *"I don't know":* Author interview, Jamal Khashoggi, Dec. 2015.

132 *emphasized in the Vision:* "2030 ru'iyat al-muwaaTin as-sa'udi" (Ar.), *Al
     Hayat*, Oct. 29, 2016.

132 *create more work for Saudis:* "2030 ru'iyat al muwaaTin: al-waTHeefa"
     (Ar.), *Al Hayat*, Oct. 29, 2016.

132 *mentioned in the Quran:* "2030 ru'iyat al-muwaaTin: ta'leem jayid wa mu-naafis" (Ar.), *Al Hayat*, Oct. 29, 2016.

132 *relatives into private hospitals:* "2030 ru'iyat al-muwaaTin: al-amaan aS-SaHHi" (Ar.), *Al Hayat*, Oct. 29, 2016.

132 *poor urban planning:* "2030 ru'iyat al muwaaTin: raSeef namshi 'alehi" (Ar.), *Al Hayat*, Oct. 29, 2016.

132 *more parking:* "2030 ru'iyat al-muwaaTin: al-baHath 'an mawqaf as-sayaara" (Ar.), *Al Hayat*, Oct. 29, 2016.

132 *commercial properties:* "2030 ru'iyat al-muwaaTin as-sa'udi: al-faSl bayn as-sakani wa at-tijaari" (Ar.), *Al Hayat*, Oct. 29, 2016.

132 *more soccer fields:* "2030 ru'iyat al muwaaTin: 500 mal'ab qurat al-qadam" (Ar.), *Al Hayat*, Oct. 29, 2016.

132 *more parks:* "2030 ru'iyat al-muwaaTin: Hadaa'iq 'aama liltanaffus fiha" (Ar.), *Al Hayat*, Oct. 29, 2016.

132 *more trees:* "2030 ru'iyat al-muwaaTin: ashjaar, mazeed min al-ashjaar" (Ar.), *Al Hayat*, Oct. 29, 2016.

132 *a half-meter tall:* "2030 ru'iyat al-muwaaTin: al-Haq fi al-HuSool 'ala al-ma'loomaat" (Ar.), *Al Hayat*, Oct. 29, 2016.

132 *conference to explain his plans:* "2030 ru'iyat al-muwaaTin: al-Haq fi al-HuSool 'ala al-ma'loomaat" (Ar.), *Al Hayat*, Oct. 29, 2016.

132 *"benefit from the news and reports":* "2030 ru'iyat al muwaaTin: al-Haq fi al-HuSool 'ala al-ma'loomaat" (Ar.), *Al Hayat*, Oct. 29, 2016.

133 *"know how to deal with him":* Author interview, Jamal Khashoggi, Nov. 2016.

133 *"more than an oil well":* "laa takhaafu trumb . . . wa lakin ista'idu lahu" (Ar.), Al Hayat, Nov. 11, 2016.

133 *insults, from the administration:* Khashoggi spoke at the Washington Institute for Near East Policy on Nov. 10, 2016; his remarks are at "A New President and the Middle East," Policy Watch 2724, The Washington Institute for Near East Policy, Nov. 15, 2016.

133 *"not that of the Kingdom of Saudi Arabia":* "Saudi ministry: Views by Jamal Khashoggi do not represent kingdom," *AlArabiya*, Nov. 19, 2016.

134 *"That's ridiculous!!!":* MMS-JK, Nov. 20, 2016.

134 *"Done":* Ibid.

134 *"Bored and worried":* MMS-JK, Dec. 12, 2016.

134 *trouble would blow over:* Author interview, Azzam Tamimi, Feb. 2019.

135 *"worry about your freedom all the time":* MMS-JK, Feb. 20, 2017.

135 *"won't happen if I stay":* MMS-JK, Ibid.

135 *"I can't guarantee that":* MMS-JK, June 2, 2017.

136 *"so SAD what's happening":* MMS-JK, June 12, 2017.

136 *"Bye":* MMS-JK, July 21, 2017.

LORD OF THE FLIES

In reporting on Saud al-Qahtani's rise, I read through scores of Hacking Team emails released by Wikileaks. Where I have used findings in them from other other researchers and journalists, I have noted them below.

137 *"Regards saud"*: Email released by Wikileaks. Email ID: 569313. Dated March 27, 2012. https://wikileaks.org/hackingteam/emails/emailid/569313

137 *"the king office"*: Ibid.

137 *"guests for the Royal Court"*: Ibid.

138 *"most known Hack Forum users"*: "How 'Mr. Hashtag' Helped Saudi Arabia Spy on Dissidents," *Vice*, Oct. 29, 2018.

138 *"RAT THAT CAN INFECT MAC PC"*: Ibid.

138 *he lived in Saudi Arabia:* Ibid.

138 *or failed to show up:* Email released by Wikileaks. Email ID 14112. Dated Sept. 23, 2013. https://wikileaks.org/hackingteam/emails/emailid/14112

138 *"90% of them are not up to it"*: Ibid.

138 *media monitoring under King Abdullah:* "Royal Order: Appointing Saud Al-Qahtani as Advisor, at the Royal Court," *SPA*, Nov. 12, 2015.

138 *hacker had hacked him:* "Lord Of The Flies: An Open-Source Investigation Into Saud Al-Qahtani," *Bellingcat*, June 26, 2019.

138 *"good man and look trusted!!!"*: Ibid.

139 *to secure their accounts:* Ibid.

139 *when he did it himself:* Ibid.

139 *posting while drunk:* Ibid.

139 *"drink tackila and dance lol"*: Ibid.

139 *could help him prevail:* Author interviews, American officials and an associate of the royal family, May 2019.

139 *with the rank of minister:* "Royal Order: Appointing Saud Al-Qahtani as Advisor, at the Royal Court," *SPA*, Nov. 12, 2015.

139 *"as soon as possible please"*: Email released by Wikileaks. Email ID 1150286. Dated June 29, 2015. https://wikileaks.org/hackingteam/emails/emailid/1150286

140 *"will protect our privacy"*: Email released by Wikileaks. Email ID 1118843. Dated July 1, 2015. https://wikileaks.org/hackingteam/emails/emailid/1118843

140 *guy seemed paranoid:* Ibid.

140 *"bad cop and lesser bad cop"*: Author interview, Dennis Horak, Nov. 2018.

141 *"pro-active thought authoritarianism"*: Author interview, Alexi Abrahams, Oct. 2018.

141 *"Lord of the Flies"*: "Who is Saudi al-Qahtani, Saudi Arabia's Steve Bannon," *The New Arab*, Aug. 23, 2017.

142 *suggest names for it:* Saud al-Qahtani (@saud1978), "al-hashtaaq ar-rasmi # al-qaaima as-sawda" (Ar.), Twitter post, Aug. 17. 2017. https://twitter.com/saudq1978/status/898265869368807424

142   *"starting now"*: Saudi al-Qahtani (@saud1978), "as-sa'udia wa ashiqaauha" (Ar.), Twitter post, Aug. 17, 2017. https://twitter.com/saudq1978/status /898259368696725504

142   *would be punished or prosecuted*: Saudi al-Qahtani (@saud1978), "wa'ad: santajalla al-ghimma 'an al-khaleej" (Ar.), Twitter post, Aug. 17, 2017. https://twitter.com/saudq1978/status/898257245183463424

142   *state could unmask them*: Saudi al-Qahtani (@saud1978), "hal al-ism al-musa'aar yaHmeek" (Ar.), Twitter post, Aug. 18, 2017. https://twitter .com/saudq1978/status/898379274788491265

142   *"the faithful crown prince"*: Saudi al-Qahtani (@saud1978), "wa ta'taqid ani aqdaH min rasi" (Ar.), Twitter post, Aug. 17, 2017. https://twitter.com /saudq1978/status/898273541367451648

142   *to guide their coverage*: Author interviews, Saudi journalists, 2017–18, and American officials, May 2019.

142   *could shift the conversation*: Author interview, Abrahams.

142   *that the government wanted delivered*: "Saudis' Image Makers: A Troll Army and a Twitter Insider," *NYT*, Oct. 20, 2018.

142   *to take them offline*: Author interview, Abrahams.

142   *"a wasteland"*: Author interview, Marc Owen Jones, Oct. 2018.

142   *the arrest in a series of tweets*: Turki al-Roqi (@turkialroqi) published an account of his ordeal at "al-maqaal al-akheer lil-SaHafi al-maTruud" (Ar.), Twitter article, Feb. 26, 2017. https://twitter.com/turkialroqi/status /835869428675915776

143   *details that could identify users*: "Saudis' Image Makers: A Troll Army and a Twitter Insider," *NYT*, Oct. 20, 2018.

143   *to work for the government*: Ibid.

144   *"austerity and the royal decrees"*: "Consulting Firms Keep Lucrative Saudi Alliance, Shaping Crown Prince's Vision," *NYT*, Nov. 4, 2018.

144   *al-Alkami was arrested*: Prisoners of Conscience (@m3takl_en), "The writer and media figure Khaled al-Alkami," Twitter post, Aug. 25, 2018. https://twitter.com/m3takl_en/status/1033288874611695616

144   *"with whom the document was shared"*: "Saudis' Image Makers: A Troll Army and a Twitter Insider," *NYT*, Oct. 20, 2018.

144   *returned to the kingdom*: "Saudi Arabia's missing princes," *BBC*, Aug. 15, 2017.

144   *in order to have Obaid extradited*: "The Khashoggi killing had roots in a cutthroat Saudi family feud," *WaPo*, Nov. 27, 2018.

144   *Morocco and flown home*: "hatha howwa hawiyat al-ameer as-sa'udi al-maqbood 'alehi bial-mudeeq wa al-maTloob lada ar-riyaaDH" (Ar.), rue20.com, Aug. 14, 2017. The prince was Saud bin al-Muntasir Bin Saud.

144   *after al-Muzaini's arrest*: Author interview, relative of Salem al-Muzaini, May 2019.

144   *by the Central Intelligence Agency*: "CIA Intercepts Underpin Assessment Saudi Crown Prince Targeted Khashoggi," *WSJ*, Dec. 1, 2018.

145 *spelling out how to do it:* Author interview, Saudi official, Oct. 2018.

145 *belonging to MBS and his father:* "It Wasn't Just Khashoggi: A Saudi Prince's Brutal Drive to Crush Dissent," *NYT*, March 17, 2019.

145 *his group really took off:* Author interviews, U.S. officials and a Saudi with knowledge of group's development, May 2019.

145 *in some way or another:* Author interview, Stéphane Lacroix, who analyzed a list of the detainees, Sept. 2017.

145 *in the dispute with Qatar:* The economist was Essam al-Zamil; the poet was Ziyad bin Naheet.

145 *"including the Muslim Brotherhood":* "More arrests in a parent Saudi campaign against critics: Activists," Reuters, September 12, 2017.

146 *"the good of their peoples":* Salman al-Awda (@salman_alodah), "rabbuna laka al-Hamd" (Ar.), Twitter post, Sept. 9, 2017.

146 *would return soon:* Author interview, Abdullah al-Awda, May 2019.

146 *"has been revealed, unfortunately":* Khalid al-Awda (@Khalid_aloadah), "#i'tiqaal_ash- sheikh_salmaan_al-'oda" (Ar.), Twitter post, Sept. 11, 2017. https://twitter.com/khalid_aloadah/status/907157189831389184

146 *too, was arrested:* Author interview, Abdullah al-Awda, May 2019.

146 *"this is not good":* "Twitter Gives Saudi Arabia a Revolution of Its Own," *NYT*, Oct. 21, 2012.

146 *would seek the death penalty:* "Saudi Arabia Seeks Death Penalty in Trial of an Outspoken Cleric," *NYT*, Sept. 4, 2018.

AN INSIDER IN EXILE

147 *what to do with his life:* Author interview, Maggie Mitchell Salem, Oct. 2018.

148 *infidel drinkers at the bar:* Ibid.

148 *kept in touch over the years:* Ibid.

148 *mental and emotional health:* Ibid.

149 *"and no tweep silenced":* Jamal Khashoggi (@JKhashoggi). "a'oud lil-kitaba wa at-taghreed, shukran li ma'aali wazeer al-i'laam li musaa'idihi" (Ar.), Twitter post, Aug. 13, 2017. https://twitter.com/JKhashoggi/status/896515210135179265

149 *"its positive role and image":* "Jamal Khashoggi's final months as an exile in the long shadow of Saudi Arabia," *WaPo*, Dec. 22, 2018.

149 *and send it to Riyadh:* Author interview, friend of Khashoggi familiar with the project, Aug. 2019.

149 *necessary for society to progress:* "ana sa'udi wa laakin mukhtalif" (Ar.), *Al Hayat*, Sept. 8, 2017.

149 *"its campaign against Qatar":* Author interview, Jamal Khashoggi, Sept. 2017.

149 *"think they'll do to me?":* Author interview, Azzam Tamimi, Feb. 2019.

150 *"long been a trusted adviser":* MMS-JK, Sept. 14, 2017.

150 *"we push you online":* Ibid.

150 *"strategic, not impulsive"*: MMS-JK, Nov. 24, 2017.

151 *"I'm not kidding"*: MMS-JK, Sept. 14, 2017.

151 *"He has done ugly things."*: Ibid.

151 *submitting it to* The Washington Post: MMS-JK, Sept. 15, 2017.

151 *"no idea who you are"*: Author interview, Maggie Michell Salem, Oct. 2018.

152 *"have more than you need"*: Ibid.

152 *the attacks from home*: Ibid, and author interviews, two others who saw him at the event.

152 *"We Saudis deserve better"*: "Saudi Arabia wasn't always this repressive. Now it's unbearable," *WaPo*, Sept. 18, 2018.

153 *forced her to do so*: Author interviews, Azzam Tamimi, Ayman Nour, Feb. 2019.

153 *"They were very nice"*: MMS-JK, Sept. 26, 2017.

154 *"Qatar and the Brotherhood"*: MMS-JK, Sept. 28, 2017.

154 *"coming to your office"*: MMS-JK, Oct. 2, 2017.

154 *"means a lot"*: Jamal Khashoggi (@JKhashoggi), "taHt qibbat kongres ha-thihi yujad muSalli" (Ar.), Twitter post, Oct. 13, 2017. https://twitter.com/JKhashoggi/status/918942205896740864

154 *"and I'll do it"*: Jamal Khashoggi (@JKhashoggi). "zurtu al-yawm SaHeefat al-waashinTon bost" (Ar.), Twitter post, Oct. 10, 2017. https://twitter.com/JKhashoggi/status/917801128628244481

155 *"'and I can write freely'"*: Jamal Khashoggi (@JKhashoggi), "al-yawm 'eid ash-shukr, munaasiba yaHtafil fiha al-amreekeeyoon bi ghad an-naTHar 'an deenihim" (Ar.), Twitter post, Nov. 24, 2017. https://twitter.com/JKhashoggi/status/933832735327752192

155 *"I'm out"*: MMS-JK, Dec. 8, 2017.

DRIVING A LIFE

In October 2017, I interviewed nine women who had participated in the 1990 driving protest: Madeha Alajroush, Monera Alnahedh, Nourah Alghanem, Asma Alaboudi, Norah Alsowayan, Fawzia al-Bakr, Meshael al-Bakr, and two others who asked to remain anonymous. All quotes by them in the text are from these interviews.

I also benefited from these books:

Aisha al-Manea and Hind al-Sheikh, *as-sadis min nofembar* (Ar.) (Beirut: Jadawel, 2013).

Manal Al-Sharif, *Daring to Drive: A Saudi Woman's Awakening* (New York: Simon & Schuster, 2018).

157 *prevent attacks on students*: Robert Lacey, *Inside the Kingdom: Kings, Clerics, Modernists, Terrorists, and the Struggle for Saudi Arabia* (New York: Penguin Books, 2009), pp. 237–38.

158 *"are out of the question"*: The Unesco consultant was Suad El Fatih El
     Badawi. "Girls' Education in Saudi Arabia," Unesco, 1969.
158 *to the Education Ministry*: Lacey, *Inside the Kingdom*, pp. 237–38.
159 *informing him of their plans*: al-Manea and Hind al-Sheikh, *al sadis min
     nofembar*.
161 *"advocates of vice"*: Ibid.
163 *"do the right thing"*: "Saudi Arabia to allow women to drive for the first
     time," CBS, Sept. 27, 2017.
164 *"a great fantasy"*: Abdulrahman bin Musaid (@abdulrahman). "tabee'ee
     faraHhun bi 'itaa'ihin haqan mashruu'an sabaqna Taalabna bihi" (Ar.),
     Twitter post, Sept. 29, 2017. https://twitter.com/abdulrahman/status
     /913706456234496000

A HOLOGRAM FOR THE CROWN PRINCE, PART ONE

166 *his childhood hero*: Richard Branson, "Just enjoyed a fascinating visit to
     Saudi Arabia, a country where great change is taking place step by step,"
     blog post, Virgin.com, Sept. 29, 2017.
166 *even touched down*: "Saudi Arabia Is Open for Business, but Not Every-
     body's Buying," *NYT*, Oct. 27, 2017.
166 *to lay eggs*: Branson, "Just enjoyed."
166 *"bringing its citizens with him"*: Ibid.
167 *pay cuts to civil servants*: "Saudi Arabia Restores Public Sector Perks Amid
     Grumbling," *NYT*, April 23, 2017.
167 *would occur in 2018*: "A young prince is reimagining Saudi Arabia. Can he
     make his vision come true?" *WaPo*, April 20, 2017.
167 *"forces that he wants to unleash"*: "Saudi Aramco's IPO is a mess," *The Econ-
     omist*, Oct. 19, 2017.
168 *"for the future of civilization"*: MBS on state at the Future Investment Ini-
     tiative, Oct. 25, 2017, online at "The pulse of change: Inside the most
     ambitious urban projects of the twenty-first century," YouTube, Oct. 25,
     2017. https://www.youtube.com/watch?v=GMgtr_L7vpQ
169 *a new iPhone*: Ibid.
169 *"we will do inside NEOM"*: Ibid.
169 *"new way of life to emerge"*: Royal Court handout obtained by author, Oct.
     2017.
169 *"name from outer space"*: "Saudi Crown Prince Details Plans for New City:
     Transcript," *Bloomberg*, Oct. 26, 2017.
170 *the proposed cities*: "Saudi Arabia Is Open for Business, but Not Every-
     body's Buying," *NYT*, Oct. 27, 2017.
170 *$1 billion in his space companies*: Richard Branson, "Change is happening
     on a number of fronts in Saudi Arabia," blog post, Virgin.com, Oct. 26,
     2017.

170 *"Immediately"*: MBS on state at the Future Investment Initiative, Oct. 25, 2017.

170 *"to all traditions and peoples"*: Ibid.

170 *corruption and Westernization:* For a well-researched narrative account, see Trofimov, Yaroslav, *The Siege of Mecca: The 1979 Uprising at Islam's Holiest Shrine* (New York: Doubleday, 2007).

170 *"Before 1979"*: "Saudi Arabia's Arab Spring, at Last," *NYT*, Nov. 23, 2017.

172 *"until the events of 1979"*: "Saudi Arabia's heir to the throne talks to 60 Minutes," *60 Minutes*, March 19, 2018.

172 *put them to the sword:* Michael Crawford, *Ibn 'Abd Al-Wahhab* (London: Oneworld Publications, 2014) ebook.

172 *they considered blasphemous:* Alexei Vassiliev, *The History of Saudi Arabia* (New York: NYU Press, 2000). The estimates of those killed range from 2,000 to 4,500.

172 *from performing the pilgrimage:* Michael Darlow and Barbara Bray, *Ibn Saud: The Desert Warrior Who Created the Kingdom of Saudi Arabia* (New York: Skyhorse Publishing, 2010) ebook.

172 *denied that the practice existed:* Robert Lacey, *The Kingdom: Arabia and the House of Saud* (New York: Avon Books, 1981), pp. 344–45.

173 *girls' education sparked riots:* Lacey, *The Kingdom*, p. 363.

173 *Saudi National Day:* Collections of the Fatwas and Letters of His Eminence Sheikh Mohammed bin Ibrahim Abdul-Latif Al al-Sheikh, published by the Government Publication in Mecca, 1978. In the text, I have opted to render his last name as al-Sheikh as opposed to Al al-Sheikh, for the nonspecialist reader.

173 *torn limb from limb:* Sandra Mackey, *Inside the Desert Kingdom* (New York: W. W. Norton & Company, 2002), pp. 13–15.

174 *"something that they are not part of"*: "Crown Prince Mohammed bin Salman Talks to *TIME* About the Middle East, Saudi Arabia's Plans and President Trump," *TIME*, April 5, 2018.

174 *"you will find Iran"*: Ibid.

WE HAVE REASON TO BELIEVE OUR PRIME MINISTER HAS BEEN KIDNAPPED BY SAUDI ARABIA

To reconstruct Saad Hariri's ordeal in Saudi Arabia, I interviewed more than twenty people who were directly involved in different parts of it, including Lebanese security officials, political allies of Hariri, ambassadors and other Beirut-based diplomats, and officials from the United Nations. They spoke on condition of anonymity, for fear of angering the Saudis, unless cited below.

While my reporting did not corroborate all of their findings, other works I found helpful included "Quand 'MBS' prennait Hariri en otage" (Fr.), Le Magazine, *Le Monde*, Nov. 17, 2018, and the series of articles published in

Lebanon under the headline "ayaam ar-reetz: waqaa'e ghayr manshuura min qiSSat ikhtiTaaf sa'ad al-Hareeri," *Al-Akhbar*, Nov. 6. 2018.

Saad Hariri declined to be interviewed.

176 *Lebanese national airline:* Saad Hariri, (@saadhariri). "iSraarina 'ala taHqeeq al-injaazaat al-jawiya" (Ar.), Facebook post, Nov. 1, 2017. https://www.facebook.com/saadhariri/videos/10156742505548294/

178 *"other than its great people":* Hariri's full speech at "Lebanon's Prime Minister Hariri resigns" (Ar.), YouTube, Nov. 4. 2017. https://www.youtube.com/watch?v=y9KiP86kzeg

178 *"May God protect you":* Author interviews, political allies of Hariri, 2018.

179 *Hariri's resignation only in person:* "Hezbollah says Saudi Arabia forced Lebanese PM to quit," Reuters, Nov. 5. 2017.

179 *"you hate your country":* Author interviews, Lebanese security officials, 2017, and "Why Saad Hariri Had That Strange Sojourn in Saudi Arabia," *NYT*, Dec. 24, 2017.

179 *"The Hostage":* Al-Akhbar, front page, Nov. 6, 2017.

179 *had gone too far:* Author interviews, U.S. and Lebanese officials, 2018–19.

180 *idea was dangerous and said no:* Author interviews, Lebanese security officials and foreign diplomats with access to intelligence reports, 2018.

180 *"not pledges of allegiance":* Nouhad Machnouk speaking at a televised press conference, November 9, 2018. Nouhad Machnouk (@Nohad Machnouk). "#al-mashnouq, lasna qaTee' ghanam li tantaqil mulkiyitina min shakhSin ila aakhar" (Ar.), Twitter, Nov. 9. 2017. https://twitter.com/NohadMachnouk/status/928657440324964352

181 *the State Department in Washington:* Author interviews, U.S. officials, 2018, and "Why Saad Hariri Had That Strange Sojourn in Saudi Arabia," *NYT*, Dec. 24, 2017.

181 *return of their prime minister:* U.S. and Lebanese officials, 2017–18.

181 *show on its TV station:* The details and quotes about Yacoubian's background and trip to Riyadh are from author interviews, July 2018 and Feb. 2019, unless otherwise noted.

182 *something was amiss:* Author interviews, political allies of Hariri briefed on the plan, 2018–19.

182 *"I am not sure of anything":* All quotes from Yacoubian's interview with Saad Hariri are from "Inter-views" (Ar.), *Future TV*, Nov. 12, 2017. https://www.youtube.com/watch?v=AoeuOz8KddE

183 *"ambiguous situation" in Saudi Arabia:* "NBN TV to boycott Hariri's interview," *National News Agency* (Lebanon), Nov. 12, 2017.

184 *"of a Hollywood movie":* Author interview, senior foreign diplomat in Beirut, Aug. 2018.

185 *"Of my own free will!":* MBS and Saad Hariri on Stage at the Future Investment Initiative in Riyadh, Oct. 2018, available at "muHammad bin salmaan mumaazihan al-Hariri" (Ar.), YouTube, Oct. 24, 2018. https://www.youtube.com/watch?v=d13mgOcfZwc

GUESTS OF THE KING

My reconstruction of the Ritz crackdown is based on dozens of interviews with associates, relatives, and employees of detainees; Saudi officials; and foreign officials who tracked the events, in addition to other sources cited below. Most spoke on condition of anonymity for fear of jeopardizing their interests or endangering themselves or their relatives in Saudi Arabia.

186 *was woken up by a surprise phone call:* The story of Alwaleed's summons is based on interviews with three close associates, 2017–18, later corroborated by "Prince Alwaleed Reveals Secret Deal Struck to Exit Ritz After 83 Days," *Bloomberg Businessweek*, March 20, 2018.

187 *$300,000 loan from his father:* "Prince Alwaleed And The Curious Case Of Kingdom Holding Stock," *Forbes*, March 5, 2013.

187 *making the prince a fortune:* "The mystery of the world's second-richest businessman," *The Economist*, Feb. 25, 1999.

187 *covers made by his staff:* "Prince Alwaleed And The Curious Case Of Kingdom Holding Stock," *Forbes*, March 5, 2013.

187 *Alwaleed in the back:* "I Just Can't Wait to Be King," *Forbes*, March 12, 2009.

187 *a mini–Grand Canyon:* "A Week With Prince Alwaleed," *Forbes*, March 27, 2009.

188 *clothing bonuses of $10,000:* "I Just Can't Wait to Be King," *Forbes*, March 12, 2009.

188 *thought they were funny:* Author interviews, associates of Alwaleed, and "THE DWARF-THROWING BILLIONAIRE WHO'S BUYING UP AMERICA: Tales Of The Mysterious Saudi Prince Alwaleed," *Business Insider*, Jan. 12, 2012.

188 *buying homes or clearing debts:* See "A Saudi Titan Watches Wall Street's Meltdown," *TIME*, Sept. 4, 2008, and "I Dined With Alwaleed in the Desert Days Before His Arrest," *Bloomberg*, Nov. 7, 2017.

188 *net worth at $18.7 billion:* "#45 Prince Alwaleed Bin Talal Alsaud," *Forbes* billionaires net worth, March 20, 2017.

188 *to await his meeting:* Author interviews, two associates of Waleed al Ibrahim, Nov. 2017.

189 *suspicious and rushed off:* Author interview, associate of Mutib bin Abdullah, Nov. 2017.

189 *Zara and Gap franchises:* The shopping magnate was Fawaz al-Hokair.

189 *"richest black person in the world":* The Saudi-Ethiopian was Mohammed al-Amoudi. "The Black Billionaires 2012," *Forbes*, March 7, 2012.

189 *flew to Riyadh that night:* Author interview, relative of Saleh Kamel, Nov. 2019.

190 *was led by MBS:* "King Salman Orders New Anti-Corruption Drive In Saudi Arabia," press release, Center for International Communication, Nov. 4, 2017.

191 *"tendency to squander it"*: Embassy Riyadh. "Saudi Royal Wealth: Where Do They Get All That Money," Wikileaks cable: 96RIYADH4784_a. Dated Nov. 20, 1996. https://wikileaks.org/plusd/cables/96RIYADH4784_a.html

191 *due to unpaid loans:* Ibid.

191 *for next to zero work:* Ibid.

191 *"royal rake-offs":* Ibid.

191 *"Al Saud Inc.":* Ibid.

192 *government land to private citizens:* Embassy Riyadh. "Crown Prince Sultan Back the King in Family Disputes," Wikileaks cable: 07RIYADH296_a. Dated: Feb. 12, 2007. https://wikileaks.org/plusd/cables/07RIYADH296_a.html

192 *"since Adam and Eve":* "Interview: Bandar bin Sultan," *Frontline*, PBS, Oct. 2001.

192 *"a prince, or whoever he is":* "WATCH & READ: Mohammed Bin Salman's full interview," *AlArabiya*, May 3, 2017.

192 *"the public interest":* "Anti-graft committee will 'create new era of financial transparency' in KSA," *Arab News*, Nov. 6, 2017.

193 *"'milking' their country for years":* Donald Trump (@realdonaldtrump), "I have great confidence in King Salman and the Crown Prince of Saudi Arabia," Twitter post, Nov. 7, 2017. https://twitter.com/realdonaldtrump/status/927672843504177152

193 *told him to withdraw:* Alwaleed bin Talal (@Alwaleed_Talal). "@realDonaldTrump You are a disgrace not only to the GOP but to all America," Twitter post, Dec. 11, 2015. https://twitter.com/Alwaleed_Talal/status/675390247165915137

193 *"U.S. politicians with daddy's money":* Donald Trump (@realdonaldtrump), "Dopey Prince @Alwaleed_Talal wants to control our U.S. politicians with daddy's money," Twitter post, Dec. 12, 2015. https://twitter.com/realdonaldtrump/status/675523728055410689

193 *on his win:* Alwaleed bin Talal (@Alwaleed_Talal), "President elect @realDonaldTrump, whatever the past differences, America has spoken," Twitter post, Nov. 9, 2016. https://twitter.com/Alwaleed_Talal/status/796341367106637828

193 *in a room by himself:* All quotes and details from author interview, former Ritz detainee, May 2019. His tale of confinement corresponded with those from relatives of other detainees.

194 *fill in later as it chose:* Details on the negotiation and settlement process from multiple author interviews with relatives and associates of Ritz detainees, 2018–19.

194 *more accounts a few days later:* "Saudi Arabia makes fresh arrests in anti-graft crackdown: sources," Reuters, Nov. 8, 2017.

194 *with no explanation:* "Palestinian billionaire Masri back in Jordan after release in Saudi Arabia: family source," Reuters, Dec. 19, 2017.

195 *power grab as "ludicrous"*: "Saudi Arabia's Arab Spring, at Last," *NYT*, Nov. 23, 2017.

196 *"he wants to destroy it"*: Author interview, relative of Ritz detainee, Dec. 2017.

196 *revealed to be the mystery buyer*: The mystery buyer was unmasked by David D. Kirkpatrick in "Mystery Buyer of $450 Million 'Salvator Mundi' Was a Saudi Prince," *NYT*, Dec. 7, 2017.

196 *a proxy for MBS*: "Saudi Arabia's Crown Prince Identified as Buyer of Record-Breaking da Vinci," *WSJ*, Dec. 7, 2017, and "Saudi Crown Prince Was Behind Record Bid for a Leonardo," *NYT*, Dec. 7, 2017.

196 *"must admire art"*: "Crown Prince Mohammed bin Salman Talks to *TIME* About the Middle East, Saudi Arabia's Plans and President Trump," *TIME*, April 5, 2018.

196 *$300 million two years earlier*: The chateau was unearthed by Nicholas Kulish and Michael Forsythe in "World's Most Expensive Home? Another Bauble for a Saudi Prince," *NYT*, Dec. 16, 2017.

196 *complained about them were arrested*: These included Khaled bin Talal and Mishaal bin Abdullah.

196 *been given electrical shocks*: Ali al-Qahtani's body was described to my colleagues David Kirkpatrick and Mark Mazzetti by a Saudi official and a doctor who had seen it.

197 *speak about what had happened*: Author interview, relative of Ali al-Qahtani, Dec. 2018.

197 *and electrocuted him*: "The Invisible American in a Saudi Prison Cell," *NYT*, Nov. 21, 2018, and "Saudi Arabia Is Said to Have Tortured an American Citizen," *NYT*, Mar. 2, 2019.

197 *"my loyalty to my country"*: Author interview, former Ritz detainee, May 2019.

198 *in negotiating his "settlement"*: "Inside Saudi Arabia's anti-corruption campaign," *BBC*, Jan. 25, 2018.

198 *in Riyadh when he claimed*: Author interviews, Alan Bender, Jan. 2018.

198 *royal suite, room 628*: "Prince Alwaleed Reveals Secret Deal Struck to Exit Ritz After 83 Days," *Bloomberg Businessweek*, March 20, 2018.

198 *everything was totally normal*: "Transcript of Reuters interview with Saudi Arabia's Prince Alwaleed bin Talal," Reuters, Jan. 27, 2017.

199 *"His Royal Highness"*: Document sent to European hotel from Alwaleed's office and shown to author, March 2018.

199 *and other illiquid assets*: "Saudi Arabia says it has seized over $100 billion in corruption purge," Reuters, Jan. 30, 2018.

199 *had not yet settled*: Ibid.

200 *Maserati showroom cleaned out*: The Reuters report was "As a Saudi prince rose, the Bin Laden business empire crumbled," Reuters, Sept. 27, 2018.

200 *given oversight roles*: Ibid.

200 *replaced with artificial turf*: Ibid.

200 *"It was a shitty experience"*: Ibid.

201 *locked up the seller*: Author interviews, regional media executives, 2018.

201 *called "Istidama,"*: Ibid.

201 *properties seized in the Ritz*: "Saudi Crown Prince Discusses Trump, Aramco, Arrests: Transcript," Bloomberg, Oct. 5, 2018.

201 *the company about $25 million*: Author interviews, regional media executives, 2018.

201 *wanted $6 billion from him*: "The Price of Freedom for Saudi Arabia's Richest Man: $6 Billion," *WSJ*, Dec. 23, 2017.

201 *"I say, is a traitor"*: "Prince Alwaleed Reveals Secret Deal Struck to Exit Ritz After 83 Days," *Bloomberg Businessweek*, March 20, 2018.

201 *"know what happened to him"*: Author interview, money manager, March 2018.

202 *"to live in Saudi Arabia"*: Author interview, associate of Ritz detainee, Feb. 2018.

A NIGHT AT THE OPERA

203 *"table and play with you"*: Author interview, Jamal Khashoggi, Dec. 2017.

203 *"and for the country"*: Saudi Arabia's crown prince is acting like Putin, *WaPo*, Nov. 5, 2017.

204 *"miles from NEOM, are silenced?"*: "Saudi Arabia's Crown Prince wants to 'crush extremists.' But he's punishing the wrong people," *WaPo*, Oct. 31, 2017.

204 *sparked the Qatar boycott*: "Saudi Arabia is creating a total mess in Lebanon," *WaPo*, Nov. 13, 2017.

204 *"Alluding to MBS"*: MMS-JK, Jan. 1, 2018.

204 *column about the Ritz*: "What Saudi Arabia could learn from South Korea about fighting corruption," *WaPo*, Jan. 8, 2018.

204 *work it in while editing*: MMS-JK, Feb. 1, 2018. The names appeared in "Saudi Arabia's crown prince already controlled the nation's media. Now he's squeezing it even further," *WaPo*, Feb. 7, 2018.

204 *"Yes, we are"*: MMS-JK, Oct. 31, 2017.

205 *"more effect than being angry"*: MMS-JK, Jan. 22, 2018.

205 *"best friend I have"*: MMS-JK, Sept. 25, 2017.

205 *"maybe for good, from home"*: MMS-JK, Jan. 24, 2018.

206 *"the official government groupthink"*: "Saudi Arabia's crown prince already controlled the nation's media. Now he's squeezing it even further," *WaPo*, Feb. 7, 2018.

206 *"Out"*: MMS-JK, Feb. 9, 2018.

206 *"I'm out"*: MMS-JK, March 13, 2018.

207 *"plan events on the weekend"*: Author interview, Fahad al-Abdullatif, March 2018.

208 *entertainment abroad each year*: "Saudi Arabia eyes billions of dollars in entertainment investments," Reuters, Jan. 22, 2019.

208 *"their religious duties"*: William Eddy, "F.D.R. Meets ibn Saud, William A. Eddy," America-Mideast Educational & Training Services, Inc., 1954.

208 *The princes loved it:* Ibid.

208 *"in neighboring countries"*: Ahmed al-Khateeb at event attended by author, Feb. 2018.

209 *"carry it out with your help"*: Ibid.

209 *$64 billion:* Ibid.

210 *"'don't have to hide anymore'"*: All quotes from Ameera al-Taweel from author interview, Feb. 2018.

210 *"'Cover your face'"*: Author interview, Lina Bulbul, Feb. 2018.

211 *"who thought more like us"*: Author interview, Ibtihal Shogair, Feb. 2018.

211 *"corrupts morals and destroys values"*: "mudakhila mumayaza Hawl al sinima wa al Hafalaat al ghinaa'iya," YouTube video, Jan. 13, 2017. https://www.youtube.com/watch?v=HiloBQJSgLo

211 *"debauchery and atheism"*: "al sa'udiya wa sajaalaat al sinima wa al Hafalaat," *Al-Sharq Al-Awsat,* Jan. 15, 2017.

211 *"at the current time"*: "munhiyan al jadal bayn 'al mana' wa al 'awda," *Sabq.org,* Jan. 16, 2017.

211 *first-time offenders, or both:* "CIC Release: Saudi Arabia's New Anti-Harassment Law Goes Into Effect 'Within Days,'" Press release, Center for International Communication, June 1, 2018.

212 *to pull her away:* "Girl arrested for hugging male singer in Saudi concert—Saudi Arabia," YouTube video, July 14, 2018. https://www.youtube.com/watch?v=GUrWK5yX6Q8 The concert was by Majid al-Mohandis in the city of Taif.

212 *dangerous dare by her girlfriends:* "fataat Haflat maajid al-muhandis" (Ar.), *Okaz,* July 15, 2018.

212 *"cinema in their pocket anyway"*: Author interview, Saudi educator, Feb. 2018.

213 *"they'll go crazy"*: Author interview, Saudi cleric, Nov. 2017.

214 *"people will get used to it:* Author interview, Saudi cleric, Nov. 2017.

215 *"population is under 30"*: "Saudi Arabia Gets an Arab Spring of Its Own," *NYT,* Nov. 23, 2017.

216 *"remote control stops working"*: Author interview, Saudi cleric who worked for the security forces, May 2016.

CHARM TOURS

217 *hidden away in embassy storage:* Author interview, two U.S. officials, July, Aug. 2019.

218 *eventually faded away:* Two former Trump administration officials, May, July 2019. The White House declined to comment.

218 *"long way in a short time"*: "Mohammed bin Salman Interview: 'British and Saudi people will be much safer if we have a strong relationship,'" *The Telegraph*, March 5, 2018.

218 *honor for a foreign visitor*: Ibid.

218 *for oil and fighter jets*: "Coming to America: The Saudi Prince's Charm Offensive," *Bloomberg*, March 19, 2018.

219 *expressed favorable views*: Gallup Country Ratings, Feb. 1–10, 2018.

219 *"Should We Believe Him?"*: "The Saudi Crown Prince Thinks He Can Transform the Middle East. Should We Believe Him?" *TIME*, April 5, 2018.

219 *"death" could stop him*: "Saudi Arabia's heir to the throne talks to *60 Minutes*," *60 Minutes*, March 19, 2018.

220 *"would have been arrested"*: "Saudi Women, Unveiled," *60 Minutes*, March 18, 2018.

220 *"middle school science project"*: Author interview, former Trump administration official, May 2019.

220 *"anywhere in the world"*: "Remarks by President Trump and Crown Prince Mohammed Bin Salman of the Kingdom of Saudi Arabia Before Luncheon," White House transcript, March 20, 2018.

221 *from the Saudi desert*: "Saudis Woo Hollywood During Crown Prince Visit," *WSJ*, Apr. 5, 2018.

221 *humanitarian crisis in Yemen*: "Oprah, Rupert Murdoch, Harvard: Saudi Prince's U.S. Tour," *NYT*, April 6, 2018.

221 *Dwayne "The Rock" Johnson*: "Prince Mohammad Does Hollywood," *Vanity Fair*, April 6, 2018.

221 *"his Royal Highness and family"*: Dwayne Johnson (@DwayneJohnson). "An historic night it was. A pleasure to have a private dinner with the Crown Prince of Saudi Arabia, Mohammed bin Salman," Facebook post, April 4, 2018. https://www.facebook.com/DwayneJohnson/posts/an -historic-night-it-was-a-pleasure-to-have-a-private-dinner-with-the -crown-prin/10156608161399384/

221 *George Bush, but* two: Associates of the Bushes to Peter Baker, Feb. 2019.

222 *SoftBank on solar power*: "A Wild Ride Behind the Scenes as Saudi Crown Prince Does America," Bloomberg, April 2, 2018.

222 *"ended up like North Korea"*: "A young prince is reimagining Saudi Arabia. Can he make his vision come true?" *WaPo*, April 20, 2017.

222 *"countries like Egypt and Jordan"*: "Saudi Crown Prince: Iran's Supreme Leader 'Makes Hitler Look Good,'" *The Atlantic*, April 2, 2018.

223 *"Let the Germans pay"*: William Eddy, "F.D.R. Meets ibn Saud, William A. Eddy," America-Mideast Educational & Training Services, Inc., 1954.

223 *father and the future king*: Bruce Riedel, *Kings and Presidents: Saudi Arabia and the United States since FDR* (Washington, D.C.: The Brookings Institution, 2018), p. 46.

223 *"are almost nonexistent"*: Mohammed bin Salman interview with Dawood Al-Sirian, *AlArabiya*, May 3, 2017.

224 *"Hitler of the Middle East"*: "Saudi Crown Prince: Iran's Supreme Leader 'Makes Hitler Look Good,'" *The Atlantic*, April 2, 2018.

224 *"for them in Iran"*: Mohammed bin Salman interview with Dawood Al-Sirian, *AlArabiya*, May 3, 2017.

224 *"a conflict to be fairly resolved"*: Author interview, Rob Malley, Sept. 2018.

224 *were sworn to silence*: "A Wild Ride Behind the Scenes as Saudi Crown Prince Does America," *Bloomberg*, April 2, 2018.

224 *"shut up and stop complaining"*: "Saudi Crown Prince: Palestinians should take what the U.S. offers," *Axios*, April 29, 2018.

225 *"not be for public consumption"*: Author interview, Joel C. Rosenberg, Nov. 2019.

225 *Israel's capital "painful"*: "Saudi prince denies Kushner is 'in his pocket,'" *WaPo*, March 22, 2018.

BLACK PANTHER

For the *Black Panther* screening, I interviewed four attendees.

For the stories of Loujain Al-Hathloul, Fahad Albutairi, and the other detained activists, I interviewed Al-Hathloul's siblings Alia, Walid, and Lina and two relatives of other detainees; spoke with U.S. officials who tracked the issue; and consulted numerous reports by Human Rights Watch. Direct quotes from Al-Hathloul's siblings are attributed in the text.

226 *would be driving by 2020*: "How will women change the automotive market in KSA," PWC Press Release, March 8, 2018.

227 *"feeling more freedom"*: Author interview, Rehab Alhuwaider, March 2018.

227 *nine thousand people in 2016*: "Car accidents kill over 9,000 people in 2016," *Arab News*, May 11, 2017.

228 *"to be behind the wheel"*: Author interview, Rahaf Alzahrani, March 2018.

228 *three hundred cinemas and two thousand screens*: "Cinema estimated to contribute $24 billion to Saudi economy," *AlArabiya*, Dec. 12, 2017.

229 *movie theaters in ten years*: Author interview, Adam Aron, April 2018.

229 *"would you have picked?"*: Ibid.

230 *"Seinfeld of Saudi Arabia"*: "Fahad Albitairi, the Seinfeld of Saudi Arabia, is back," *The National*, March 21, 2013.

230 *published in* Vanity Fair: "See Meghan Markle and Emma Watson Honored for Their Humanitarian Work in Vanity Fair U.K.," *Vanity Fair*, March 31, 2017.

230 *spot number three in 2015*: "The 100 Most Powerful Arab Women," *Arabian Business*, Feb. 26, 2015. The magazine rated her fifty-two in 2016 and forty-three in 2017.

230 *for both her and her husband*: "A Clarification," LoujainHathloul.com, March 24, 2016.

231 *live and work where they chose*: The videos are available at Loujain Al-Hathloul (@LoujainHathloul), "HaaDra al dawra al taasi'a wa as-sitoon

lil-lajna al-ma'niya bi al-qaDaa' 'ala at-tameez Didd al-mar'a" (Ar.), Twitter, Feb. 27, 2018. https://twitter.com/LoujainHathloul/status/96843597
5461441536

231 *"views to government agencies"*: Ibid.

232 *"I am"*: Author interviews, three people who were present at the time,
2018–19.

232 *branding them "traitors"*: Ahkbar Al-Saudia (@saudinews50), "at-taareekh
yubaSSiq fi wujuuh al-khawana" (Ar.), Twitter photo, May 19, 2018.
https://twitter.com/saudinews50/status/997633595601838080

232 *the death penalty:* "al-taHqeeq ma' 7 yaquud al-aakhareen" (Ar.), *Okaz*,
May 20, 2018.

233 *"WhatsApp"*: Abdullah Jaber (@jabertoon), cartoon, Twitter image, May
7, 2018.

233 *"good for the Saudi economy"*: "The Prince Who Would Remake the
World," *NYT*, June 21, 2018.

233 *arrested soon afterward:* "Prominent Saudi women's rights activist detained
as driving ban lifted": sources, Reuters, June 27, 2018.

233 *as a "historic moment"*: "First Licenses Issued to Saudi Women as Lifting
of Ban on Women Driving Fast Approaches," Press release, Center for
International Communication, June 3, 2018.

234 *"gotten their freedom"*: Alwaleed bin Talal (@Alwaleed_Talal), "wa
akheeran! al-aan as-saa'a 12:01 min SabaaH al-yawm" (Ar.), Twitter post
and video, June 24, 2018. https://twitter.com/Alwaleed_Talal/status/1010
632476828594177

234 *not comment on women's rights:* "Is the End of Saudi Arabia's Driving Ban a
Rebrand or a Revolution," *TIME*, June 28, 2018. The driver was Aseel
Al-Hamad.

234 *journalists could follow along:* Ibid.

234 *on fire outside her house:* "salma al-barakaati lil-madeena: abnaa' al-Hay
aghraquuni bi sh-shataa'im" (Ar.), *Al-Madina*, July 4, 2018.

234 *opened an arson case:* imaarat munTiqat makka (@makkahregion), "shurTat
makka al-mukarrama: hareeq muta'mida fi siyaarat muwaaTana fi qariyat
(al-Samad)" (Ar.), Twitter post, July 3, 2018. https://twitter.com/makkah
region/status/1014056674741583872

234 *arrested two suspects:* imaarat munTiqat makka (@makkahregion),
"#imaarat_makka: al qabD 'ala shakhSain aHraqaa markabat sayida"
(Ar.), Twitter post, July 4, 2018. https://twitter.com/makkahregion/status
/1014587187944394752

234 *the one she had lost:* "salma al-barakaati: lan atanaazil 'an haqi fi man Ha-
raqu siyaarati" (Ar.), *Al-Madina*, July 19, 2018.

234 *members of the Rapid Intervention Group:* Author interviews, U.S. officials
with access to intelligence reports, May 2019, and "It Wasn't Just
Khashoggi: A Saudi Prince's Brutal Drive to Crush Dissent," *NYT*, March
17, 2019.

235 *and given electric shocks:* "Saudi Arabia: Detained Women Reported Tortured," Human Rights Watch, November 20, 2018.

235 *"not even God":* "My Sister Is in a Saudi Prison. Will Mike Pompeo Stay Silent?" *NYT*, Jan. 13, 2019.

235 *Saudi women truly equal:* "Change can happen in Saudi Arabia," CNN, Sept. 27, 2017.

235 *summon medics to treat her:* Author interviews, U.S. officials with access to intelligence reports and "It Wasn't Just Khashoggi: A Saudi Prince's Brutal Drive to Crush Dissent," *NYT*, March 17, 2019.

OH CANADA

The story of Jamal Khashoggi and Omar Abdulaziz is based on multiple interviews with Abdulaziz in 2018–19 and others who heard Khashoggi talk about him, and Abdulaziz's WhatsApp history with Khashoggi, which the former shared with the author. Some messages have been edited for grammar, spelling, and clarity. All other quotes from Abdulaziz were to the author.

237 *listen to the people:* "What Saudi Arabia's crown prince can learn from Queen Elizabeth II," *WaPo*, Feb. 28, 2018.

237 *building new ones:* "Why Saudi Arabia's crown prince should visit Detroit," *WaPo*, March 20, 2018.

237 *"just as intolerant of dissent":* "By blaming 1979 for Saudi Arabia's problems, the crown prince is peddling revisionist history," *WaPo*, April 3, 2018.

238 *"like my balanced criticism":* MMS-JK, March 27, 2018.

238 *"discussion and debate":* "Saudi Arabia's reformers now face a terrible choice," *WaPo*, May 21, 2018.

238 *"voices and silhouettes":* "My Fiancé Jamal Khashoggi Was a Lonely Patriot," *NYT*, Oct. 13, 2018.

238 *"can't control himself":* MMS-JK, June 25, 2018.

238 *"I'm so down":* MMS-JK, Ibid.

239 *young leader's mistakes:* Author interview, Ayman Nour, Feb. 2019.

239 *"want a reformed system":* "How free expression is suppressed in Saudi Arabia," *The Economist*, July 26, 2018.

239 *economic reports translated into Arabic:* Author interview, Azzam Tamimi, Feb. 2019.

239 *looking for funding:* Author interviews, Tamimi, and Radwan Masmoudi, Oct. 2018.

240 *"we'll just go quiet":* Khashoggi's full lecture is at "CSID 19th Annual Luncheon Jamal Khashoggi," YouTube video, May 2, 2018. https://www.youtube.com/watch?v=MUq4FC31Rlg

240 *eavesdrop on my conversations:* Author interviews, Ron Diebert and Bill Marczak of Citizen Lab at the University of Toronto, Oct. 2018. They inspected the message and concluded it was from hackers connected to Saudi Arabia.

240 *Saudi dissidents in London:* "Exclusive: Saudi Dissidents Hit With Stealth iPhone Spyware Before Khashoggi's Murder," *Forbes*, Nov. 21, 2018. The dissidents were Yahya Assiri, who ran a human rights monitor, and Ghanim Al-Masarir, who had a satirical YouTube program.

240 *researcher for Amnesty International:* "Amnesty International staff targeted with malicious spyware," Amnesty International, Aug. 1, 2018, and author interview, Yahya Assiri, July 2019.

240 *struck up a friendship with Khashoggi:* "The Kingdom Came to Canada," Citizen Lab, Oct. 1, 2018.

240 *"doing their job or to silence critics":* Author correspondence, NSO Group spokesperson, Aug. 2019. The company said its technology has helped governments save "an untold number of lives" by helping prevent terrorist attacks, stop drug and sex trafficking, and rescue kidnapped children. It says it investigates reports of misuse and responds appropriately, including by shutting down its clients' ability to use its products.

241 *make online videos:* OA-JK, Nov. 8, 2017.

241 *"make it permanent":* OA-JK, Dec. 6, 2017.

241 *pay the programmer:* OA-JK, Jan. 8, 2018.

241 *build its website:* OA-JK, Mar. 28, 2018.

241 *"enjoying private life":* OA-JK, March 6, 2018.

242 *"analyzing the man's mentality":* OA-JK, May 21, 2018.

242 *refused to go:* Author interview, Omar Abdulaziz, Oct. 2018, who also provided a sample recording of his conversations with the envoys.

242 *"Saudi Arabia is against you":* OA-JK, June 21, 2018.

242 *get the project going:* Author interview, Omar Abdulaziz, April 2019.

243 *"know everything about you":* Ibid.

243 *to see the big boat:* Author interview, former Trump administration official, May 2019.

243 *pondering eternal life:* Author interviews, foreign businessmen who met with MBS, Sept. 2018.

243 glow-in-the-dark sand: "A Prince's $500 Billion Desert Dream: Flying Cars, Robot Dinosaurs and a Giant Artificial Moon," *WSJ*, July 25, 2019.

243 *residents at all times:* Ibid.

244 *"where we can watch everything":* Ibid.

244 *"flying cars in 2030!":* Ibid.

244 *her constraints had been loosened:* Author interviews, Saudi royal and Saudi who socializes with royals, summer 2018; Michael Field, Tree of Al-Saud, Arabian Charts, version 24.6.

244 *"doesn't deserve to live":* "Une princesse saoudienne ordonne de 'frapper' et 'tuer' un artisan Parisian" (Fr.), *Le Point*, Oct. 4, 2016.

244 *held him for four hours:* Ibid.

244 *soon fled to Saudi Arabia:* "La soeur du prince saoudien MBS va être jugée à Paris" (Fr.), *Le Point*, June 13, 2019.

244 *put her under house arrest:* Author interview, Saudi princess, summer 2019.

244 *reported to be under house arrest:* Ibid and Michael Field, Tree of Al-Saud, Arabian Charts, version 24.6.

245 *"both Raif and Samar Badawi":* Chrystia Freeland (@cafreeland), "Very alarmed to learn that Samar Badawi, Raif Badawi's sister, has been imprisoned in Saudi Arabia," Twitter post, Aug. 2, 2018. https://twitter.com/cafreeland/status/1025030172624515072

245 *to be released:* Canadian Embassy, Riyadh (@CanEmbSA), "tash'ur kanada bi qalaq baaligh izaa' al-i'tiqaalaat al-iDaafiya" (Ar.), Twitter post, Aug. 5, 2018. https://twitter.com/CanEmbSA/status/1026049114088333313

245 *trade and investment:* Saudi Foreign Ministry (@KSAmofaEN), "#Statement | The negative and surprising attitude of #Canada is an entirely false claim and utterly incorrect," Twitter thread, Aug 6, 2018. https://twitter.com/KSAmofaEN/status/1026241364604932096

245 *at Canadian hospitals:* "Saudi Arabia Escalates Feud with Canada Over Rights Criticism," *NYT*, August 8, 2018.

245 *Canada's domestic affairs:* Saudi Foreign Ministry (@KSAmofaEN), "#Statement | Any other attempt to interfere with our internal affairs from #Canada," Twitter post, Aug 6, 2018. https://twitter.com/KSAmofaEN/status/1026241374516113409

245 *between 2015 and 2017:* AlArabiaya (@AlArabiya), "taqareer li naashiTeen tuTaalib kanada bi taHseen waDa' as-sujanaa'" (Ar.), Facebook video, Aug. 6, 2018. https://https://www.facebook.com/AlArabiya/videos/1980290395340575/

246 *"a racist country":* "muHallil sa'udi: sukaan kanada al aSleeyeen ma'dumeen" (Ar.), YouTube video, Aug. 7, 2018. The commentator was Ayed al-Rasheedi. https://www.youtube.com/watch?v=sadHOojSy9g

246 *account down and apologized:* "Saudi Arabian group apologizes for posting image appearing to threaten Canada with 9/11-style attack," *CBC*, Aug. 6, 2018.

246 *"The fig leaf has fallen":* "al-mamlaka 'aaSiya 'ala at-ta'aamor" (Ar.), *Al-Riyadh*, Aug. 10, 2018.

246 *"poking a teddy bear":* Author interview, former Trump administration official, May 2019.

246 *confirmed the hack:* "The Kingdom Came to Canada," Citizen Lab, Oct. 1, 2018.

247 *"God help us":* "OA-JK, Aug. 7, 2018.

LOOKING FOR LOVE

The story of Jamal Khashoggi and Hanan al-Atr is based on author interviews with and documents and photos provided by al-Atr in March 2019, and on conversations with others Khashoggi told about the relationship. All quotes from al-Atr were to the author.

The story of Jamal Khashoggi and Hatice Cengiz draws heavily from interviews my *NYT* colleague Carlotta Gall did with Cengiz in October 2018 and April 2019 and from my own correspondence with Cengiz. Details taken from other Cengiz interviews and her own book are cited below.

For the events surrounding what happened to Jamal Khashoggi in the consulate, I interviewed a range of Saudi and Turkish officials, as well as two people who had heard audio from the hours before, during, and after his killing. I also relied on:

"Annex to the Report of the Special Rapporteur on extrajudicial, summary or arbitrary executions: Investigation into the unlawful death of Mr. Jamal Khashoggi," United Nations Human Rights Council, June 19, 2019, henceforth cited as "U.N. Report."

Ferhat Ünlü, Abdurrahman Simsek, and Nazif Karaman, *Diplomatic Vahset: Kasikçi Cinayetinin Karanlik Sirlari* (Tu.) (Istanbul: Trurkuvaz, 2018). While my reporting did not corroborate all of the book's allegations, it contained a helpful collection of documents and its authors shared with me parts of their trove of surveillance footage of Khashoggi and the Saudi agents moving around Istanbul, which helped establish many details of the narrative.

Information from other sources is cited below.

248 *filed for a divorce:* MMS-JK, Nov. 1, 2017.

248 *he get a dog:* MMS-JK, Oct. 3, 2017.

249 *"talk about democracy":* Author interview, Mohamed Soltan, Dec. 2018.

249 *"free me from her?":* MMS-JK, Feb. 23, 2018.

249 *fifty-ninth birthday:* An enduring mystery is Jamal Khashoggi's three birthdays. His Saudi passport has January 22, 1958, as his date of birth. He celebrated his birthday with his family on March 23, and told al-Atr his real birthday was March 23, 1958. Hatice Cengiz said they had been planning to celebrate his birthday on October 13. It is not clear why he told her he celebrated his birthday then.

249 *"thousands like her":* MMS-JK, April 22, 2018.

251 *"Mr. Jamal":* "Kaşıkçı'nın nişanlısı anlatıyor" (Tu.), *Habertürk*, Oct. 26, 2018.

251 *never mentioned his Egyptian wife:* There is some debate among Khashoggi's friends about whether he divorced al-Atr. She says he did not.

251 *"willing to say":* MMS-JK, Aug. 6, 2018.

251 *"does indeed still care":* "Saudi Arabia cannot afford to pick fights with Canada," *WaPo*, Aug. 7, 2018.

251 *"when it comes out":* MMS-JK, Aug. 7, 2018.

251 *suspicions to rest:* Declan Walsh interview with Jamal Khashoggi, Sept. 2017.

252 *"choose their political representatives":* "The U.S. is wrong about the Muslim Brotherhood—and the Arab world is suffering for it," *WaPo,* Aug. 28, 2018.

252 *"working on it tonight":* MMS-JK, Aug. 28, 2018.

252 *preventable cause:* "Remarks by the Secretary-General to the Pledging Conference on Yemen," United Nations Office At Geneva, April 3, 2018.

252 *to war crimes charges:* "44 Small Graves Stir Questions About U.S. Policy in Yemen," *NYT,* Aug. 15, 2018.

253 *restore the kingdom's dignity:* "Saudi Arabia's crown prince must restore dignity to his country—by ending Yemen's cruel war," *WaPo,* Sept. 11, 2018.

253 *providing information to diplomats:* "Saudi economist who criticized Aramco IPO Charged with Terrorism: activists," Reuters, Oct. 1, 2018.

253 *"Next of kin":* Sinan Onuş and Mehmet Akif Ersoy, *Cemal Kaşıkçı—Hayatı, Mücadelesi, Sırları* (Tu.) (Istanbul: Kopernik Kitap'tan, 2019).

253 *He'll know what to do:* Ibid.

253 *"understood me like you do":* Carlotta Gall interview with Hatice Cengiz, April 2019.

253 *walked out holding hands:* Surveillance footage shown on Turkish television.

254 *"Saudis are good people":* Author interview, Azzam Tamimi, Feb. 2019 and "Jamal Khashoggi Disappears, a Mystery Rattling the Middle East," *NYT,* Oct. 7, 2018.

255 *"one of the people sought":* U.N. Report.

255 *"top secret" mission:* Ibid. The Saudi Consul General in Istanbul was Mohammed al-Otaibi.

255 *near the consul's office:* Ibid.

255 *three more Saudi agents:* Ibid and author interview, Turkish security official, April 2019. The three men were Naif Hasan Alarifi; Mohammed Saad Alzahrani; Mansour Othman Abahussain.

255 *hotel near the consulate:* Information from Ferhat Ünlü, Abdurrahman Simsek, and Nazif Karaman, *Diplomatic Vahset: Kasikçi Cinayetinin Karanlik Sirlari* (Tu.) (Istanbul: Trurkuvaz, 2018), corroborated by Turkish security officials. The three agents were Khalid Ayed Alotaibi, Abdulaziz Mohammed Alhawsawi, and Meshaal Saad Albostani.

255 *checked into another hotel:* Ibid.

255 *because of repair work:* Ibid.

256 *so they could not record:* Ibid.

256 *stopped taking Aktay's calls:* All quotes in this section from Yasin Aktay are from author interview, Feb. 2019.

257 *"We have nothing to hide":* "Saudi Crown Prince Discusses Trump, Aramco, Arrests: Transcript," Bloomberg, Oct. 5, 2019.

257 *published a blank column:* "This should be a column by Jamal Khashoggi," *WaPo*, Oct. 4, 2018.

257 *to be found:* "Find Jamal Khashoggi," *NYT*, Oct. 5, 2018.

257 *Khashoggi leaving the building:* Consul quote and visit details from "Saudi Arabia opens up consulate after journalist vanishes," Reuters, Oct. 6, 2018.

257 *"Why did he go?":* Author interview, Yasin Aktay, Feb. 2019.

257 *the Turkish state mobilized:* Ibid.

258 *to damage MBS:* Ibid.

258 *his body taken offsite:* "Exclusive: Turkish police believe Saudi journalist Khashoggi was killed in consulate—sources," Reuters, Oct. 6, 2018.

258 *had been dismembered:* The friend was Turan Kislakci, cited in "Jamal Khashoggi Disappears, a Mystery Rattling the Middle East," *NYT*, Oct. 7, 2018.

259 *"are absolutely false":* "Personal Message Sent by HRH the Ambassador," Press Release from the Saudi Embassy in Washington, Oct. 9, 2018.

259 *had audio and video:* "In Jamal Khashoggi Mystery, Turkey Says It Has Audio and Video of His Killing," *NYT*, October 11, 2018.

259 *same time as Khashoggi:* "The Jamal Khashoggi Case: Suspects Had Ties to Saudi Crown Prince," *NYT*, Oct. 16, 2018.

259 *MBS's palace in Jeddah:* The three Royal Guard officers were Abdulaziz Mohammed al-Hawsawi, Muhammed Saad Alzahrani, and Thaar Ghaleb al-Harbi, who had received the promotion. Ibid.

259 *mobile autopsies and dissection:* Ibid.

259 *United Nations in New York:* Ibid.

259 *spoken with university officials:* "Why Is There So Much Saudi Money in American Universities?" *The New York Times Magazine*, July 3, 2019.

259 *online as an engineer:* The purported engineer was Mustafa al-Madani.

260 *local collaborator to dispose of:* Author interview, Saudi official, Oct. 2019.

261 *Khashoggi sightings around the city:* "Surveillance footage shows Saudi 'body double' in Khashoggi clothes after he was killed, Turkish source says," *CNN*, October 23, 2018. A senior Saudi official acknowledged that the man had been sent as a body double. The body double was Mustafa al-Madani and his companion was Saif Saad al-Qahtani.

261 *"should be in big trouble":* "Trump Says Saudi Account of Khashoggi Killing Is 'Worst Cover-Up' in History," *NYT*, Oct. 23, 2018.

261 *plans for the Middle East:* Author interview, former Trump administration official with knowledge of the calls, May 2019.

261 *were usually cleaner:* Author interview, former Trump administration official and two other U.S. officials, May 2019.

261 *and detain him:* Author interview, former Trump administration official, May 2019, and "Crown Prince sought to lure Khashoggi back to Saudi Arabia and detain him, US intercepts show," *WaPo*, Oct. 10, 2018.

262 *denied knowing anything:* Author interview, former Trump administration official with knowledge of the calls, May 2019.

262 *"enemy of the state":* "Statement from President Donald J. Trump on Standing with Saudi Arabia," White House press release, Nov. 20, 2018.

262 *as a dangerous Islamist:* "Saudi Crown Prince described slain journalist as a dangerous Islamist in call with the White House," *WaPo,* Nov. 1, 2019.

262 *in the dark about what was said:* Author interview, three U.S. officials, May 2019.

262 *"it's bad, bad stuff":* "In Shift on Khashoggi Killing, Trump Edges Closer to Acknowledging a Saudi Role," *NYT,* Oct. 18, 2019.

262 *"as evil as it gets":* "Trump doubts Saudi account of journalist's death: 'There's been deception, and there's been lies,'" *WaPo,* October 20, 2018.

262 *No. Too heavy:* The narrative of what happened in the consulate is from U.N. Report and from an author interview, Turkish security officials, April 2019. All quotes from the Turkish audio are from U.N. Report unless otherwise noted.

263 *"drink coffee and smoke":* Author interviews, Turkish security officials, May, Aug. 2019.

263 *"hear from me for a while":* Ibid.

264 *"attempt to resuscitate him":* U.N. Report.

264 *flushed it down the toilet:* Author interviews, Turkish security officials, May, Aug. 2019.

264 *determined to be a saw:* The U.N. investigator could not determine whether the sound came from a saw, and a Saudi official insisted that the team had not brought a bone saw, but had used implements available in the consulate, without specifying what they were. U.S. officials briefed on the intelligence never raised questions about the saw.

264 *al-Qahtani about MBS:* "According to 'Tell Your Boss': Recording Is Seen to Link Saudi Crown Prince More Strongly to Khashoggi Killing," *NYT,* Nov. 12, 2018, Mutrib said, "Tell your boss" that the deed was done. According to "'I can't breathe.' Jamal Khashoggi's last words disclosed in transcript, source says," *CNN,* Dec. 10, 2018, Mutrib said "Tell yours, the thing is done, it's done." The author assumes one was a quote and one was a summary of Mutrib's remarks, but was not able to determine which was which.

264 *large black plastic bags:* Turkish surveillance footage shared with author.

265 *pleased with himself:* "Surveillance footage shows Saudi 'body double' in Khashoggi clothes after he was killed, Turkish source says," CNN, Oct. 23, 2018.

265 *were all gone:* U.N. Report, Turkish security official.

A HOLOGRAM FOR THE CROWN PRINCE, PART TWO

The wedding was for Prince Sultan bin Saud bin Mohammed bin Saud al-Kabeer and Princess Lulwa bint Bandar bin Khalid al-Faisal. I reconstructed the scene from an author interview with a female attendee, Oct. 2018, and social media posts by other guests.

267 *grown apart more recently:* "The Saudi royal family circles its wagons in the Khashoggi crisis," *WaPo*, Oct. 24, 2018.

267 *how much the Turks knew:* Author interview, Yasin Aktay, Feb. 2019.

267 *"to get out of this one":* Author interview, Saudi royal, Oct. 2018.

268 *"today before tomorrow":* "al-ameer aHmad bin 'abdul'aziz" (Ar.), YouTube video, Sept. 5, 2018. https://www.youtube.com/watch?v=m7MKfZFXhn4

268 *"sell arms and buy oil":* Author interview, Saudi princess, Oct. 2018.

268 *"go on foreign holidays":* Author interview, associate of the royal family, Oct. 2018.

269 *date by three decades:* "kalimat khaadim al-Haramain ash-shareefain al-malik salmaan bin 'abdul'aziz" (Ar.), YouTube video, Feb. 24, 2019. https://www.youtube.com/watch?v=yvjyVpi7Ok4. The remarks were at the European Union–Arab League summit in Egypt. It should have been the 1967 borders.

269 *"No. 1 and No. 2":* Author correspondence, associate of the royal family, Oct. 2018.

269 *"in the global economy":* "Saudi Arabia Totally Rejects Any Threats and Attempts to Undermine the Kingdom: Official Source," press release, Center for International Communication, Oct. 14, 2018.

269 *"into the arms of Iran":* "U.S. sanctions on Riyadh means Washington is stabbing itself," *AlArabiya*, Oct. 14, 2018. The commentator was Turki Aldakhil, who later became the Saudi ambassador to the United Arab Emirates.

270 *he named Mohammed bin Salman:* "Custodian of the Two Holy Mosques Directs Formation of Ministerial Committee to Restructure the General Intelligence Presidency," *SPA*, Oct. 20, 2018.

270 *cleaned, inside and out:* Author interview, Turkish security official, May 2019, and "Annex to the Report of the Special Rapporteur on extrajudicial, summary or arbitrary executions: Investigation into the unlawful death of Mr. Jamal Khashoggi," United Nations Human Rights Council, June 19, 2019, heretofore cited as "U.N. Report."

270 *refused to hand them over:* Ibid.

270 *toxicology and genetics:* Ibid.

270 *inside until 4 A.M.:* U.N. Report.

270 *appeared to be bleach:* "Trump suggests 'rogue killers' murdered Saudi journalist," *AP*, Oct. 16, 2018.

270 *reacted less than expected:* Ibid.

271 *technicians were gone, too:* Ibid.

271 *obstruction of justice:* Ibid.

271 *inside the U.S. government:* Author interview, former Trump administration official, May 2019.

271 *denied this:* Author correspondence, White House spokespeople, July 2019.

271 *The White House agreed:* Author interviews, two U.S. officials briefed on the discussions, May 2019.

271 *leaked to the news media:* "Trump administration to end refueling of Saudi-coalition aircraft in Yemen conflict," *WaPo*, Nov. 10, 2018.

272 *death penalty for five of them:* Saudi Ministry of Justice Spokesman Shaalan al-Shaalan, press conference, Riyadh, Nov. 15, 2018, and "'aam / al-naa'ib al 'aam: tawjeeh at-toham ila 11 shakhSan min al-mawqufeen fi qadiyat jamaal khaashoqji" (Ar.), *SPA*, Nov. 15, 2018.

272 *"execution of the operation":* "Treasury Sanctions 17 Individuals for Their Roles in the Killing of Jamal Khashoggi," U.S. Treasury Department press release, Nov. 15, 2018.

272 *between intelligence services:* Author interviews, three current and former U.S. officials, May 2019.

272 *"is called America First":* "Statement from President Donald J. Trump on Standing with Saudi Arabia," White House press release, Nov. 20, 2018.

273 *"make a stance against that":* "Sir Richard Branson uses Hollywood star to discuss disappearance of Saudi journalist Jamal Khashoggi," YouTube video, Oct. 17, 2019. https://www.youtube.com/watch?v=iYFigjU9qQA.

273 *Saudi tourism projects:* "Virgin's Branson halts talks on $1 billion Saudi investment in space ventures," *Reuters*, Oct. 12. 2018.

273 *CEOs of Blackstone Group:* "Blackstone and BlackRock Chiefs Withdraw From Saudi Conference," *NYT*, Oct. 15, 2018.

273 *and Uber:* "Uber CEO Khosrowshahi pulls out of Saudi conference over disappearance of journalist," CNBC, Oct. 12, 2018.

273 *Saudi research grant:* "Western walkout of Saudi 'Davos in the Desert' conference over Jamal Khashoggi undermines kingdom's modernization plans," *WaPo*, Oct. 12, 2018.

273 *MBS's foundation:* Author correspondence, Gates Foundation spokesperson, Nov. 1, 2018.

273 *ran for the exits:* "Two more Washington lobbying firms drop representation of Saudi Arabia in wake of alleged killing of Jamal Khashoggi," *WaPo*, Oct. 15, 2018.

273 *over a kneeling Khashoggi:* Screenshot taken by the author Oct. 2018.

274 *"illicit appropriation":* "World Economic Forum Objects to Misuse of the 'Davos' Brand," press release, World Economic Forum, Oct. 22, 2018.

274 *"the last few weeks":* Lubna Olayan, on stage at the Future Investment Initiative, Oct. 23, 2018.

274 *$1 billion investment:* "Saudi's PIF invests more than $1 billion in electric carmaker Lucid Motors," Reuters, Sept. 17, 2018.

274 *names behind their ties:* "$30 billion in Saudi Deals Even As Investors Denounce a 'Horrendous Killing,'" *NYT*, Oct. 23, 2018.

274 *unveiled at the conference:* "Saudi Crown Prince Discusses Trump, Aramco, Arrests: Transcript," Bloomberg, Oct. 5, 2019.

275 *"desperate at the moment":* "Imran Khan: Pakistan cannot afford to snub Saudis over Khashoggi killing," *Middle East Eye*, Oct. 22, 2018.

275 *$6 billion aid package:* "Saudis offer Pakistan $6 billion rescue package to ease economic crisis," Oct. 23, 2018.

275 *$2.5 billion in economic support:* "Gulf states pledge $2.5 billion aid package to Jordan," Reuters, June 11, 2018.

275 *crown prince of Bahrain:* The crown prince of Bahrain was Salman bin Hamad Al Khalifa.

275 *"the great Saudi people":* Mohammed bin Salman on stage at the Future Investment Initiative, Oct. 24, 2018. https://www.youtube.com/watch?v=JRxP-81dgOo&t=1591s

276 *Peking duck:* "$30 billion in Saudi Deals Even As Investors Denounce a 'Horrendous Killing,'" *NYT*, Oct. 23, 2018.

276 *"Hotel California":* Tasneem Alsultan (@tasneemalsultan), "Hotel California played at the Ritz Hotel, Riyadh," Twitter post and video, Oct. 23, 2018. https://twitter.com/tasneemalsultan/status/1054820499669372928

AFTERWORD

278 *find the magic solution:* According to one smart assessment, to turn Saudi Arabia into a non-rentier state, the kingdom would need to create 3.65 million jobs in twenty years while more than tripling the share of Saudis working in the private sector and reducing the share of them in government jobs. "Even under ideal conditions, it will be impossible to become 'post-rentier' by 2030 and hard to imagine it even by 2050," the author concluded. See Steffen Hertog, "What would the Saudi economy have to look like to be 'post-rentier'?" POMES Studies, pp. 29–33.

279 *the desired $2 trillion mark:* "Saudi Aramco hits Crown Prince's $2 trillion goal despite valuation doubts," Reuters, Dec. 12, 2019.

279 *a few thousand pilgrims:* "In Mecca, a fortunate few pray for a pandemic-free world," Reuters, July 30, 2020. The kingdom's Hajj minister said the month before the event that about about 1,000 pilgrims would attend. During the Hajj, local media reported as many as 10,000.

280 *estimated $67.6 billion:* "Trends in World Military Expenditure, 2018." Stockholm International Peace Research Institute, April 2019.

280 *"locked and loaded":* Donald Trump (@realDonaldTrump). "Saudi Arabia oil supply was attacked," Twitter post, Sept. 16, 2019. https://twitter.com/realdonaldtrump/status/1173368423381962752

280 *allowed for indirect diplomacy:* "Saudi Arabia and Iran Make Quiet Openings to Head Off War," *NYT*, Oct. 4, 2019.

282 *"matters into their own hands":* Notes from a conversation between MBS and evangelical Christian leaders in Riyadh on Nov. 1, 2018, provided to the author by Joel C. Rosenberg, the delegation's head.

282 *"have to be willfully blind"*: "A 'Smoking Saw' Links Saudi Prince to Khashoggi's Murder, Senator Says," Bloomberg, Dec. 4, 2018.

282 *"responsible" for Khashoggi's death*: "Senate Votes to End Aid for Yemen Fight Over Khashoggi Killing and Saudis' War Aims," *NYT*, Dec. 13, 2018.

283 *real estate worth millions*: "Saudi Arabia Giving Jamal Khashoggi's Children Money and Real Estate," *NYT*, Apr. 2, 2019.

283 *others to prison terms*: "Saudi Death Sentences in Khashoggi Killing Fail to Dispel Questions," *NYT*, Dec. 23, 2019.

283 *pardoned the killers*: Salah Khashoggi (@salahkhashoggi). Twitter post and image, May 22, 2020. https://twitter.com/salahkhashoggi/status/1263613366247075841

283 *from seven to twenty years*: "'aam/al-niyaaba al-'aama: Sudoor aHkaam niha'iya bihaq thamaaniya ashkhaaS mudaaneen fi qaDiyat maqtal jamaal khaashoqji," SPA, Sept. 7, 2020. https://www.spa.gov.sa/2130930

284 *"where is his body?"*: Hatice Cengiz (@mercan_resifi). "This is my statement in response to the ruling today," Twitter post and image, Sept. 7, 2020. https://twitter.com/mercan_resifi/status/1302993904430710786

284 *"young girls know about these things"*: All information here about Rahaf Alzahrani from author interview, Aug. 2019.

286 *She refused:* "Saudi woman activist rejects release deal tied to denying torture: family," Reuters, Aug. 13, 2019.

PHOTOGRAPH CREDITS

INDEX